Features to Help You Remember

After every major topic, you will find the Check Back feature. Here you are asked questions and given projects to try. They are designed to help you discover how well you understood the material that you just studied.

End of Chapter Exercises

At the end of every chapter, there are four types of questions. These questions are designed to let you test yourself on how well you understand the chapter, to get you to stretch your geography skills, and to allow you to demonstrate how ready you are to move on to new material.

Understanding the Concepts

Research and Communication Skills

Map and Globe Skills

Applications

Features to Help You Use this Book

Every so often you will see an arrow and circle like this. Inside the circle is a page number. If you turn to that page you will find more information about the topic you were reading about. It's a great way to stretch your understanding of what you're studying.

Map Appendix: On pages 288 to 310 is a set of maps you will need to help you understand and do the work in this book.

Skills Appendix: On pages 311 to 327 is a set of explanations for many of the skills you will need to do the tasks in the book. This appendix will refresh your memory on how to make bar graphs, how to read latitude and longitude, and many other skills. Take a look at it when you are stuck on how to do something.

Glossary: On pages 328 to 331
A glossary is like a mini-dictionary. It gives words and very brief meanings. As you read this book, you will see words that are printed in bold print. Many of these words are explained in the glossary. Other terms are also explained, so if you're not sure what a word means, try the glossary first.

Index: On pages 332 to 335
An index is a list of terms that you can find in the book and on what pages they are f[illegible]
This is a quick way of finding something in the book, like social trends or quaterna[illegible]ies.

Emin Margosian

gage

HUMAN GEOGRAPHY

Discovering Global Systems and Patterns

Graham Draper • Lew French • Andrea Craig

Contributing author Patricia Healy

gage EDUCATIONAL PUBLISHING COMPANY
A DIVISION OF CANADA PUBLISHING CORPORATION
Vancouver · Calgary · Toronto · London · Halifax

Canadian Cataloguing in Publication Data

Draper, Graham A.
Gage human geography 8

Includes index.
ISBN 0-7715-8226-9

1. Human geography – Juvenile literature. I. Craig, Andrea. II. French, Lew. M. Title.

GF43.D72 2000 304.2 C99-932914-6

We acknowledge the financial support of the Government of Canada through the Book Publishing Industry Development Program for our publishing activities.

We hope you find this Geography book helpful, informative, and easy to use. If you have any comment that will help us improve our next edition of this book, please let our editorial team know.

Gage Educational Publishing Company
164 Commander Blvd., Toronto, ON MIS 3C7
fax 416-293-0757 e-mail info@gagelearning.com

Project manager: Joseph Gladstone
Production editor: Francine Geraci
Photo research: Leesa Price
Copy editor: Jeff Siamon
Proofreader: James Gladstone
Cover and text design: Dave Murphy/ArtPIus Limited
Page layout: Leanne Knox/ArtPlus Limited
Art director: Donna Guilfoyle
Maps and illustrations: Renné Benoit, Donna Guilfoyle, Ryan Koetstra, Sue Ledoux, Dave McKay, Kristi Moreau, and Jane Whitney

ISBN 0-7715-**8226-9**

2 3 4 5 FP 04 03 02 01 00

Written, printed, and bound in Canada.

Consultants and Reviewers

The authors and the publisher wish to thank the consultants and reviewers for their input — advice, ideas, directions, and suggestions — that helped to make this learning resource more student-friendly and teacher-useful. Their contributions in time, effort, and expertise were invaluable.

Reviewers and consultants who helped develop the model for the Gage geography series

Andrea Bishop
Angelo Bolotta
James Burrell
Terril Butterworth
Chris Callaghan
Sue Case
Mike Costelloe
Mike Filip
Fiona Hopkins
Wendy Murtagh
Ken O'Connor
Peter Olczak
Yette Powrie
Wayne Stewart
Alison Sutherland
Dennis Wendland
David Whipp
Barb Wilson
Chris Zannuttini

Reviewers on the grade 8 Human Geography text

Gary Baldwin
Teacher
Kawartha Pine Ridge DSB

Mike Ball
Program Facilitator
Durham DSB

Mary Jo Bell
Teacher
Limestone DSB

James Burrell
Teacher
Toronto DSB

Ian Craig
Former Principal
York Region DSB

Nadine Cuccaro
Curriculum Consultant
Renfrew County DSB

David Ferren
Teacher
Niagara DSB

Brad Hilliard
Teacher
York Region DSB

Linda Sloan
Consultant
Ottawa-Carleton CDSB

John Smith
Principal
Peel DSB

Equity Consultants: Kennard Ramphal
Patricia Healy

Contents

To the Student

Welcome to Gage Human Geography!

There are over six billion people on earth and every one of those six billion needs the physical environment to satisfy basic human needs - air to breathe, water to drink, food to eat, shelter from the elements. Then there are the many things we want - televisions, cars, paper, toothpaste, movies, chocolate - the list goes on and on. As well, we build cities, roads, airports, bridges, homes, and office buildings. As we use the earth's resources to provide for these needs and wants, we change it. Understanding those changes is extremely important if we ever hope to solve the world's major problems like hunger, poverty, pollution, and overcrowding.

Human geography is the science that explores the connections between humankind and the physical environment and the changes caused by those connections. The aim of human geographers is to better understand people and our impact on the earth. To help organize our studies in human geography, we use five themes or strands.

The themes are outlined on the inside covers of this text. Take some time now to review them.

Throughout this book, you can find many Web sites to use in your research. Sometimes these sites get changed, or reorganized, or even removed completely from the Web. This will be a challenge for you. If the site has been changed, try to find similar information at the changed site. If the site has been reorganized, try to find the new correct path. If the site has been removed from the Web, use a search engine to discover an alternate site.

There are special features in this book to help you with your human geography studies. Look at the inside of the front cover and you can read about them.

We, the authors, wish you every success in your investigation of human geography.

Graham Draper, Lew French, Andrea Craig

Patterns in Human Geography

EXPECTATIONS

- identify and explain patterns in human geography and describe how human activities are affected by these patterns
- demonstrate an understanding of employment patterns and trends
- use a variety of geographic representations, tools, and technologies, to gather, process, and communicate geographic information

1 As cities become more and more crowded, new problems arise. What problems do you see arising from this situation?

2 Explain the meaning of this cartoon.

3 These immigrant children have their basic needs taken care of. What are human basic needs? Do people have a right to them?

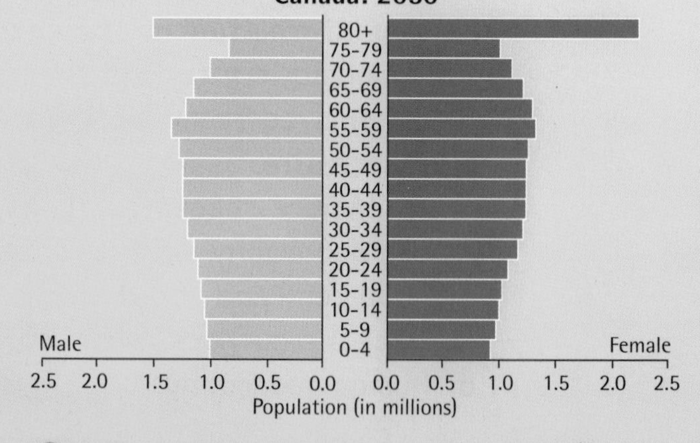

4 Population pyramids show what a country's population is like according to sex and age. What does this pyramid predict Canada's largest age group will be in 2050?

5 Humans change the environment. What might have been on this land before all these roads were built?

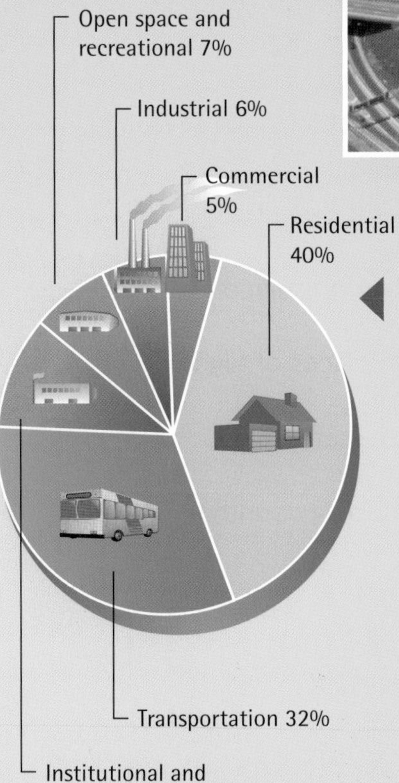

6 This graph illustrates how city land is usually used. Does land use in your community match this pattern?

MOVEMENT/PATTERN

7 Robots will be used more and more for many different types of jobs. What are some jobs robots are doing now?

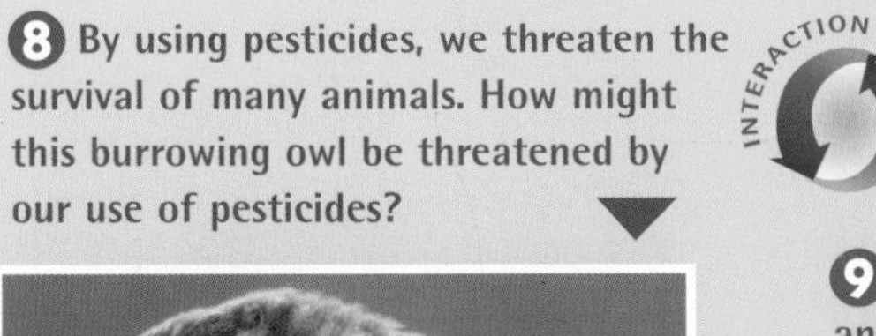

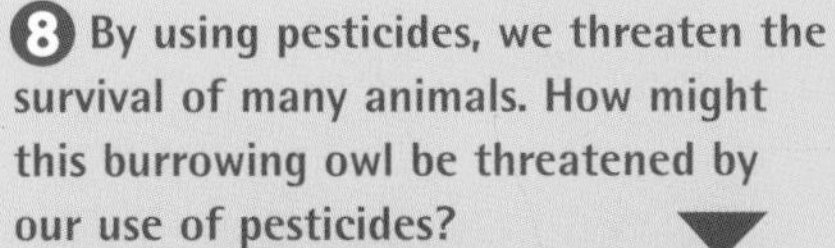

8 By using pesticides, we threaten the survival of many animals. How might this burrowing owl be threatened by our use of pesticides?

INTERACTION

9 Many different cultures make up our world and our country. What are some of the different cultures reflected in your school?

1 Where People Live: Population Distribution and Density

EXPECTATIONS

- identify and explain patterns in human geography, and describe how human activities are affected by these patterns
- demonstrate an understanding of the factors affecting population distribution
- identify and describe the characteristics common to places of high and low population density
- identify three main patterns of settlement: clustered, scattered, and linear
- compare the characteristics of developed and developing countries

Growing Pains

For thousands of years in human history, the earth was home to relatively few people. At the end of the last Ice Age — about 10 000 years ago — there were somewhere near ten million people worldwide. It wasn't until about 1950 that the population started to grow quickly. In the 1990s, world population grew by around 80 million people a year. Official estimates by the United Nations predict that by the year 2050 the world's population will have grown to around nine billion people, and that it will continue to grow over the next two centuries.

In 1998, the United Nations also predicted that by October 1999, a child would be born to bring the world's population to six billion — a huge number to grasp. How many years would it take to count to six billion at a rate of one number per second? (*Hint:* There are 86 400 s in a 24-h day.)

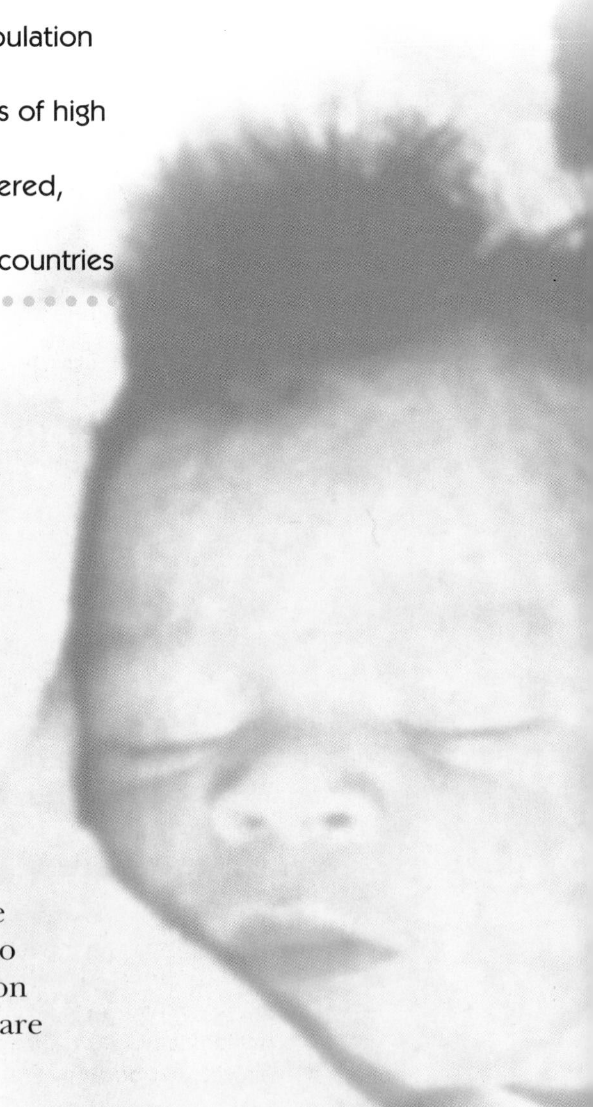

Figure 1.1
The world's 6 billionth child may have been born into your community. However, chances are much greater that he or she lives in an economically developing part of Africa or Asia — and will die at a young age.

Counting Heads

Demography is the study of human population. *Demographers* are scientists who study data on population and issues related to where — and how well — people live. Geographers and demographers try to help us understand why people live where they do and why some countries have population problems. As part of their work, demographers help countries, regions, and cities predict what the population will be in the future. They are hired by governments and businesses to make recommendations about how to provide services and goods for people.

Fact File

Eighty percent of the world's people live in countries that are economically developing, and 97% of all population growth occurs in these countries. The United Nations uses the term **economically developing** to refer to countries that are not as industrialized as Canada or the United States, mainly in Africa, Asia (except Japan), and Latin America.

SEE PAGE 180

GO TO

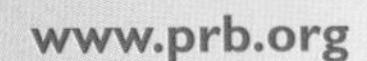

www.prb.org

Visit this Web site to discover many free books about world population growth. Write down the name of a free book you would want to look at. Copy the details on how to get that book.

ENVIRONMENT

> *"Population growth is the primary source of environmental damage."*
>
> **Jacques Cousteau, oceanographer and environmentalist**

The Census

How are all the people in a country counted? Every five years, governments collect information about the number of people living in their region. Every 10 years a more detailed **census** is carried out: people are hired to conduct door-to-door surveys in their neighbourhoods, collecting information about age, ethnic background, language, family size, and other facts. Statistics Canada is the branch of government responsible for the Canadian census.

Connections to Demographics

If we could shrink the earth's population to a village of 100 people, with all the existing human ratios remaining the same, it would look like this:

There would be

62 Asians
10 Europeans
14 from the Western hemisphere (8 from North America)
13 Africans
1 Oceanian

52 would be female
48 would be male

70 would be non-white
30 would be white

70 would be non-Christian
30 would be Christian

6 people would possess 59% of the entire world's wealth
80 would live in substandard housing
70 would be unable to read
50 would suffer from malnutrition

1 would be near death
2 would be near birth

1 would have a college education

1 would own a computer.

Go to www.statcan.ca

Select the language you wish to work in. Click on Canadian Statistics. Click on Census and then on Canadian Statistics on the left side of the screen. Explore one of the topics under The People. Find two interesting facts about Canada's people and share them with your classmates. When will the next census take place in Canada?

Figure 1.2

World population growth, 1800 to 2150 (estimated). What do demographers mean when they say there has been a population "explosion"?

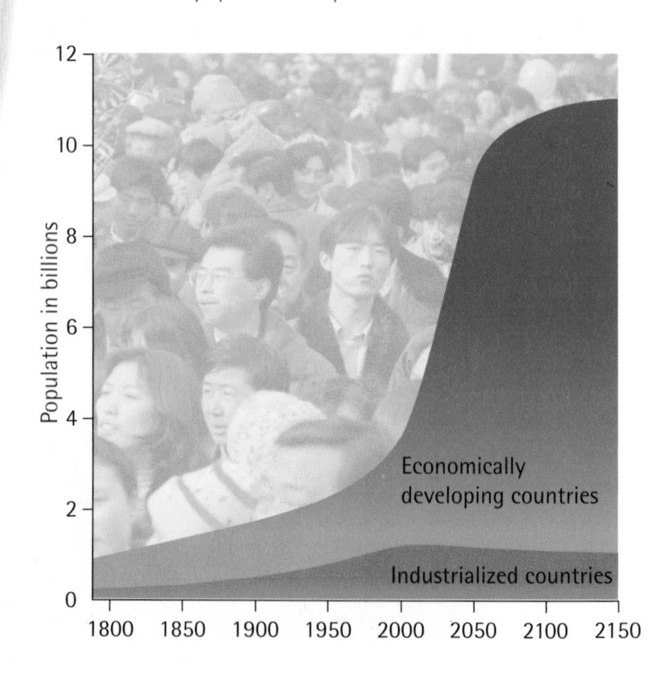

It's Your World

World Population Milestones	
World population reached:	**World population may reach:**
1 billion in 1804	7 billion in 2013 (14 years later)
2 billion in 1927 (123 years later)	8 billion in 2028 (15 years later)
3 billion in 1960 (33 years later)	9 billion in 2054 (26 years later)
4 billion in 1974 (14 years later)	
5 billion in 1987 (13 years later)	
6 billion in 1999 (12 years later)	

When did the number of people living on "spaceship earth" first reach one billion people? How long did it take in the 1980s to add one billion inhabitants? In the 1990s?

Fact File

The most northerly permanent settlement in Canada is at Alert on Ellesmere Island, Nunavut, at latitude 83° north.

Population Distribution

Look at the map of world population density on page 290 of the map appendix. As you can see, people are not evenly distributed on the earth's surface. Although settlement does not occur everywhere, very few places are completely free of the impact of human activities. There are even permanent, year-round research bases in Antarctica.

Where people live is called **population distribution**, and how many people live within a given area is called **population density**. While these terms may seem very similar, Figure 1.3 shows the difference: both regions A and B have the same population density, but the population distribution is different for each.

SEE PAGE 51

SEE PAGE 147

Figure 1.3

Regions A and B both have the same population density — 12 people per square kilometre — but different patterns of population distribution. Region A shows an unequal distribution, or **cluster**, of people. In region B, the population is more evenly distributed, or **scattered**, throughout the area.

Population Density

The population density of a place tells us how many people live in an area, usually measured by the average *number of people* for each square kilometre (km^2). You can calculate this by dividing the number of people living in a country or region by the *land area* in which they live.

For example, Australia has a population of 19 million and an area of 7 682 000 km^2:

$$\frac{19\ 000\ 000}{7\ 682\ 000} = 2.47 \text{ people per km}^2.$$

Bangladesh has a population of 120 million and an area of 144 000 square km^2:

$$\frac{120\ 000\ 000}{144\ 000} = 833.3 \text{ people per km}^2.$$

As these two examples show, population density varies greatly from place to place. In fact, population densities around the world range from less than one person per square kilometre to thousands of people per square kilometre.

Fact File

Australia has over 50 times more land area than Bangladesh but only $\frac{1}{6}$ the population.

Figure 1.4

Population density of 24 countries.

Country/ Territory	Population (people/km^2)
Australia	2.5
Bangladesh	833.3
Belgium	336.6
Bermuda	1 260.0
Brazil	20.1
Canada	3.3
China	122.0
Hong Kong	6 435.7
Egypt	66.4
France	107.8
Greenland	< 0.1
Iceland	2.7
Israel	277.6
Japan	331.0
Macau	20 338.0
Mongolia	1.6
New Zealand	13.5
Nigeria	121.4
Russia	8.6
Saudi Arabia	10.6
Singapore	5 474.5
Sudan	12.0
United Kingdom	238.9
United States	29.5

Figure 1.5

Population density in Osaka, Japan contrasts sharply with the density of the rural area shown in Figure 1.6.

Figure 1.6

What kinds of economic activity do you think the people who live in this community would be engaged in?

SEE PAGE 97

SEE PAGE 99

Countries that are large in area but have small populations — like Canada and Australia — are said to have a low or **sparse** population density. Countries with large populations living in a small area — like Bangladesh, where people are packed more closely together — have a high population density or a **dense** population. A **moderate** population density is somewhere in the middle, averaging from 15 to 150 people per square kilometre. France, with 107.8 people per square kilometre, is considered to have a moderate population density.

Fact File

Cities are places with the highest population densities in the world. Around 75% of people in developed countries live in cities.

Understanding population density — in other words, how close or how far apart people live from one another — can help communities plan what services are needed and where to build new schools, houses, businesses, and transportation routes. Knowing population density also helps us make comparisons among different regions of the world.

1. Predict the number of people that may live on planet earth in 100 years.
2. How old will you be when the earth is expected to have nine billion people?
3. What is the ratio of people who live in economically developing countries to those who live in developed, industrialized countries?
4. Calculate the population density of your classroom by finding the number of people per square metre.

Why Do People Live Where They Live?

We have seen that there are patterns to where people live in the world. The natural environment, the level of economic development, and the history of a region are some of the factors that work together to create these patterns.

Natural Environment

ENVIRONMENT SEE PAGE 160

The natural environment has a significant influence on where people live and the number of people that can live in a region. About 71% of the world's surface area is water. This leaves only 29% of the world as land surface. Of this 29%, less than half can support human settlement. Approximately 90% of the people on earth live on 10% of its land area. The rest is too rocky, too steep, too dry, too cold, or too swampy to support many people.

Figure 1.7

Helicopters bearing special "cone collectors" gather seeds in Ontario's wilderness lands. The seeds will be planted in nurseries, and the young trees that grow from them will be used to replenish the province's forests. Why do the forests need replenishing?

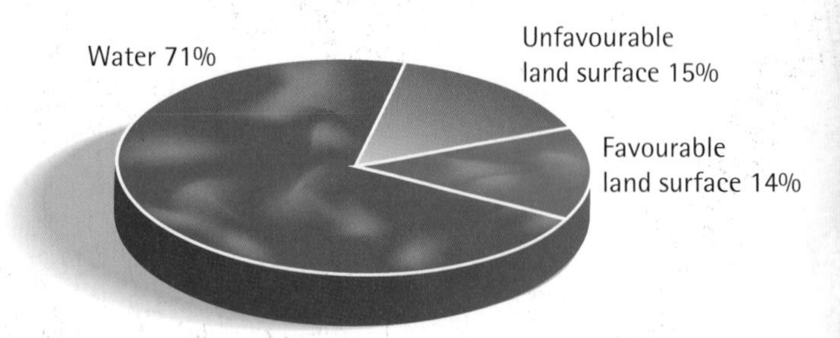

Figure 1.8

The earth's surface. Most of the world's population lives on less than one-half of the planet's land area.

It's Your World

In 1998, the Ontario government developed a "Lands for Life" policy to protect the province's wilderness. Lands for Life uses a round table process in which government representatives meet with local citizens, businesses, and environmental agencies to hear many different points of view about land use. What do you think the population density of northern Ontario's wilderness lands might be, sparse, moderate, or dense?

Fact File

Agriculture — from the Latin *agri* ("field") + *cultura* ("cultivation") — developed over 10 000 years ago in what is now northern Iraq, when people first learned how to grow wheat and barley.

Places with good **arable** land — which have fertile soil, a moderate climate, and water for growing crops — attract large numbers of people. The location of other natural resources, such as fish and forests, will also attract settlement. Natural resources provide the materials necessary for food, shelter, and trade.

Many densely populated areas are found in river valleys, coastal regions, and flat or gently rolling plains. For example, the Great Lakes–St. Lawrence Lowlands region of Canada has very fertile soils, a moderate climate, and relatively flat lands that are good for agriculture and the establishment of cities and transportation networks. People tend to move to locations where these favourable characteristics and opportunities are found.

Areas with unfavourable environments — rugged terrain, extreme climate, limited water supply, limited resources, or infertile soils — usually have sparse population densities. The Himalayan mountain range in India or the Gobi desert of Mongolia are examples of regions that have a sparse population density as a result of their unfavourable conditions for human settlement.

Figure 1.9

This area of outback in the Northern Territories of Australia, known as The Olgas, has conditions too extreme for human habitation, but it does attract tourists from all over the world.

Figure 1.10

A plum orchard in southwestern Ontario. Why do you think the agricultural community around Hamilton is known as "Fruitland"?

We Like to Live Near Water

People tend to live where there is access to water, since it is the basis of life. Areas that have adequate water for people, animals, crops, and industries can support large populations. Many of the world's largest cities are ports that developed in coastal areas — for example, New York, Cairo, Shanghai, Toronto, and Chicago.

Besides its fertile land, another favourable factor that has attracted people to the Great Lakes–St. Lawrence Lowlands is its excellent waterways for shipping, industry, and agriculture.

Figure 1.11
Toronto Island, located in Toronto's harbour, has private homes, public parklands, and some businesses. How might the mix of activities affect this community's economic development?

Figure 1.12
The Welland Canal runs from Port Colborne on Lake Erie to Port Weller on Lake Ontario, and is a major link of the Saint Lawrence Seaway. The canal was built between 1912 and 1932, and was deepened in 1972. It has eight locks to overcome the 100-m difference in height between lakes Erie and Ontario. Why do you think this canal was built?

Economic Development

Fact File

Ecology is the study of our home, planet earth; *economy* is its management. Both words come from the Greek *oikos*, "home." Ecology and economy should work together.

A region's level of economic development has a significant impact on its population patterns. For example, many people in less industrialized countries tend to have larger families, and so the populations in these countries grow more rapidly. On the other hand, people in industrialized nations tend to have higher levels of technological development as a result of better access to education, health care, and more job opportunities. Because of these conditions, people in economically developed countries tend to have smaller families and live in regions with sparse or moderate population density. (Two economically developed countries that are exceptions to this general rule are Japan and the Netherlands.)

REGION

Before 1800 most people lived in rural areas. With the **Industrial Revolution**, many people began moving to cities to work in the factories that were springing up there.

SEE PAGE 116

In recent years, the growth of cities in economically developing countries (such as Mexico and Malaysia) has been very rapid; fewer than 50% of people in these countries live in rural areas.

"Concern for the ecology, the endangered habitat of the human race, will increasingly have to be built into economic policy. And increasingly, concern for the ecology and ecological policies will transcend national boundaries."

Peter F. Drucker, author

Fact File

Although Asia is home to the largest total number of people, Africa is the continent that is growing the fastest. Meanwhile, populations in some countries in eastern Europe — such as Hungary — are shrinking.

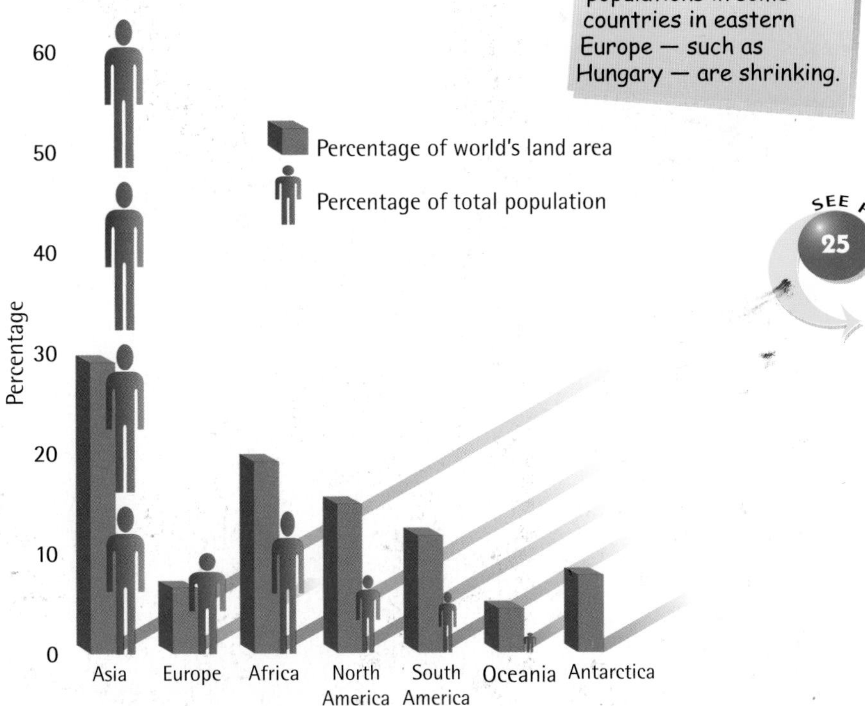

SEE PAGE 25

Figure 1.13

This graph compares the area of continents to their populations. Which continents have the largest share of people?

History

INTERACTION

The history of a region influences the number of people that live there. Areas that were settled earliest — for example, because of a favourable natural environment or access to water transportation — may have larger populations. This is because these settlement sites have existed for a longer period of time. Only in the last 300 or so years have large numbers of people from other continents moved to North and South America. This is a short time compared with how long people have been living in Europe, Africa, and Asia, all of which have higher population densities than North and South America.

SEE PAGE 209

GO TO

http://sunsite.unc.edu/expo/1492.exhibit/Intro.html

This site is called "1492: An Ongoing Voyage" and focusses on the cultures of the early Americas, Christopher Columbus, and the European claims in the western hemisphere. Look at the drawing on the opening screen. If the First Nations peoples decided not to let the Europeans land, describe two ways in which your life today would be different. Explore this site to follow the fascinating changes that have taken place in the Americas since 1492.

Figure 1.14

Tokyo is one of the largest cities in the world. Because of the huge numbers of people using the subway system, there is massive congestion during rush hours. At some stations, white-gloved "pushers" have been hired to push people into the trains. Imagine travelling in this crowded subway every morning. What might be one solution to this problem of overcrowding?

Figure 1.15

These ancient Egyptian statues were moved from Aswan to nearby Abu Simbel by the United Nations Educational, Scientific, and Cultural Organization (UNESCO) when they were threatened by floods from the building of the Aswan High Dam. Many people also were relocated when the dam was built. What effects do you think this forced migration had on them? Can you think of a situation in Canada in which people were forced to relocate because of human development?

SEE PAGE 207

It's Your World

Factors affecting population patterns work together. For example, farming in North Africa began thousands of years ago close to the Nile River in Egypt, where plenty of water and fertile soil could grow enough food to support many people. Overall, Egypt's population density is 56 people/km^2, which is moderate. Yet, if you look at a map of world population density (page 290 of the map appendix), a startling pattern can be seen in the shape of a narrow finger of land around the Nile, which has a very dense population. This population pattern can be described as **linear**.

For centuries, many people drowned when the Nile flooded its banks each year. Technological development allowed the building of the Aswan High Dam in the 1960s and 1970s. The dam reduced the risk of flooding by creating a "controlled flood" – Lake Nasser, an artificial lake nearly 500 km long. It also helped irrigate over 400 000 ha of farmland and established one of the world's largest hydro-electric generating stations, allowing for an even denser population in the region.

REGION

1. Give two reasons why it is useful to understand population distribution and density patterns.
2. Where in Canada is good arable land found? How has this affected where people live?
3. Why do people prefer to settle close to water?
4. Which continent has the highest population growth? Which has the largest total population?

CASE STUDY

Australia

SEE PAGE 151

In the late 1700s, England sent thousands of its prisoners to work on farms in Australia. When they were released, they were offered a choice of returning to England or staying in Australia. Many were offered provisions for 18 months and a grant of land if they stayed. Because most of these people were poor and had no opportunities for work in England, they chose Australia — and their descendants remain there today. About 94% of Australians are of European descent, mainly of British or Irish background.

REGION

Figure 1.16

Location of Australia.

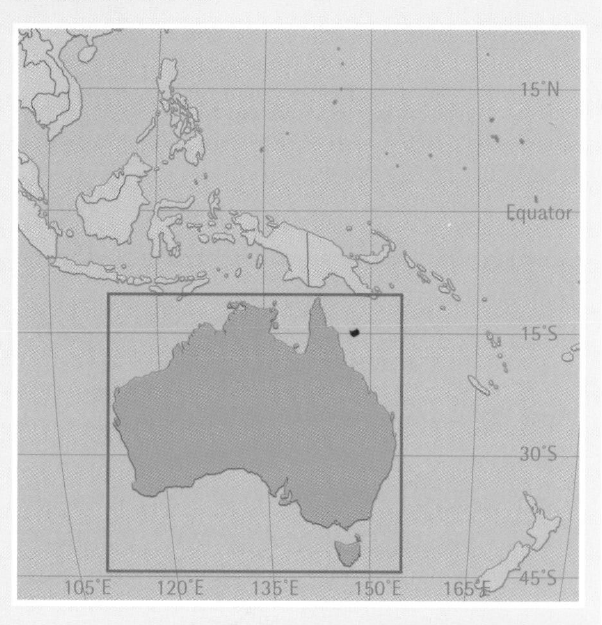

Figure 1.17

The Great Barrier Reefs, along the coast of Queensland, are the world's largest coral reefs. How might increasing population density and tourism affect the plants and animals that are part of the reefs' ecosystem?

The first English settlement was at Botany Bay in 1788. This settlement grew and became the large city of Sydney. From 1788 to 1850 Britain transported over 160 000 prisoners and poor people to Australia. In 1850, the population of Australia was 400 000 people and 13 million sheep.

This changed dramatically when gold was discovered in New South Wales in 1851 and later in Victoria. The discovery of this natural resource led to the industrialization of Australia. During the 1850s, the population tripled.

Fact File

Four out of every five Australians (80%) live in one of the densely populated coastal cities that are situated on only 3% of the country's land area.

The prisoners from Britain were not the first inhabitants of Australia; at that time, about 300 000 Aborigines lived there, just as their ancestors had done for thousands of years. The British arrivals brought new diseases such as cholera and smallpox. They also caused social and cultural disruptions to the local society, and the population of Aborigines declined dramatically. Today Australia has a population that includes about 150 000 Aborigines. Some live in the "outback" in the centre of Australia or in the Northern Territories. Many work on ranches or farms, or have moved to cities in the more densely populated southeast and southwest.

Most of Australia is sparsely populated with a very low population density in the centre of the continent. The eastern, southeastern, and southwestern coasts are locations where most people choose to live.

INTERACTION

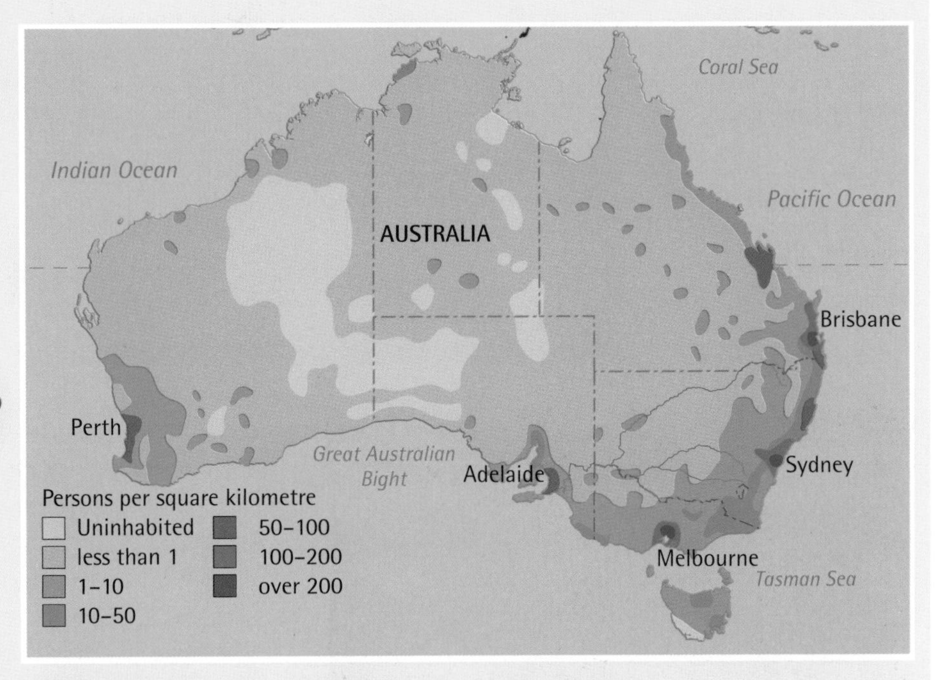

Figure 1.18

Describe the population patterns shown on this map.

> ***"The more you know, the less you need."***
> **Aborigine saying**

Figure 1.19

A celebration of National Aboriginal Week in Darwin, Australia. Australian Aborigines did not receive the right to vote until 1967. How does that compare with Canada's treatment of its First Nations people?

Figure 1.20

Dry climate and flat land throughout most of Australia are suited to livestock farming, especially sheep.

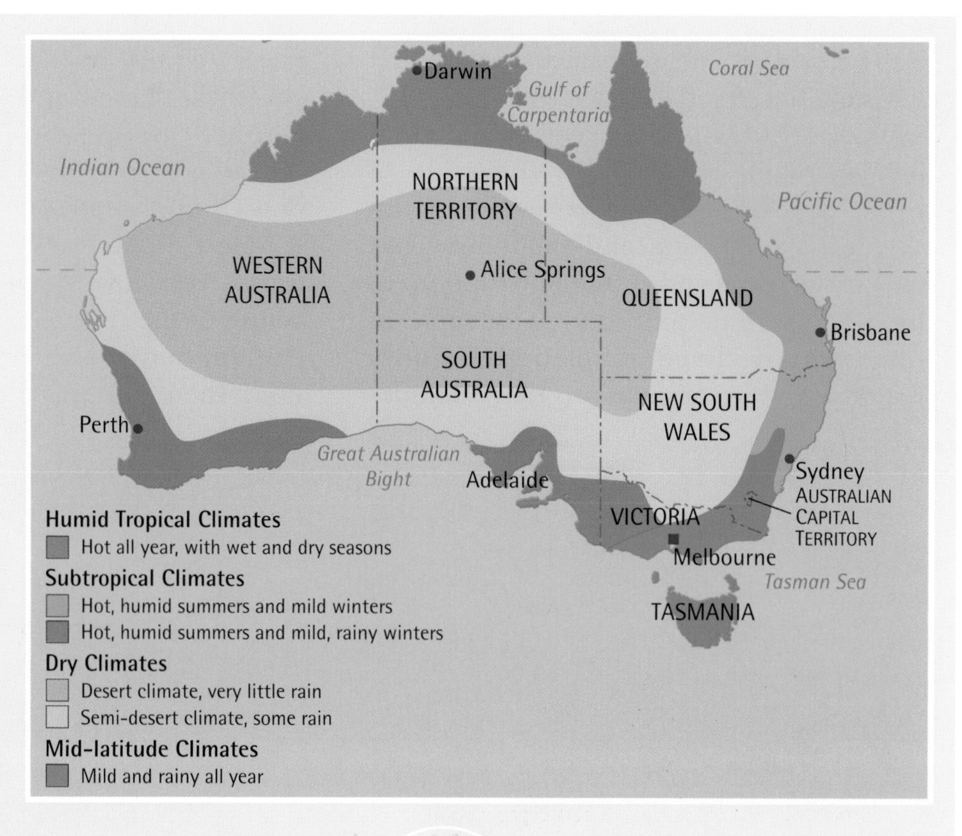

Figure 1.21

Sheep farming in Australia.

How to Speak "Strine" (Australian Slang)

billibong – water hole
billy – container for boiling tea
bloke – man
bonzer – great, terrific
chook – chicken
dingo – Australian wild dog
dinki-di – the real thing
jumbuck – sheep
mob – flock of sheep
outback – remote bush in rural area
sheila – woman
station – sheep ranch
swag – bedroll and belongings
up a gumtree – in a mess
waltz matilda – carry a swag

Australia wins the awards for the flattest continent, the driest continent (two-thirds of the land is desert or semi-desert), and the most urbanized continent (85% of the people live in cities). The only parts of Australia with enough rain to support forests are the northern and southeastern coastal plains. The southeastern part of the continent has the most and best arable land. Australia is also the leading industrial country, and the most economically developed, in the southern hemisphere.

The settlement of Canada began at about the same time as that in Australia. Today, Canada has a population of over 30 million, while Australia's is less than 20 million. One reason for Australia's slower growth was its government policies in the early 1900s, which allowed immigration from only some countries in Europe.

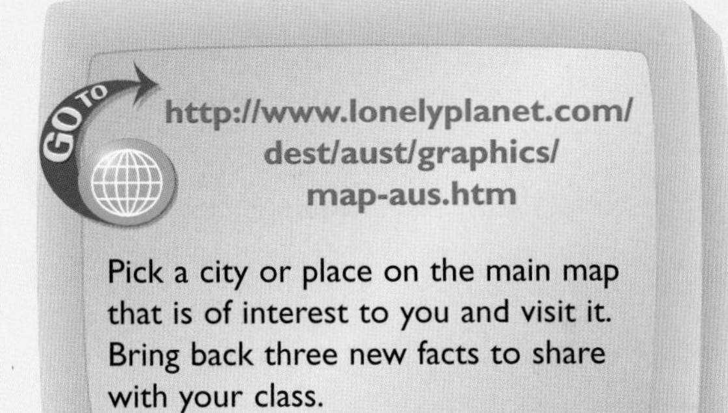

Fact File

In the Australian outback, the population density averages less than one person per square kilometre.

Figure 1.22

Alice Springs, Australia receives 253 mm of precipitation a year, while Melbourne receives 650 mm. Which months make up the peak growing season in this part of the world? Why?

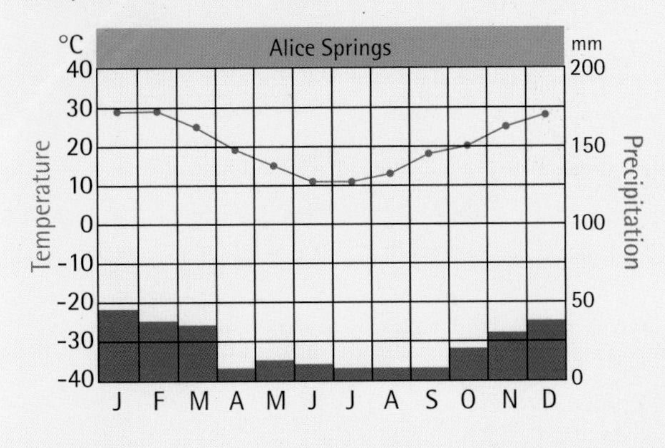

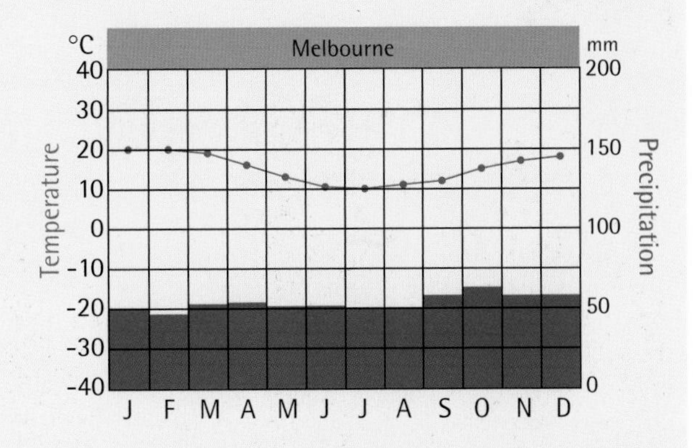

1. What is the population density of most of Australia?
2. Where are most of Australia's cities located?
3. Using the map of Australia's climate regions in Figure 1.20, suggest reasons to support your answers to questions 1 and 2.
4. Natural environment, history, and level of economic development are factors that influence population patterns. Looking at the Case Study on Australia, can you think of any other factors that may influence population patterns? Explain.

Understanding the Concepts

1. Which factor that influences population patterns do you think is the most important? Give reasons for your explanation.

2. Draw a timeline to show the number of years it has taken to add each additional billion to the world's population. (*Hint:* Use the data from the It's Your World on page 7 ["World Population Milestones"].)

3. What is the name given to the vast rural area in the centre of the Australian continent? What natural features explain the very sparse population of this area?

4. Write a well-constructed paragraph explaining to a friend how population density varies around the world.

5. Do you agree with the quote by Jacques Cousteau on page 5? What other factors contribute to environmental damage?

6. Design a chart to compare living conditions in an area of high population density with living conditions in an area of sparse population density (refer to Figures 1.5 and 1.6 on pages 8–9).

Research and Communication Skills

7. Develop a survey of five or six questions to conduct a census of your class. Brainstorm with other class members to decide what information you would like to collect, e.g., the distance people travel to school; type of transportation used; number of brothers and sisters each person has; number and type of pets. Graph and display the results.

8. Why do you think New York City became the largest city in the United States? Consider all factors that influence populations, e.g., location, resources, history.

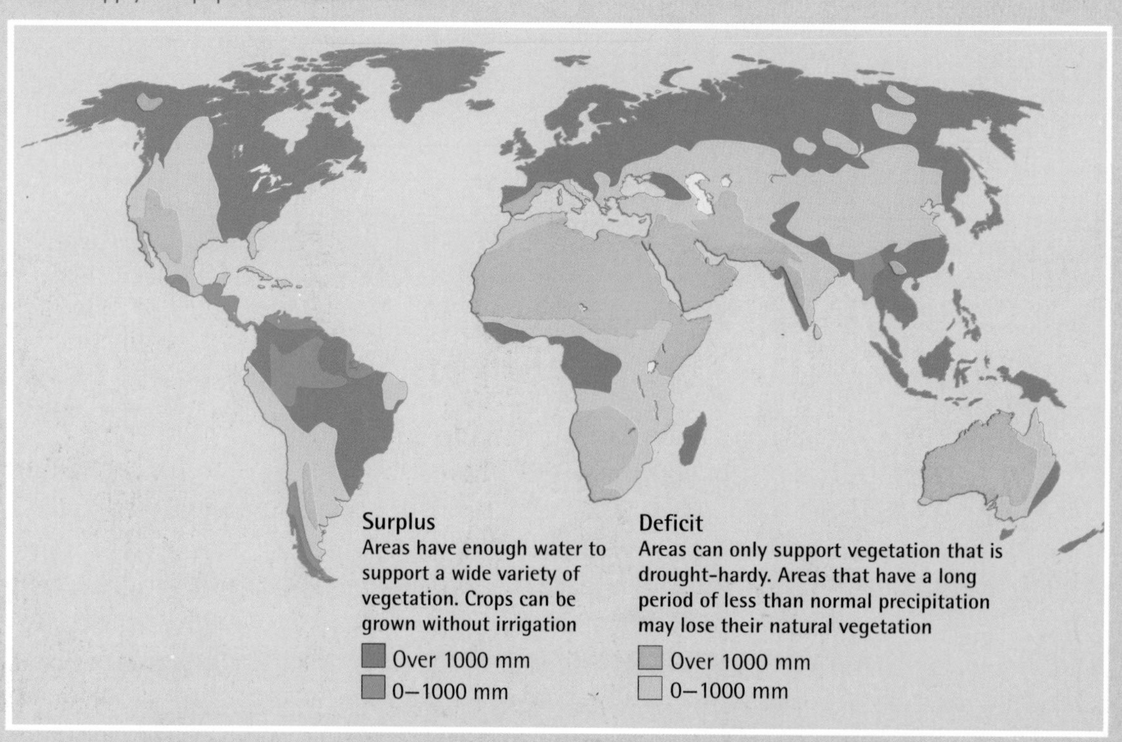

Figure 1.23

World map of water deficiency (drought) and surplus (flooding). What correlations can you observe between water supply and population distribution?

Map and Globe Skills

9. Look at the map of world population density (page 290 of the map appendix). The darkest shades of colour show places with the highest population density. What patterns do you notice? Which parts of the world are uninhabited? Using an atlas, name the countries that appear to have the highest populations and population densities.

10. The patterns of world population distribution show some amazing correlations (similarities) to patterns found on maps of the natural environment. Compare Figure 1.23 with the map of world population distribution (page 290, map appendix). What patterns do you observe? Use an atlas to find other world thematic maps (e.g., reliefs, landforms, climates, soils) and compare them with regions of dense, moderate, and sparse population on the map of world population distribution.

11. Using an atlas to obtain a physical or relief map of Australia, find out where people living in the cities of Melbourne and Canberra would be able to ski or snowboard. At what time of year would this be possible?

12. Using a thematic map of urbanization in an atlas, identify the 12 largest cities in the world. Which of these are located on water? Which are major seaports?

13. Use an atlas to locate those countries in the world that have the top 10 total populations and those with the 10 highest population densities. Are there any countries that can be found on both lists?

Applications

14. Do you think that world population distribution will change over the next 50 years? Give reasons for your explanation.

15. What changes in population density do you predict over the next 50 years? Give reasons for your opinions.

16. "The natural environment is the most significant factor that influences where people live." Do you agree or disagree with this statement? Give supporting reasons for your point of view.

17. Why is it impossible to get a truly accurate number for the present world population?

18. Consider your community as a place to live. What are the favourable and unfavourable factors about its location?

Figure 1.24

Sydney Harbour is Australia's major seaport and the home of its famous Opera House.

How People Live: Population Characteristics

EXPECTATIONS

- demonstrate an understanding of the terms describing population characteristics, such as birth, death, and literacy
- demonstrate an understanding of the correlation between population characteristics
- compare the characteristics of developed and developing countries

Number One!

6TH YEAR IN A ROW!

Canada still rated best place to live — U.N.

This headline, from a daily newspaper in September 1999, should make us feel fortunate to live in Canada. But who decides which is the best country to live in? And how is this decided?

The United Nations selects a number of factors that tell how people live in 175 of the world's countries: such things as how long people can expect to live, how many people can read and write, and how much money people earn. These factors are expressed as **statistics**. Statistics is the science of collecting, interpreting, and presenting different kinds of data in number form. The United Nations combines these statistics into its **Human Development Index**, which gives a general picture of living conditions in each country.

Figure 2.1

Canada is a huge and diverse country. Do you think everyone in all parts of Canada would agree that we're "number one"? Why or why not?

Figure 2.2

These countries rate the highest and the lowest scores on the United Nations Human Development Index.

10 Highest Scores	10 Lowest Scores
Canada	Sierra Leone
France	Niger
Norway	Burkina Faso
USA	Mali
Iceland	Burundi
Finland	Ethiopia
Netherlands	Eritrea
Japan	Guinea
New Zealand	Mozambique
Sweden	Gambia

http://www.undp.org/hdro/98hdi1.htm

This site lists 175 countries rated by the U.N. Which country is listed number two? 65th? Last? Give one reason why you think that country was listed last.

Canada may top the list for the highest quality of life in the world, but the United Nations Human Development Report raises some concerns about Canada's poor record on child poverty and its treatment of First Nations peoples.

Figure 2.3

More than 15% of Canadian children live in poverty, such as these First Nations children living on a reserve in Alberta. Why do you think that, in such a rich country like Canada, some people are so poor?

SEE PAGE 147

Number Crunching

Statistics is the science of counting events, such as how many TVs are bought in a year, or how many people are in the military in a country, or the amount of energy each person uses. When these statistics are mapped, they show global patterns. Statistics are used as a tool by geographers as they collect, analyse, and interpret this numerical information in order to understand the past and present, solve problems, manage resources today, and plan for tomorrow.

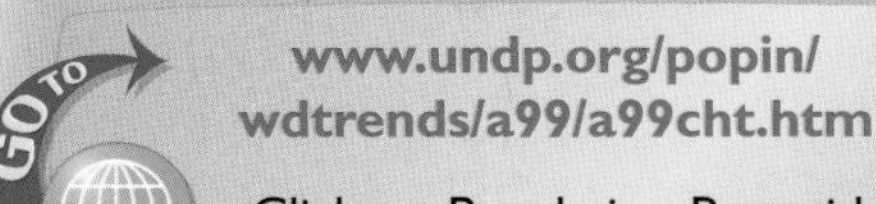

GO TO www.undp.org/popin/wdtrends/a99/a99cht.htm

Click on Population Pyramids: Age Structure, 1999 and 2050. There are four sets of graphs: World, More Developed Regions, Less Developed Regions, and Least Developed Regions. Figures are given to show how each region looked in 1996 and how it will probably look in 2050. What trends can you see?

Population Characteristics

Factors that tell us how a population is changing or how well people live in a country are called **population characteristics**. Everyone who plans for the future — large corporations, hospitals, retail stores, school systems, **non-governmental organizations** like UNICEF or Amnesty International, as well as individuals — needs information about population characteristics. There are many different population characteristics, such as birth rates, death rates, literacy rates, and life expectancy. They are like pieces of a giant puzzle. Geographers put all the pieces together to get a clearer picture of what a country is like and how well its people live.

SEE PAGE 5

"Demography, the study of human populations, is the most powerful — and underutilized — tool we have to understand the past and to foretell the future."

David K. Foot, "Boom, Bust and Echo"

Figure 2.4

Every family is different. Do you think there is a "best" size for a family? Why?

Fact File

The fertility rate in Africa is 5.8 children per woman. Remember that this is an average of all the countries in Africa. Niger and Uganda are the countries that have the highest fertility rates, with an average of more than 7 children born per woman.

Figure 2.5

Why do you think the fertility rate, on average, has decreased worldwide?

Counting the Babies

How many children are there in your family? The average number of children born in Canada is about 1.55 per family. That is the average number of babies born in a woman's lifetime in the country. This is called the **fertility rate**. The average fertility rate for the whole world now stands at 2.7 births per woman. During the 1950s, the average was more than five births per woman. Women everywhere in the world are now having fewer babies. The decline is greatest in developing countries. The current fertility rate is highest in Africa.

Figure 2.6

Fertility rates for selected countries. What ideas do you have that might explain the decrease in fertility rates over the last 25 years?

Country	1975	1998
Albania	2.3	1.3
Australia	2.2	1.8
Brazil	5.8	2.6
Canada	1.8	1.5
China	5.8	1.9
Germany	1.5	1.0
Guatemala	6.4	5.1
India	5.7	3.4
Indonesia	5.2	2.9
Mexico	6.2	3.9
Rwanda	8.7	6.6
Tunisia	6.0	2.9
Yemen	8.5	7.6

Going Up or Going Down?

One reason a country's population changes is that people are born and die each year. The **birth rate** tells us the number of babies who are born each year for every 1000 people in a country. The **death rate** tells us the number of people who die each year for every 1000 people in a country. If the number of births is greater than the number of deaths, then the population will go up. Sometimes the death rate goes up sharply for one year because of a major catastrophe, such as a severe natural disaster, an **epidemic**, or a war.

When the population goes up because the birth rate is higher than the natural death rate, it is called a **natural increase**. When birth rates are lower than death rates, a country's population will actually go down. A number of countries in Europe have decreasing populations. More people are dying than there are babies being born. Birth rates are falling everywhere in the world, but death rates are falling even faster because of advances in medicine, greater access to medical care, and improved living conditions.

SEE PAGE 282

Fact File

World's 10 most populous nations, 2025 (estimate)
- China
- India
- USA
- Indonesia
- Pakistan
- Nigeria
- Brazil
- Bangladesh
- Ethiopia
- Russia

SEE PAGE 156

Getting a Fix on the Numbers

Canada has a birth rate of 13 per 1000 or 13/1000. Canada's death rate is 7/1000. Because the death rate is lower than the birth rate, Canada has a natural increase every year. To calculate the natural increase of a country, find the difference between the birth rate and the death rate.

Figure 2.7

Natural increase in Canada's and Malawi's populations.

Canada

$$\frac{13}{1000} - \frac{7}{1000} = \frac{6}{1000} = 0.006 \times 100 = 0.6\%$$

Birth rate – Death rate = Natural increase for Canada
For every 1000 people who live in Canada, six more people are added to the population each year.

Malawi 

$$\frac{50}{1000} - \frac{20}{1000} = \frac{30}{1000} = 0.030 \times 100 = 3\%$$

Birth rate – Death rate = Natural increase for Malawi
For every 1000 people who live in Malawi, 30 more people are added to the population each year.

Figure 2.8

Do you think it is important that Canada's population grow a great deal? Why?

Figure 2.9

On a typical day in Canada, about 1100 babies are born and about 600 people die. Some 610 people come to Canada as immigrants while 135 people emigrate from Canada to other countries.

GO TO

www.statcan.ca/english/Pgdb/

This is the Web site for Statistics Canada. Click on Population under The People. Click on Population at this screen, too. Click on Population Density, Births and Deaths for selected countries. Which country has the highest natural increase? The lowest?

The global population growth was 1.8% in the early 1980s and has now gone down to 1.33% per year. The United Nations predicts that this may drop to 1% by the year 2025. Most industrialized countries, like Canada, have a low natural increase or, like Italy, a decreasing population. Most developing countries, like Malawi, have higher rates of natural increase, usually averaging between 2% and 3%. It is important to remember, though, as you study these figures, that the statistics represent real people (including geography students!), living real lives.

MOVEMENT/PATTERN

Another factor that causes the population to change is immigration. Some people move out of a country, while others move in. The difference between the number of people leaving (emigrating) and those coming in (immigrating) is called the **net migration**. The population growth of a country depends upon both natural increase and net migration.

Fact File

Net migration for Canada:

Years	Immigration	Emigration	Net
1976-86	1 216 551	555 807	+ 660 744
1987-97	2 339 155	440 144	+1 899 011

SEE PAGE 271

Doubling Time

Imagine the changes in your living conditions if the number of people in your family doubled over the next few years. Would there be enough room? Would there be enough money? If your family grew that quickly, you would certainly be forced to make many adjustments in your life. When a country's population is growing quickly and it doubles in size quickly, people have to make adjustments in how they live. There could easily be many problems for the government in providing food, housing, education, health care, a healthy natural environment, and other basic requirements. It is important to know how fast a population is growing so that governments can plan for the future.

The faster the population is growing, the shorter the amount of time it will take for the country's population to double. The average **doubling time** for industrialized, more developed countries is 500 years. For the less industrialized, less developed countries the average is only 37 years. The population of many African countries will double in less than 25 years. This big gap in numbers (from 500 years to 37 years) clearly shows the difference in population growth between developed and developing countries.

Fact File

If Canada's population continues to grow at current rates, it will take 116 years for the population to double.

Figure 2.10
Rush hour in New Delhi, India.

It's Your World

Paul Ehrlich, a Stanford University professor who has written books on population issues, travelled to New Delhi, India. This description from his book, *The Population Bomb*, provides a vivid picture of life in some parts of developing countries: "My wife and daughter and I were returning to our hotel in an ancient taxi ... . As we crawled through the city, we entered a crowded slum. The temperature was well over 37°C, and the air was a haze of dust and smoke. The streets seemed alive with people. People eating, people washing, people sleeping. People visiting, arguing, and screaming. People thrusting their hands through the taxi window, begging. People defecating and urinating. People clinging to buses. People herding animals. People, people, people, people."

Figure 2.11

What information would you need to help you determine whether China's one-child policy is working?

It's Your World

Close to one-fifth of all the people in the world live in China. The Chinese government tries to get people to limit their family size to only one child. This population policy is an attempt to slow down China's population growth. China's natural increase is only 1.1%, but because it has such a large population to begin with (1.2 billion), the total number of people included in that increase is huge.

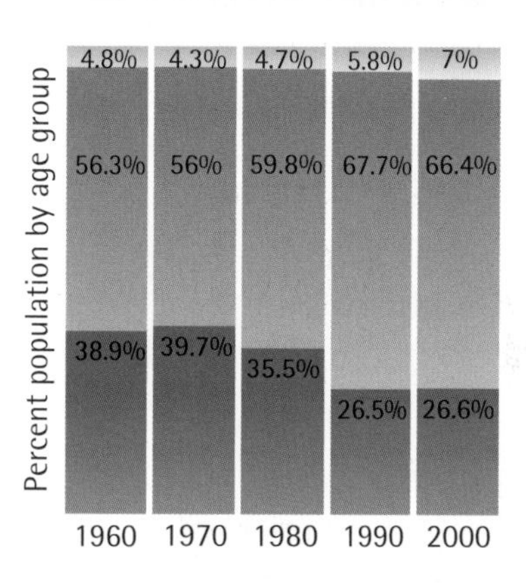

Figure 2.12

Population breakdown for China by age.

1. Name three population characteristics that tell us whether a country's population is changing (growing, stable, or shrinking).
2. Which parts of the world are experiencing a very high increase in population?
3. Explain the difference between natural increase and fertility rate.
4. Why is the doubling time so low in African countries? Explain, referring to specific population characteristics.
5. Which parts of the world are experiencing a population decrease?
6. Identify two responsibilities that you think governments have with respect to population growth.

A Different Kind of Pyramid

Population pyramids are a type of graph that give information about the number of people in each age group and the balance of males and females in a country's population. The pyramid is divided down the middle to show males on the left and females on the right. Each graph is a series of horizontal bar graphs stacked on top of one another. The youngest people in a society are shown in the bars at the bottom of the graph. The oldest people are on the top.

SEE PAGE 263

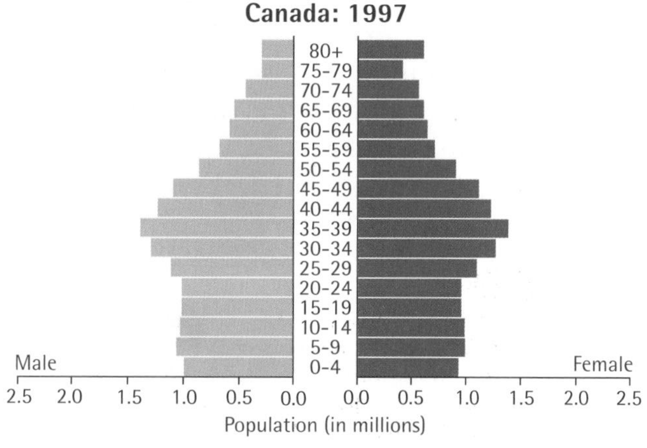

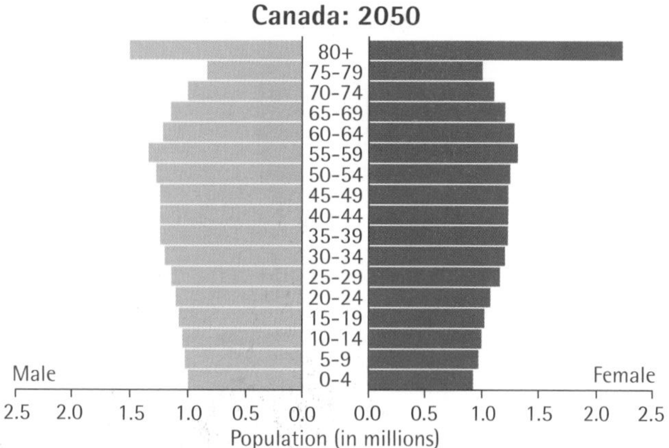

Figure 2.13

Population pyramids for Canada. Locate the bars that represent Canada's "baby boom" generation. What impact does this group have on the shape of the population pyramid predicted for 2050? Suggest why the bar for females over 80 is larger than the bar for males over 80 in the 2050 graph.

The Human Pyramid

Fact File

Uganda is the world's "youngest" country, with almost half of its population under age 15. Italy is the world's "oldest" country, with half its population over 40.

Population pyramids are useful for studying issues related to the age and sex distribution of populations of different countries. For example, if you want to predict some of the things that will happen in a country, it helps to know about age groups. If more people are old, then you know that you must plan for the needs of senior citizens.

Countries with rapidly growing populations have very different age structures from those that grow slowly. A rapidly growing population has a wide base at the bottom (a large number of young people) and a narrow top (not many older people). This type of population pyramid is typical of developing countries. A population pyramid that has a narrow base and fairly equal numbers of people in all age groups represents a more developed country.

It's Your World

If your parents were born between 1946 and 1965, they are part of a large group of children born after World War II known as the "baby boom" or "baby boomers," who have had a big influence on North American society. More families meant more houses were needed. More children meant more schools had to be built. This big surge in the population created changes in every aspect of Canadian life.

Figure 2.14

Describe one or two differences between the population patterns shown on the two graphs. Which of the graphs shows a greater increase in total population to 2050? Use the information from the graph to explain why.

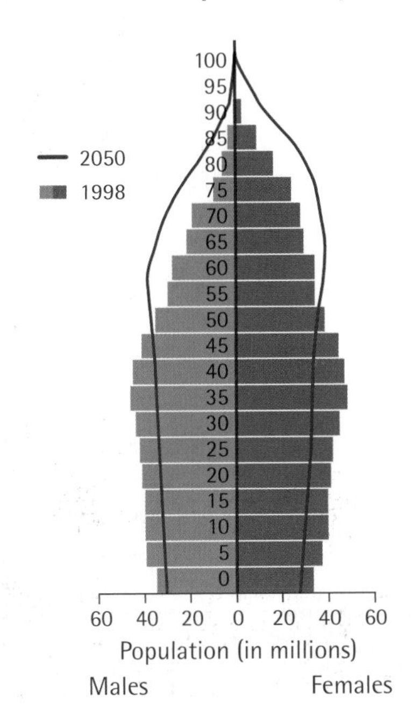

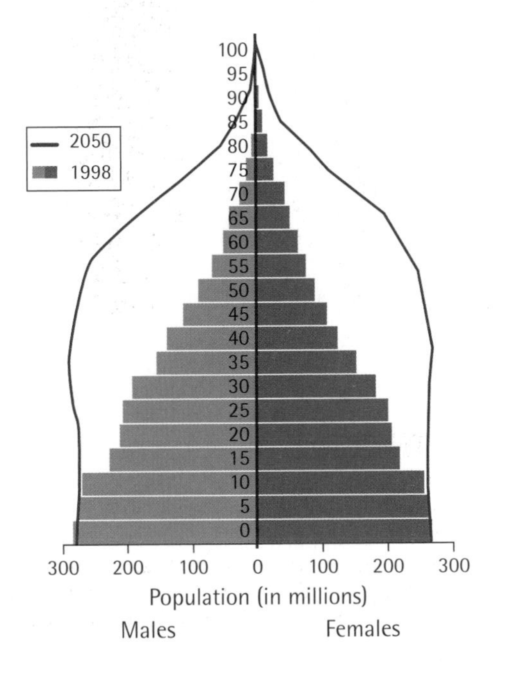

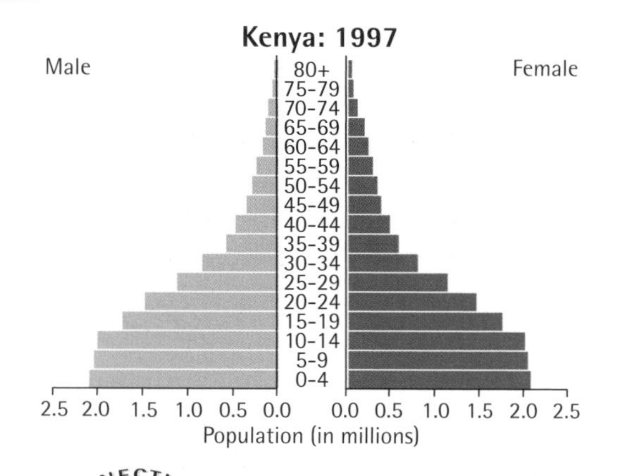

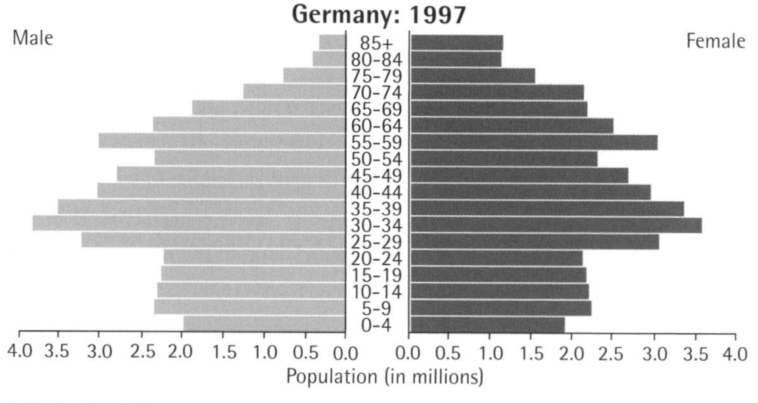

Figure 2.15

Compare these population pyramids with those in Figure 2.13 on page 30. Identify whether each of the three countries (Canada, Kenya, and Germany) has a population that is increasing quickly, increasing slowly, decreasing, or stable.

Connections to Demographics

Population characteristics are interconnected. Most developing countries have a large percentage of their population under 15 years of age. These countries will experience a rapid growth in population, as there are far more young people who will soon be having children (adding to the population) than there are old people who are dying. Even if the fertility rate goes down and these young people have fewer children than their parents did, the fact that there are so many of them to start with — who will have children in the next few years — will keep the population growing for another 60 or 70 years. If medical treatment, sanitation, education, and food and water quality improve in the developing world, life expectancy will increase and death rates will continue to decrease. You might expect these two factors to cause a further increase in population. However, demographers have discovered that these improvements in quality of life usually result in a slowdown in total population growth. In other words, when people have a better quality of life, they tend to have fewer children.

SEE PAGE 5

SEE PAGE 156

GO TO www.census.gov/ftp/pub/ipc

This Web site offers population pyramids for many countries for 1997 and estimates for the years 2025 and 2050. Click on www/. Make a note of the world's population. (Return to this site in a week to see how fast the world's population is changing!) Next, click on International Data Base (IDB). Choose Population Pyramids. Select Canada, then go to the bottom of the page and click on Submit Query. Do the same for Afghanistan. Based on these graphs, write a paragraph comparing Afghanistan and Canada. Print your work, if possible.

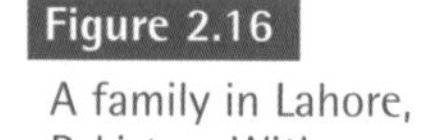

Figure 2.16

A family in Lahore, Pakistan. With a fertility rate of 5.2, Pakistan has one of the highest population growth rates in the world.

Comparing Quality of Life

The United Nations rated Canada as the best place to live in the world from 1994 through 1999 because most Canadians have clean drinking water, abundant food, comfortable housing, and full-time employment. We often take these things for granted, although most Canadians know there are significant differences in standard of living around the world. There are areas of the world where many people do not have access to these basic requirements. A number of additional population characteristics help us to measure standard of living or quality of life.

Fact File

Canadians are getting fatter! The number of overweight Canadians in 1999 increased to 34%, up from 22% of the total population in 1985.

Life Expectancy

Life expectancy is the number of years that a baby born in a particular year can be expected to live under current conditions. Life expectancy at birth is a key indicator of the health and quality of life of a society. Where many people do not have access to the basic requirements for a good quality of life, such as health care, clean water, and abundant food, one can expect to live, on average, to around 50 or 60 years of age. Countries that have lower economic stability or that are engaged in war have even lower life expectancies.

Fact File

As a grade 8 student in Canada today, you will probably
- complete high school, and possibly go on to college or university
- marry by the time you are 30–34 years old
- have one or two children
- have an annual family income of $40–50 thousand
- live at least 78 years
- enjoy good health most of your life.

Figure 2.17

Population characteristics for selected countries. Which country listed here has the lowest life expectancy? Suggest why this is so.

Country	Life expectancy (years)	Per capita income (US$)	Doubling time (years)	Literacy rate (% of pop.)	Birth rate (per 1000)	Infant mortality (per 1000)	Persons per motor vehicle
Bangladesh	57	230	35	38	31	97.7	1200.0
Brazil	66	3 370	41	83	25	37.0	9.0
Canada	78	19 570	116	99	13	5.6	1.6
China	70	530	66	82	17	45.5	225.0
Ethiopia	50	130	23	36	46	125.7	800.0
Iceland	79	24 590	68	100	17	5.3	1.8
India	59	310	37	52	29	63.1	225.0
Japan	80	34 630	315	99	10	4.1	2.1
Mexico	73	4 010	32	90	27	25.8	9.0
Norway	78	26 480	182	100	14	5.0	2.2

Life Expectancy for Canadians Reaches New High

Life expectancy for Canadians has reached a new high, 75.1 years for men and 81.4 years for women, according to a study released in 1999. Only the Swiss and Japanese live longer. Men are more likely to die earlier because of heart disease, accidents, cancer, and suicide.

Based on these statistics, to what year would a baby born in Canada today live?

Fact File

Although many people claim to have lived to an exceptionally old age, they often lack birth certificates or other proofs. However, in 1997, Jeanne Calment died in Arles, France, at the age of 122 years — the greatest authenticated age to which any human has lived.

"The most striking advances against poverty have been in health. Average life expectancy in developing countries has risen significantly."

World Development Report, World Bank, 1996

Literacy Rate

Literacy (the ability to read and write) is important in helping people to learn and to improve their quality of life. The **literacy rate** is a measure of the population over 15 who can read and write. More than one billion adults in the world cannot, because they do not have access to basic education. In many less developed countries, children spend a great deal of their time producing food or working

Fact File

In Brazil, illiterate women have an average of 6.5 children, while women with a secondary school education have an average of 2.5 children.

It's Your World

The Caucasus Mountains is a region that is noted for its large population of very old people. While it is difficult to authenticate the actual ages of the villagers there, it is certain that many people are over 100 years old. This finding seems surprising, because they live in a relatively remote region and work hard in the fields to produce food despite their advanced years. One man claims to be 168 years old; his wife says she is 120. They say they were married in 1897. What factors do you suppose might account for the unusually long life expectancy in this small part of the world?

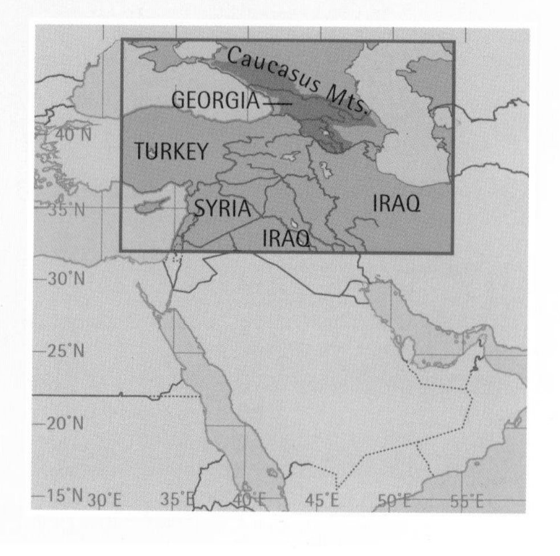

Figure 2.18

Before 1990, Iraq was the world's third largest supplier of oil. Over the last decade, however, the United Nations has prohibited all trade with Iraq because of its invasion of Kuwait. As a result, the per capita income of Iraqis has fallen, and food supplies have been rationed. These women are lining up to receive one chicken each for their families' dinner.

to earn money, leaving little time or money for school. While world literacy rates are improving, fewer than 10% of children in most developing countries get as far as secondary school. In some countries, girls are not given the opportunity to go to school at all. Statistics show that women who have received a basic education and are literate tend to have fewer children, resulting in a lower fertility rate.

Earning Power

SEE PAGE 124

One statistic that is often used to measure quality of life is **per capita income** — the average amount of money earned by each person in a country for one year. Per capita income is calculated by dividing all the money earned in a country in a year by the number of people in that country. Because this figure is an average, it can be misleading. For example, Kuwait has a high per capita income because it is rich in oil, which it sells to other countries. This brings in a lot of money for some. However, most Kuwaitis earn low wages. There are a few very rich people, and many more who are not.

Fact File

	Kuwait	Canada
World GNP rating	51st	7th
GNP per capita	$16 400	$20 758
Inflation	8%	1.3%
Unemployment	1.5%	6.9%

A Different Kind of Gross

Gross domestic product (GDP) is the total value of all goods and services produced in a year in a given country. **GDP per capita** is calculated by dividing the country's total GDP by the number of people living in the country. GDP is sometimes used instead of per capita income. Per capita GDP is just one of many population characteristics that can be used to indicate the difference between developed and developing countries.

SEE PAGE 125

> *"If everybody lived like today's North Americans, it would take at least 5 additional planet Earths to produce the resources, absorb the wastes, and otherwise maintain life support. Unfortunately, good planets are hard to find."*
>
> Mathis Wackernagel & William Rees, "Our Ecological Footprint"

Fact File

	Haiti	Canada
Life expectancy	57	79
Literacy rate	45%	99%
Per capita income	$300	$28 000

Figure 2.19

Two views of Haiti, one of the world's poorest countries. Population characteristics indicate a very low quality of life; for example, only 30% of the population has potable (drinkable) water. Overcrowded slums like this present serious, seemingly unsolvable problems. for people who live in such poverty. What are two things you think a poor country like Haiti can do to help erase its poverty?

ENVIRONMENT

INTERACTION

Connections to Math

Everything in our world today is more interconnected than ever before. One statistical indicator is often related to another. For example, if a high number of people in an area smoke cigarettes, there is likely to be a high number of cases of lung cancer. As the number of cigarettes smoked goes up, so does the number of lung cancer cases. The two sets of statistics are related or interconnected. As you see different stories in the news, think about how they could very well be connected.

SEE PAGE 177

Scatter Graphs

A **scatter graph** is a good way to show a relationship or interconnection between two population characteristics. Sometimes this is called a **correlation.**

Figure 2.20 shows the relationship between life expectancy and birth rates, using 20 countries as a sample. Dots on the graph are plotted to show the location of the two sets of data, birth rate on the x-axis and life expectancy on the y-axis. A "line of best fit" (the line that comes closest to as many of the dots as possible) is drawn on the graph so that it follows the overall trend of the dots. If all the dots are close to this line, then these two characteristics have a *strong correlation.* If the dots are scattered, with many of them farther away from the line, then there is a *weak correlation* between the two characteristics. If the line extends from the upper left to the lower right, there is a *negative correlation* (when one of the numbers goes up, the other goes down). If the line extends from the lower left to the upper right, there is a *positive correlation* (when one number goes up, the other one does as well).

> ***"The gap between the haves and the have-nots is widening, and it is showing up in the state of their health."***
>
> **Allan Rock, Canadian Minister of Health**

Country	Birth Rate	Life Expectancy
Australia	14	78
Brazil	25	66
Bulgaria	9	71
Canada	13	78
China	17	70
Colombia	27	69
Egypt	30	64
Ethiopia	46	50
France	12	78
India	29	59
Indonesia	24	63
Jamaica	24	74
Japan	10	80
Nepal	39	55
Poland	12	72
Rwanda	44	47
Syria	44	66
Thailand	20	70
Vietnam	30	65
Zambia	45	49

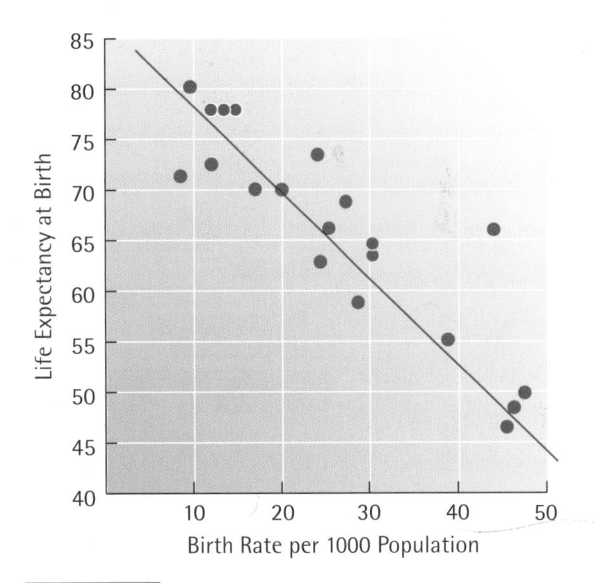

Figure 2.20

This scatter graph shows the relationship between birth rate and life expectancy for 20 countries. There is a strong negative correlation between birth rate and life expectancy. This means that the higher the life expectancy, the lower the birth rate. Countries with high life expectancies will have low birth rates. Do you think that this is a characteristic of a developed or developing country?

Most of the world's leaders seem to be concerned about the prospect of continued population growth. In 1994, they met at a United Nations conference on population and development in Cairo, Egypt to discuss and find solutions for population problems and issues. Many countries promised to work toward slowing population growth and promoting sustainable population that won't use up the earth's resources at a rapid rate, leaving enough for future generations. They agreed to spend money on voluntary family planning programs and other projects that would improve people's quality of life. Not many of these promises have been kept. How do you think this failure may affect your life?

"No other phenomenon casts a darker shadow over the prospects for international development than the staggering growth of population."

Lester B. Pearson, Canadian prime minister and winner of the Nobel Peace Prize, 1957

INTERACTION

SEE PAGE 179

Fact File

Since this comment was made by Pearson in 1969, almost two billion people have been added to the world's population.

Figure 2.21

The gap between developed and developing countries. These figures are averages for 25 developed countries and 150 developing countries. Why are averages sometimes misleading?

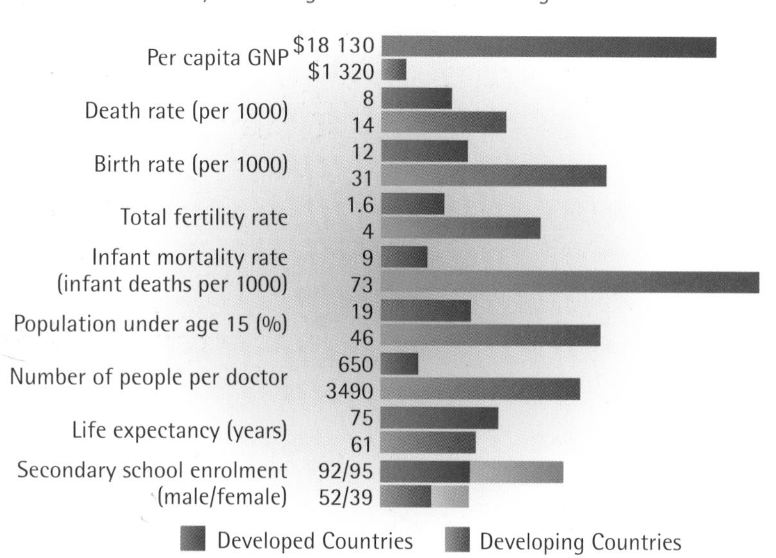

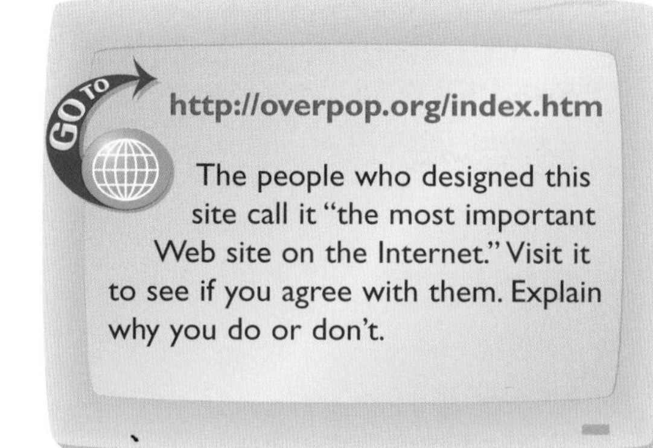

1. Draw a sketch that shows the shape of a population pyramid for a typical developed and a typical developing country.
2. Use the statistics to the left of the scatter graph in Figure 2.20 on the previous page to identify the countries that appear as the highest and lowest dots on the graph.
3. Look at Figure 2.21. What relationship does there appear to be between per capita income and secondary school enrolment?
4. Why do you think women generally can expect to live longer than men?

We're All in It Together

"The future... will depend on the outcome of the quiet, and perhaps not so quiet, war between the comfortable and the underclass."

John Kenneth Galbraith, economist

Most Canadian students are aware of developing countries as television, magazines, and newspapers bring information into our living rooms. Although this may provide a snapshot view of parts of these countries, the focus is usually on hunger and poverty. This view can be narrow and misleading. What you rarely see in the media are the millions of people in developing countries who succeed in school, work hard at jobs, raise families, and pursue their hopes and dreams much as people in developed countries do. One interesting difference might be in the sheer amount of "stuff" that we, in developed countries, have as we buy more and more material goods to satisfy our wants.

Population characteristics show that the new millennium has started with a relatively small number of rich countries that have stable or declining populations and a large number of poorer countries that are growing quickly. More people means using up the earth's natural resources more quickly and producing more and more garbage and pollution.

Figure 2.22

The future of many less developed countries is looking better because more young people are attending school. What is the connection between education and a country's future?

1. Select a population characteristic that is a good indicator of quality of life from Figure 2.17 on page 33. Explain how the characteristic you have chosen tells us how well people live.
2. Why is it important to know about the size of different age groups, such as the percentage of the population under 15, in a country's population?
3. List three problems that may result from rapid population growth.
4. What solutions have the world's leaders suggested for slowing the growth of world population?
5. Why do Canadians not get an accurate picture from the news media of life in developing countries?

CASE STUDY

Youthquake — Prospects for the Future

More than a billion teenagers in the world are just entering their reproductive years. Demographers sometimes refer to this group as a "youthquake" because of the population growth that will occur in the future, as this huge group — one-sixth of the people on the planet — begins to reproduce. There is a strong need for these young people to have access to reproductive health information and services that improve their quality of life.

Over 95% of these teens live in less developed countries, where governments are already struggling to meet current needs for social services, education, jobs, family planning information, and health care. Millions of teens live on their own or on the streets. The decisions that young people everywhere make will help to determine the planet's future. Their families and their education will play an important role in helping today's youth make these decisions.

The stories of Manoj and Ilse show many strong contrasts in the lives of the world's youthful population.

▼▲▼▲▼▲▼▲▼▲

My name is Manoj and I'm 13 years old. I live in a village in Bihar province, India with my mother, father, brother, and two sisters. My older sister, Riasa, died a few years ago of measles. My country, India, grows enough food to feed us all, but the food is not evenly distributed. Many of my friends — and sometimes my family and I — go to bed hungry at night.

My father works very hard. He works about 60 hours a week for part of the year, in the rice fields, scattering fertilizer by hand.

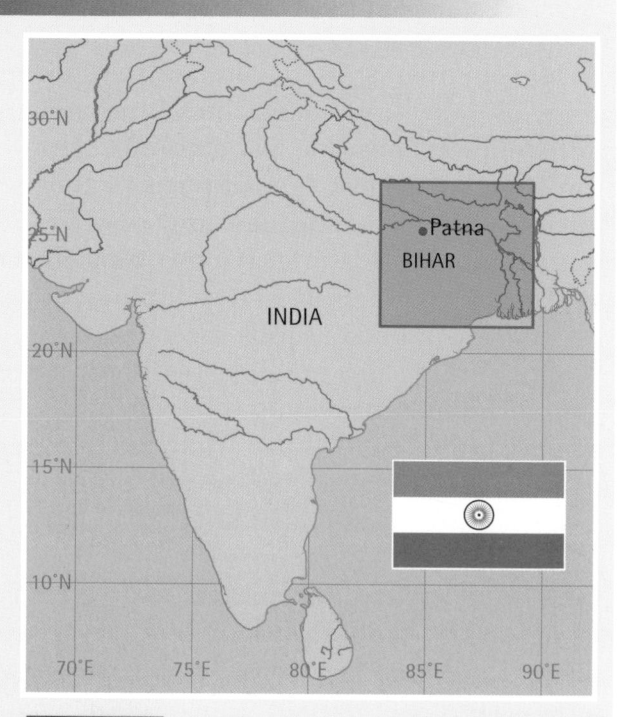

Figure 2.23
Location of India

My mother works about 80 hours a week in the house, keeping the family clean, fed, and clothed, going to collect animal dung or wood for fuel, or walking to the market.

I am lucky because I am still at school, although this is my last year. The secondary school is too far away from my village and anyway, my parents can't afford to send me. There would be expenses for uniforms, supplies, and school fees. Dilip, my younger brother, goes to school, too. He and his classmates sit outside in the shade, as the school is too small for everyone. We can't afford books or writing paper. We write on small pieces of slate. My parents have promised that Lakshmi and Gita, my two younger sisters, may attend school for two or three years. After that they will be needed at home to help Mother. Father thinks one of them may have to be sent to work in Patna, a large town, to earn money for the family.

Last year, I visited a doctor to get medicine to cure my malaria. That was the first time I had ever been to see a doctor. The medical clinic is a two-hour walk and the doctor is not always there, although health care workers usually are.

> *"Live simply, so that others may simply live."*
>
> **Mohandas Ghandi, statesman and peacemaker, 1869–1948**

Figure 2.24

Manoj helps his little brother with his schoolwork in Bihar, India.

Our house is made of mud with a tile roof. We have three wooden beds, four blankets, two wooden chairs, a bicycle, a solar-powered radio, metal and ceramic pots, a large basket, bags of rice, and jars of spices. Our statues of our Hindu gods protect our home. We are really proud of owning our own well. It's in the courtyard of the house. We don't have electricity yet, but the government says we should get it in our village soon.

I'm a good bike rider and when Father lets me, I ride the bike to the wrestling club in the village. Sometimes, when I have time, I make toys for my sisters from discarded items I pick up around the village.

My parents have picked out the girl I will marry when I'm 16. I must decide whether to try and find work in the fields, which are owned by a landlord from the next town, or move to a large city and look for work there. I hope when I have children that they will have a better life than mine. My greatest wish would be to be able to get a cow to provide milk for the family and to go to school in the city to improve my chances of getting a good job.

Figure 2.25

Fifteen percent of the world's people live in India. The large population is putting great pressure on the environment because of **deforestation**, water pollution, over-irrigation of the soil to grow rice (which causes soil to become salty and infertile), and many other problems.

Hi. I'm Ilse and I'm 14 years old. I live in Marburg, Germany with my mother and father. Mother is a professor at Philipps University in Marburg. She works about 40 hours a week. Father is a mechanical engineer in a nearby city. He takes a high-speed train to work, where he spends about 40 hours over a four-day work week. He has three days off in a row every week.

Our house, which is three storeys high, is in town, close to a park. Inside, it's like any other house with all the regular stuff — a new car, three bicycles, a motorcycle, a computer, two television sets, three cameras, two CD players, camping equipment, books, and games. But the thing I hold dearest is a photograph album of my grandparents. Grandfather died of a heart attack last year.

Figure 2.26
Location of Germany

Figure 2.27
Germany is Europe's largest and most industrialized country. Automobile industries and technological and scientific know-how are important aspects of the economy. Germany faces some serious pollution problems, including acid rain and air and water pollution.

Figure 2.28

Ilse, of Marburg, Germany, can look forward to a long and healthy life. How does her life compare with yours?

My school, which is just around the corner, is neat. I really like it. Because I love working with machines, I will probably attend the same technical college my father went to. My soccer team won't win the district championship this year, but we did make the finals. I won't play next year because I won't have time. I'm starting karate lessons, and I'll be working part time at the library. And, to tell the truth, I like having more time to go with my friends to movies and parties. When I graduate, I'm pretty sure I'll be able to get a good-paying job.

SEE PAGE 231

CONNECTIONS TO History Germany was divided into two countries following World War II. West Germany became a free-market democracy allied with the West; East Germany became a communist-ruled command economy allied with the USSR. The collapse of the East German government in 1989 paved the way for reunification of the two countries in 1990. However, the differences in wealth between the east and west continue to cause tensions among the population.

Figure 2.29

Population breakdown for Germany by age

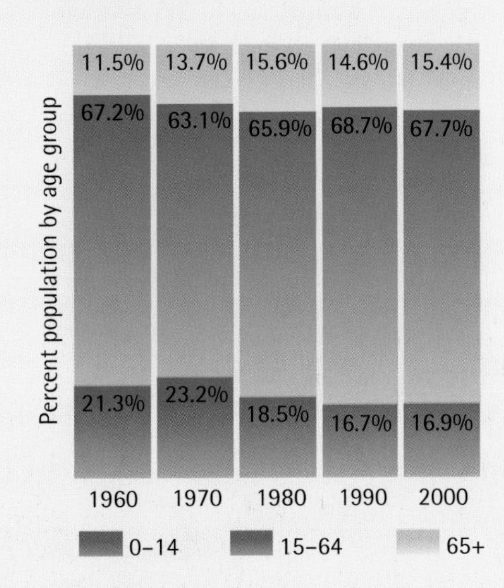

1. Why are the group of people in the world under age 15 known as the "youthquake"?
2. What problems might result from the high population density of Germany?

Understanding the Concepts

1. Because you are reading this, you are considered literate. Suggest two reasons for the difference in literacy rates between Canada and the developing country of your choice.

2. Create a population characteristics connections web. Choose any five population characteristics and write them on a piece of paper. Draw small circles around each. Draw lines between the characteristics that seem to be related to one another. Label each line with the word *strong* or *weak*, *negative* or *positive* to show the correlation between the population characteristics.

3. Create a quality of life ideas web. Put the phrase *Quality of Life* in a small circle at the centre of a half page of paper. Write down all the ideas that come to mind when you think of quality of life, scattered around this phrase on the paper. Draw lines to show the connections between all the ideas.

Figure 2.30

A maternity hospital in Bombay, India. Why might a higher quality of life lead to a lower birth rate?

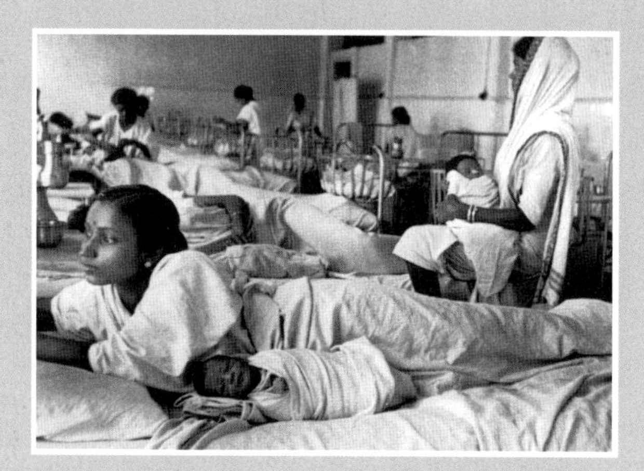

Research and Communication Skills

4. Make a sketch, collage, poster, or hanging mobile to show the characteristics of Canadian life and life in a developing country. Work with a partner to decide on a format. Decide who will portray Canadian life and who will portray life in a developing country. Add labels and a title to your work.

5. Refer to the Case Study on pages 40–43. From the account of the lives of Manoj and Ilse, what diseases do you think are more typical in developed and developing countries? Suggest how the difference could be related to differences in quality of life.

6. Select two population characteristics from Figure 2.17 on page 33. Draw a scatter graph and plot the locations of the countries in Figure 2.17 on it. Write an analysis of your graph to explain the correlation between the two characteristics and the differences between developed and developing countries.

7. Construct a population pyramid for your own community, a community close to where you live, or another community of your choice. Add labels and a title to your graph.

GO TO **http://www.statcan.ca/english/profil/PlaceSearchForm1.cfm** to begin your search for population data. This site offers statistics by age and sex for each community. You will be asked to type in the name of your community and province in the search space.

Map and Globe Skills

8. Use the map of world literacy rates on page 298 of the map appendix.

   a) Look for the location of countries with high, moderate, and low literacy rates. Describe the global patterns that can be found on this map.

   b) Next, describe the global patterns that are found on a map with reference to another population characteristic of your choice. Are the global patterns you have described for both maps similar or different?

   c) Explain the reason for your answer.

Applications

9. Refer to Figure 2.14 on page 31. Using the line that represents the year 2050, predict what will happen to the population of developed and developing countries by the time you are 60 years old.

10. Use the statistical data in Figure 2.31 to construct a population pyramid for India. Describe and explain the reasons for the patterns (shape) shown by the pyramid. Compare your pyramid to the pyramids for Germany and Kenya in Figure 2.15 on page 32.

11. You have been given the chance to spend a month visiting a young person in a developing country, such as Manoj in India. Write a letter home to a friend describing your visit.

12. Imagine that you are a demographer. Write a report that describes the population characteristics of the community in which you live. Make one recommendation to the local government on how to provide better services to the age group of your choice.

13. Why is an investigation of population characteristics a useful tool for predicting the future?

Figure 2.31

India's population by age and sex, 1998

	Age	Total	Male	Female
		984 004	**508 625**	**475 379**
Young	00–04	118 063	60 537	57 526
	05–09	112 794	58 189	54 605
	10–14	108 478	55 852	52 626
	15–19	99 655	52 492	47 163
Middle aged	20–24	90 423	48 132	42 291
	25–29	81 543	41 792	39 751
	30–34	72 790	36 317	36 473
	35–39	63 790	32 474	31 316
	40–44	54 995	28 525	26 470
	45–49	45 884	24 033	21 851
	50–54	37 589	19 796	17 793
	55–59	29 711	15 550	14 161
Old	60–64	22 959	11 884	11 075
	65–69	18 208	9 230	8 978
	70–74	13 222	6 646	6 576
	75–79	8 154	4 220	3 934
	80+	5 746	2 956	2 790

3 Human Imprints: How People Use the Earth

EXPECTATIONS

- identify and explain patterns in human geography, and describe how human activities are affected by these patterns
- identify three main patterns of settlement: linear, scattered, and clustered
- demonstrate an understanding of how site and situation influence settlement
- identify and describe types of land use

Deforestation

Nature — It's Indispensable!

Imagine the chaos that would result if, every few years, our climate underwent huge changes; if there were no natural protection from the sun's ultraviolet radiation; or, if we ran out of energy and natural resources.

So far, nature has taken care of us. The earth's climate is stable, and the ozone layer protects us from UV radiation. When we need energy to heat our homes and transport us from place to place, our natural resources provide oil and gas and other fossil fuels. Forests offer trees, not only for heating, but also for lumber, paper, furniture, and other products — not to mention a place of beauty to enjoy.

We need food and water. All the food chains that support animals, including humans, are based on plants that change sunlight, carbon dioxide (CO_2), nutrients, and water into energy that keeps us alive.

ENVIRONMENT

"The sheer exuberance and beauty of nature is a source of joy and spiritual inspiration."
Mathis Wackernagel & William Rees, "Our Ecological Footprint"

Collapse of fisheries on Canada's east coast

Figure 3.1

Warning signs! Are we demanding too much of nature? Are we using the land wisely, or are we putting future generations at risk? There are many indications that the way people use the earth may be damaging the support systems that we cannot live without.

Soil erosion

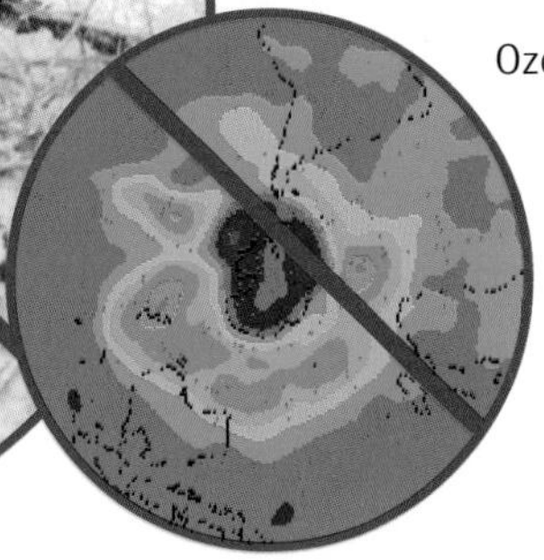

Ozone layer depletion

Species extinction

Pollution

Fact File

The earth's ozone layer forms when UV radiation from the sun comes into contact with oxygen in the atmosphere. In recent decades, a hole has appeared in the ozone layer over Antarctica, largely as a result of human activities.

GO TO **www.epa.gov/ozone/science/hole/holehome.html** to see an animated explanation of the Antarctic ozone hole.

SEE PAGE 97

It's Your World

Almost 80% of Canadians live in towns and cities. Some of us living in cities tend to forget that we are all part of nature. Have you ever gone camping in a national or provincial park, or spent time at a summer camp? If you have, you probably experienced sights, sounds, and smells that made you feel closer to nature than when you were in the city. In the city, you tend to move quickly on streets and highways, which hide or eliminate natural spaces like creeks and forests. When you move quickly, you may miss the colours of autumn foliage, the song of a bird, or the texture and smell of a tree.

INTERACTION

Use It Wisely!

Land is an important part of nature's interconnected systems. Of the 50 or so billion hectares of our planet's surface, a little more than 8 billion hectares of land is suitable for our use. There are more than 6 billion people (and counting) living on planet earth. If the population were evenly distributed, each of us would have about 1.4 hectares of land to supply us with *all* our needs. That's not much land per person. We would be wise to consider looking after it and using it in sustainable ways. We must also remember that there are many other plant and animal species that share this land with us.

"On the slopes of Mt. Everest, even in the ice of Antarctica, we have left our imprint on once-pristine wilderness."

Michael Tobias, journalist

SEE PAGE 5

A Bird's Eye View

If you were high in the air, riding in a hot-air balloon and looking down at the land, the world would look very different. This "big picture" view would give you evidence of how humans make imprints on the land. You would see many different patterns related to settlement and land use.

Settlement patterns show how people arrange themselves as they live on the land, usually in either urban or rural regions. **Land use** is the range of different ways in which people use the earth's surface.

Figure 3.2

Human imprints often form patterns on the land. Which activities can be seen in these photos? Describe the patterns they form.

Settlement Patterns

Most people live in **habitations** of one form or another. These habitations are arranged in a variety of ways to form distinct settlement patterns on the earth's surface. Settlements vary in size, density, function or purpose, and arrangement on the land. They reflect the type of economic activity that is found within them, for example, a port city, a mountain resort, or a mining town. Larger settlements, like cities, usually have a wide variety of economic activities. We say that these settlements are **economically diversified.**

Geographers study settlement patterns to understand how people in different parts of the world are distributed and how closely they live together. They examine how settlements are connected to their natural setting, and investigate relationships as people, goods, and ideas move from one settlement to another. Based on this information, they help solve economic and social problems related to where people live and how they use the land.

"Settlements exercise a powerful influence in shaping the world's different cultural, political, and economic systems."
National Geographic Standards Foundation, "Geography for Life"

SEE PAGE 99

The World's Biggest Settlements

Cities are the largest and most densely populated forms of settlement. Although every city is unique in shape, size, and appearance, almost all cities have sprawled out from a central historic core onto open space and agricultural land.

Cities in most parts of the world are growing quickly. As cities grow into the surrounding countryside, they change forever the land- and water-based ecosystems that exist there. The people in growing cities use up increasing amounts of the earth's resources, and deposit many different kinds of wastes. Some cities grow outward and meet the boundaries of other cities to form one continuous urban area. For example, in Japan, the three cities of Tokyo, Kawasaki, and Yokohama grew into one another to form one big **megalopolis** (super-city).

> *"Cities are the most spectacular achievements of human civilization."*
> **Mathis Wackernagel & William Rees, "Our Ecological Footprint"**

> *"Spreading cities in every country march across the globe, devouring half a million hectares of land every day."*
> **Prof. Peter Newman, Murdoch University, Australia**

Canada is one of the countries in the world that is noted for its expertise in satellite technology. Radarsat is Canada's first earth observation satellite. Launched into orbit 800 km above the earth in 1995, it collects photographs of the earth from space twenty-four hours a day. Geographers use the high-resolution images to study land use and settlement patterns, monitor the environment, and manage natural resources.

Fact File

Almost 50% of people in developing countries live in cities.

Figure 3.3

Countries, corporations, and even the public may buy the services of Radarsat. For around $5000, the satellite will take a picture of your house from space.

What Shape are You In?

Geographers use maps, aerial photographs, and satellite images as tools to describe and analyse settlement patterns. They look at the way in which the land is divided among its owners, as well as the way buildings and different-sized settlements are arranged on the land. Patterns are often described according to their shape.

There are three main types of settlement patterns in rural areas: linear, scattered, and clustered.

Figure 3.4

Three types of settlement patterns.

a) Linear

Sometimes called *strings*. This pattern consists of groups of houses or villages that form a long line, which can be straight (usually along a road or railway) or wavy (as found along the edge of a river or lake, or in a long, narrow valley).

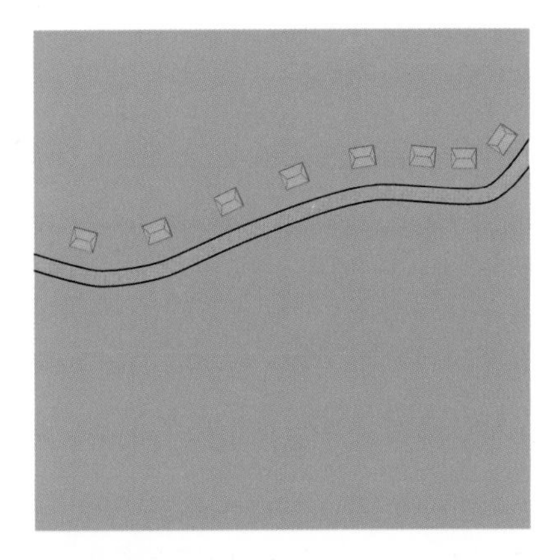

INTERACTION

b) Scattered

Sometimes called *dispersed*. This is the main pattern found in agricultural regions of North America. Each house sits alone, with just a barn or another outbuilding, on a piece of land quite separate from its neighbours.

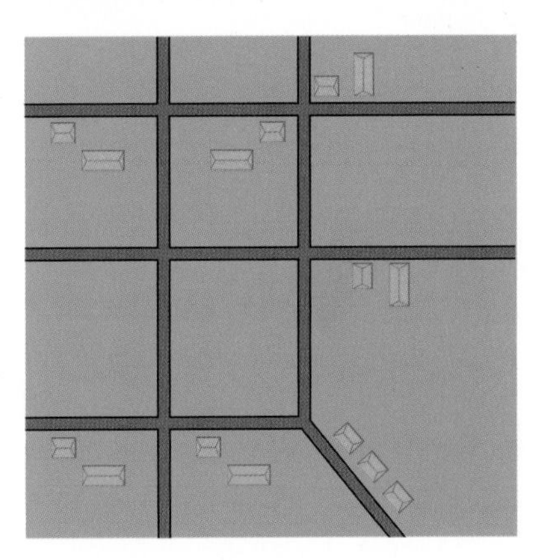

c) Clustered

Examples of this pattern could be a group of houses close together, as found in tiny hamlets or villages in agricultural areas, or a concentration of gas stations, motels, and restaurants at a highway intersection.

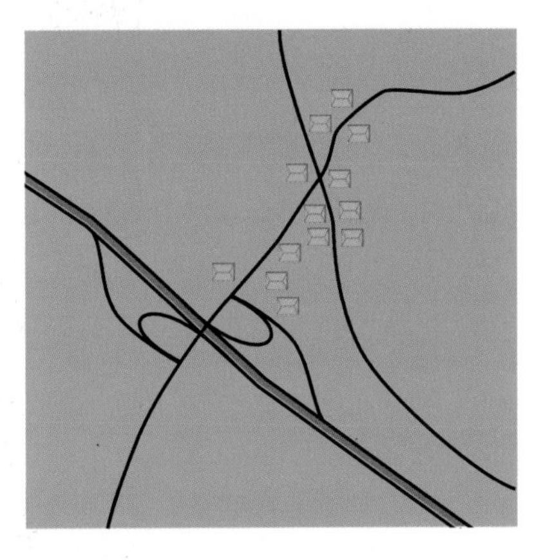

Change is Constant

In order to understand the geography of our country today, it helps if we look at the past. Early settlement patterns left an imprint on the land that affected future growth and development of human activities. Figure 3.6 shows several stages of development as settlement took place in the Prairies of central and western Canada. At one time all urban communities were rural. When settlers, seeking new land and a new life, moved in, they changed forever the long history that native people had of living in harmony with the land. Communities formed clusters in a linear pattern along the railways that were built to link Canadians from coast to coast. Species after species disappeared, and ecosystems were changed or destroyed.

SEE PAGE 208

Fact File

The ruins of Machu Picchu were discovered by the U.S. explorer Hiram Bingham in 1911.

Connections to Archeology

The ruins of Machu Picchu sit high up in the Andes Mountains in Peru, overlooking the narrow Urubamba River valley. Tourists ride a rickety train or hike for days to view this historic remnant from the 1500s. This fascinating and mysterious imprint of the Inca Empire consists of the stone ruins of homes and temples. The building stones weigh many tonnes and fit together perfectly. No one knows for sure why this ancient mountaintop city was abandoned, or whether some Incas may have used it to hide from the Spanish as the invaders stripped gold and other resources from this part of South America. Although many questions are unanswered, the human imprint remains.

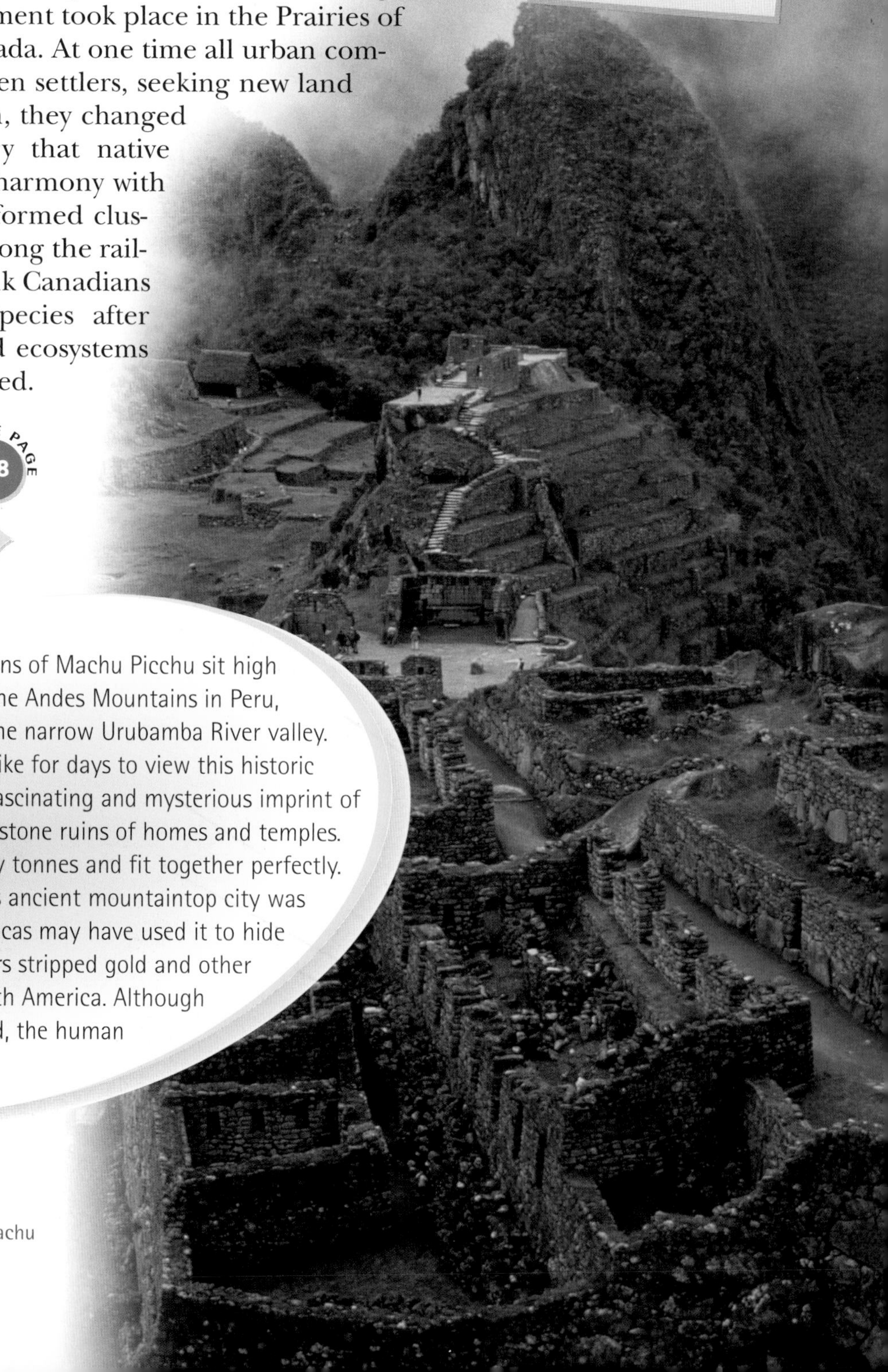

Figure 3.5

Ancient human imprints such as Machu Picchu are still visible on the land.

Figure 3.6

Changing settlement patterns and land use in the Prairies. What do you think will look different in 100 years?

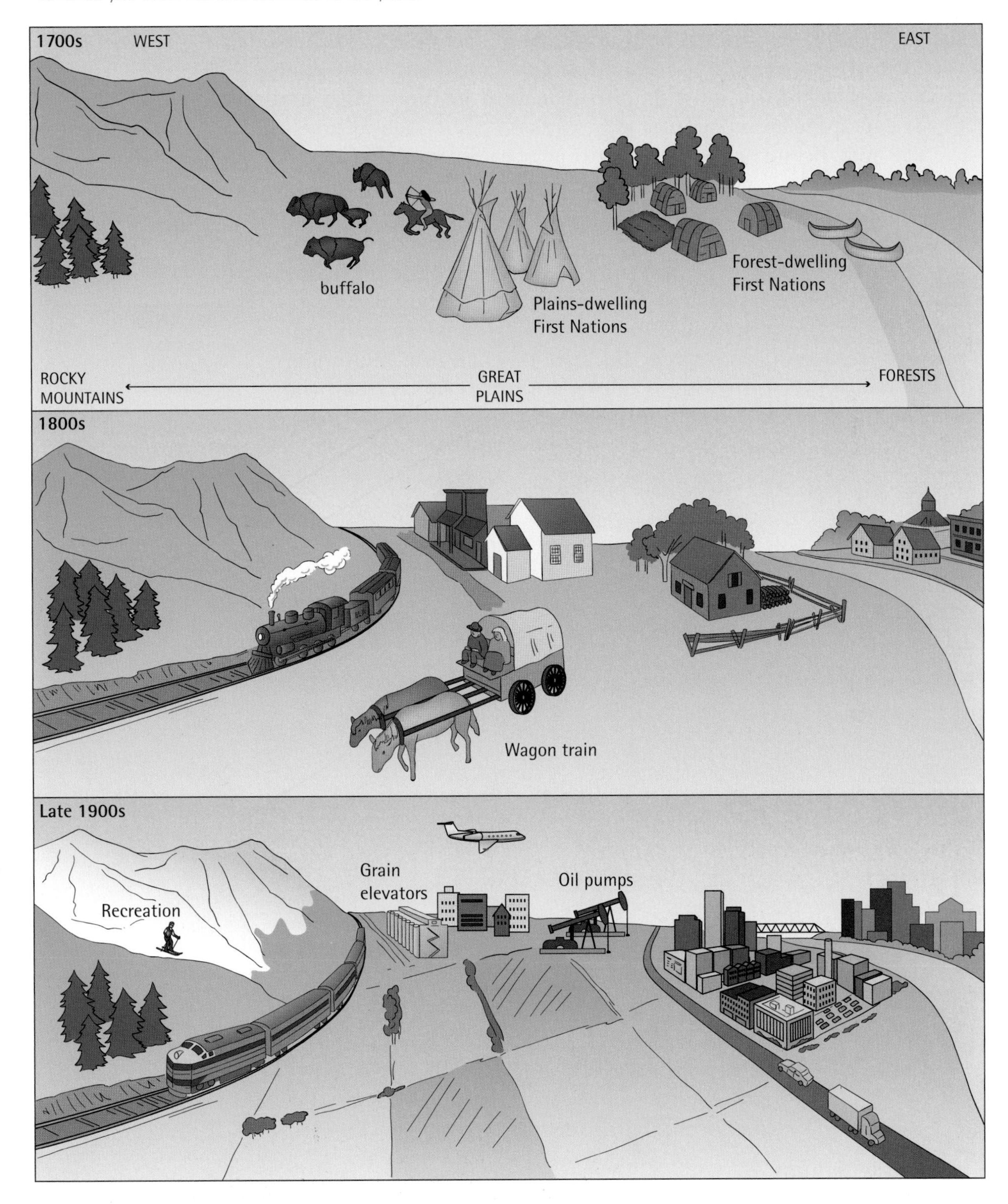

Changing Patterns

Settlement patterns in the Prairies were transformed radically in the 1900s because of population growth, exploitation of resources such as oil and natural gas, and advances in technology. Perhaps you have driven "out west" on a family holiday and noticed the grain elevators that are the most dominant feature in the villages and towns that are scattered along the Canadian Pacific Railway line.

You may be surprised to learn that over 80% of these grain storage buildings have been closed. The ones that are left are disappearing quickly as farmers now take their grain, often by truck, to larger storage facilities in bigger urban centres or to wherever they can get the best price. As a result, basic services in many small towns — such as the general store, the farm equipment dealer, the post office, and the bank — have closed. Some towns have even disappeared. Because of changing technology in agriculture, farms on the Prairies are much larger than they were in the past. As a result of these human activities, the settlement patterns they create are constantly changing.

Figure 3.7
A grain elevator in Biggar, Saskatchewan. What kinds of structures do you think will eventually be built to replace the grain elevators that have been closed?

1. Create a graphic organizer (such as a word web or Venn diagram) to show how you are connected to, and dependent upon, nature.
2. In one sentence, identify the relationship between the size of an urban area and the number and variety of economic activities found there (economic diversification). Start your sentence with the following words: *The larger the size of a city ...*

Land Use

Most Canadians, like most people in the world, live in urban areas. The growth of towns and cities will probably continue over the next century. When urban areas spread out and grow into the surrounding rural areas, the result is **urban sprawl.**

Land use changes as technology changes. In the past, when people travelled by water, horse, or cart, settlements could extend only as far as people could travel in a day. The invention of the automobile allowed people to travel farther in a day, and so made urban sprawl possible.

Extensive transportation networks are now necessary to move people around. Many people still commute to the city from the suburbs and surrounding towns, spending as much as three hours each day driving back and forth to work. That's fifteen hours a week, or two whole work days, spent just going to and from work.

Open space and recreational 7%
Industrial 6%
Commercial 5%
Residential 40%
Transportation 32%
Institutional and public buildings 10%

ENVIRONMENT

Figure 3.8
Land uses in a typical city.

CONNECTIONS TO Ecology

Since January, 1999 cyclists from the Afribike Centre in downtown Johannesburg, South Africa, have been riding their bicycles in large groups of 30 or more through the streets of the city once a month to promote awareness of this sustainable transportation method. They are taking action to encourage officials to build bicycle lanes on roads leading into the city, provide bike access to commuter trains, and pass laws to protect cyclists. They also provide low-cost bicycles, tools, and workshops to encourage people to start using their bikes.

Fact File

Most people in Canada prefer cars to other forms of transportation. The average Canadian travels about 18 000 km a year — over 88% of it in a personal vehicle.

Figure 3.9
This photo shows two kinds of energy use: the truck uses fossil fuels, while the wind farm uses the power of the wind to generate electricity. What are two advantages and two disadvantages of each method?

How People Use the Land

Patterns and imprints that people make on the land are affected by their activities and choices. Land use patterns result from many decisions made by planners, developers, governments, and individuals. Poor decisions can result in badly planned cities that eat up valuable agricultural land, destroy natural habitat for other species, and contribute to pollution. Public transit is often not a convenient option for suburban commuters, forcing people into their greenhouse gas–emitting, resource-depleting cars.

Rural land use includes land that is forested or used for primary industries like forestry, agriculture, and mining. Recreational land and parks outside cities, as well as wetlands (swamps and marsh) and wilderness areas, are considered rural.

Figure 3.10

Types of urban land use include residential, commercial, industrial, institutional, transportation, recreational, and open-space developments.

a) In which of these types of residential land use is population density higher? Which type do you think has the most impact on the natural habitat of the region? Why?

b) Many products and services are available in a shopping mall, where people can shop in climate-controlled comfort. However, malls are surrounded by asphalt parking lots. These use up a great deal of land and indirectly contribute to pollution. What steps could planners take to lessen this land use practice?

c) Manufacturing, in which raw materials are turned into finished products such as steel or cars, is one type of industrial land use that requires a large amount of land. It also requires easy access to water, rail, or highway transportation routes. This type of land use can be a source of air, water, and noise pollution. Are there factories in your area? What do they produce?

d) At industrial parks like this, high-value products like computers and electronic equipment are manufactured. Many industrial parks are located in the suburbs, where land is less expensive than in the city. So, these businesses spread out around a city, using a great deal of space for parking and landscaping. They also require land for easy access to highways and expressways, as trucking is the main method of transporting their goods. Do you think this is a good use of land? Explain.

e) Institutional land use includes public buildings, such as schools, churches, hospitals, and government offices.

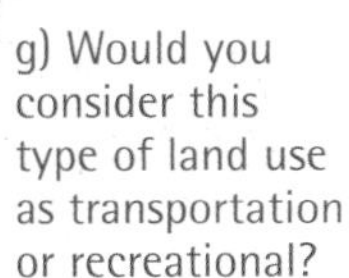

f) Almost one-third of all the land within towns and cities is used for getting people and things from one place to another. Parking lots, train and bus stations, airports, and docks are all considered transportation land use. How did the car change the way cities are planned?

g) Would you consider this type of land use as transportation or recreational?

h) Recreational land includes parks, playing fields, golf courses, and arenas. Cemeteries and farmland that is not being used to grow crops but is sitting vacant waiting for future development are considered open space.

Town planners, with input from politicians and citizens, create an official plan for how they want their community to grow. They produce land use maps that illustrate the official plan and show where different land uses will be allowed in the future. Laws, called zoning bylaws, are passed by the municipal or regional government, to make sure the official plan is followed. Sometimes developers apply to have an amendment made to the official plan, so they can have the zoning bylaw and designated land use changed to build something else.

Fact File

Land use maps are produced from remote sensing data from satellite images, aerial photography, and field studies. Geographers use them to analyse patterns on the land, as well as for environmental assessment and planning for the future.

Land Use Conflicts

Problems occur when people hold different views about what land use decisions should be made. Poor planning can result in land use conflicts. For example

- a school might be built near a busy road
- a hospital might be built close to a noisy industrial area
- a new subdivision might be built close to a landfill site where the smell, noise, and constant garbage truck traffic cause discomfort.

A mix of commercial and light industrial land uses provides jobs and services for people living nearby and is, therefore, most desirable. When mainly residential land use occupies a large area, as in the suburbs of large cities, people are forced to use their cars to go to work, to the library, or to the grocery store. This contributes to more pollution.

Connections to Architecture Some architects are now designing new suburban developments to include a mix of land uses and higher population densities. Instead of designing the community for cars, the focus is on people walking and cycling. Garages are often built in back lanes to keep cars out of the way, allowing people to use the front of their houses for better communication with neighbours.

Figure 3.11

Which do you think was built first: this chipboard factory, or the houses that surround it? What makes you think this? Identify two advantages and two disadvantages of this kind of mixed land use.

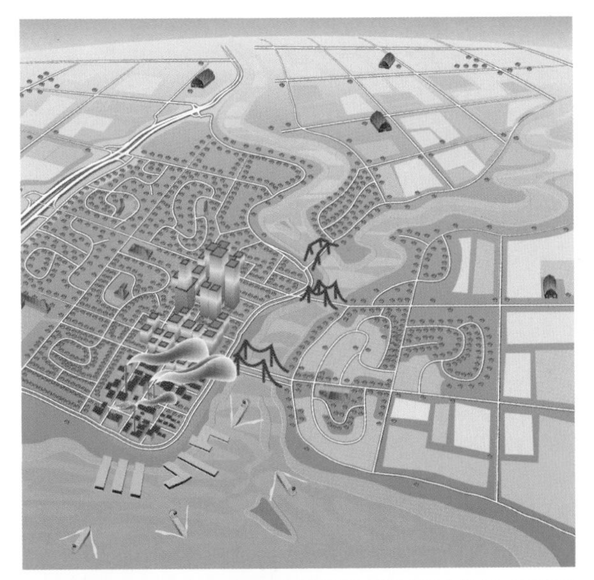

Site and Situation

ENVIRONMENT

Although people use technology to alter the natural environment, such as building bridges and dams on rivers, the physical features of the environment also have a strong influence on people, places, and patterns. Site and situation are terms used by geographers to describe the location of a town or city.

SEE PAGE 118

Site refers to the physical features in the area where the city is located. This could be a flat plain on the edge of a lake or a narrow valley in the mountains. Mountains, deserts, and other harsh natural environments are more of a challenge to settlers. Settlements most often grow to become large cities when they are located in wide river valleys, at the joining of two rivers, or on a lake or ocean coastline with a good harbour. Fertile soil, moderate climate, and abundant natural resources also promote the growth of cities.

SEE PAGE 141

Situation refers to the general position of a city in relation to transportation routes, other cities, and natural resources such as good farmland.

Figure 3.12

Identify the features of the site in each of these settlements. Explain how the physical setting has influenced the settlement that occurred. What features have influenced the size of each settlement and the economic activity found in it?

Check Back

1. Using two specific examples, explain how land use may change as technology changes.
2. Explain the difference between settlement patterns and land use. How do they depend on each other?
3. What land use changes would result if many people within a community chose to use bicycles instead of cars?
4. What are two choices that you and your family could make to lessen the impact of your activities on the land? How will these choices affect land use patterns?

CASE STUDY

Montreal, Quebec: Imprints and Patterns from Space

From space, the "big picture" view of any city looks as though a giant designed a large stamp with many different patterns on it and pushed it onto the earth's surface. That giant is us! Cities all over the world have a similar appearance on satellite images.

This photograph, taken from a Canadian satellite, shows

- how Montreal is connected to its natural setting (site)
- relationships between the city and other cities, transportation routes, and surrounding natural resources (situation)
- settlement patterns on the land, both rural and urban
- different land uses and the patterns they make on the land.

Figure 3.13

Satellite images of urban areas help us to picture how cities grow and spread over the surrounding countryside, changing the land forever.

Fact File

As a satellite orbits around the earth, usually at an altitude of about 900 km above the surface, it continually scans an area that is 185 km wide.

Settlement Patterns

Of the many factors that work together to produce distinct settlement patterns on the earth's surface, the most important are the physical features of the natural environment; history; technology; and government policy.

Site can influence the original location of a city, its shape, the location of its land uses, and its problems. For example, to avoid the barrier of the Lachine Rapids, the Lachine Canal was built to carry ships farther inland to the St. Lawrence River.

Fact File

The original settlement in what is now Montreal was Hochelaga, a village of First Nations people on the south shore of the St. Lawrence River. This site is now part of the Kahnewake Indian Reserve.

GO TO **www.montrealcam.com/en-socom.html** for a view of downtown Montreal from the top of Mount Royal, as well as several other live camera shots of the city.

Figure 3.14

Using the map, find the line on the satellite image that represents the old Lachine Canal.

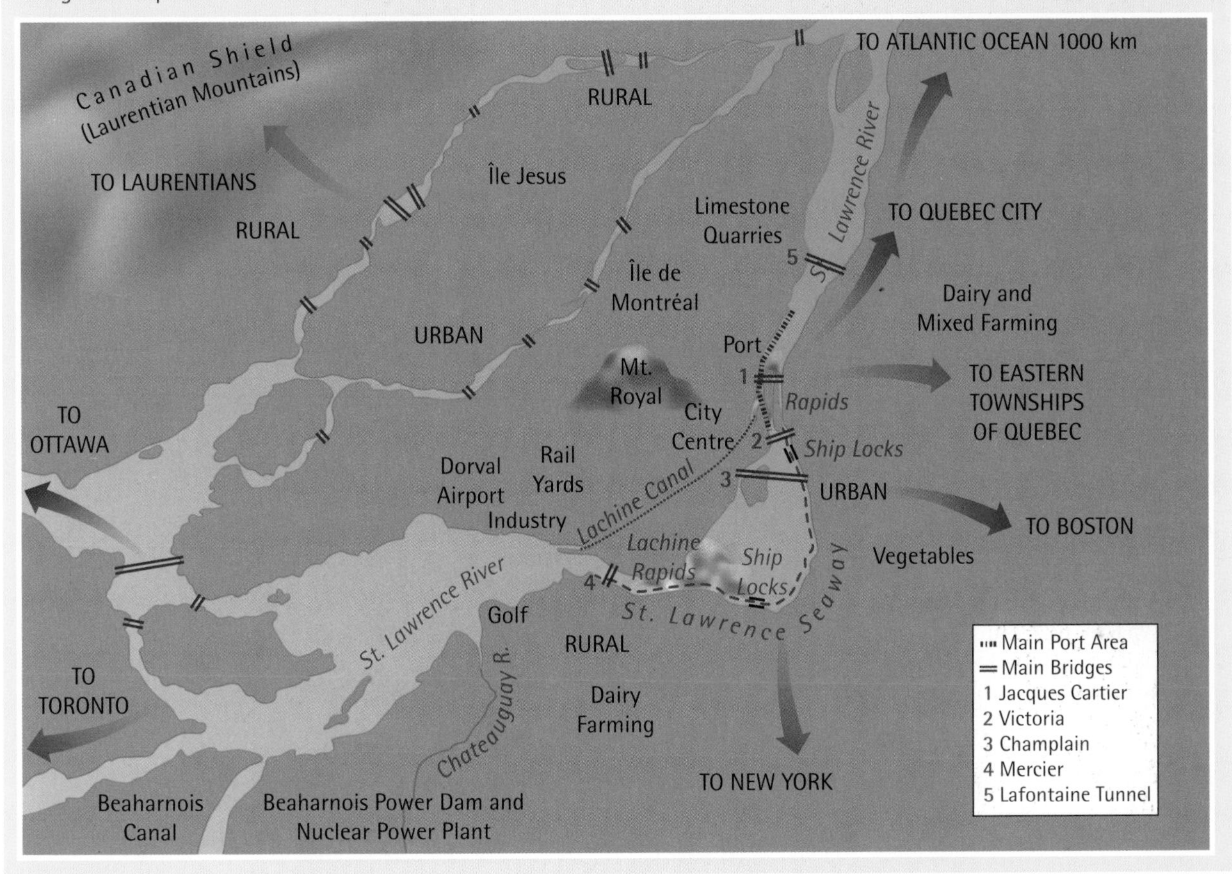

Figure 3.15

Factors that influenced the settlement of Montreal. Which do you think was most important in influencing the location of the city?

Physical Features
- good agricultural land
- good water supply
- easy transportation routes

History
- first farms were long and narrow, built in a linear pattern along the river
- later farms had no river access

Government Policy
- in the 1700s, France gave land to settlers based on long, narrow lots
- governments later added roads, power lines, and other features

Technology
- railroads and cars changed settlement patterns
- town is now more spread out
- houses built along roads and rail lines form a linear pattern

Figure 3.16

Features of Montreal's site. How do you think these features influenced settlement patterns?

Features of the Site
- islands in the St. Lawrence River, which helped to shape the city
- river for fresh water and transportation
- rapids that were a barrier to water transportation
- flat, fertile agricultural land once the forests were cut down
- a series of rock terraces or step-like features on the main island (Île de Montréal), which provided a good vantage point for defence
- a large hill (Mount Royal), which is the remnant of an ancient volcano and now provides some green open space, as well as a scenic location for expensive housing developments
- sedimentary (limestone) rock layers, which provided building stones for many of the early buildings

Fact File

Montreal is the second largest city in Canada after Toronto. It is the second largest French-speaking city in the world.

Figure 3.17

Many tourists are attracted to Montreal, which is renowned as a charming and exciting cosmopolitan city.

Site and Situation

Because the Great Lakes–St. Lawrence Lowlands provide flat land and fertile soils, much of the land has been cleared for agriculture. This favourable land base can also support a dense population. Parts of the island on which Montreal is situated are the most densely populated in Canada.

An important aspect of the relationship between the city and its surroundings is Montreal's location on the St. Lawrence River. This location is 1600 km from the Atlantic Ocean — far enough inland so there are no tides to rise and fall. It also provides a gateway to the middle of North America. Before Montreal could take full advantage of this feature, canals and the St. Lawrence Seaway had to be built. This enabled large ocean-going ships to enter the Great Lakes and continue on to other port cities, like Toronto, Thunder Bay, and Chicago.

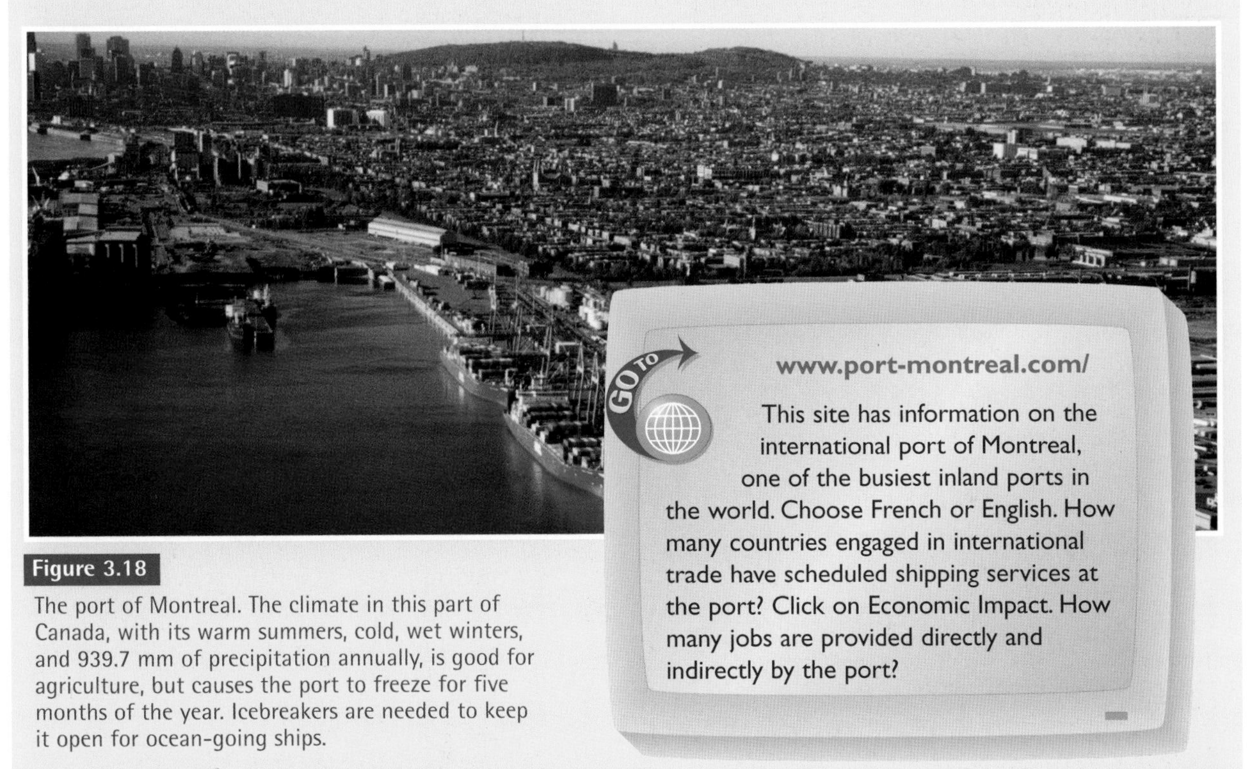

Figure 3.18

The port of Montreal. The climate in this part of Canada, with its warm summers, cold, wet winters, and 939.7 mm of precipitation annually, is good for agriculture, but causes the port to freeze for five months of the year. Icebreakers are needed to keep it open for ocean-going ships.

GO TO

www.port-montreal.com/

This site has information on the international port of Montreal, one of the busiest inland ports in the world. Choose French or English. How many countries engaged in international trade have scheduled shipping services at the port? Click on Economic Impact. How many jobs are provided directly and indirectly by the port?

1. Which feature of Montreal's site do you think has been the most important for determining the shape of the city?
2. List five cities in North America that have transportation links to Montreal.
3. Identify where the following types of settlement patterns occur on the satellite image in Figure 3.13 (page 60): linear, dispersed, clustered.
4. List the features of the site and situation of Montreal that you can locate using the satellite image in Figure 3.13 and the map in Figure 3.14 (page 61).
5. Which type of land use would most likely be located around the old Lachine Canal and the port of Montreal?

Understanding the Concepts

1. Describe the site and situation of the community in which you live. Sketch a map to illustrate the main features of both. What factors have influenced the shape of your community?

2. Construct a chart or other organizer to compare the characteristics of two different types of settlements, for example, a small rural village in a farming community and a neighbourhood within a large city. Compare types of housing, population density, patterns on the land, economic activities, and services, such as theatres and restaurants.

3. Classify each of the land uses in Figure 3.19 below under the appropriate urban land use category: residential, commercial, industrial, institutional, transportation, parks/open-space, recreational.

Figure 3.19

Skateboard park	Drive-in movie
Scrap metal yard	Nuclear generating station
Sewage treatment plant	Greenhouse
Senior citizens' home	Museum
Conservation area	Golf course
Cemetery	Hospital
Sports complex	Airport
Woodlot	Shopping mall
Industrial park	Apartment building
University	Amusement park
Cement-block plant	Prison
Railway yard	Convenience store

4. Which of the land uses in Figure 3.19 would you want close to your home? Which ones would you not want to live close to? Explain your reasons for at least two of the land uses.

Research and Communication Skills

5. Write a paragraph that outlines the advantages and disadvantages of living in either a rural or an urban area. Add a concluding sentence that explains where you would prefer to live — now and in the future.

6. Find the Web site of your town or city, or the city nearest to where you live, by typing your community name into an Internet search engine such as Alta Vista or Lycos. Look for demographic information. What are the population growth trends in your region? Will the population increase or decrease? What impact will the situation in your community have on future land use?

GO TO **www.altavista.digital.com or www.lycos.com/** to begin your search. Or, try both search engines, and compare the results from each.

7. Conduct primary research by contacting the planning department of the municipal or regional government closest to where you live. Investigate what actions are being taken to reduce the impacts of urban sprawl, or what process is in place to deal with any land use conflicts that arise in your community.

Map and Globe Skills

8. Find the location of the Okanagan Valley on a map of British Columbia in an atlas. Draw a sketch that includes Okanagan Lake, the surrounding mountains (use the coloured elevation/land height legend to help with this), and the towns of Enderby, Armstrong, Vernon, Kelowna, Peachland, Summerland, Penticton, Oliver, and Osoyoos. Describe and explain the settlement patterns shown by these towns.

9. Use tracing paper over the satellite image of Montreal to sketch the islands and the St. Lawrence River. Decide on an appropriate colour legend for the following types of land use: agricultural, recreational, open-space, residential, city-centre, industrial, and institutional. Shade each area of the image to create a land use map.

Applications

10. On page 59, you learned that settlements most often grow into large cities when they have certain basic requirements of site and situation. Review these requirements from the text and use an atlas to test this theory on two of the world's largest cities, such as New York, Mexico City, Tokyo, Saõ Paulo, or Bombay.

11. Contact your local government office to find a land use map of your community. Does your community fit the pattern of a typical Canadian city shown in Figure 3.8 (page 55)? Explain why or why not.

12. Ask your parents or caregivers to help you attend a meeting of the local government to investigate what land use decisions are being discussed in your area.

13. Design the ideal residential community with a well-planned mix of different land uses. Show your design using a labelled land use map, sketch, or three-dimensional model.

GO TO www.studentsguide.com/montreal/montreal.html

Click on Montreal Region Maps to find a land use map of the city to help you.

Figure 3.20

Largely unplanned growth to accommodate its 20 million residents and the absence of environmental controls on factories have made Mexico City one of the world's worst sites for air pollution.

4 People at Work

EXPECTATIONS

- demonstrate an understanding of employment patterns and trends
- identify some employment and workplace issues, and describe their impact on the present-day Canadian workforce
- research job trends and predict the skills needed to meet the challenges of the future
- describe how mechanization and technology have changed the Canadian economy
- identify and give examples of the three major types of industries, and describe how the distribution of these industries has changed

What About the Future?

Imagine riding on a train speeding through time. You race from year to year into the future, not sure where the train will take you. You see amazing new sights outside the windows. While it is hard to predict what the future holds, one thing is certain: much will change, even more quickly than now. You will be affected by these changes, and you will need to adapt to them.

Sometime in the next five to ten years, you will probably enter the work market. Whether you do this directly from high school or after a post-secondary school education, the workplace that you will enter will be very different from the one your parents experienced. It is difficult to predict what types of jobs people will be doing in the 2000s, because constant change means that many future jobs have not even been invented yet.

> *"There are those that wait for the future to happen; those that go out and make the future happen for them; and those who are simply left to wonder what happened!"*
>
> **Frank Feather, futurist**

Figure 4.1

The changing work market.

Old Workplace (Industrial Era)	New Workplace (Information Era)
People finished their education and went on to one main career	People will have several careers in life and will retrain every few years
Career path a steady, progressive climb in a company, based on promotions	Career path will move in and out of different jobs, with more opportunities to work with a variety of other people
More people work for medium- to large-sized companies	More people work for small- to medium-sized companies or are self-employed
Few people work at home	More people are working from home offices
Job security rests in one career or company with one main job skill	Performance contracts (workers hired on a project-by-project basis) require a broad range of skills
Success often based on seniority or how long one worked for a company; more interest in financial success	Success based on performance and ability to adapt quickly; more interest in a balanced, satisfying life

"As the information economy spread prosperity across Canada, people became less concerned with material survival. Instead, the emphasis is on higher values concerned with the quality (rather than the quantity) of life."

Frank Feather, futurist

Figure 4.2

The changing nature of work. Can you suggest a reason for the predicted decline in services after 2000?

SEE PAGE 167

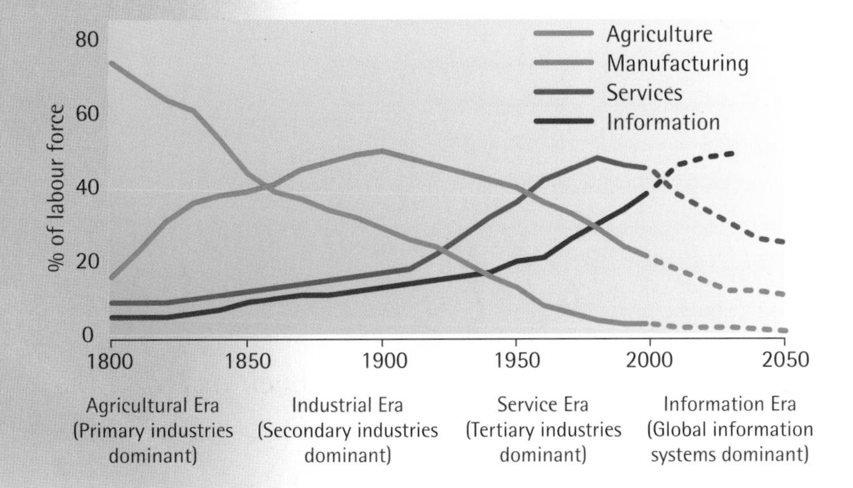

It's Your World

Banking has changed dramatically all over the world in the past decade. People use bank machines and debit cards and can do their banking from home on personal computers (PCs). New banking jobs are being invented, and new skills are needed to provide people with different kinds of personal services. Ask your grandparents or other older people in your community how banking was different many years ago.

Trends

There are many factors that cause industries to grow or decline. Some of these factors are related to economic or **demographic trends**. A trend is when things change in a general direction. Figure 4.3 shows you that changes in the work market mean a trend toward more and more people working in part-time jobs. Geographers, economists, and other scientists use such trends to help them predict what the future will be like.

Two major demographic trends in Canada are the aging of the population and the existence of the **baby boom cohort**. They will continue to have a significant impact on employment and the workplace.

SEE PAGE 271

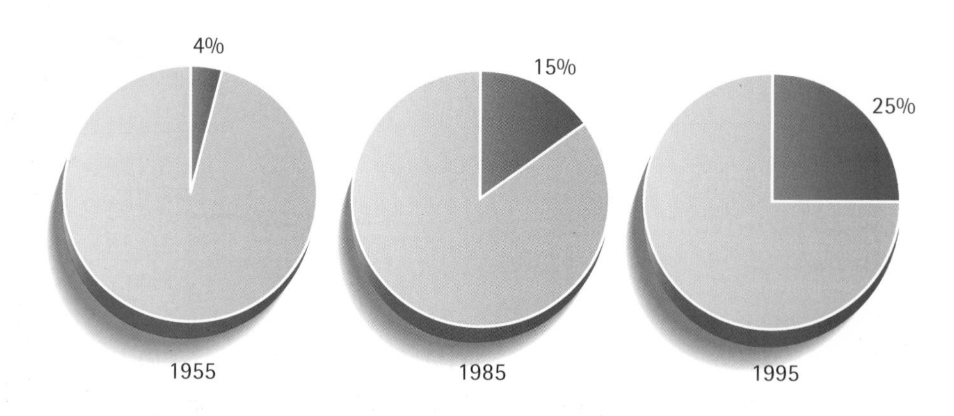

Figure 4.3

Part-time workers as a percentage of Canada's workforce. The average income for part-time workers in 1996 was just over $13 000 a year. Use the trend shown in these graphs to predict how Canada's workforce may change in the next 10 years. What impact will this trend have on Canadian workers?

Computers Are Changing Society

Computers are changing the way we live and work. Many things we used to do outside the home can now be done at home by using the computer, such as working, shopping, or sending a letter.

> *"I think two key factors — population and technology — will determine the landscape of tomorrow's workplace."*
> **John A. Challenger, futurist**

Social Trends

One social trend shows that Canadians want to spend more time at home on their computers than watching television. Another important trend is people's desire to spend more time enjoying outdoor activities like hiking, kayaking, or snowboarding. These social trends are creating many new jobs in Canada's economy.

Fact File

Between 1990 and 1999, part-time jobs increased by 24%, three times faster than the growth in full-time employment. Self-employment has also increased at a rapid rate. About 43%, or 775 000 more Canadians, were self-employed in 1999 than in 1990.

Economic Trends

The economic trend is toward a more global economy. For example, parts for our cars are made in many companies, often in different countries, and sent here for final assembly. Most of your running shoes are made in Asia. This trend is causing a great deal of change. It creates new jobs and makes other jobs disappear.

Figure 4.4

These trends are occurring in all parts of the developed, industrialized world

- more jobs are part-time
- more people are self-employed
- more people work from home
- more women work outside the home while still doing unpaid work in the home
- more workplaces are getting by with fewer employees
- more people hold more than one job
- more jobs are created in small or medium-sized companies than in large corporations

Demographic Trends

Demographics affect the market in two main ways

- by changing the jobs that are needed in the economy and that are available to workers
- by changing the workforce in some way, such as its age structure or how people are distributed in different ethnic groups.

> *"Don't count on the economy to produce new jobs; you've got to produce them yourselves."*
>
> **Angus Reid, pollster, author, "Shakedown"**

Figure 4.5 shows how demographics have affected several generations of Canada's workforce.

Fact File

From 1990 to 2000, the top 500 manufacturing corporations in the United States eliminated five million jobs — over 25% of their total workforce.

Figure 4.5

Canada's workforce, 2000.

Pre-Baby Boomers (born up to 1946)
Retired or soon to retire; had no trouble finding careers, but some are losing their jobs as the workplace changes. They have lived through one or two world wars and an economic depression in the 1930s. Their needs include health care, travel and recreation, crafts, and hobbies.

Baby Boomers (born 1947–1960)
Because there are so many of them, they face competition for jobs, and some are in debt. They will continue to influence demand for services (e.g., high-tech home entertainment and computers for their children) and recreations such as golf and birdwatching as they retire.

Generation X (born 1961–1966)
The X stands for "excluded." They earn less, and accumulate less wealth, than boomers. They grew up at a time when many companies were downsizing. X-ers prefer audio, visual, and computer media to print, and are more attuned to the new marketplace than older workers – yet still find it difficult to get jobs.

Baby Bust (born 1967–1979)
Like the X-ers, they also find it difficult to get good jobs. Many settle for "McJobs," such as in fast-food restaurants. Others have created their own jobs, working as consultants or finding a market for a unique product. They are the first generation of cellular phone users, and are more likely to shop and bank on the Internet.

Baby Boom Echo (born 1980–1995)
This cohort is just starting to enter the work market. They have the advantage of having grown up in the new Information Age economy. They will not find it as difficult to get jobs as Generation X did.

Millennium Kids (born 1995– and into the future)
These are the children of the baby busters. They will make their way into the work market starting in 2015.

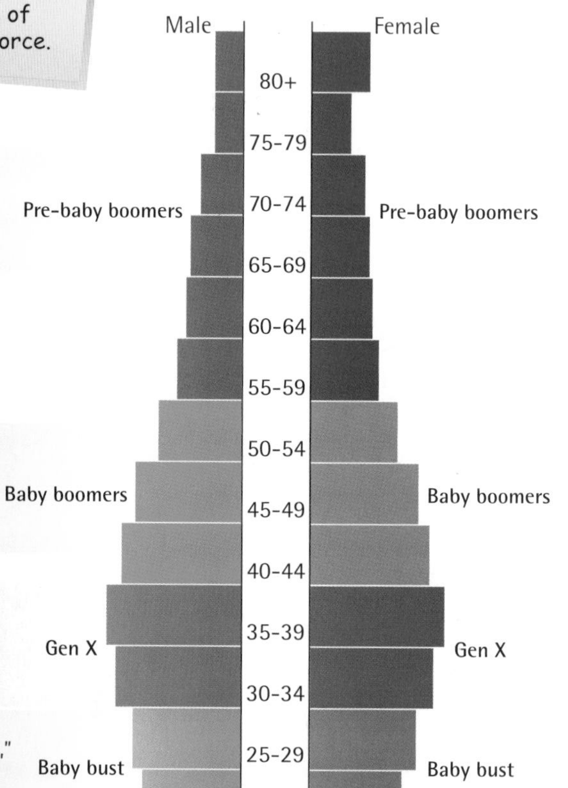

The changing work market has introduced some new words into our language.

Downsizing: Many companies, particularly big corporations, have had to cut costs so they can compete on world markets. They have chosen to lay off many workers, or "downsize." Managers in the middle layers of companies and workers replaced by technology have been most affected. In the future, fewer managers will be required. People will work in teams that are responsible to one another and that produce on their own initiative.

SEE PAGE 193

Outsourcing: Instead of employing large numbers of workers, many companies are hiring temporary workers, or people who work for other companies, to perform tasks on a project-by-project basis.

The Great Job Shift

Canada's economy is shifting from one based on industries that produce goods — such as manufacturing, mining, construction, and agriculture — to an economy based on providing services, including trade, transportation, health care, and finance.

SEE PAGE 167

> ***"People work any time and all the time, with no one keeping track of their hours, but with everyone watching their output."***
> **William Bridges, former Microsoft employee**

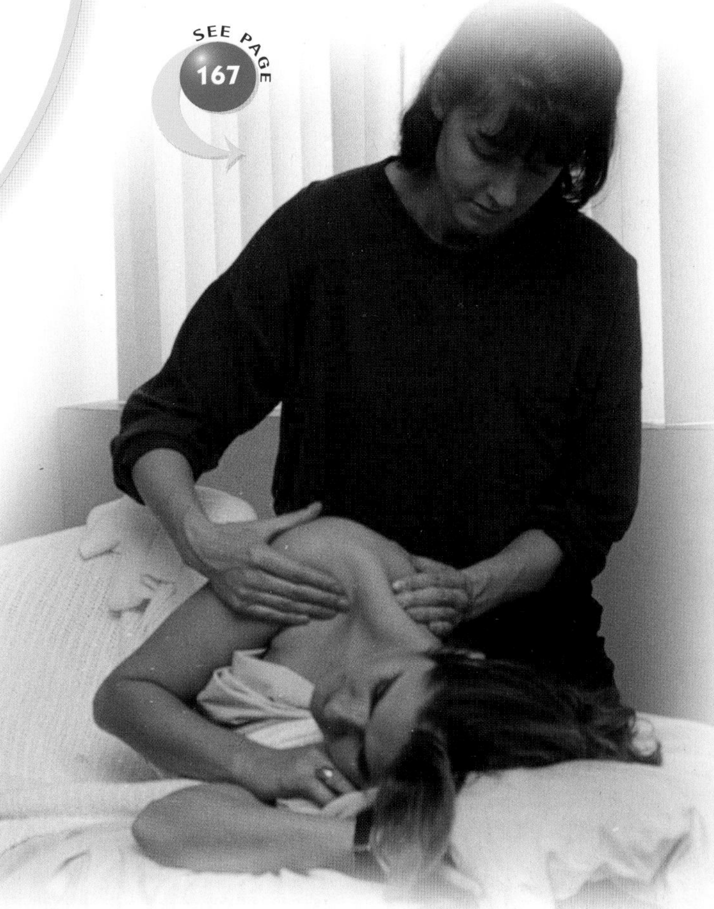

Figure 4.6

More Canadians than ever are working in personal services such as massage therapy and fitness training, retail sales, tourism (e.g., hotels and restaurants), and entertainment (e.g., theatres and video stores).

1. Figure 4.1 (page 67) and Figure 4.4 (page 69) provide information on how the workplace is changing. Which characteristics of the changing workplace have affected people in your family? Which have not affected them?
2. Refer to Figure 4.2 (page 67), and describe the trends in agriculture and in information systems.
3. Into which cohorts on the population pyramid in Figure 4.5 do you and your parents fit?

Changes in Canada's Traditional Industry Sectors

Deciding which sector of the economy a job fits into can be confusing. Workers in service industries are not always employed in the service (tertiary) sector. For example, a cook (a service job) may work in a logging camp (forestry is a primary industry). Or, a sales person (also a service job) may work for a manufacturing company (secondary industry). Some people, such as clerical staff (secretaries, payroll clerks), work in all sectors of the economy.

Figure 4.7

Primary industry — trends for the future.

SEE PAGE 168

Farming
- Fewer and fewer farmers
- Larger farms owned by big companies
- Computers used in all aspects of farming
- Factory-like raising of animals in large, crowded areas
- Robots replacing farm machines
- New crops invented through **biotechnology**
- Concerns about soil depletion, pesticide use, and safety of **bioengineered** foods
- Typical jobs of the future: geneticist, computer programmer, plant biologist

Forestry
- Fewer and fewer loggers and mill workers
- Pulp and paper mills and saw mills increasingly automated
- Laser-guided saws and robots moving wood to machines
- Concerns about overuse of forest resources and the impact of **clearcutting**
- Typical jobs of the future: wildlife biologist, forest conservation officer

Mining
- Fewer ore drillers, blasters, mining engineers
- Robots and computers will take over
- New materials such as plastics will replace metals in many products
- Growth in mining the ocean floor
- Typical jobs of the future: new-material engineer, **polymerization** scientist

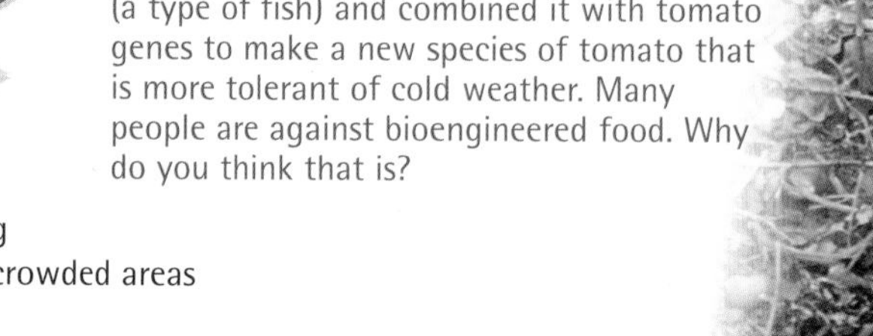

Figure 4.8

Scientists have taken a gene from a flounder (a type of fish) and combined it with tomato genes to make a new species of tomato that is more tolerant of cold weather. Many people are against bioengineered food. Why do you think that is?

Figure 4.9

Mining in the future will rely increasingly on robots rather than humans. Can you think of one advantage and one disadvantage of this trend?

Primary Industries

SEE PAGE 169

Employment is declining in Canada's primary industries, such as mining, farming, and forestry. Before the Industrial Revolution, most people were farmers and were self-employed. People grew most of their own food and made their own clothing.

Many of the future jobs that will be created in the primary sector of the economy will require advanced training and specialized skills, such as research skills or skills in design and engineering. Farmers, for example, are now using infrared satellite images to see where to install drainage tiles or add more fertilizer on their fields. They need the "know-how" to use this technology in their work.

GO TO

www.statcan.ca/

Choose the language you wish to work in. Click on Canadian Statistics. Under the Economy section, click on Primary Industries. Now choose Fishing and Trapping. Look at the top chart. Which year had the highest catches for all areas? Which year had the lowest? What trend do you see in these figures?

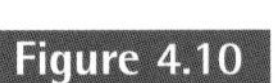

Figure 4.10

Fish are now bred in hatcheries such as this one and used to replenish dwindling stocks. Can you think of two reasons why fish stocks decline?

Fishing

- Fewer fishers, small shipbuilders, machinists, navigators
- Large factory trawlers will continue to "scoop" up fish
- Increase in aquaculture and intensive fish farming
- Concerns about depletion of fish stocks, impacts of aquaculture (use of antibiotics, production of wastes, escape of fish that breed with wild stocks)
- Typical jobs of the future: marine biologist, oceanographer, **aquaculture** farmer/consultant

Energy

- Energy demand will continue to increase
- Switch away from oil and coal
- Continued development of Canada's reserves of natural gas
- Jobs will shift to alternative fuel sources such as solar, hydrogen fuel cell, wind, **biomass**, and **nuclear fusion**
- Concerns about greenhouse gas emissions from burning fossil fuels and hazardous (nuclear) waste disposal
- Typical jobs of the future: air quality analyst, solar cell technician, hazardous waste engineer, energy auditor

Figure 4.11

Traditional sources of energy such as coal, oil, and nuclear power — generated at plants like this Candu reactor — will be used less and less. Name one advantage and one disadvantage to this trend. What are the alternatives?

Figure 4.12 A blind worker on a computer assembly line. While many manufacturing industries have slowed in recent years, the demand for computers has increased steadily.

Secondary Industries

SEE PAGE 171

Jobs in this sector of the economy, mainly in manufacturing, are a product of the Industrial Age of the past 200 years. More recently, better machines for making things, including robots for routine work, have reduced the number of jobs needed in this sector. Growth in manufacturing has also slowed down somewhat because the largest age group in society, the boomers, already has much of what it needs. Some manufacturing industries have been relocated to other countries, mainly developing countries such as Mexico or Taiwan, but some have just disappeared altogether.

> *"As Canada becomes more of a service economy, resourceful young people will continue to invent new services to fill new needs created by demographic change."*
>
> **David K. Foot & Daniel Stoffman, "Boom, Bust, and Echo 2000"**

Tertiary Industries

SEE PAGE 172

Canadian society is becoming more dependent on services, including those related to processing information and communication technologies. Our economy is now called an information economy. People need to locate, read, understand, and process information, both at work and in everyday life. Literacy skills continue to be very important, because so much of modern communication depends on reading and writing.

Fact File

In 1990, 650 000 people worked in the automobile manufacturing industry in Canada. By 1995 — just five years later — there were fewer than 500 000 working in this industry.

Employment Trends in the Information Economy

“Many workers, such as visible minorities, women, aboriginal people, and people with disabilities, have already adjusted to [new] employment situations, whether by choice or necessity ... and thus have a subtle advantage.”

William Bridges, former Microsoft employee

New jobs have been invented to develop computer hardware (the computers themselves: monitors, printers, hard drives, scanners) and computer software (the programs that people use on their computers). There are many other computer-related jobs, such as Internet Webmaster and network maintenance specialist.

Today, one in every eight workers in Canada is a **knowledge worker** — the fastest-growing type of worker to appear in the past 25 years. Knowledge workers, who deal with information, have now become essential in most industries, and they will continue to replace factory workers. By 2010, it is estimated that close to 70% of the workforce will be knowledge workers. These are people — like social scientists (including geographers and psychologists), applied scientists, educators, system designers, and engineers — who are involved in designing, planning, and developing ideas.

SEE PAGE 173

Fact File

Everything we know today will account for only 0.5% of all knowledge in 2050. In 2050, almost all of what people know will have been discovered between 2020 and 2050.

Connections to Careers

Some careers in the tertiary sector related to the Information Age include investigation, publishing, advertising, data bank services, computer software consulting, law, laboratory research, engineering, photography, and education. Some careers in the secondary sector include the manufacturing of computer equipment, fax machines, and photocopiers.

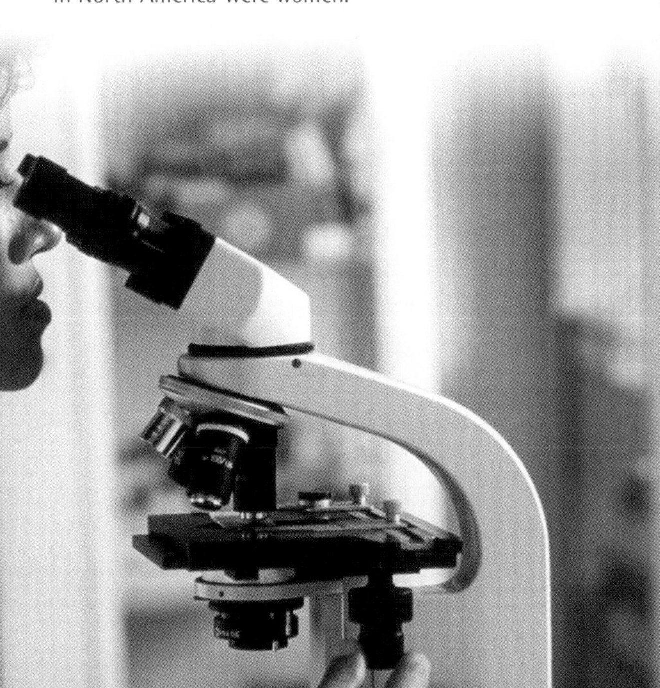

Figure 4.13

In 1998, more than 60% of technicians, engineers, and technical sales support staff in North America were women.

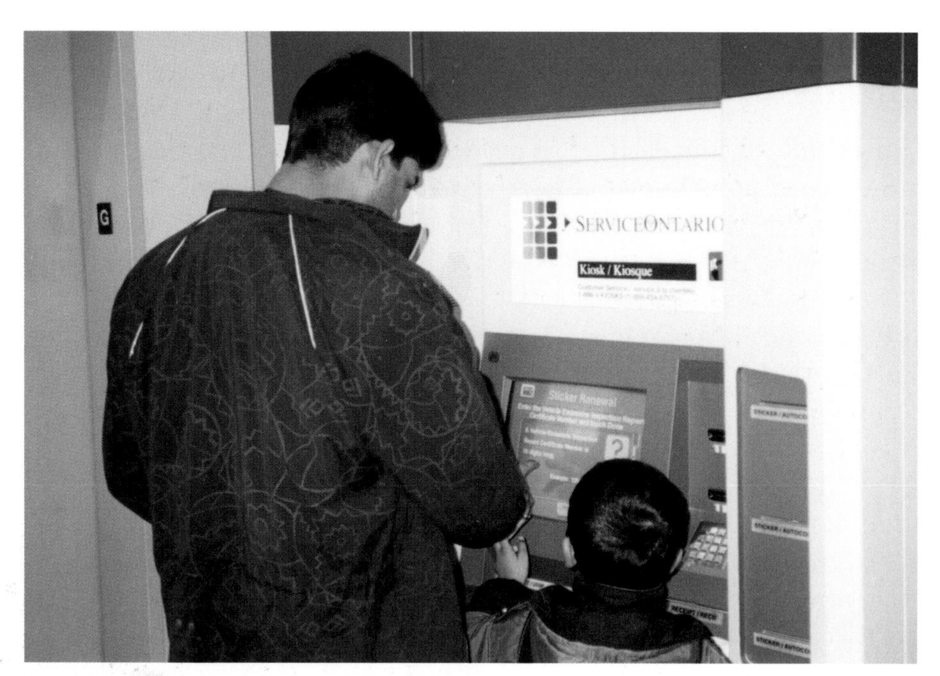

Figure 4.14

Even renewing your driver's licence can now be done by computer at a mall.

SEE PAGE 122

The Power of Technology

There has been a shift away from the Industrial Revolution to what is called the Information Revolution. We are also living with a Technology Revolution. The technology that was developed in the 1900s — from the automobile to space flight and the Internet — has been awesome. It is difficult to predict what other surprising technological devices people will create next.

Personal computers with e-mail and Internet access, as well as fax machines, have made it easier to work at home. Home-based business is a trend that is expected to continue. Computers are also doing much of the work that used to be done by people in many areas, such as banking and assembling the parts of a product in manufacturing industries.

So, today's auto mechanic requires not only technical knowledge about cars, but also the ability to use computers for repair and maintenance of most newer auto models.

Another impact of rapid change in technology on the workforce is that an individual worker needs to have knowledge about many different areas, including the latest in technology. Workers will need to retrain every few years to keep up to date and satisfy their customers. This will create a demand for more education and training.

Fact File

The increased participation of women in the paid workforce has resulted in the need for services that replace some of the unpaid work women did in the home, such as cleaning and child care.

"Sophisticated computers will likely displace humans in the same way that work horses were eliminated by the introduction of tractors."

Wassily Leontief, economist, Nobel Prize winner

SEE PAGE 181

Robots are Here to Stay!

In 1999, there were more than 12 000 robots performing all kinds of jobs in Canada. Robots build cars and many other assembly-line products, handle hazardous chemicals, and defuse bombs. In the future, it is predicted that many Canadian households will have robots to perform routine tasks.

Many companies favour the use of technology because it saves money. Machinery may seem expensive, but costs less than workers do. It is estimated that 90 million jobs in the United States, out of a potential workforce of 124 million people, may be in danger of being eliminated by machines in the future.

Connections to Literature

In his 1950 novel *I, Robot*, science fiction writer Isaac Asimov proposed three laws of robotics:

1. A robot may not injure a human or, through inaction, allow a human to come to harm.
2. A robot must obey the orders given by humans, except where such orders would conflict with the First Law.
3. A robot must protect its own existence, as long as this does not conflict with the First or Second Law.

What law would you add to this list?

Figure 4.15

Researchers have developed small submarine robots that are equipped with sensors and monitoring equipment to explore the physical, biological, and chemical nature of the oceans. Autonomous underwater vehicles (AUVs) can monitor wastes, explore for oil and gas, and research the role played by oceans in climate change. Students at Florida Atlantic University have helped to design and test these bright yellow robots, which were used to help locate the position of the sunken Titanic.

Problems at Work

An *issue* is a large and complicated problem that generates discussion among people with different views. Many workplace issues will have a significant impact on Canadians over the next few years. We have seen how the workplace is changing and the many factors that are responsible. We have investigated how changing technology can have good and bad impacts on the workforce. Other trends that have become issues are the impact of the aging baby boomers, who are about to retire; increasing concern for protection of the environment; and the impact of **globalization** and immigration on Canada.

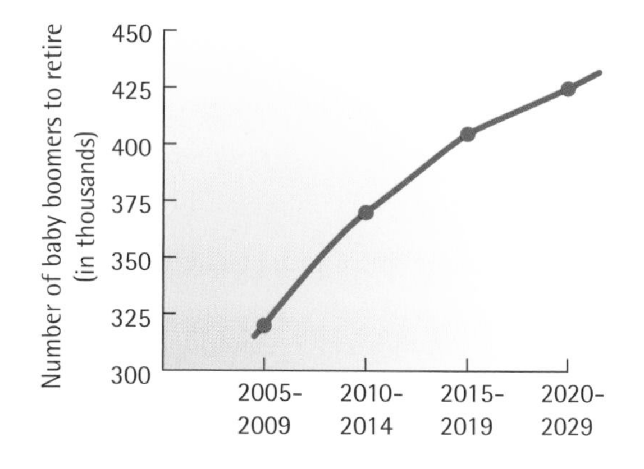

Figure 4.16

As the baby boomers get older, the number of people over 65 will increase to 25% of the total population by 2040. What opportunities for new business will arise because of this?

Up with the Environment!

Environmental protection industries are one of the fastest-growing areas for jobs, not only in Canada but around the world. The market for environmentally friendly products and services in Canada has grown tremendously. Governments and companies hire workers to help them become more efficient and less polluting.

SEE PAGE 191

SEE PAGE 216

ENVIRONMENT

Figure 4.17

Solar panels on the Manitoba Legislature Building and wind turbines, like this one in Saskatchewan, are renewable, non-polluting energy sources.

SEE PAGE 26

Help wanted! In the 2000s, there will not be enough young people to fill all the jobs Canada has to offer. Demographers and economists have investigated how major trends will work together to produce a labour shortage in the next few years. Natural increase will remain low, the baby boom generation will retire and leave the workforce, and there will not be enough new immigrants to fill all the jobs. More workers will be needed because of the predicted growth in international trade. The unemployment rate in Canada, which in the late 1990s stood at around 7% to 8% of the population, will go down to around 3% by 2010.

Landscape Research Analyst
$48 700–$58 800

Environmental, Geotechnical, Water & Waste Water Engineers required to assist in upcoming projects

Director, Information Services The candidate will have excellent computer skills and be an effective communicator, both written and oral...

Global Trade

Our planet is shrinking! People can hop on an airplane and be anywhere in the world in a few hours. Satellites can beam images instantaneously to television sets any place on earth. Many of the products that we use in our daily lives, such as appliances, running shoes, and jeans, are imported from whichever country can make them for less.

Canada has a reputation around the world for expertise in a number of areas including satellite technology, **fibre optics**, and transportation equipment from snowmobiles to subway cars. We have an ethnically diverse country with connections to every part of the world. Because of these factors, Canada can look forward to increased world trade, which is one of the areas in the economy that is growing. This will contribute to the creation of many new jobs in marketing, advertising, and transportation of Canadian products to the export market, as well as special career fields such as international law.

Increased world trade will also result in more competition, however. This will put pressure on industries and businesses to cut their costs even more. Because workers in North America are expensive, companies are likely to try to reduce their workforce to as few as possible.

Fact File

Between 1992 and 1997, jobs for computer programmers and systems analysts increased by 92% in Canada to 267 000. This compares with 9% growth in Canada's economy as a whole. People in these jobs earn, on average, about $300 more a week than workers overall.

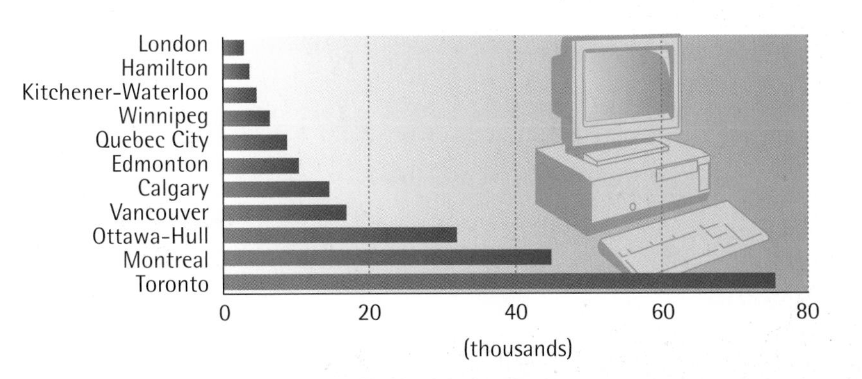

Figure 4.18
Number of computer programmers/systems analysts in Canada, 1999.

Global Skills

People who hope to work in global trade will not only need to understand trends and respond to them very quickly. They will also need language skills and an awareness of the varying rules of etiquette in different countries.

As immigration continues to add to Canada's population, ethnic diversity has led to growth in a variety of food products, restaurants, stores, and newspapers, as well as many services needed by people new to the country. Some immigrants need language and educational services. Others, especially those who come as business- or entrepreneurial-class immigrants, start businesses in Canada and employ workers.

> *"Companies can no longer think in terms of 24 time zones. Now there are only three — the Americas, Asia, and Europe. If customers are sleeping in one time zone, they are awake and ready to buy in others. But if your company is sleeping, those customers will take their business elsewhere."*
>
> **John A. Challenger, futurist**

SEE PAGE 279

INTERACTION

Figure 4.19

Seventy percent of Canada's immigrants now come from Asia, Africa, and Latin America.

Challenges of the Future

Most careers of the future will require some important general skills. One of the most important is the ability to communicate effectively. Problem solving, decision making, and creative thinking are also skills that will be in demand in the new work market. You will need to be able to work well with others as part of a team, and be flexible and adaptable in order to meet the challenges of rapid change.

> *"Because technology and the economy change so rapidly, the hot jobs forecasted today may not be hot for long. Even computer skills are no magic bullet. ... Rather than pressuring children to prepare for a particular job, parents should help them identify and nurture their areas of interest and ability."*
>
> **Barbara Moses, "Career Intelligence"**

GO TO **http://worksearch.gc.ca/**

Click on Staying Marketable. Now, click on New World of Work, and then on Survival Tips. What is tip #1? Explore other parts of the site, as it has a lot of information about the world of work you will be entering.

Blueprint for the Future is a series of career fairs for First Nations students. The objective is to introduce youth to the wide range of potential careers and to spark an interest that will lead to good, solid career choices by aboriginal students.

Since 1996, two career fairs have been held each year in different cities across Canada. Approximately 1200 students from across a given province attend some 90 workshops conducted by professionals of diverse career backgrounds including, but not limited to, health, medicine, business, sciences, technology, finance, and manufacturing.

Speakers have included recipients and jury members of the National Aboriginal Achievement Awards, local and national business leaders, and local and national aboriginal and non-aboriginal leaders. In each seminar students receive practical information on career options, educational requirements, and employment trends. Supported by both the public and private sectors, the career fairs have been highly successful and are noted for their high level of organization.

Figure 4.20

Evan Adams (left) and Ted Nolan with participants of the Blueprint for the Future Aboriginal Youth Career Fair, Winnipeg, 1999.

1. What impact has the baby boomer generation had on manufacturing industries in the secondary sector of the economy?
2. What does it mean to be literate? What does it mean to be computer literate?
3. Explain how the workplace issue of downsizing is related to the global economy.

CASE STUDY

GIS—An Expanding Career Area in the Information Economy

GIS is an acronym (a word made from the initials of other words) for Geographic Information Systems. It is a powerful computer-based technology that is predicted to be used in the future as widely as word processing is today. A GIS is a combination of a computer, specialized software, and geographic data (information) about places. It is a tool that allows the operator to see and analyse patterns and interconnections among many different layers of data that are applied to maps of a particular location.

GIS is in great demand in the marketplace in business and industry, government, and institutions, in planning, environmental management, and municipal services. Tens of thousands of jobs over the next few years will be created in the GIS field.

Why are people with GIS skills in such demand? Well, think of all the types of questions people in everyday jobs might ask, and think about how GIS might help them answer these questions.

INTERACTION

Figure 4.21

The questions and problems that can be analysed and solved using GIS are seemingly endless!

Job	Question	GIS Answer
Urban planner	Where should we build a bicycle trail in our community?	GIS can show where there are sites with fewer steep slopes and more scenic views.
Mayor of a city	Where should a new landfill site go?	GIS can show available land areas that are far away from populated areas, yet near to transportation links.
Police officer	Why do certain parts of my city experience more crime than others?	GIS can map out crime sites and compare these to areas of high population density and urban decay.
Environmentalist	What damage will occur if that river floods its banks?	GIS can create a map showing what buildings are too close to a river, and also predict the total flooded area.
Sales manager	How do I divide up my sales territories so my sales people have an equal number of customers?	GIS can look at where customers live and draw boundaries so that each sales person has the same number of customers.

Figure 4.22

GIS can help select appropriate sites for landfill garbage disposal. Can you think of other problems that GIS might help to solve?

GIS Career Profile

Michelle Laronde is from the Mohawk Nation near Montreal. She has a university degree in geography and environmental studies and a GIS diploma from Sir Sandford Fleming College. Michelle has been a Geographic Information Systems technician for the last three years. Her skills allow her to analyse problems in natural resource management. She is currently working with a team studying a watershed project. They are using different layers of information on maps of the watershed area to find the location of major sources of river pollution. They are also trying to determine the impact of water pollution on the local ecosystem and on the drinking water of local residents.

GO TO

www.city.london.on.ca/

This is an interactive site using GIS to help you find things in the city. Click on Living in London. Then, click on Visiting London. In the window, choose Maps of London, and then click on the Tutorial button. Explore the various options to experience the power of GIS!

GIS Application Profile

The Crime Analysis and Mapping Unit of the Philadelphia Police Force consists of a team of three GIS specialists and one police officer. The unit serves the needs of 7000 officers and 1000 other employees. They produce maps of crime densities for a variety of different crimes and analyse the patterns that result. As areas of higher crime are identified, police can respond and deal with criminals. For example, by analysing a map showing where cars had been stolen, police were led to the location of a vehicle "chop shop," where stolen cars were taken apart and the parts sold.

1. Why are people who work in the GIS field called knowledge workers?
2. What aspects of Michelle Laronde's career profile and the Philadelphia Police's application profile fit the pattern of current employment trends?
3. Is GIS going to become more important or less important in the future? Explain.

Understanding the Concepts

1. List three advantages and three disadvantages for people who work at home.
2. What is the main demographic trend in Canada? What opportunities for new jobs does this create?
3. Why are jobs in the GIS field increasing so rapidly?

Research and Communication Skills

4. **a)** Ask your parents, your grandparents, or other senior citizens in the community what skills were the most important ones needed at the time when they entered the workforce. Make two lists of skills, one for those needed 50 years ago and one for those needed 15 years ago.

   b) Compare these skills to those that are needed in the workplace today.

   Which skills are different? Are any of the skills you listed in part (a) the same as those needed today?

5. **a)** Visit the Statistics Canada Web site at <www.statcan.ca/>. Choose the language you wish to work in. Click on Statistical Profile of Canadian Communities at the bottom of your screen. Type your community's name in the window. Click on the Search button. If your community is not listed, use the name of a larger community near you. Is the population increasing or decreasing? Now, click on Income and Work.

   b) Create two circle graphs to show the proportion of the community that is employed in primary, secondary, and tertiary industries, one graph for males and one for females.

   c) Create two additional circle graphs to show the same data for Ontario (one for males and one for females).

   d) Write an analysis of your graphs that answers these questions:
   - Which type of industry (primary, secondary, or tertiary) provides the most jobs in your community? Which type provides the least?
   - What do you notice about the difference in patterns of female and male employment in your community? What reasons can you give for these differences?
   - Compare employment patterns in your community to those in Ontario.
   - Suggest reasons for any similarities or differences between your community and Ontario.

6. Write a two-paragraph scenario of a typical day in the life of a worker in the year 2020. In your scenario, refer to at least four employment trends that will affect workers of the future.
7. Conduct research using the business report of newspapers and weekly magazines to find some examples of downsizing (workers being laid off) as a workplace issue in Canada's industries. What reasons for layoffs have been given by the companies? Identify at least two different points of view regarding this issue.

Map and Globe Skills

8. Look at the labels on your clothes. Find out where they were made. Draw the item of clothing on the country of its origin on an outline map of the world. Describe the globalization of business based on your map.

Applications

9. Create a poster to illustrate at least four jobs that may be created as a result of the social trend in which more people are enjoying outdoor activities.

10. Conduct a survey of all the workers in your school. Classify them into different job categories of your choice. What percentage of the total workforce in your school would be considered "knowledge workers"?

11. Write a poem or perform a skit with other members of your class to show your prediction of how a technology of the future could change the Canadian economy.

12. Investigate a career or type of work that interests you to find out the skills and educational requirements needed and a description of the day-to-day work done by someone in that field.

Figure 4.23
What economic, social, and demographic trends do these goods suggest to you?

5 Connections and Consequences

EXPECTATIONS

- identify and explain patterns in human geography, and describe how human activities are affected by these patterns
- demonstrate an understanding of the factors affecting urbanization, industrialization, transportation, and improvements in agriculture
- compare the characteristics of developed and developing countries

Riding the Wave

You have read in the first few chapters of this text that there are waves of change sweeping over the world. You have seen that changes, which are not easy to predict, will affect everyone's future in some way or another. These changes seem to be increasing at an ever faster rate. Many people feel that even the pace of daily life is getting faster.

This chapter investigates some of the factors that are causing change in agriculture, urbanization, industrialization, and transportation. However, it is hard to separate these four areas of society, because the factors that affect one area affect them all. To make things even more complicated, the characteristics of agriculture, urbanization, industrialization, and transportation vary a great deal from one part of the world to another. With agriculture, for example, a variety of types and methods produce a wide range of foods and products. Each of these elements can have different characteristics that pose many different problems.

SEE PAGE 49

Figure 5.1

How can you prepare yourself to "surf the waves" of future change?

Links in the Web

The issues listed in Figure 5.2 are closely related to agriculture, but they are also linked to urbanization, industrialization, and transportation. They are interconnected with one another and with the factors causing them to change.

Differences from Place to Place

In developing countries, farm land and wealth are unevenly distributed among people. The gap between rich and poor is wide within the developing countries and between developed and developing parts of the world.

There are also great differences in the amount of money a farmer may have and the farm's **productivity**, or amount of food produced per hectare. Even within Canada, many different types of farming have developed, affecting human activities and the environment in a number of ways.

GO TO

www.agview.com

Click on Sustainable Agriculture, Sustainable Farming Connection, then 1000 Ways to Sustainable Farming. Finally, click on What is Sustainable Farming. Follow the areas through several screens by clicking on "next." List some of the many ways to farm sustainably.

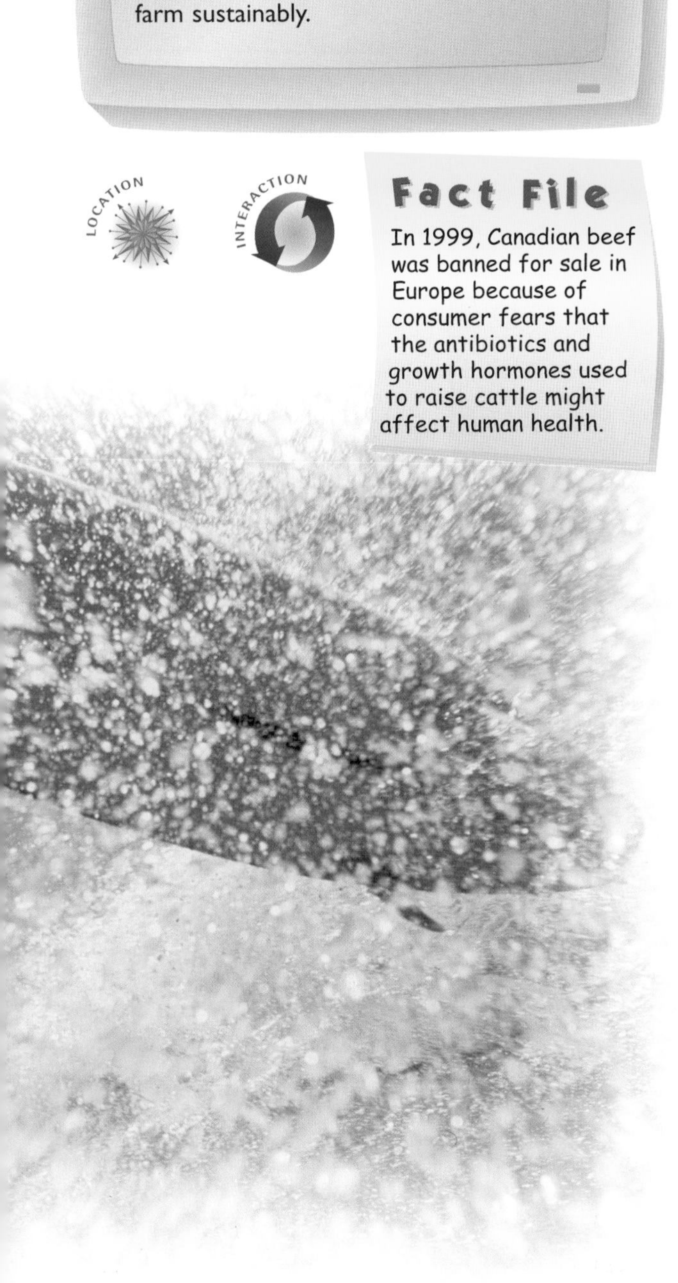

Fact File

In 1999, Canadian beef was banned for sale in Europe because of consumer fears that the antibiotics and growth hormones used to raise cattle might affect human health.

Figure 5.2

Changes in agriculture, urbanization, industrialization, and transportation often introduce many issues and concerns. For example:

- *Food security* – Food shortages are likely to occur as world population grows.
- *Water quality* – Animal wastes and agricultural chemicals could end up polluting lakes and rivers.
- *Water use* – Over-irrigation can cause soils to lose their fertility.
- *Pesticide use* – Overuse may kill many beneficial species as well as pests, possibly affecting human health.
- *Soil quality* – High-technology farming methods, along with heavy use of fossil fuels and chemical additives, may cause long-term damage and erosion.
- *Farm ownership* – Communities may change as traditional family farms are transformed into corporation factory farms.
- *Urban growth* – Good farmland may disappear as cities sprawl into the countryside.
- *Genetic engineering* – New bioengineered foods may pose a threat to the health of people and ecosystems.

Dealing with Issues

Even the most knowledgeable experts working in governments, industries, organizations, institutions, and the United Nations find these problems very complicated and difficult to solve. We can walk on the moon and land on Mars, but humans still struggle in their efforts to create a better world. By studying these issues and concerns, we can better understand our connections and relationships within our community and with the world. We can also gain a greater awareness of social and economic problems and attempt to find solutions as we work toward a sustainable future.

Figure 5.3

The average farmer in Canada or Australia has more than 200 ha of land and access to high technology. In parts of Asia and Africa, however, the average farmer has only 1 ha and still uses traditional methods of subsistence farming.

SEE PAGE 115

Figure 5.4

How do you think these two farming methods compare with regard to amount of food produced, efficiency, costs to farmers, and impact on the environment? What other criteria could be used to compare them?

Fact File

The annual per capita consumption of meat in kilograms in Canada is 70, in the United States is 110, in China is 22, and in India is 1.

Figure 5.5

Range-fed cattle provide more food energy than it takes to raise them. Between 10 and 20 times more energy is used to raise cattle on beef **feedlots** than is produced in food energy. The energy for producing food comes from things like the electricity used in automated feeding systems and the fuel used to run machinery.

Factors Causing Change

There are many factors that cause change. They are often grouped under the following headings: *social, political, cultural, economic,* and *environmental,* but these factors do not work alone. They are very closely connected to one another (interconnected) because each of them depends on what is happening with the others (interdependent). Of the many factors that work together to influence change, two important ones are *demographics* (human patterns and social trends) and *changing technology.*

Figure 5.6

Characteristics of social, political, cultural, economic, and environmental factors causing change. Many of the factors that cause change are the result of numbers of decisions made every day by people around the world. In turn, people feel the impact of these decisions. Each individual decision is important.

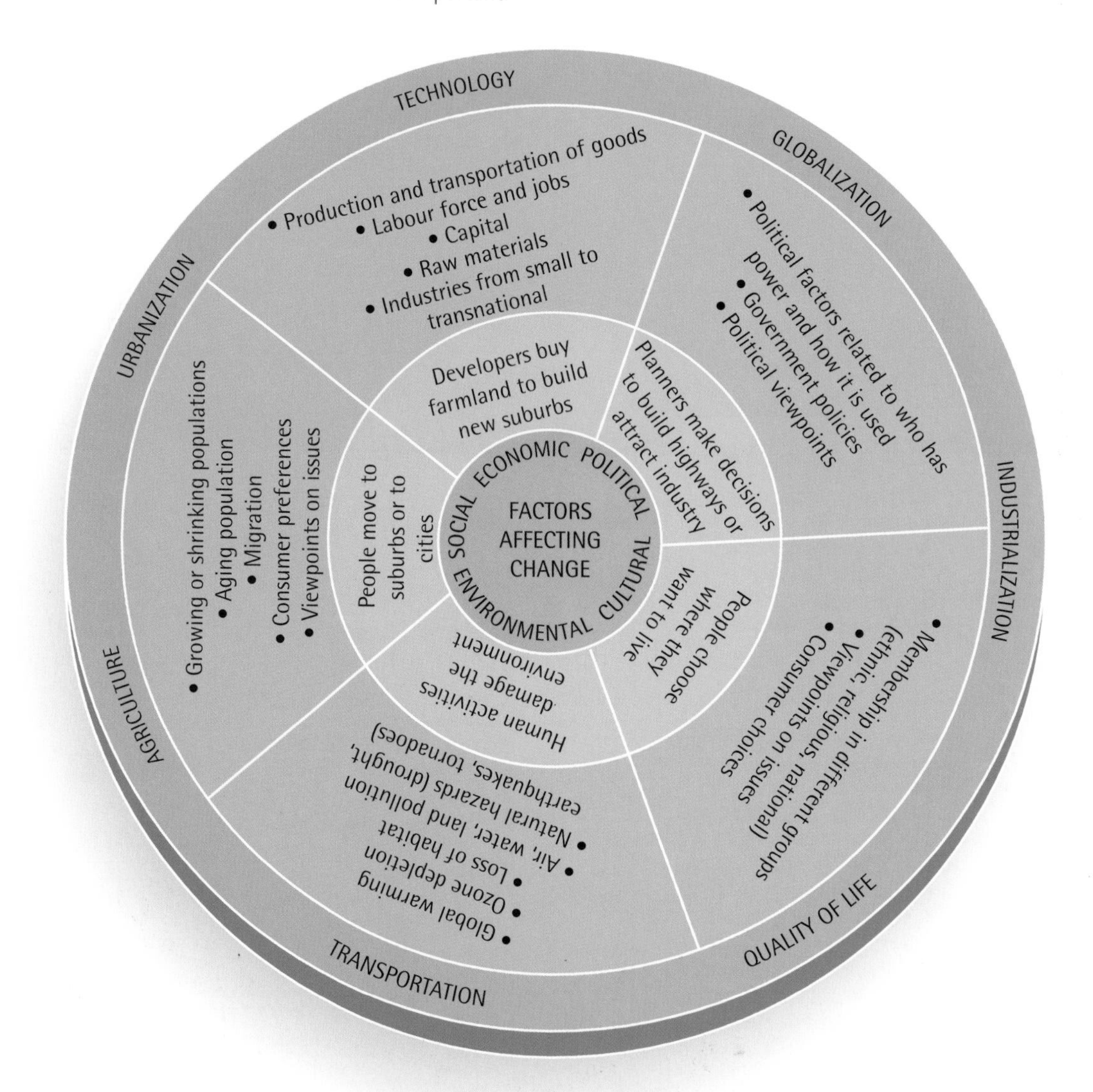

A 1999 study found that 38% of the children under 10 living in Toronto live in poverty – up from 23% in 1991. Around 1000 children live in shelters with their families. Although government and many citizens disagree on the actual percentage of children living in poverty, some poverty activists feel that any number is too high in a country like Canada.

SEE PAGE 23

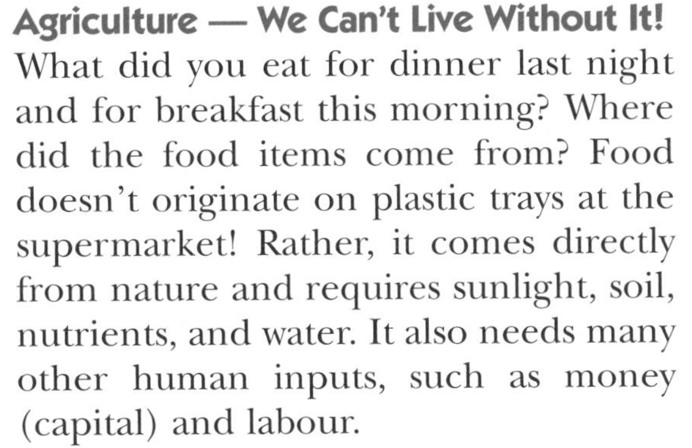

Agriculture — We Can't Live Without It!

What did you eat for dinner last night and for breakfast this morning? Where did the food items come from? Food doesn't originate on plastic trays at the supermarket! Rather, it comes directly from nature and requires sunlight, soil, nutrients, and water. It also needs many other human inputs, such as money (capital) and labour.

Agriculture in Canada is affected by many factors, including world demand for food, prices that farmers get on the market, government policies on agriculture, trade agreements with other countries, how much money is spent on agricultural research, and consumer preferences.

The next time you're in a supermarket, spend a few minutes looking around at the great variety of available products — an amazing kaleidoscope of colours, shapes, and sizes. Technological advances in high-speed transportation and refrigeration bring us products from every region of the world. Many of these foods are **processed** by adding substances that maintain freshness, colour, and consistency.

Fact File

North Americans spend more than $5 billion each year on special diets and diet foods to lower their caloric intake, while millions of people around the world are seriously malnourished.

Figure 5.7

A Philippine family enjoy their dinner together. More than a billion people in the world go to bed hungry, and not all of them live in developing countries. Poverty and other social and economic conditions are the causes.

Figure 5.8

Industrialization related to agriculture has resulted in thousands of processed food products. Processing potatoes into potato chips can reduce the nutritional value of the food and greatly increase the price.

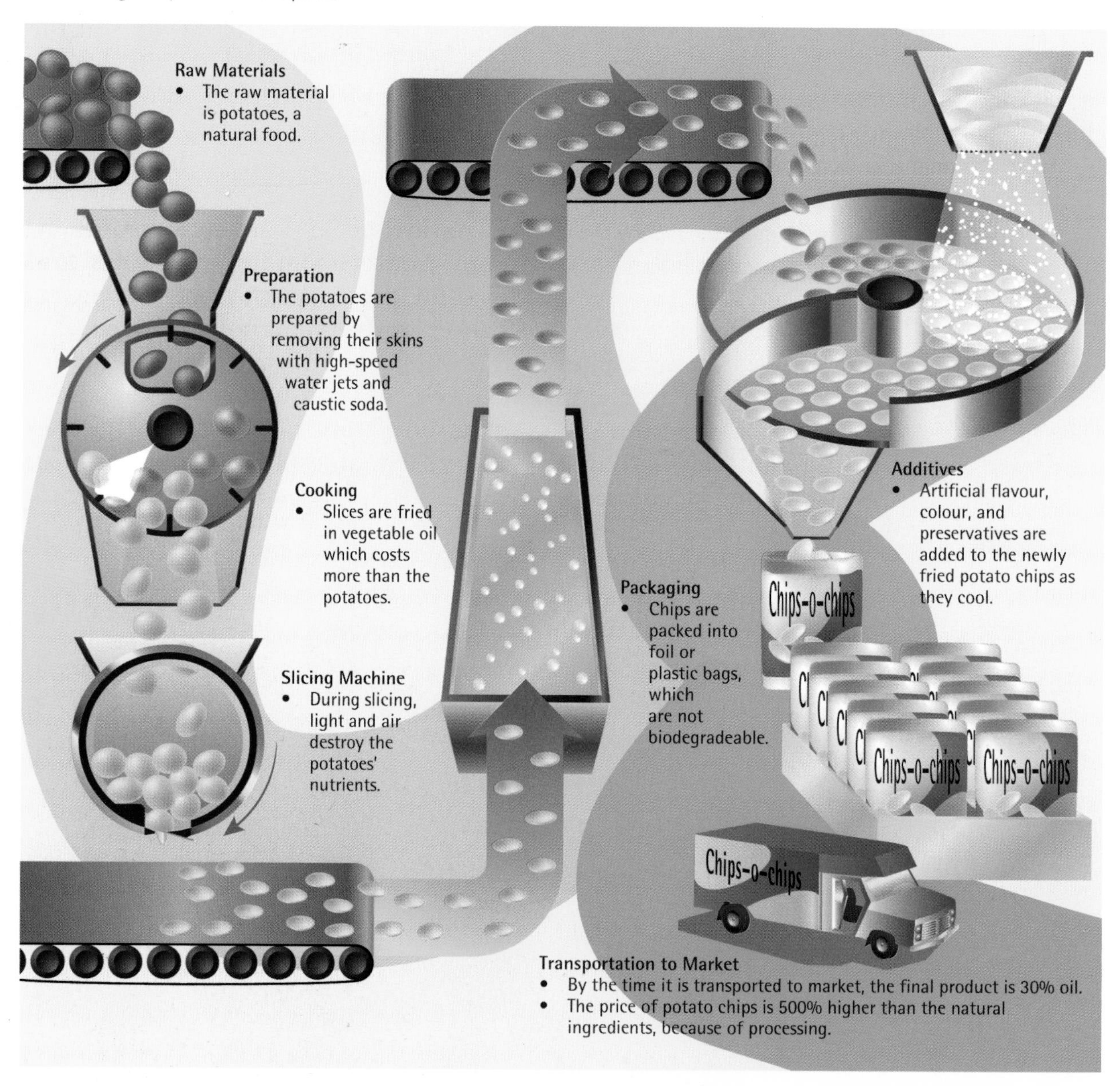

1. Choose one of the agricultural issues listed in Figure 5.2 (page 87) and show how it is connected to (a) growth of cities and (b) demographics. Explain your choices.
2. List three factors that affect agriculture. Indicate whether you consider each to be mainly a social, cultural, political, economic, or environmental factor.

Fact File

All the grain that is fed to livestock around the world — about 40% of the total grain produced — would feed five times as many people as it does after it is converted into meat.

More Mouths to Feed!

Over the past century, there has been enough food in the world to feed everyone. However, not everyone has the same access to food, because it is unevenly distributed. In many developed countries, there are food surpluses, while in many developing countries, there are food shortages.

SEE PAGE 4

Meeting the Challenge

As farmers and fishers fall behind world population growth, we must consider some serious questions about our survival: How many people can the earth support? How can we take better care of the resources we have? There are many ways to meet the challenge of working toward a balance between people and food on the earth

- protect croplands from being changed to other uses
- invest more in agricultural research
- reduce the world's consumption of animal products
- encourage home gardening.

Figure 5.9

As world population continues to grow, the demand for food will increase. The earth's long-term ability to meet the growing demand for food is of major concern.

Down on the Factory Farm

Because most of the world's arable land is already being used to grow food, increasing the amount of food will require ever more intensive farming on the same land. Many farmers believe that more inputs of seed, fertilizer, chemical pesticides, tools, and machinery will have to be applied. On the other hand, many people and international institutions are concerned about the devastating effect that modern, industrial agriculture (sometimes called "agribusiness") can have.

Fact File

Tobacco production uses large amounts of pesticides and depletes soil nutrients faster than many other crops.

Agribusiness is Not the Answer

Large-scale, highly mechanized agribusiness may not be the most beneficial way to farm in all parts of the world. Growing just one crop, known as **monoculture**, reduces biodiversity; the intensive use of fossil fuels, synthetic fertilizers, and pesticides causes pollution; and farm machinery can cause soil erosion.

"If the million hectares of land used to produce tobacco were turned over to growing grain, it would not only provide enough grain to support world population for six months, but it would also reduce death rates and sharply lower health care costs."

Lester R. Brown, Worldwatch Institute

Figure 5.10

In Canada, the use of pesticides threatens the survival of the burrowing owl. What other animals in your area are on the endangered list? Alternatives to pesticides include crop rotation, natural pest predators, and crops that are naturally resistant.

Figure 5.11

Millions of farmers in developing countries, and more and more farmers in developed countries, are practising organic farming.

Figure 5.12

There are more than 200 commercial farmers in Ontario using organic farming methods, and the organic food market has doubled every year in Canada over the last decade.

Organic Farming

Imagine eating an apple without having to wash it! **Organic farming** is a method of growing food and livestock without using synthetic pesticides, fertilizers, antibiotics, or growth hormones. Instead, it relies on a variety of natural methods to maintain healthy soil and food production. Organic farmers must also feed organic grains to their livestock and use compost and composted manure as fertilizer.

A Growing Business

SEE PAGE 169

Because this type of farming requires more labour, and because it is not mass produced, organically produced food is often more expensive. Many farmers all over the world, however, are finding that organic farming can improve production and local economies, as well. Over 25% of the rice farmers in Indonesia, for example, now use organic methods. Their **yields** are increasing, and more jobs are provided in the fields. In Germany, over 45 000 ha are farmed organically.

Fact File

If wealthy people in the world reduced the amount of meat they ate by just 10%, 65 million tonnes of grain would be available for people to eat.

Technology

Human inventiveness, intelligence, and creativity result in thousands of new inventions every year. New technology is often seen as a solution for many of the problems facing the world. Most technology, however, has good and bad consequences.

For example, during the Green Revolution in the 1950s and 1960s, technology was developed to produce more food, especially in developing countries. Agricultural researchers invented new seeds for higher-yield crops that were more resistant to damage from drought and pests. The Green Revolution resulted in large gains in food production. But, critics are concerned about the environmental damage that these agricultural practices can have.

Fact File

Agriculture uses over 50% of the available global fresh water supply. More efficient irrigation methods are being developed, but some parts of the world are already severely short of water and are using underground water supplies faster than they can be replenished.

Figure 5.13

Irrigation of a large potato field. While we need to increase the amount of food we produce on the world's agricultural land, we need to be careful that the technology used does not damage our life support systems of water, soil, and air.

Figure 5.14

"Carpet bombing" using pesticides. Modern, large-scale farming methods, including high-energy inputs and use of synthetic fertilizers and pesticides, can contribute to deterioration of water, air, and soil quality.

1. Explain two factors that make it difficult for everyone in the world to get enough nutritious food to eat.
2. If you were a world leader, list two steps that you would take to improve agriculture in order to produce more food for people who are hungry.
3. List three alternatives to the intensive use of chemicals on the world's croplands.
4. What do you think will happen to organic farming by the year 2010?

Swelling Cities

Advances in technology, particularly in the areas of transportation and building, have influenced the shape and function of cities and the increasing numbers of people who live in them. This process is called **urbanization**. The developing world is now experiencing urbanization in the way that developed countries did in the early 1900s.

> ***"Urbanization means good news and bad news. ... It contributes to national economic and social development [but] it is almost impossible for governments to follow rapid growth with water, energy, and other basic services."***
>
> **Jorge Wilheim, deputy secretary-general, Habitat II**

SEE PAGE 50

The world's urban population is growing quickly. Just 50 years ago, there were 2.5 billion people worldwide. In developing countries, 85% of the population lived in rural areas; in developed countries, that figure was only 38%. In all, fewer than 30% of the world's population lived in cities. But, this has changed. By the early 2000s, for the first time ever, *half* of the more than six billion people now on earth live in towns and cities.

SEE PAGE 217

Fact File

The United Nations predicts that, within the next 25 years, more than 60% of the world's 8.5 billion people will live in urban areas.

Many of the world's leaders met in Istanbul, Turkey in June, 1996 to attend Habitat II. This was a conference that focussed on managing the world's cities and the problems facing them. One recommendation made was for governments to spend more money on programs to improve rural and agricultural areas so people would be less inclined to leave their farming lifestyle and move to cities.

Figure 5.15

How will cities provide the food, shelter, and services needed by people in the future when so many go without these things today?

Figure 5.16

Young girls assemble straw mats in Nouakchott, Mauritania. The quality of life in city slums can be dismal. Many people, including children, are forced to work in terrible conditions in factories. Some live on the street, begging and scavenging food to survive. Despite these conditions, people still see the city as a better place to live, and so urbanization continues.

Fact File

Only 15% of the people living in rural areas in Canada live on farms.

Rural Inhabitants "Vote with Their Feet"

Changes in agriculture, transportation, and industrialization are contributing to the push of people out of rural areas and to the pull of people toward cities. As more and more industries developed in cities in the early 1900s, people were attracted away from farms to the new jobs that these businesses provided. Today's farming inventions mean that fewer people are needed to work on farms.

In developing countries, people leave rural areas for a number of reasons:

- *High fertility rates* —Too many children are born for small farms to support.
- *Small farms* — Farms are divided up into smaller and smaller plots that cannot support enough people, as new generations inherit traditional farms.
- *Economic opportunities* — More jobs are found in cities.
- *Natural disasters* — Earthquakes or volcanic eruptions cause serious damage in rural areas, forcing people away from their homes and villages.
- *Violent conflicts* — War and other political upheavals affect land use.

GO TO **www.freethechildren.org**

This Web site was created by a Thornhill, Ontario student named Craig Kielburger, who has become famous as an activist. He has raised awareness of child labour conditions in cities and towns in developing countries. Click on Projects. What are some of the projects in which this "children helping children" organization is involved? How could you get involved?

Fact File

The United States produces 25% of the world's greenhouse gases, which cause global warming.

Megacities

Another aspect of urbanization is the growth of huge masses of people and the proliferation of buildings. "Megacities" have spread out over the countryside, swallowing up farmland, towns, and cities. These massive urban areas, such as Saõ Paulo, Shanghai, and Mexico City, have serious human and environmental problems that have become global issues of concern. These issues of urbanization include

- poverty
- environmental problems
- traffic congestion
- lack of services such as electricity, water, sewage, and garbage disposal
- deteriorating **infrastructure**, which includes roads and bridges, access to adequate housing, and access to food.

The trend to the rapid growth of megacities is starting to slow down in developing countries, except in China. However, megacities in developed countries will grow much more slowly, if they grow at all.

SEE PAGE 294

Figure 5.17

Beijing is one of China's most traffic-congested and polluted cities; Los Angeles is the most polluted city in the United States. By looking carefully at these photos, can you suggest one measure that each city might take to reduce the problem of congestion and smog?

Economic Factors and Trends

Most new industries are located in cities, because cities have services, transportation, workers, and markets close by. The challenge for humankind is to control and direct industrialization — and cities' growth — in sustainable ways.

> ***"Today more human beings are in touch with one another than ever before. Billions more, without even knowing it, are becoming entangled across great distances in global webs that are transforming their lives."***
>
> **Richard J. Barnet & John Cavanagh, "Global Dreams, Imperial Corporations and the New World Order"**

Globalization

Globalization is a major trend that is sweeping the world. It affects a wide range of activities in agriculture, urbanization, industrialization, and transportation. Globalization includes the spread of

- media and entertainment, especially satellite TV
- electronic communication
- rising levels of trade
- international investment
- travel and migration
- new worldwide organizations
- increased personal consumption and spending
- rapid changes in technology in all areas
- growth of transnational corporations.

SEE PAGE 216

Figure 5.18

In Canada, as in most other industrialized countries, agriculture, industry, and technology are strongly influenced by globalization. Products have to be of high quality and available at low prices in order to compete with other countries in the global marketplace.

Figure 5.19

Transnational corporations operate in all areas of the economy, from large oil companies and car manufacturers to electronic and entertainment companies and food conglomerates, like Coca-Cola, Pepsico, Nike, Ford, Sony, Mitsubishi, and Microsoft.

Fact File

Transnational corporations control 80% of the world's trade and 80% of the world's croplands.

The Big Players

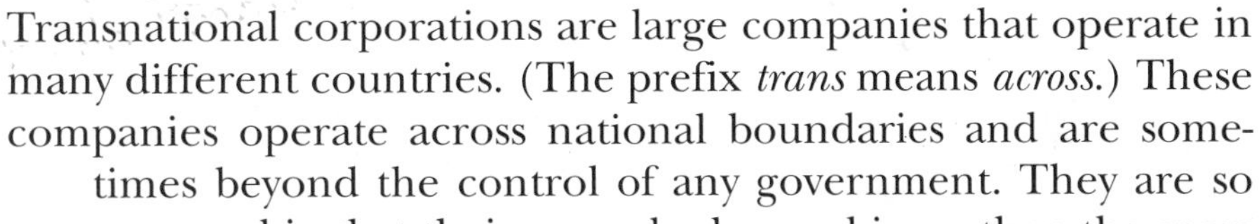

Transnational corporations are large companies that operate in many different countries. (The prefix *trans* means *across.*) These companies operate across national boundaries and are sometimes beyond the control of any government. They are so big that their annual sales are bigger than the gross domestic products of many developed countries. For example, Philip Morris, a transnational tobacco corporation and **food conglomerate**, owns Kraft General Foods and produces many common brand-name food products such as Kraft, Post, Maxwell House, Oscar Mayer, Jell-O, and Miller.

"Multinational corporations are the main agents of globalization. They control information, markets, investment, financial flows, and employment practices. ... Globalization does create wealth, but not for everyone."

Daryl Copeland, author

Governments, particularly in developing countries, sometimes give in to the demands of transnationals operating within their borders simply because they provide many jobs and boost the economy. The top 200 transnational companies, however, employ less than 1% of the world's total workforce. Many companies have "downsized" even more in the last few years.

A Tale of Four Cities

SEE PAGE 273

Canada's big cities are alive and well! They are continuing to grow even faster than small and medium-sized towns and cities. Many immigrants new to Canada are drawn to Calgary, Montreal, Toronto, and Vancouver. In addition, people from other provinces tend to move to these cities to look for work.

> *"... The city itself provides a vivid theatre for the spontaneous encounters and challenges and embraces of daily life."*
>
> **Lewis Mumford, "The City in History"**

Figure 5.20

Percentage of population growth during the 1990s. Vancouver, Calgary, and Toronto were all well above the Canadian average.

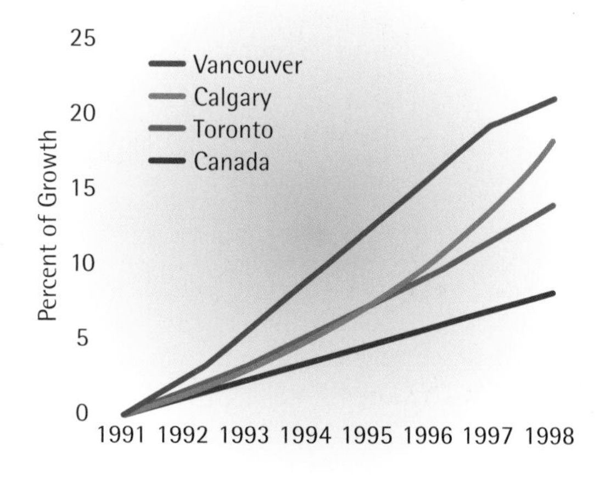

Figure 5.21

Percentage of Canada's population living in small towns and rural areas. These numbers have dropped steadily in the last 25 years.

SEE PAGE 50

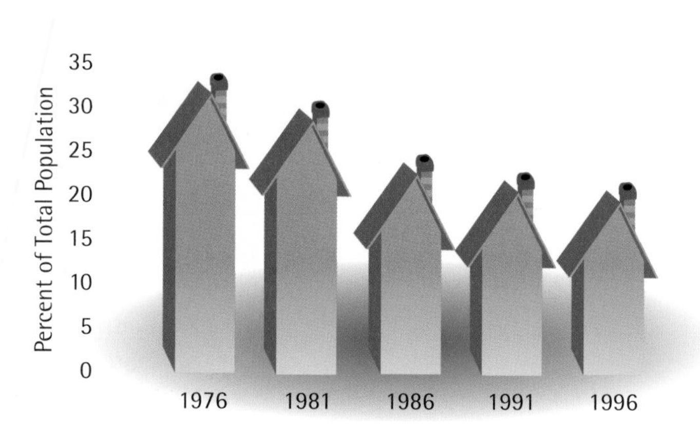

Fact File

In 1997, 192 cities around the world were ranked by a company based in Geneva, Switzerland according to how pleasant it was to live in them. Vancouver ranked 1st, Toronto 3rd, and Montreal 15th. Megacities such as Tokyo, Mexico, and New York rank much farther down the list.

Figure 5.22

Over the past 25 years, Calgary's population has nearly doubled – from 470 000 people to over 800 000. City dwellers everywhere make intensive use of the earth's natural resources, but this is especially so in developed countries. What problems can this create?

Figure 5.23

Making cities work more sustainably is an urgent challenge for humans today. Cleaner energy technologies, greater efficiency in transportation, and better recycling will help to reduce the "ecological footprint" of people living in cities. What is one thing you can do to help reduce your city's "ecological footprint"?

It's Your World

Do you feel safe walking in the city closest to where you live? Most parts of the downtown area of Canada's four largest cities are safe and busy places, where people live and work. By contrast, the downtown core of some U.S. cities seem empty and unsafe after working hours. Cities such as Buffalo and New York have launched urban renewal programs to address some of the poverty, crime, and decay in the city centre. Land uses that attract people – such as stadiums, hotels, concert halls, convention centres, and condominiums – are often included in such renewal projects.

Industrialization has gone hand in hand with urbanization. Most industrial activities produce large quantities of wastes, some of them hazardous. This has brought wealth and well-being to many, but the tremendous concentration of people and activities requires co-operation among government, industry, and individual citizens if cities are to remain pleasant and healthy places to live.

> ***"If a city's streets are safe from barbarism and fear, the city is tolerably safe from barbarism and fear."***
>
> **Jane Jacobs, "The Death and Life of Great American Cities"**

The "Greening" of Cities

People around the world are starting to improve the appearance of their cities and make them more resource-efficient and less polluting. Urban geographers and planners have outlined some ideas for developing more sustainable cities. These include:

- Change land use planning. Cities and suburbs can be created with a mix of different land uses. This trend would result in green, safe, diverse, and lively communities close to public transportation facilities.

Figure 5.24

In a vibrant city, housing, work, shopping, schools, and recreation facilities are all within easy walking distance.

- Change transportation planning. Travel by walking, biking, and public transit can made easier so that people will be encouraged to use their cars less.

MOVEMENT/PATTERN

Figure 5.25

Vancouver's Skytrain is an example of effective urban transportation planning.

- Encourage the building of safe, conveniently located, and affordable housing for people in all economic groups.

Figure 5.26

Houses that are close to the street and to one another create a sense of shared space and community, even in a big city.

- Restore natural environments, such as woodlots, rivers, and wetlands, in cities that have been damaged.

Figure 5.27

Parkland trails are inviting to hikers and bikers alike. Cleanup campaigns, such as clearing aluminum cans from parks and lakesides, can help minimize the bad effects of human activities on the environment.

- Support local agriculture and community gardens within cities.

Figure 5.28

Planting trees is one way to beautify an urban environment. Can you suggest two other activities that might make our cities greener, more pleasant places?

- Promote recycling and other programs to conserve energy and water and reduce waste and pollution.

Figure 5.29

What happens to your waste paper after it leaves your recycling box? This shredded material will be used to make a variety of new paper products.

"The well-being of the planet in the coming century will be decided to a significant degree by cities and their citizens."

Trevor Hancock, urban consultant

1. Identify an example of how environmental factors have affected changes in:
   a) agriculture
   b) industrialization
   c) transportation.
2. List four things that urban citizens can do to help make cities more sustainable.

CASE STUDY

High-Tech Farming

One sunny August day, Terry Gates put his John Deere combine in neutral and paused amid his 1620 ha of wheat and barley near the town of Nipawin, 100 km east of Prince Albert, Saskatchewan. As the motor idled, Terry inserted a data cartridge into a dashboard-mounted computer. Seconds later, a colour display appeared on the monitor.

Global Positioning System (GPS) satellites 18 000 km above the earth gave Terry his position in a wheat field to within two metres. On the screen, among reds, greens, blues, and yellows — signifying potassium distribution in the soils — he could view a graphic rendering of the six-metre strip of land on which he tested a fungicide last summer. As he hoped, his yield per bushel had increased in that tiny patch.

SEE PAGE 77

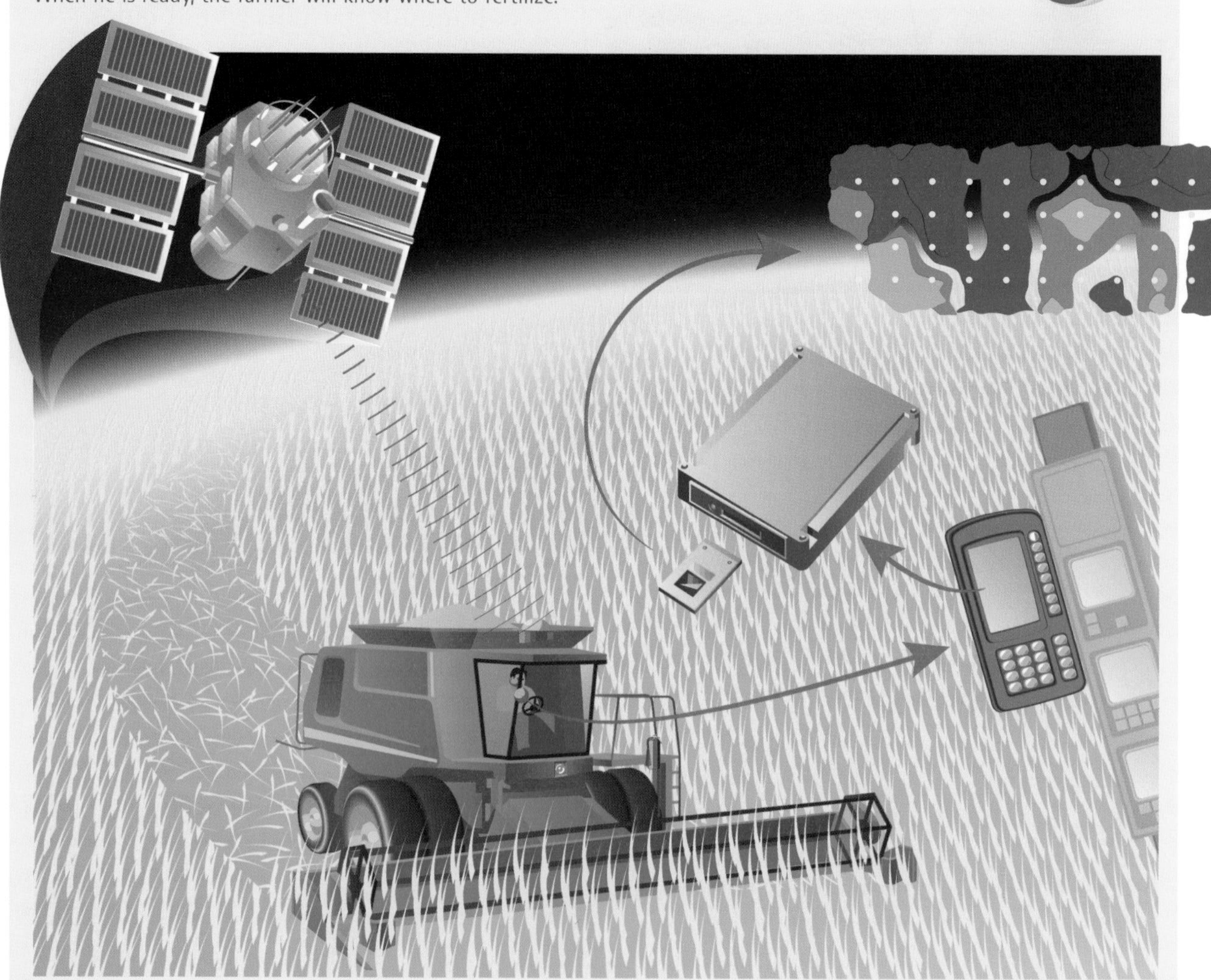

Figure 5.30

The Global Positioning System satellite beams information to a receiver fastened to the roof of the combine. The data produce an image on the farmer's computer screen (right), revealing the pattern of potassium distribution over the land. When he is ready, the farmer will know where to fertilize.

Precision farming is based on GPS, a satellite navigation system that pinpoints objects on earth by their latitude and longitude. It was used extensively in the Persian Gulf war to direct U.S. jeeps, tanks, and missiles equipped with receivers for satellite data.

There was a time when farmers laid wire to mark the boundaries of their land. Today, a new breed of "wired" farmers use the GPS to push the boundaries of what they can produce from their land. Where once owners experimented with hybrid crops and tinkered with heavy machinery, the modern farm is going high-tech.

In Terry's case, a white 15-cm receiver mounted on his combine cab picks up signals from the sky, allowing him to map his fields precisely and pass the data to the onboard computer. He can also enter important information — data about soil moisture, topography, locations of weeds and insects, and past chemical-use patterns — so he can compare the current situation with the past.

Now, instead of carpet-bombing his fields with herbicides and fertilizer, this precision farmer is armed with information that allows him to spot-spray. This saves money and helps the environment, since smaller amounts of chemicals are needed.

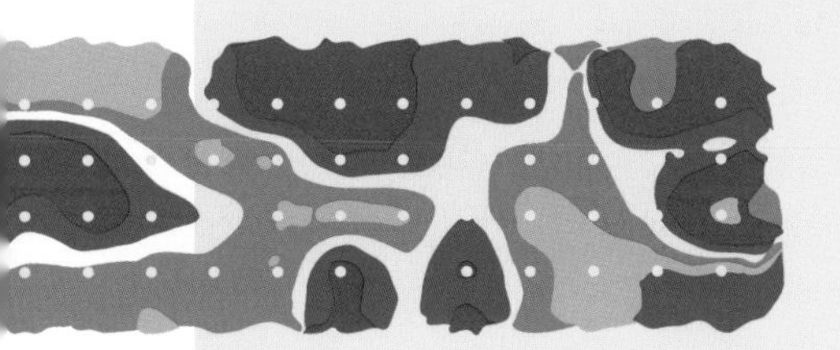

1. Which characteristics of globalization, listed on page 100, are illustrated by this case study of Terry Gates and his high-tech farming methods?
2. How can the technology used by Gates be considered beneficial to the environment?
3. Create your own definition of precision farming.
4. Identify one social, political, and economic factor that has caused improvements in agriculture such as precision farming.

Understanding the Concepts

1. Describe, in your own words, the meaning of the following terms. Explain how each is connected to one of the key areas of agriculture, urbanization, industrialization, or transportation.

   Demographics
   Productivity
   Globalization
   Precision farming
   Transnational corporations
   Alternative fuels

2. Construct a chart to show how people's consumption habits in the developed world are related to agriculture, urbanization, industrialization, and transportation.

3. Create a poster that includes sketches and text boxes to illustrate several ways of bringing agriculture into the city.

4. Draw a web organizer with connecting arrows to show several of the many interconnections among agriculture, urbanization, industrialization, and transportation. Start with the four key areas in bubbles on your page. Label any factors that affect these areas in an appropriate place on the interconnecting arrows.

Research and Communication Skills

5. Imagine you are a member of a poor family living in a rural farming village in a developing country such as Mexico or India. Because your family cannot make ends meet on your small plot of land, you lose your farm to a wealthy landowner and move to a megacity. Write a postcard to a friend back in your rural village explaining what your new life in the city is like.

6. Write a two-paragraph scenario describing transportation methods used by people and freight in a sustainable city of the next century.

7. To date, no country is following a policy of complete sustainable development. As a highly respected world leader, you have been asked by the United Nations to design a set of principles for other leaders to follow when promoting development in their countries. You must decide on six principles. Here are two to give you a start; devise four more.

   a) Development is sustainable if it makes use of renewable materials.

   b) Development is sustainable if it encourages co-operative activities in local communities.

www.macalester.edu/~geograph/world-urbanization/urban.html

Browse through the world map of this informative Web site. Select a region of the world and click on one of its cities to find a wealth of information. Maps of some cities are included.

Map and Globe Skills

8. a) Use an atlas to find Canada's 10 largest cities and their populations. Locate them on a map of Canada.

   b) Place a piece of tracing paper over the map and, in an appropriate location, construct a bar graph to represent the size of the population in each city.

   c) Use your knowledge from the chapter to analyse the pattern shown by the location and size of the cities.

9. There are now 22 cities with 8 million people or more. Use an atlas to locate these cities. How many are in Asia? Which are found in developing countries?

10. a) You will need an atlas for this activity. On a full-page outline map of Southern Ontario, locate and label cities with a population of over 250 000.

    b) Use a compass to draw circles with a radius of 1 cm, centred on each city.

    c) Lightly shade in green the productive agricultural land in Southern Ontario.

    d) Write an analysis of the patterns shown on your map that includes
    - any conclusions you can draw about the location of cities and farmland
    - your predictions for the future related to the impact of urban sprawl on agriculture, taking into account that these cities are expected to double in size in the next 30 years.

Application

11. Can you name a new product that has recently arrived on supermarket shelves? What factors encourage industry to create so many new products?

12. Investigate where in your community organic food products are available. Select one or two organic items and compare them with similar supermarket items grown using industrial farming techniques. Use criteria such as cost, appearance, taste, availability, and location where grown.

13. Conduct an inventory and make a list of chemical products found in different rooms in your household. Check the labels to identify which ones require disposal at a hazardous household waste facility. Check with your local municipal government to find the facility nearest to where you live. Investigate some environmentally friendly products that can be used as alternatives.

Figure 5.31
What organically grown fruits and vegetables are available in your community? Where are they grown?

UNIT 1 Patterns in Human Geography

PERFORMANCE TASK: Concepts, Skills, and Applications

Genetically Modified (GM) Food

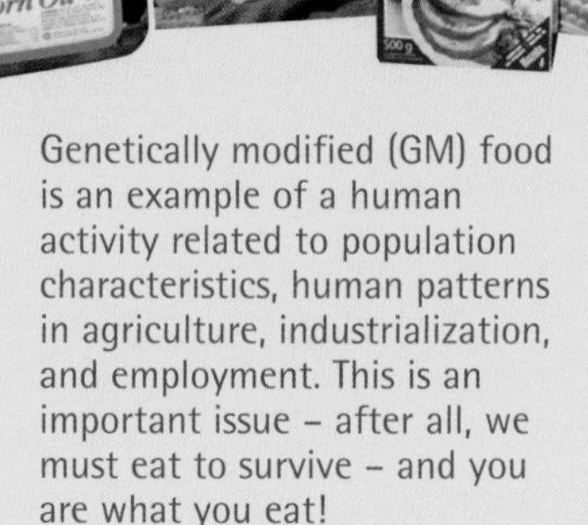

Genetically modified (GM) food is an example of a human activity related to population characteristics, human patterns in agriculture, industrialization, and employment. This is an important issue – after all, we must eat to survive – and you are what you eat!

The growth of the biotechnology industry has been called the latest and greatest agricultural revolution. Geneticists and researchers develop new plant and animal species that have been changed by adding genetic material from some other species including bacteria. Researchers hope that the new food or seeds will have the desirable characteristics of the transplanted gene. Tomatoes have had a fish gene inserted into their make-up for example to help them resist frost.

In Canada, we eat genetically modified corn, soybeans, tomatoes, potatoes, and genetically modified breakfast cereals, baked goods, and other processed foods.

> *"These genetically engineered seeds will not add to the food security of India. They will add only to the profit security of these companies."*
>
> **– Davinder Sharma, agriculture analyst, New Delhi, India**

Because of growing concerns about the possible risk to human health and the natural environment, some consumers would like to see labels on all genetically modified (GM) foods so they will know what they are eating.

In some European countries, GM foods are being eliminated because of public pressure. Many supermarkets there are now GM food free.

> *"This whole experiment is the most dangerous intervention into the earth since the dawn of history."*
>
> **– Jeremy Rifkin, lawyer, author**

The Geographic Inquiry Process (GIP)

When people want to find out as much as they can about a problem or issue in order to decide what should be done or in order to find a solution, they need a way to organize their research and make informed decisions.

The geographic inquiry process is a step by step method that is used to research a problem or an issue. Geographers, when researching a problem or an issue, find information from a wide variety of sources and subjects such as economics, ecology, biology, history, and art. This method of research, decision making, and problem solving is very useful because it also works well on research projects in other subjects.

Your Task

1. Follow the step-by-step geographic inquiry process to look at all sides of the GM foods issue.
2. Make your own personal decision about whether GM foods should be part of the food choices for Canadians.
3. Suggest two steps the federal government could take as part of a solution to the issue.

> *"Canada's system is recognized internationally as being a very, very good system and I think we've been very cautious and responsible."*
>
> **–Morven McLean, chief of plant biotechnology office at Canada's food inspection agency.**

The GIP Steps

1. Clearly state the problem with a question that provides a main focus for your research. For example, "Should genetically modified foods be a choice for Canadians?"
2. Conduct some initial research to locate sources of information. The library has many resources such as books, periodicals (magazines), and vertical files. The Internet will have many Web sites with information on the issue.
3. Choose a method to organize your information. A chart with subheadings can be very useful. Some subheadings you may wish to use for this issue are benefits (of encouraging GM foods), disadvantages, government action, suggested solutions, and impact on our future.
4. Continue your research and record the information under the appropriate subheading. Create new subheadings if necessary as you go along.
5. Evaluate the information as you find it by asking yourself these questions:
   Have I found information from a variety of points of view?
   Is this relevant to my focus?
   Is this fact or opinion?
   Is the information biased in any way?
   Who has written this and what is their purpose?
6. Include additional material in your information organizer from class discussions, documentary videos, interviewing experts, or other primary sources.
7. Carefully examine the information in your organizer. Consider the pros and cons of using GM foods in Canada. You may wish to look at the chart below for some ideas. Draw your conclusions based on the information you have gathered.
8. Depending on the conclusions you draw, suggest two alternatives either in support of encouraging people to use GM foods or in support of government controls on them.
9. Communicate the results of your inquiry. Select one way to let others know what conclusions you have reached. You may wish to write a letter to the local paper to increase people's awareness, or to the federal minister of agriculture or health with your suggestions. You may wish to do a brief oral presentation, create a poster, or pamphlet.

Fact File

Japan and South Korea, under consumer pressure, have passed a law that requires a label on all foods that contain genetically modified corn, soybeans, and bean sprouts.

Fact File

Japan and South Korea, under consumer pressure, have passed a law that requires a label on all foods that contain genetically modified corn, soybeans, and bean sprouts.

Subheading	Pros	Cons
Promise of biotechnology	May improve human health because it could increase vitamin content of foods and make them last longer, reducing spoilage	The risks and hazards to human health and the environment are unknown. May increase the risk of allergic reactions to ordinary foods
Employment trends	Thousands of jobs provided by the biotechnology industry	
Biotechnology industry		
Government action		
Global food supply		

UNIT 2

Economic Systems

EXPECTATIONS

- demonstrate an understanding of economic systems and the factors that influence them
- describe the economic relationship between Canada and the global community
- use a variety of geographic representations, tools, and technologies, to gather, process, and communicate geographic information

1 There are many different jobs people do to earn money. What are some of the jobs your friends and family do?

2 Technology has changed the way we do things. What are some new technologies that you use that were not there for your parents?

3 People everywhere need food and other basic necessities. People in different parts of the world shop at markets. Where does your family shop?

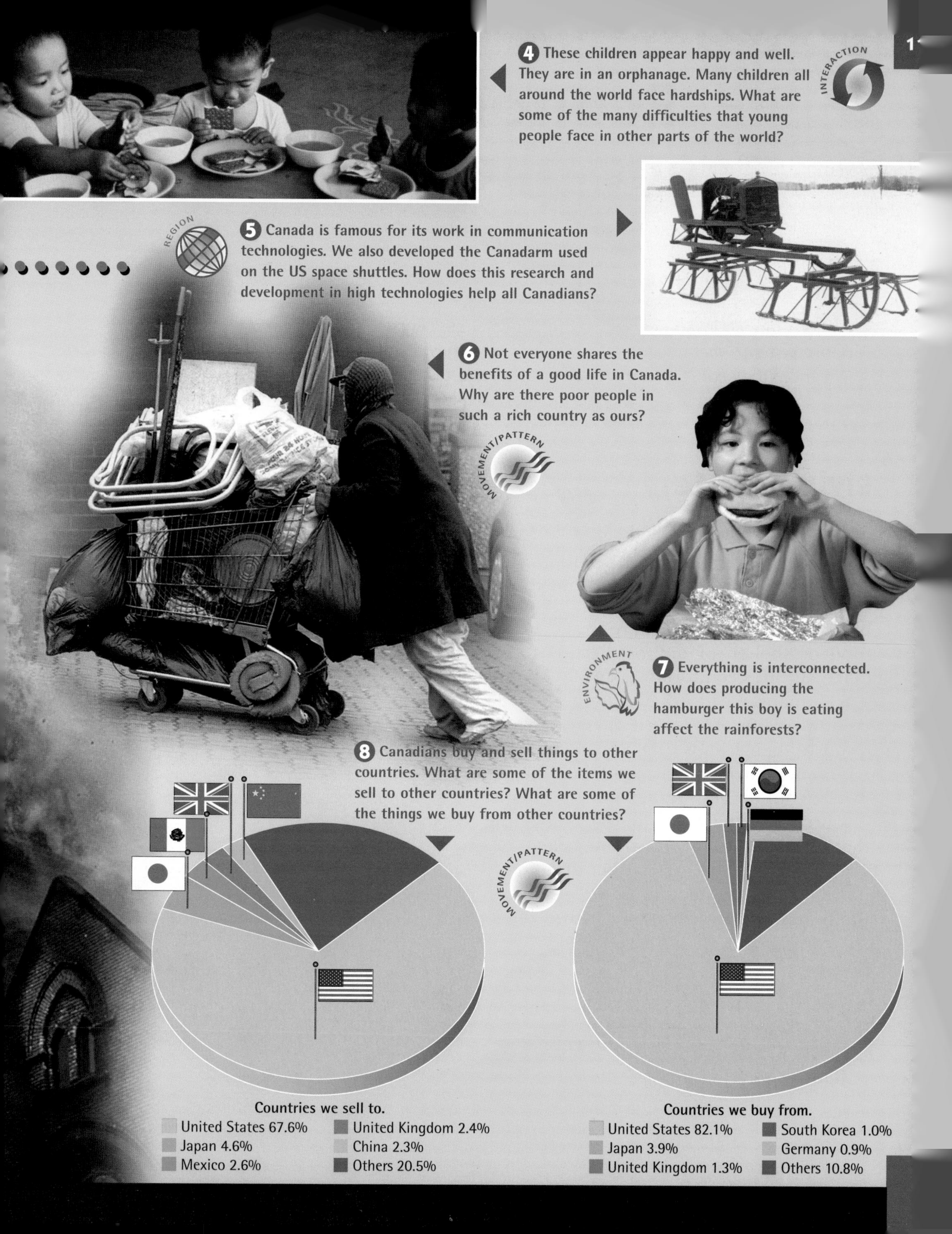

4 These children appear happy and well. They are in an orphanage. Many children all around the world face hardships. What are some of the many difficulties that young people face in other parts of the world?

5 Canada is famous for its work in communication technologies. We also developed the Canadarm used on the US space shuttles. How does this research and development in high technologies help all Canadians?

6 Not everyone shares the benefits of a good life in Canada. Why are there poor people in such a rich country as ours?

7 Everything is interconnected. How does producing the hamburger this boy is eating affect the rainforests?

8 Canadians buy and sell things to other countries. What are some of the items we sell to other countries? What are some of the things we buy from other countries?

Countries we sell to.

- United States 67.6%
- Japan 4.6%
- Mexico 2.6%
- United Kingdom 2.4%
- China 2.3%
- Others 20.5%

Countries we buy from.

- United States 82.1%
- Japan 3.9%
- United Kingdom 1.3%
- South Korea 1.0%
- Germany 0.9%
- Others 10.8%

Economic Activity and the Economy

EXPECTATIONS

- demonstrate an awareness of the fundamental elements of an economic system: what goods are produced; how they are produced; for whom they are produced; and how they are distributed
- identify patterns in the area of economics, using thematic maps

Living Better

Imagine what life would be like if people did not have to work. It might seem pleasant to spend our days doing whatever we like, as though every day were a holiday. But in reality, life would be terrible if no one worked. There would be little or no food or shelter, or any of the other things that make our lives comfortable, such as computers or TV. Humans must work in order to have a better quality of life. The work that people do to improve their lives is called **economic activity**. Economic activities include all the things that people do to get, refine, or use natural resources. The term also describes anything that people do to increase their wealth.

Economic activity exists because people have needs. Meeting needs — and wants — stimulates economic activity.

Figure 6.1

Working is part of the human experience, and is also economic activity. In what ways are these firefighters engaged in economic activity?

The Beginnings of Economic Activity

The earliest economic activity centred around food gathering. During the **Stone Age**, which lasted until about 11 000 years ago, early humans wandered in tribal or family groups, hunting animals for food and picking nuts, berries, and fruits where they could.

> *"There is no free lunch."*
> Milton Friedman, economist

An **agricultural revolution** occurred when people domesticated plants and animals. This new technology first appeared about 12 000 years ago. Having a reliable supply of food improved people's lives and provided leisure time, which could then be used to develop other activities. The demands of tending crops and herding animals also encouraged people to remain in one location, so villages and towns began to develop.

Figure 6.2

Native American women herding sheep in Arizona, USA. Herding domestic animals is an ancient form of agriculture that is still carried out in some parts of the world. Can you think of two advantages and two disadvantages of this type of life?

Fact File

The goat was the first animal that humans raised domestically — over 8000 years ago.

Continued improvements in agricultural technology — such as the plough, the tractor, and better farming techniques — led to even better lives for people. The new technology improved crop yields and food quality, and also resulted in better methods for storing, transporting, and selling food.

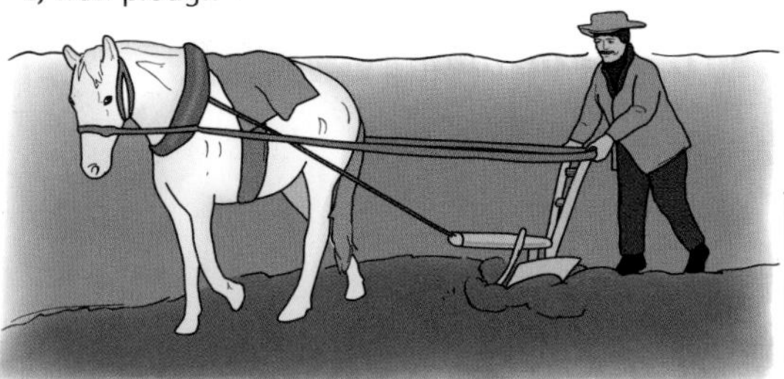

Figure 6.3

Improvements in agricultural technology have meant that much food can be produced by few people. What do you think will be the next improvement in ploughing?

One result of technological change was that some people had time to do other things besides produce food. They could become craftspeople, working with metal, wood, or cloth. Or, they could do a host of other things, including teaching, developing laws, practising medicine, or leading their growing communities. This freedom led to key developments, such as the ability to write and to understand how technology could improve people's lives.

Figure 6.4

Technology expanded once people no longer needed to direct all their energy toward food production. This page from the *Book of Kells*, an early religious work, was illustrated by Irish monks circa 500 A.D., nearly 1000 years before the printing press was invented.

Modern Economic Activities

Modern times for economic activities started around 1700 A.D. It was at this time that a second agricultural revolution took place. Farmers began to apply new scientific ideas to producing food, especially the use of machines and equipment. This spurred the development of manufacturing, and the **Industrial Revolution** was underway by the 1800s. This revolution dramatically changed economic activities. Huge numbers of people were no longer needed as food producers. Many moved to cities to find work in the new factories that were springing up there.

MOVEMENT/PATTERN

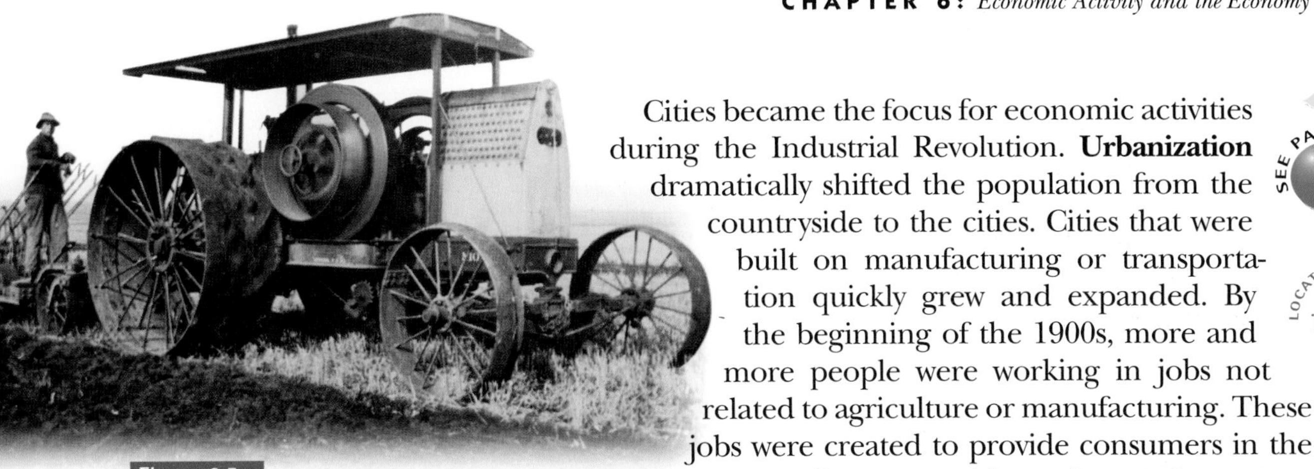

Figure 6.5

This photograph was taken on the Canadian Prairies around 1912. How do you think the purchase of this equipment changed the nature of wheat farming?

Cities became the focus for economic activities during the Industrial Revolution. **Urbanization** dramatically shifted the population from the countryside to the cities. Cities that were built on manufacturing or transportation quickly grew and expanded. By the beginning of the 1900s, more and more people were working in jobs not related to agriculture or manufacturing. These jobs were created to provide consumers in the cities and surrounding areas with services such as entertainment, shops and stores, and banking and insurance.

Today, economic activities include many different types of services and professions. As the Case Study of EuroDisney/Disneyland Paris on the next page shows, few jobs now are directly linked to producing food or providing other basic needs, such as shelter and clothing.

Fact File

Life expectancy in 1900 in Canada was 50 years. In India — which was not experiencing the Industrial Revolution — it was only 23 years. Today, life expectancy in Canada is 79 years, while it is 62 years in India.

SEE PAGE 33

It's Your World

Some small changes can have big impacts on our daily lives. Think about the zipper. The modern zipper was first patented and sold in Canada in 1913. Its inventor was Gideon Sundback, president of the Lightning Fastener Company of St. Catharines, Ontario. Think of all the different ways zippers are used in our modern way of life.

1. Review the definition of economic activity on page 114. Name five economic activities that you have performed in the past few days. Explain why you consider each one an economic activity.
2. Make a sketch or diagram to show how the range of economic activities has gone from being very narrow in the Stone Age to very broad today.
3. Technological change often stimulates economic activity, such as the factories that grew out of the Industrial Revolution. Think of what you have learned about the past 100 years. What technological change do you think has created the most economic activity over that time? Explain your answer in a well-written paragraph, including support for your opinions.

CASE STUDY

EuroDisney/Disneyland Paris

Let's take a look at a development that shows how economic activities have become very diverse in modern times. The EuroDisney/Disneyland Paris theme park was designed to meet modern needs for recreation and entertainment. Opened in April 1992, this megaproject brought American-style entertainment to the people of Europe.

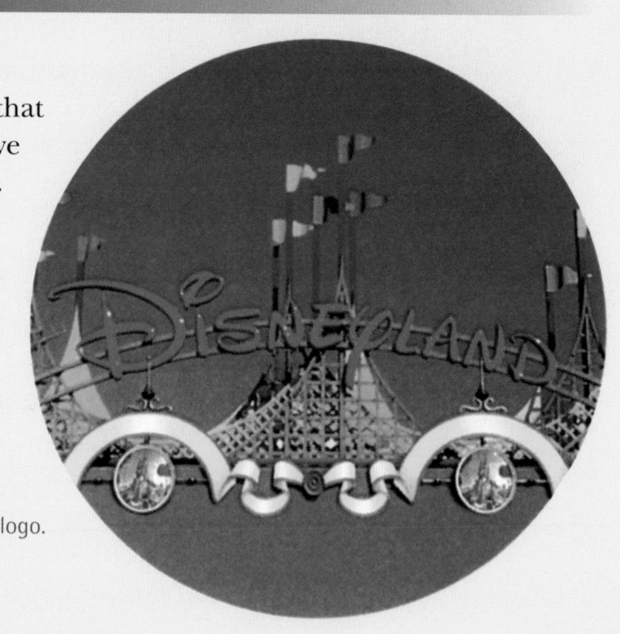

Figure 6.6

The Disneyland Paris logo.

Figure 6.7

This is the guide map for Disneyland Paris. Besides English, what other languages do you think this map is available in?

Figure 6.8

The theme hotels of Disneyland Paris. Why do you suppose the park's designers chose these names?

Hotel	Theme
The Disneyland Hotel	• a fairy tale setting introducing the world of magic
The Hotel New York	• in the style of an elegant Manhattan skyscraper
The Newport Bay Club	• a charming seaside resort
The Sequoia Lodge	• typical American national park
The Hotel Cheyenne	• highlights adventure in the American Wild West
The Hotel Santa Fe	• the atmosphere of New Mexico and the Rio Grande
The Davy Crockett Ranch	• captures the adventure of living in the heart of the forest

Designing the Park

Disney Corporation bought 2300 ha of land outside Paris in 1987. Paris was chosen because it is one of the world's most popular tourist destinations. The first stage of construction called for seven theme hotels, a "Main Street, USA" attraction, a campground, a golf course, and homes for the park's staff. The French government spent $7.5 billion to improve local transportation and enlarge the water and sewage facilities and the electrical grid.

Economic Aspects

EuroDisney/Disneyland Paris created 12 000 jobs, such as running rides and attractions, repairing equipment, picking up garbage, serving in restaurants, tending cash registers, and the like. Many of these are seasonal, part-time jobs. Probably some of the more interesting jobs are playing Disney characters. Donald Duck and Mickey Mouse are often played by women because the characters are small and women fit the costumes better.

Disney theme park for Hong Kong could bring in billions

(Hong Kong) —Mickey Mouse, the icon of Americana, will take up his first residence in communist territory, along with comrades Goofy and Donald Duck.

Ending months of speculation, Hong Kong's government and Disney Corporation announced a deal to create a theme park on one of Hong Kong's islands.

The deal will involve an investment of $3 billion, including land, on the part of the government; Disney will contribute a further $320 million. The park will create 5000 service jobs and is expected to earn more than $20 billion over the next 40 years. It could also make Hong Kong the number one tourism city in southeast Asia.

Disney believes China's new middle class will make the park a success, and the Hong Kong government agrees.

"It's a new era," said a government representative. "Mickey Mouse is coming to town."

Figure 6.9

A tea party with some Disneyland characters. To what age groups do theme parks like Disneyland Paris appeal?

To make a profit, Disneyland Paris has to attract 11 million visitors a year, or about 30 000 per day. In the summer, the daily figures are easily reached, but winters in the area are cold and damp, and attendance is much less. In fact, for the first several years of operation, attendance was a problem, and the theme park lost money. The company reached a financial crisis in 1994; some workers were laid off, and it even looked like the park would be forced to close. Fortunately, new investors were found. It was at this time that the name was changed from EuroDisney to Disneyland Paris, to try to get rid of the negative image that the park had gained. Attendance figures rose over the next several years, and the park began to make a profit in 1996.

GO TO www.disneylandparis.com/disney/smain.htm

Go to the official web site of Disneyland Paris. Click on the British flag for English. What attractions are taking place this month?

Figure 6.10

Disneyland Paris attendance, 1993–1996. If you were in charge of this theme park, what might you do to try to increase attendance?

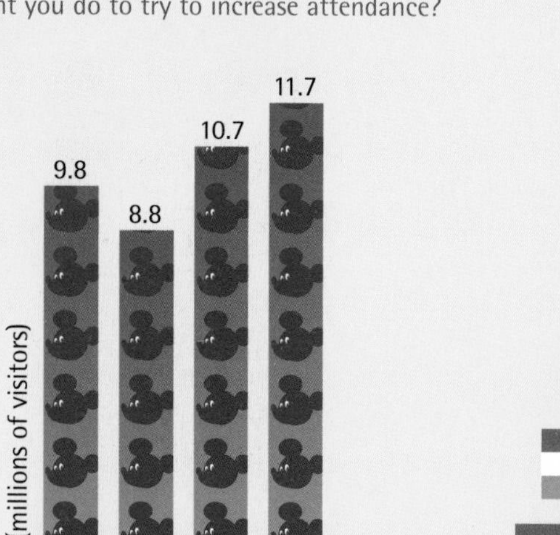

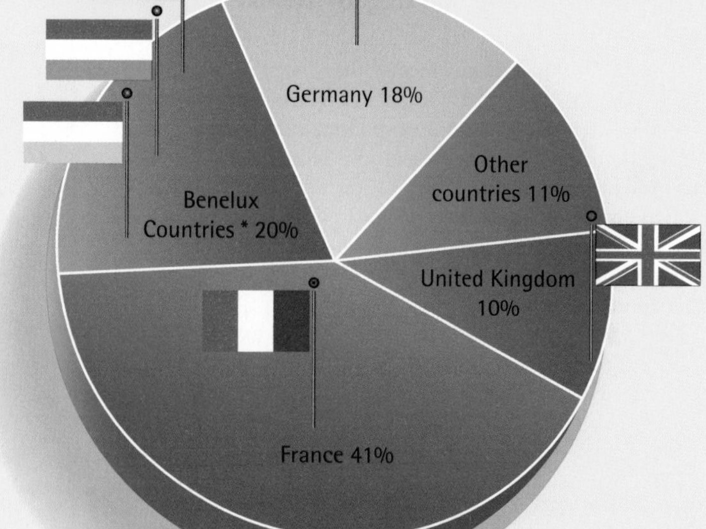

Figure 6.11

Origin of visitors to Disneyland Paris, 1996. What countries are probably included in the "Other" category?

* Belgium, the Netherlands, Luxembourg

French Reaction to the Park

Attendance at Disneyland Paris was lower than expected for several reasons.

- Many French citizens feared that their culture would be damaged by this "American invasion." In the first few years of operation, only three out of 10 visitors were French. In fact, on the park's opening day, when admission was free, officials expected 500 000 people. Less than 50 000 showed up.
- As the park was being built, Europe entered a period of economic hard times. Many people simply did not feel that they could spend money on recreation of this type.
- Word got around that prices were too high. Most visitors felt that admission fees, meal costs, and price tags for souvenirs were about 20% higher than they ought to be. This discouraged people from attending or returning. As part of their move to increase attendance figures, park officials lowered prices for admission and restaurants.

The Future

Once the theme park began to make a profit, company officials started planning Phase II of the project. This new section will open in the early 2000s. It will add an additional 1700 ha to the total site and will include

- 20 000 hotel rooms
- a convention centre
- 3500 residential units
- two golf courses.

It remains to be seen if the new, expanded park will be as successful as the other Disney theme parks. Only time will tell.

Figure 6.12 The top ten theme parks in the world are

1	Disneyland Tokyo, Japan
2	Magic Kingdom, Disney World, Florida, USA
3	Disneyland, California, USA
4	Jaya Ancol Dreamland, Indonesia
5	EPCOT, Disney World, Florida, USA
6	Disneyland Paris, France
7	Yokohama Hakkeijima Sea Paradise, Japan
8	Disney-MGM Studios Theme Park, Florida, USA
9	Universal Studios, Florida, USA
10	Blackpool Pleasure Beach, England

1. Make up two advertising slogans to promote Disneyland Paris. Make sure you point out some of the theme park's important aspects in your slogans.
2. Imagine that it is 1987 and the Disney Corporation has just purchased the land on which it intends to build its theme park. A meeting is held in a local community hall to discuss the project. Identify three reasons why people might oppose the new theme park, and three reasons why people might support it.
3. What would you consider to be the two most important economic advantages of Disneyland Paris? Give reasons to support your answer.
4. What environmental consequences could this project have? List three.

Measuring Economic Activity

Economic activity is meant to improve people's lives. Clearly, there have been great improvements over human history, beginning with the Stone Age. Your grandparents can probably point to changes within their lifetime that they see as improvements. Scientists who study economic change — geographers, economists, sociologists, and so on — need to be able to measure what has changed and by how much. Understanding change in economic activity can lead to even more improvements in the future, or can help reduce the negative impacts of economic activity, such as pollution and exploitation of children.

> *"Remember to have patience for technology to catch up to your discovery."*
>
> **Memory Elvin-Lewis, Canadian biologist**

What is the Value of Work?

The difficult part of measuring economic activity is deciding what to measure. Figure 6.13 shows that there are many different types of economic activity, and not all of them are measurable in dollars and cents. It is relatively easy to measure **formal economic activities**. These are jobs where money is paid, usually as fees, wages, or profits. Governments spend a good deal of time and energy measuring these activities because taxes are often based on the figures. It is harder to measure **informal economic activities**, in which people are trying to avoid being counted and measured by the government, such as criminal activity, and private yard sales. Bartering also fits this category. **Bartering** occurs when people exchange things of value, for instance, when car repairs are traded for painting a house.

Figure 6.13 The economic activity of a country.

All the Wealth of a Country			
"Money" Economy			"Non-Money" Economy
Formal Economy		Informal Economy	Unpaid Activities
Private sector	Public sector	(Crime, tax avoidance, yard sales, etc.)	(Child rearing, housework, volunteer work, shopping, etc.)
(Businesses and corporations)	(Governments, including education and health care)		

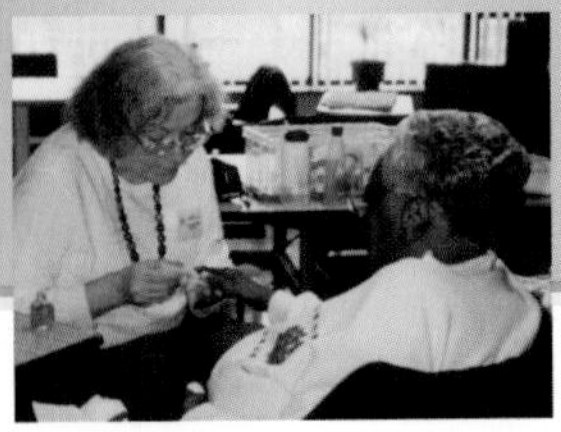

In Canada, a national income tax was first introduced in 1917 to help pay for Canada's involvement in World War I. This "temporary" tax has never been repealed. Provinces also have income taxes.

Unpaid economic activity is hard to measure, as well. What is the economic value of looking after a younger brother or sister, or an elderly grandparent? Many jobs done around the home are designed to improve living conditions and yet are unpaid, so their value is difficult to measure.

What Makes a Better Life?

Interaction

Economic activity has often been seen as producing more goods and services to make people's lives better. These goods and services are our **material wealth**. Without question, some of these help people to live longer, more comfortable lives. Automobiles, for example, are important because they give us more choices in how we live and what we can do, although they also have negative consequences such as pollution and traffic congestion.

See page 220

Improvements in our lives also occur because of **non-material wealth**, improvements that cannot easily be seen or measured as goods and services. An example is the protection of human rights in a society. Improvement in human rights is important to many people's satisfaction with their lives, but it is hard to measure the economic value of this change.

Go To

www.cfc-efc.ca/ccrc/sir.htm

This site tells you about your rights as a young Canadian, as stated by the United Nations. Select one of those rights. Report back to your class about it. Give your opinion about whether or not that right is being met in Canada.

> ***"The person who does not work for the love of work but only for money is not likely to make money nor find much fun in life."***
>
> **Charles Schwab, investment counsellor**

Figure 6.14

This table shows the percentage of growth in material wealth of Canadians from 1990 to 1997. Which appliances saw the greatest growth? Which grew by very little?

Appliance or Product	Ownership in 1990	Ownership in 1997
Air conditioners	24.4%	29.1%
Camcorders	5.6%	17.7%
Dishwashers	42.0%	48.5%
Home computers	16.3%	36.0%
Microwave ovens	68.2%	86.2%
Telephones	98.5%	98.6%
Televisions	99.0%	99.1%
Video cassette recorders	66.3%	84.7%

A problem with measuring economic activity occurs when people want to consider only material wealth. Having a car is fine, but what if the desire to have more cars means that the environment is destroyed or human rights are neglected? Many citizens of a country will not be contented, in this case. People will get the most amount of satisfaction when they have both material and non-material wealth. Having satisfaction with both material and non-material aspects of life is part of a high **quality of life**.

INTERACTION

Measuring the Wealth of a Country

Most measures of economic activity look only at the formal sector of the economy. There are a number of ways used to measure economic activity and wealth. One common way is to look at incomes — how much people earn per year. This is an important way of expressing wealth because it shows how much people have to spend on the goods and services they need and want. In Canada, the average income of families is over $56 000 per year.

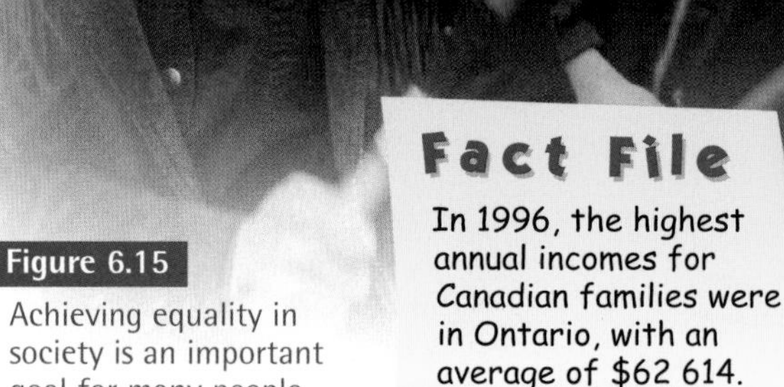

Figure 6.15
Achieving equality in society is an important goal for many people in Canada.

Fact File

In 1996, the highest annual incomes for Canadian families were in Ontario, with an average of $62 614. The lowest annual family incomes were in Newfoundland, with $43 564 the average.

Figure 6.16
This table compares the average wealth for people in selected countries. Which country's total wealth is the greatest?

Country	Gross Domestic Product (billions)	Population	GDP per Capita
Afghanistan	$ 18.1	23 738 100	$ 800
Australia	$ 430.5	18 438 800	$23 600
Brazil	$1022.0	164 511 400	$6 300
China	$3390.0	1 221 591 800	$2 800
Egypt	$ 183.9	64 824 500	$2 900
Spain	$ 593.0	39 107 900	$15 300
United Arab Emirates	$ 72.9	2 262 300	$23 800

There are two other commonly used ways to measure economic activity:

- The **gross domestic product**, or **GDP**, measures the value in dollars of all the goods and services produced *in the country* in one year. Money earned outside the country is not counted. In other words, if you added up the money spent on everyone's rent, groceries, TV repairs, dentist's fees, phone bills and the like, the total would be the GDP.
- The **gross national product**, or **GNP**, measures all the wealth earned by citizens *of the country* in one year, no matter where it was earned.

Fact File

Countries that maintain high rates of employment and good health care for their people have higher GDPs than countries that do not.

These two measurements are very large numbers that are often expressed as averages to make them more meaningful. For example, in 1996 Canada's gross domestic product was $721 000 000 000, while our GDP per capita (per person) was $25 500.

1. Explain why jobs like shopping and looking after children are considered to be economic activities.
2. Name two types of material wealth that you would not like to give up. Name two types of non-material wealth you would most like to keep.
3. **a)** Suppose you were an economics expert and someone asked you to define the term "quality of life." What definition would you give?
   b) Describe the living conditions of someone with a high quality of life. Describe a low quality of life.
4. Look at Figure 6.16, which deals with the gross domestic product for selected countries.
   a) How is it possible that China, with the highest GDP, has the second lowest GDP per capita?
   b) How is it possible that the United Arab Emirates, with the second lowest GDP, has the highest GDP per capita?
   c) Describe what your quality of life would be like if your country had a GDP per capita of only $800, as Afghanistan does.

Understanding the Concepts

1. Draw a diagram to illustrate the difference between material and non-material wealth.

2. Think about all the people you know.

   a) Name the person that you think is most interested in economic activity. What two things about his or her life support your choice?

   b) Name the person that you think is least interested in economic activity. What two things about his or her life support your choice?

   c) Name the person that you think will be the first one to visit Disneyland Paris. Give reasons for your choice.

3. Imagine a country where money has not been invented. Identify three ways in which economic activities in this imaginary country would differ from activities in a country that uses money.

Research and Communication Skills

4. What are the world's richest and poorest countries? Conduct research to find the top 10 countries in the world measured as gross domestic product per capita. Also find the bottom 10 countries. Shade and label these places on an outline map of the world. Write a paragraph in which you describe the pattern that you see on your map.

for economic and other information about countries around the world.

5. Research the Industrial Revolution. Try to find information to answer questions that begin with Who...? What...? When...? Where...? and Why...?

6. How does Canada's Wonderland theme park, located north of Toronto, Ontario, compare to Disneyland Paris? Make up a comparison chart with these headings:

Disneyland Paris	Canada's Wonderland

   Use the Case Study of Disneyland Paris on pages 118–121 to find seven facts that can be compared to Canada's Wonderland.

Map and Globe Skills

7. Refer back to Figure 6.12 on page 121, showing the top 10 theme parks in the world. On an outline map of the world, put a dot in the country of each of the parks. What pattern of dots do you see? How might you explain the pattern of dots?

for information on the Industrial Revolution.

8 Figure 6.17 shows the regions of the world where agriculture probably developed.

a) In your notebook, give each of the regions a name based on its location in the world.

b) Describe the pattern that these regions make on the map of the world.

c) What might be two reasons to explain the pattern of the development of agriculture?

d) Why do you suppose the part of the world that is now Canada was not a region that had many areas of developed agriculture?

Applications

9 Imagine that you are a TV reporter watching the 10th anniversary celebrations of the opening of Disneyland Paris. Make up the script of a one-minute report that you will give on the evening news. Make sure that you comment on the impact of the theme park on economic activities in France.

10 Look at this photograph of a young peddler in Mexico. Write a paragraph in which you identify what this photo tells us about economic activity.

Figure 6.18

In many developing nations, children — like this young street vendor in Mexico — play a significant role in the local economy. What economic and social consequences do you think result from child labour?

11 Some of the goods Canadians consume (running shoes, clothes, some sports equipment) are made in other countries by people (often children) who are poorly paid, work long hours, and work in dangerous conditions. List three things you might do to help improve the quality of life for these workers.

Figure 6.17

What continents were not important in the development of agriculture?

7 Economic Systems

EXPECTATIONS

- demonstrate an understanding of basic economic systems — e.g., subsistence, traditional, command, market — and the factors that influence them
- recognize that Canada, like most countries, has a mixed economy that includes features from more than one system
- demonstrate an understanding of how economic resources such as land, labour, capital, and entrepreneurial ability influence the economic success of a region
- identify the top trading countries in the world and the reasons for their success

Decisions, Decisions, Decisions

Most families have to make careful choices about what to buy. Can we afford to own a car? Do we really need a new computer? How much should we spend on clothes this month? The ways in which decisions about these matters are made vary from one household to the next. The same is true for societies.

People try to improve their quality of life through economic activities. The goods or services that we would like to have — that we think will improve our lives — are virtually endless. Unfortunately, our resources for obtaining these goods and services are limited. We have only so much time, energy, and money available. So, like a family that must make decisions about what to buy with their income, a society must make decisions about what to do with its limited resources. This is why we need **economic systems**.

> *"All economic systems operate within the larger economy of planet earth."*
>
> Anonymous

Figure 7.1

A shopping mall in Mississauga, Ontario and a weekly market in Banaue, Ifugao province, Philippines. Economic activities make up a good part of most people's lives. Identify an economic activity that you have done recently.

It's Your World

Think of the economic decisions needed in order for you to be able to buy a can of cola.

- Forest or other farmland, probably on a Caribbean island, had to be converted into a sugar cane plantation.
- Sugar had to be produced and shipped to Canada.
- Water had to be purified and mixed with flavourings and sugar.
- Aluminum or steel had to be produced and rolled into a long, flat strip.
- The can had to be fabricated from the metal, painted, and filled with cola.
- The cola was packaged and transported to the store where you purchased it.
- You had to decide if the purchase of the cola was in your best interest.

Economic activities are very complicated, as your purchase of a can of cola demonstrates. An economic system is needed to organize all these activities.

Deciding on an Economic System

Economic systems reflect the ways in which societies organize themselves to make decisions. Each society must answer four economic questions:

- What resources are available?
- What goods and services will be produced?
- How will they be produced?
- Who will get how much of each?

All economic decisions are really about how the society is arranged in order to produce goods and services — in other words, how resources are used to answer economic questions.

The economic system that gets established in a country is chosen on the basis of three conditions within a society

- *tradition* — the way things have been done in the past
- *ideology* — beliefs about the proper ways to do things
- *pragmatism* — practical solutions that will work.

In any society, these three conditions are found in varying degrees, so no two societies develop identical economic systems.

What will our economic system be like?

Tradition
How have we done things in the past?

Ideology
What are the things we believe in and value?

Pragmatism
What will work and be easy to manage?

Figure 7.2

Which of these factors do you think is most important in Canada?

Economic Resources

The economic resources we have to provide goods and services include **land**, **capital**, **labour**, and **technology**. *Land* takes into account all the natural resources needed to make something, such as minerals, energy, water, or land. *Capital* refers to money — the money that has to be invested in machinery, buildings, and the like. *Labour* is the human energy, efforts, and talents that go into making something. *Technology* includes all resources that are not natural resources, such as scientific knowledge, that allow decisions to be made. Economic resources are arranged differently in various economic systems.

Fact File

North Americans make up less then 5% of the world's population but consume more than 30% of its resources.

Who Decides?

Economic systems differ in terms of the people or groups of people who have a say in the decisions that are made. Decisions can be made by

- the government that is in power
- industries and businesses in the country
- institutions that are important, such as human rights or environmental groups and
- individual participants in the economic system.

In each economic system, these groups play different roles. In some countries, a particular group may be very important; in another, a similar group may be much less influential. There is a great deal of variation around the world. Looking at the differences in economic systems tells us much about societies and what they value.

Figure 7.3

The geography software that these students are running for their school project could be considered an economic resource.

Figure 7.4

Where do you fit into your economic system?

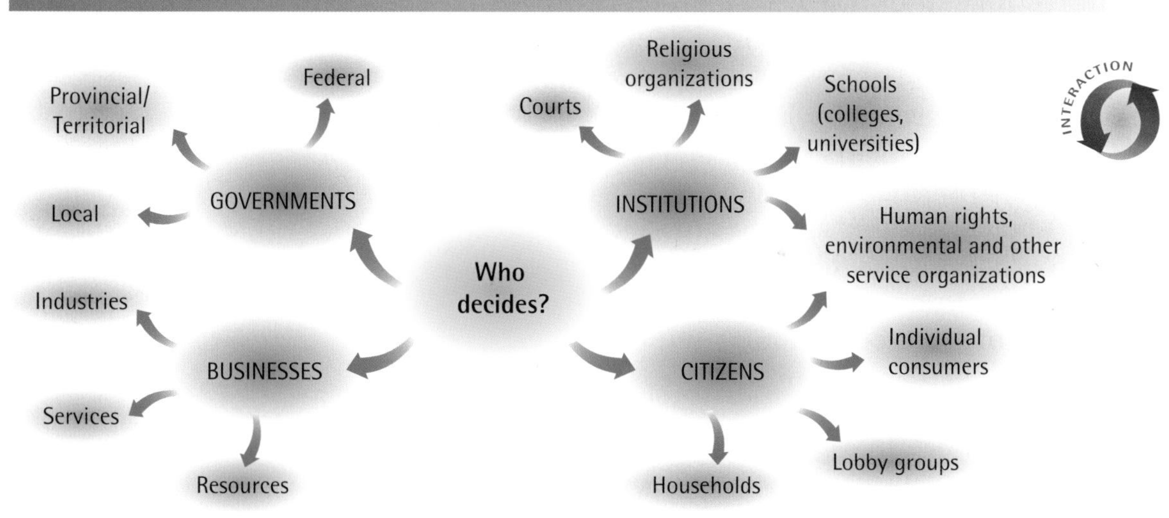

Types of Economic Systems

The economic systems around the world can be grouped into four categories, as shown in Figure 7.5.

Figure 7.5

Types of economic systems. (Look up the words "command" and "market" in a dictionary, if you are not sure what they mean.)

Type of Economy	Who Makes Economic Decisions?	Example
Traditional (no modern national example exists)	Decisions are made based on what has been done in the past. People organize their economic choices following custom and tradition.	To decide to construct a new road, elders might be consulted, and the decision would be made according to the traditions of the people.
Command (e.g., North Korea)	Decisions are made by a central authority, such as a dictator or the government. Citizens are required to carry out these decisions; personal choices are few.	A road would be constructed if the people in power decided it fit into their plans and met their needs.
Market (e.g., USA)	Decisions are made by all members of the society based on their own needs and desires. Citizens make economic choices through buying and selling in the marketplace.	Constructing a road would be a decision made by a corporation, based on whether a profit could be made. Government might or might not be involved.
Mixed (e.g., Canada)	Decisions are made within a system that has aspects of both command economies and market economies. Governments, businesses, and individuals are all included in economic planning and decision making.	The decision to construct a road would be made after discussions among governments, businesses, and consumers. The decision could rest in the hands of any or all of these groups.

Traditional Economies

Few completely traditional economies exist today. Those that continue to operate this way are in remote areas where outside influences have little impact. These societies are based on **subsistence farming** or hunting and gathering. The needs of the group are largely met by their own activity, and members have little economic contact with outsiders.

Traditional economic systems are slow to change. Since decisions today are based on what was done in the past, economic choices vary little from one generation to the next. A traditional system may have difficulty adapting to economic change. Contact with outsiders often leads to rapid change and conflict within the society. New economic ideas may not fit the old ways of life.

> ***"An economic system that stresses production, consumption, and resource depletion... [and] ignores the air, water, soil, biodiversity, and long-term sustainability of raw materials is disconnected from the real world that supports us... ."***
>
> **David Suzuki, biologist**

Figure 7.6

Many Tibetan Buddhist monks and nuns fled their native land for India when the Chinese took control of their country in the 1950s. While the Chinese government has improved the Tibetan economy in some ways (e.g., by building new roads, schools, and hospitals), it has also threatened the local people's religion, language, and culture. Can you think of a Canadian group whose heritage is in danger of being lost?

Command Economies

The Soviet Union was an example of a command economy. The country was formed in 1917 and collapsed in 1991. While it existed, the Soviet Union was run by a small group of people at the head of the Communist Party. These people made all the economic decisions for the country — supposedly for the good of all the people — and then citizens were organized to accomplish the plans. These decisions included which natural resources were to be developed, which manufacturing industries would be emphasized, and how much money would be spent on the military. All factors of production were considered to be owned by the government. Citizens had jobs, and the government's responsibility was to look after their needs.

> *"From each according to his abilities, to each according to his needs."*
>
> **Karl Marx, 1818–1883, philosopher and economic theorist**

Ideally, in a command economy, everyone works toward a common goal. Each person's efforts help to improve the country by accomplishing the decisions that have been made by wise leaders. In reality, command economies do not work that well. Part of the reason the Soviet Union collapsed was that citizens wanted to participate more in decision making. Since 1991, the countries that used to make up the Soviet Union have been adopting more mixed-economy characteristics.

LOCATION

SEE PAGE 229

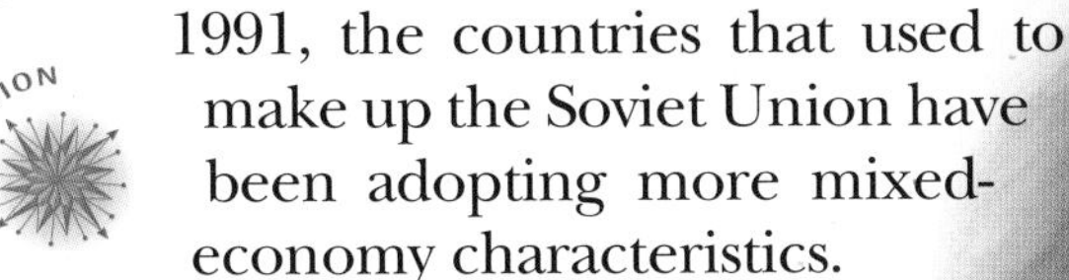

Figure 7.7

Protests against the Communist government in 1999 showed that the people of the former Yugoslavia were unhappy with a command economy.

Market Economies

In market economies, the government has very little involvement. Factors of production are largely owned by individuals and businesses. Self-interest is the guiding force. Businesses make decisions about what to produce based on what they think consumers want to buy. If they are right, they make money. If they are wrong, they lose money. Consumers have a great impact on what gets produced in a market economy. In many ways, the United States is an example of this type of economic system.

> ***"That government is best which governs the least, because its people discipline themselves."***
>
> **Thomas Jefferson, U.S. president, 1800–1809**

CONNECTIONS TO History

Many of our ideas about market economies were first discussed by Adam Smith in his book *The Wealth of Nations*, published in 1776. He argued that greed and self-interest were the most important motivating forces for all people. While these sound like unpleasant ideas around which to organize an economy, Smith reasoned that if each individual could become successful, then the whole society would be successful. How do you suppose Smith would explain homeless people and food banks in Canada today?

Market economies have been criticized because poverty often is part of life for many people. Those who are successful become wealthy and meet their economic needs. Those who do not have the talents, abilities, opportunities, or luck to be successful become poor. These societies tend to be divided into "have" and "have not" groups, and this division can cause conflict within a country.

Figure 7.8 In market and mixed economies, businesses try to get consumers to buy their products or services through advertising, as seen in this photo of Piccadilly Circus, London, England.

Mixed Economies

Most countries of the world have a mixed economy. Mixed economies have some elements of both command economies and market economies. The goal is to take the benefits of each system, but not the weaknesses. Elected government representatives, businesses, and citizens all have roles to play in managing factors of production.

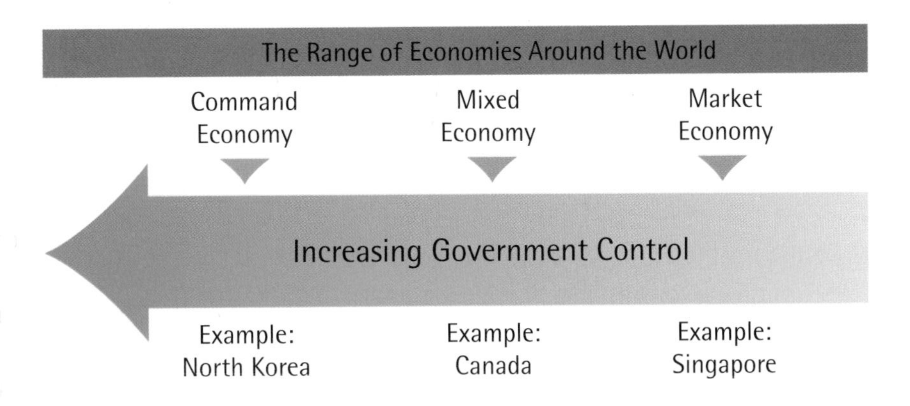

Figure 7.9

Continuum from command to market economies.

In mixed economies, governments often own resources or businesses that are run for the public good. The Canadian Broadcasting Corporation (CBC) is an example; national communication is seen as so important that the government must have a key role. Governments also set policies for the public good that affect businesses and consumers, such as requiring packaging to be in both official languages. Privately owned businesses make decisions within those policies. Businesses' actions are based on their understanding of the market and what consumers want. Consumers make choices that influence the success of businesses. Canada is a good example of a mixed economy.

LOCATION

Figure 7.10

In mixed economies, one of government's roles is to make sure that products meet a high standard of performance and safety. In Canada, for example, government inspectors visit meatpacking plants to ensure that all the meat we eat has been properly stored, processed, and packaged before it is shipped.

It's Your World

A market economy may offer little protection for the environment. Businesses may not wish to adopt environmentally friendly processes that increase the cost of doing business and thus decrease profits. Consumers do not want the higher prices that protecting the environment would mean. Governments do not have the power to compel businesses to comply with strict environmental guidelines.

In mixed economies, consumers and governments can co-operate more easily to protect the environment, work toward human rights, and strive to improve the quality of life for everyone in society. Why is Canada considered a mixed economy?

ENVIRONMENT

Figure 7.11

This sour gas plant in Alberta separates sulphur from gaseous fossil fuels, but the process is not very efficient. Every day, tonnes of sulphur are released from smokestacks as sulphur dioxide, a pollutant. Newer technology could reduce these emissions, but the expense of changing equipment would raise the costs of manufacturing, and would result in lower profits or higher prices for fertilizers, drugs, and other sulphur products.

1. Write a four-sentence paragraph in which you use the following words clearly to show their meaning: labour, command, economic system, consumers, tradition.
2. Suppose you have just discovered a wonderful new cure for the common cold. You now want to get your cure out to as many people as possible. Describe how you would do this under each of the four economic systems explained in this chapter.
3. Copy the comparison chart below into your notebook and complete it, recording your ideas about market and command economies.

	Market Economies	Command Economies
Who makes economic decisions?		
Who owns the factors of production?		
What role do consumers play in economic decisions?		

4. Identify two advantages and two disadvantages for:
   a) command economies
   b) market economies
   c) mixed economies.

CASE STUDY

North Korea — A Command Economy

When World War II ended in 1945, the Asian country of Korea was freed from Japan. U.S. troops moved into the southern part of the country, and forces of the Soviet Union were in the north. The Soviet Union established a communist government in North Korea, while South Korea set up a democratic government. Because of political differences, conflicts between the two Koreas became so great that a war broke out in 1950. The boundary between the two countries was drawn at the 38th parallel of latitude when the war ended in 1953. North and South Korea have remained deeply suspicious of each other since that time.

LOCATION

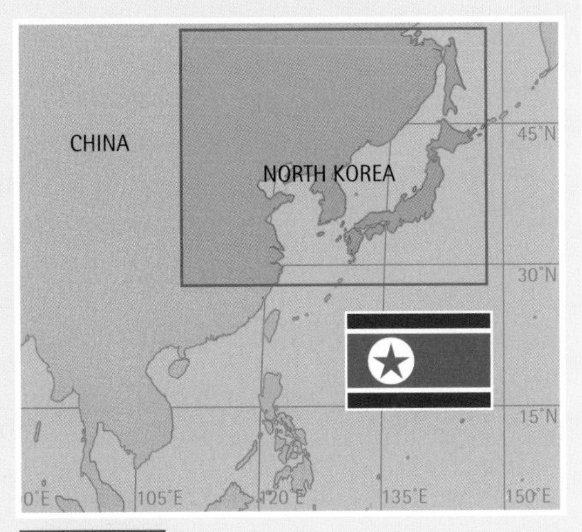

Figure 7.12 Location of North Korea.

Figure 7.13 Facts and figures about North Korea, 1998

Characteristic	North Korea	Comparison to Canada
Area	120 540 km^2	A little smaller than Nova Scotia and New Brunswick combined
Population	24 137 000	About four fifths of Canada's population
GDP per capita	$900	Canada's gross domestic product per person is $25 500
Important industries	Machine building, military products, chemicals	Canada's important industries are minerals, food products, wood and paper products, automobiles
Farm land	14% arable, plus 12% irrigated	Only 5% of Canada can be used for crops
Foreign trade	Imports $1.3 billion; exports $0.8 billion	Canada's imports: $198.8 billion; exports: $208.8 billion
Military spending	Up to 33% of GDP	Canada's spending: 1.6% of GDP

Fact File

In North Korea, all media are heavily censored by the government, which also restricts ownership of telephones, VCRs, and computers to state institutions.

SEE PAGE 24

Characteristics	North Korea	Canada
Birth rate	22.7 births/1000 people	12.4 births/1000 people
Life expectancy at birth	67.5 years for males 73.8 years for females	75.6 years for males 82.5 years for females
Televisions	50 per 1000 people	703 per 1000 people
Telephones	46 per 1000 people	590 per 1000 people

Figure 7.14 Comparison of living conditions in North Korea and Canada. Using these data, how would you describe the quality of life in North Korea?

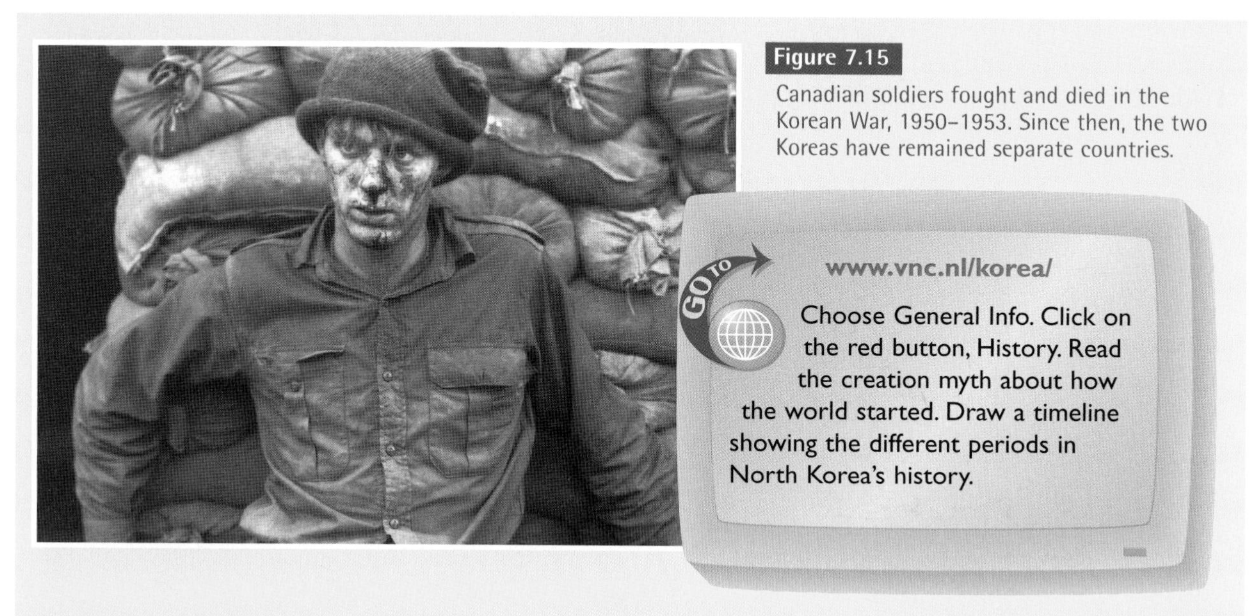

Figure 7.15

Canadian soldiers fought and died in the Korean War, 1950–1953. Since then, the two Koreas have remained separate countries.

Economic System

North Korea has a command economy that is tightly controlled by the communist government. The government's policy has always been one of national self-reliance, meaning that the country strives to meet all its economic needs on its own. These policies can be seen in several ways.

Agriculture

INTERACTION

Farming is concentrated in the lowlands of the west coast, where a longer growing season, adequate rainfall, and good soil allow the best cultivation of crops, particularly rice. Agriculture was **collectivized** by the government after the war. This means that farmers no longer had ownership of the land. **Co-operative farms** were set up in which farmers worked together, pooling their time and resources. The output from the farms was distributed by the government to the rest of the country. In the decades following the Korean War, agricultural production increased because collectivization was more efficient than farmers working separately.

Industries

SEE PAGE 103

Most industries are owned by the state. National planning committees decide which goods the factories will produce. At the end of the Korean War, priority was given to building an industrial base that met all the country's needs for such items as machinery and transportation equipment. This strategy of **industrialization** pushed the economy forward at record growth rates in the 1950s and 1960s. Consumer goods were given a low priority and, to this day, few are available.

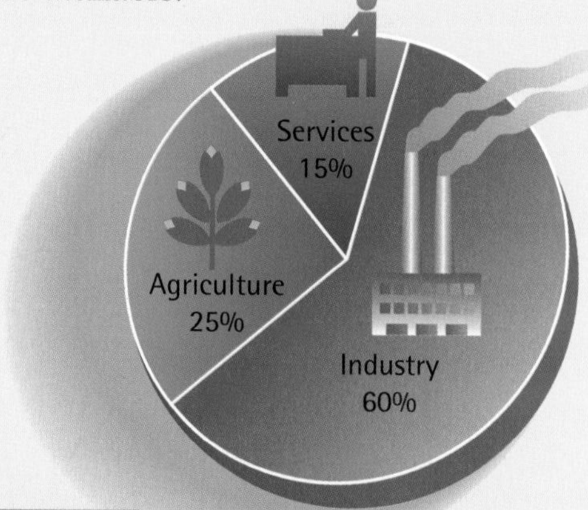

Figure 7.16

The economic structure of North Korea's economy, by percentage of GDP. In Canada, services make up about two-thirds of our gross domestic product. Why do you suppose that sector is so low in North Korea?

Military Spending

Long-standing suspicion of South Korea has caused the North Korean government to spend a great deal of money on its military. The government considers a strong military the best defence against attack by South Korea or its allies. Military equipment is one of the largest industrial sectors. Until the Soviet Union collapsed in 1991, it was an important supplier of weapons and technology for North Korea.

Economic Problems Faced by North Korea

The farms have been unable to feed North Korea's growing population. Throughout the 1990s, crop failures and flooding resulted in widespread hunger and famine. An estimated two million people died of hunger in the 1990s.

Because of the government's focus on self-reliance, the North Korean economy has become isolated from the world. Manufacturing companies have not had to compete with other companies and are inefficient. Their few products are of poor quality. Throughout the 1990s, the GDP fell because industries became so unproductive.

North Korea has suffered severe energy shortages. Much of its energy has come from imported oil. With declining national wealth, the country cannot afford to buy oil, and the country's power supply has become unreliable.

South Korea's economy raced ahead of North Korea's faltering economy in the 1980s and 1990s. North Koreans recognize that their material wealth and quality of life are poor in comparison with their neighbours to the south.

Figure 7.17

This photo, taken at the border between the Koreas, shows only barbed wire and marching guards on the north side. The military has taken a large part of North Korea's spending since the country was created. Why does North Korea need a large military force?

Figure 7.18

Famine relief in a North Korean orphanage. In such an industrialized country, why are people hungry?

The Future

Widespread famine, a rapidly worsening economy, and dissatisfaction among the people would seem to mean that change is necessary in North Korea. However, the communist party that controls the country has other ideas, as Figure 7.19 points out. The future for the command economy of North Korea does not look bright.

> *"The government solution to a problem is usually as bad as the problem."*
>
> **Milton Friedman, economist**

Figure 7.19

A newspaper article reporting on conditions in North Korea in 1998. What is the attitude of the government toward the country's problems?

NORTH KOREA SAYS NO REFORMS, NO OPENNESS

SEOUL — Despite massive economic difficulties and widespread famine, North Korea vowed today to stick to its isolationist ways. The ruling Workers' Party reaffirmed that self-reliance will continue to be the backbone of the communist country's economic policy.

"It is a foolish daydream to try to revive the economy by introducing foreign capital, not relying on one's own strength," said the article in the party's newspaper.

Stricken by three years of famine, North Korea has been relying on outside aid to feed its 24 million people, including help from longtime enemy South Korea. A U.S. congressional delegation to North Korea has said the famine has killed up to two million people.

The article warned that capitalistic economic reforms would only cause catastrophic results, as shown in some former Soviet-bloc countries. "We will . . . set ourselves against all the attempts to induce us to join an 'integrated' world," the article said. "We have nothing to 'reform' and 'open.'"

The article admitted that North Korea faces serious economic difficulties but said that the country will revitalize its economy "one sector after another as ants gnaw a piece of bone."

1. Suppose you had just written the Case Study about the command economy of North Korea. What are three different titles you might have given this Case Study?
2. You are a farmer in North Korea just after the Korean War ended. Your farm has been collectivized by the government. Write a diary entry stating your feelings and opinions about this event.
3. In your opinion, what is the greatest problem that North Korea faces? Explain your choice in a four-sentence paragraph.
4. Imagine that you had the opportunity to offer one suggestion for improving North Korea to the president of the country. What would be your suggestion? Explain your reasoning.

CASE STUDY

Singapore — A Market Economy

Singapore came into existence in 1965 when it gained independence from Malaysia. At that time, it established a market economy.

Singapore is a very small nation with few natural resources other than its people. To compete most effectively, the country concentrates on manufacturing high-value goods, such as computers. It also ships other countries' goods to the rest of the world.

Singapore's economic survival depends on open international trade — the free flow of goods into and out of the country. More than 96% of imports enter Singapore duty free. Exports are treated in the same way.

Singapore's success is also partly due to its excellent communications system, political stability, and disciplined work force. Its economic advantages have given the people of Singapore a quality of life not that different from Canadians'.

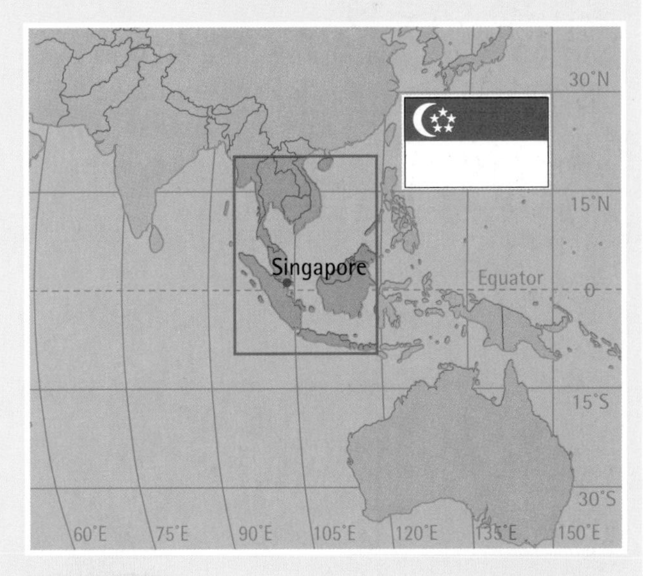

Figure 7.20
Location of Singapore.

Fact File

Singapore currently makes more than 40% of the world's computer disk drives.

Figure 7.21 Facts and figures about Singapore, 1998.

Characteristic	Singapore	Comparison to Canada
Area	647.5 km^2	The city of Toronto is over eight times larger than the country of Singapore
Population	3 440 700	This is about the same population as Montreal
GDP per capita	$21 200	Canada's GDP per person is $25 500 per person
Important industries	Oil refining, electronics, oil drilling equipment, rubber products	Canada's important industries are minerals, food products, wood and paper products, automobiles
Farm land	2% arable	5% of Canada can be used for crops
Foreign trade	Imports $134.9 billion Exports $127.0 billion	Canada's imports: $198.8 billion Exports: $208.8 billion
Unemployment rate	2.0%	Canada: 9.4%

Location Advantages

Singapore has an excellent deep-water harbour and a location on major shipping routes through Asia. It is the busiest port in the world in terms of shipping tonnage. At any one time, there are more than 800 ships in the port. Over 100 000 vessels call at the port annually. Four hundred shipping lines, with links to more than 600 ports worldwide, operate out of Singapore.

SEE PAGE 59

GO TO www.sg/

Find three exciting things to do and see in Singapore. List three major differences and three major similarities between your community and Singapore.

MOVEMENT/PATTERN

Singapore is a major trans-shipment hub, a warehousing and distribution centre for the Asia–Pacific region (including North America). Goods in smaller quantities are shipped to the port from around the region. Here they are organized and loaded onto larger vessels heading to ports anywhere in the world. Singapore's **entrepôt** (warehousing) trade is particularly important in rubber, oil products, spices, timber, manufactured goods, and machinery. Singapore is also the major shipbuilding, ship repair, and oil-rig building centre in Southeast Asia. It is the third largest oil-refining centre in the world.

Figure 7.22

Where Singapore earns its wealth (percentage of GDP). Which sector contributes most to the country's economy?

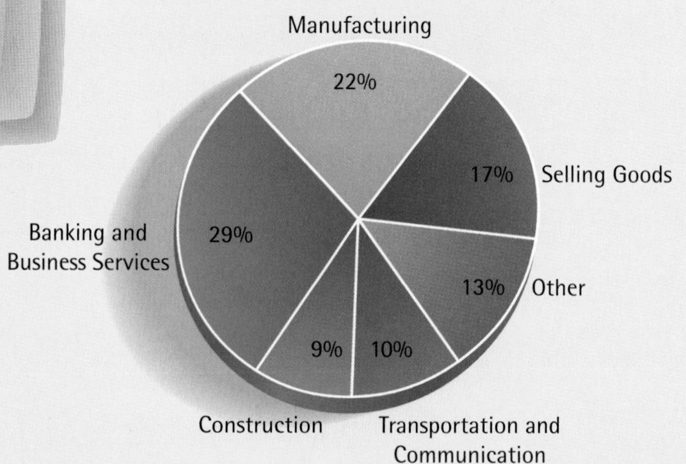

Figure 7.23

Singapore's important trading partners. Why do you suppose some of the same countries show up on both lists?

Top Export Destinations		Top Sources of Imports	
Country	Percentage of Exports	Country	Percentage of Imports
United States	20.3	Japan	21.9
Malaysia	14.2	Malaysia	16.5
European Union	14.0	United States	16.2
Hong Kong	8.7	European Union	11.5
Japan	7.5	Thailand	4.1
Other	35.3	Other	29.8

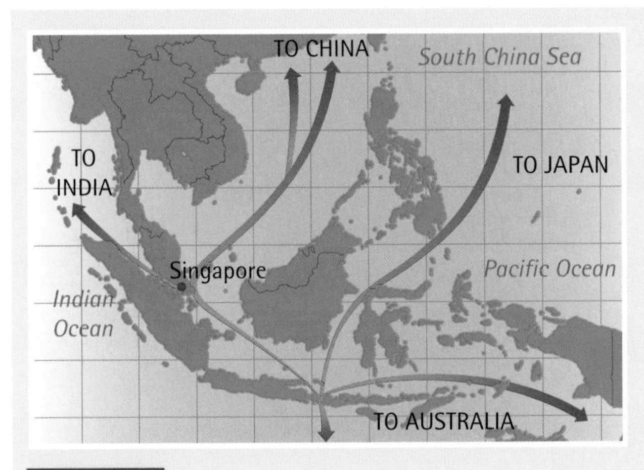

Figure 7.24

What about Singapore's location makes it such an important port?

The Future

In some ways, Singapore is a victim of its own economic success. The country used to be seen as a place to do business at low cost. However, wages and standards of living have risen in recent years. Other costs of doing business, such as rents, have also gone up. Costs are now higher than in other countries, particularly China and Vietnam, which often offer tax breaks, cheap land, and even cash grants for business investors. For example, computer disk-drive manufacturers are starting to invest in China.

To help ensure Singapore's success, the government is spending money on a number of transportation projects, including airport improvement. The government attempts to improve conditions for businesses without getting involved in business itself.

Singapore's government is also concerned about improving the technological skills of the population. While most citizens are literate, the number of people who have advanced education or technological training is far less than in countries such as Canada or the United States. In order for Singapore to attract high-tech businesses, it must improve the skill level of the population. This will be a priority for the government.

Overall, the future of this market economy looks bright. Still, a big question remains concerning the impact of Singapore's economy on the environment and the country's quality of life.

Figure 7.25

Singapore's airport. Why would an efficient airport be an important facility in a market economy?

1. Suppose you work for a computer software company and have just been transferred to Singapore. Devise three questions about doing business in Singapore that you would like answered before you go.
2. Give three advantages for Singapore in adopting a market economy.
3. Make a sketch to show how a trans-shipment hub operates. Include information in your sketch about where goods come from, where they are going, and services that are supplied while the goods are en route.

Understanding the Concepts

1. Copy the following table into your notebook. Match the term in column A with an appropriate term in column B.

Column A	Column B
Capital	Practical solution
Collectivization	Investment money
Command economy	Based on custom
Entrepôt	Meeting own food needs
Pragmatism	Communism
Subsistence farming	Co-operative farming
Traditional economy	Trans-shipment hub

2. Think about the advantages and disadvantages of the four types of economic systems described in this chapter. Design a poster to advertise the system that you personally think is the most effective way to organize an economy. What kinds of images will you wish to include in your poster?

Figure 7.26

Posters are a dramatic way to make a point or to persuade others. This poster from the Soviet Union says, "Come join us, comrade, at the collective farm!" To whom do you think this poster was addressed?

3. Copy the following headings into your notebook. For each heading, review the Case Studies in this chapter and compare the economic systems of North Korea and Singapore.

Characteristics	North Korea	Singapore
Type of economy		
Decision makers		
Main economic activities		
Quality of life for people		
Problems		
The future		

Research and Communication Skills

4. Besides North Korea, name five other countries in the world that have command economies. (*Hint*: A command economy does not need to be a communist country. Countries that are run by dictators may also be command economies.)

5. Using the Internet, locate a shipping company operating in Canada that also operates out of Singapore. Find out the type of products normally carried by this shipping company.

6. Choose one country that interests you and conduct research to find out the type of economy that it has. Write a short report in which you describe the type of economy, giving some evidence that convinces you of its type.

Map and Globe Skills

7. Look at the map of Asia on page 288 in the map appendix of this book. On a sheet of blank paper, draw a circle with a radius of approximately 3000 km. Cut out the circle. Centre the circle over Singapore.

   a) List all those countries that are all or partly inside the cut-out area (i.e., within 3000 km of Singapore).

   b) Cross off the list those countries that do not have access by ocean to Singapore.

   c) What does your list tell you about Singapore's location in Asia?

Applications

8. Review the four economic questions that all societies must answer, as listed on page 130. Explain how Canada as a society has answered these questions.

9. Imagine that a war in the Middle East has just caused a severe shortage of oil, the major energy supply for both North Korea and Singapore.

   a) What actions do you think the government of North Korea will take to solve this problem?

   b) What actions do you think the government of Singapore will take to solve the problem?

   c) Which country's actions are likely to be more effective? Explain your answer.

10. You have been hired by a company that plans school trips to other countries. They need pamphlets that will attract school groups to book trips to North Korea, Japan, China, and Singapore. Design a pamphlet for one country, making sure to include points of interest for school groups. Add colour and pictures to your pamphlet.

Figure 7.27

In Singapore, rickshaws and bicycles are as common a sight as automobiles. China has outlawed rickshaws. Can you think of three possible reasons why?

World Patterns of Rich and Poor

EXPECTATIONS

- demonstrate an understanding of how economic resources influence the economic success of a region
- identify economic patterns, using thematic maps
- identify the top trading countries in the world and the reasons for their success
- compare the characteristics of developed and developing countries

Who's Rich and Who's Poor?

You have seen pictures of starving children, and read of poor families in other countries who must struggle to get shelter, food, and clothing. Why is it that some people have so little, while Canadians, as a country, have so much? This chapter looks at patterns of rich and poor around the world. We will try to understand the economic conditions that create these patterns and differences.

All countries have economic resources — land, labour, capital (money), and technology — but not all countries have an equal share of these resources. Also, countries organize their economic resources in different ways.

INTERACTION

Some countries, like Canada, succeed in organizing their economies to benefit their citizens. Their citizens have material and non-material wealth, such as protection for human rights and the environment.

Figure 8.1

Photographs of desperate people in other parts of the world, like this family in Kosovo whose home was destroyed, show that not everyone has the same advantages as people in Canada. What do you think could be done to help these people?

Other countries are not as successful, so that people have few advantages. These people have a low quality of life. When looking at the world as a whole, we can discover some distinct patterns.

Figure 8.2

Even rich countries like Canada have poor people. Why do you think this is?

Avoiding Miscalculations

Before we can identify economic patterns, we must decide how we will measure a country's economy. We might use an economic measurement, such as gross domestic product (GDP) per capita. GDP is the average of all the wealth in the country created in one year divided by all the people. The problem is that this figure is an average. It cannot tell us how much of the population actually enjoys a decent life. Figure 8.3 shows how deceptive averages can be. What we need is a measurement that takes into account both the material and the non-material wealth of countries.

Figure 8.3

This bar graph shows how averages can sometimes lead to misunderstanding about conditions in a country.

- There are 10 people in this society. The graph shows their incomes.
- The gross domestic product of this society (the sum of all the incomes) is $2000 (9 x $100 + $1100).
- The GDP per capita (per person) is calculated as GDP divided by the number of people, or $2000/10 = $200.
- According to our statistic, the average income in the country is $200, yet 9 out of the 10 people earn only half that amount. Averages can give a false measurement of conditions in a country.

SEE PAGE 40

Who Has the Good Life?

The Human Development Index (HDI) is an economic measurement that was designed to measure the average quality of life of a country's citizens, not just their incomes. The United Nations introduced the HDI in 1990. It takes into account many factors, such as people's ability to purchase food and essential non-food items needed for survival, like warm clothing in colder climates. Other factors considered are the availability and quality of education and health care.

The best score a country can get in the Human Development Index is 1.0. This would be a country that is doing extremely well on all items that the HDI takes into account. Canada's score in 1998 was 0.96, indicating that conditions were very good, but not perfect.

Fact File

Throughout the 1990s, Canada was ranked first by the United Nations on the Human Development Index out of all the countries in the world.

It's Your World

Indexes are used in many situations. An important index used in Canada is the Consumer Price Index (CPI). This index is calculated using prices of many goods and services that Canadians use in day-to-day living. The costs of food, shelter, transportation, and household expenses are all taken into account. As well, the CPI incorporates the cost of recreation, personal care products, and other items. Often, changes in the CPI are used to figure out how much people should get as raises in their salaries.

Fact File

An index is an indicator or sign, usually expressed as a number, that gives relative values (amounts) for a particular measurement.

Fact File

The HDI is not just based on incomes. Two examples prove this:

	HDI rank	GDP/capita
Costa Rica	34	US $ 5 969
Kuwait	54	US $23 848

Figure 8.4

The top and bottom countries on the Human Development Index, 1998.

Top 10 Countries			Bottom 10 Countries		
Rank	Country	Score	Rank	Country	Score
1	Canada	0.960	165	Gambia	0.291
2	France	0.946	166	Mozambique	0.281
3	Norway	0.943	167	Guinea	0.277
4	United States	0.943	168	Eritrea	0.275
5	Iceland	0.942	169	Ethiopia	0.252
6	Finland	0.942	170	Burundi	0.241
7	Netherlands	0.941	171	Mali	0.236
8	Japan	0.940	172	Burkina Faso	0.219
9	New Zealand	0.939	173	Niger	0.207
10	Sweden	0.936	174	Sierra Leone	0.185

Figure 8.5

Average Human Development Index scores for groups of countries, 1998.

HDI Category	Life Expectancy (years)	Literacy Rate (%)	GDP per Person (US dollars)	HDI Average Score
High (e.g., Canada, United States, France)	73.5	95.7	$16 241	0.897
Medium (e.g., Brazil, Egypt, Indonesia)	67.5	83.2	$3 390	0.670
Low (e.g., Bangladesh, Kenya, Pakistan)	56.7	50.8	$1 362	0.409

Figure 8.6

A high quality of life includes more than just material goods. It also includes the knowledge that the future will likely be prosperous and comfortable. That is why an education is so important in providing people with the skills and knowledge for their future.

It's Your World

The fact that Canada consistently places at the top of the Human Development Index does not go unnoticed by governments in this country. Frequent mention is made of the HDI by the prime minister and government officials when bragging about their achievements in office. Do you think any one political party or economic group should take credit for our high HDI rating? Why (or why not)?

GO TO

http://bized.ac.uk/stafsup/options/aehumandevecgro.htm

This site is a worksheet developed by a student in a junior high school in Singapore. Follow the instructions to do a comparative analysis of the HDI of various countries. Canada is included.

1. a) On an outline map of the world, shade in green those 10 countries that are at the top of the HDI ranking. Shade in red those 10 that are at the bottom.
   b) Describe the pattern of the countries shaded in green. Describe the pattern of the countries shown in red.
   c) On the basis of this map, determine which regions of the world have a generally high quality of life. Which regions have a low quality of life?
2. Look at the Fact File on page 148. Explain why a country with a high per capita income, such as Kuwait, can rank much lower on the HDI than a country with a lower per capita income.
3. a) Use the data in the chart in Figure 8.7 to construct a scatter graph illustrating the number of televisions per 1000 people. (For help, see page 314 of the skills appendix.) The vertical axis of the graph will show the HDI score, while the horizontal axis will show the number of televisions. (The scatter graph in Figure 8.8 is constructed the same way using HDI score and number of physicians, so you can use it as a model.) Make sure to title your graph, and use as many labels as necessary.
   b) List two conclusions that you can draw from your scatter graph.

Figure 8.7

Human Development Index and other economic statistics for selected countries.

Country	Human Development Index	Number of Physicians / 10 000 People	Number of Televisions / 1000 People
Bangladesh	0.371	2	6
Brazil	0.809	9	209
Canada	0.960	22	703
China	0.650	16	204
Congo	0.519	3	7
Egypt	0.612	18	111
France	0.946	28	638
Jamaica	0.735	5	145
Russia	0.769	38	380
South Korea	0.894	12	351
Spain	0.935	41	404
Yemen	0.356	1	28

SEE PAGE 37

Figure 8.8

This is a scatter graph drawn using HDI scores and number of physicians for these selected countries. What pattern do you see in the scatter graph?

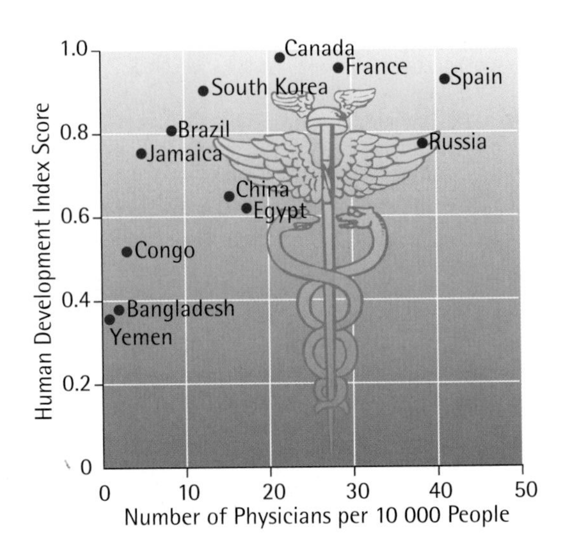

Explaining Poverty

Figure 8.4 on page 148 shows the countries with the best and worst qualities of life. Some parts of the world, such as most of North America and Europe, have high qualities of life (e.g., people live longer and in better health). Economic conditions in these places have allowed the people a comfortable life. Other regions have low qualities of life (e.g., people often suffer many diseases and die young). Economic factors in these places have made it much more difficult for people to achieve a good quality of life.

In this section of the chapter, we will look at reasons why most citizens of some countries do not share a high quality of life.

Looking at the Past

What happened in the past often influences what happens today. Most countries with a low quality of life, such as those in Africa and Asia, were once **colonies** of European countries, including England, Spain, Portugal, and France. The colonies were controlled by these European "mother countries."

The European countries established governments and economies to suit their own purposes. This sometimes included making slaves of the local people. The Europeans were able to do this because they had better technologies, particularly military equipment. They controlled the colonies through military might.

Figure 8.9

The slave trade had a huge impact on Africa. The young and strong were targeted by slavers, stripping away generations from the continent. Millions of young men and women were forced into terrible lives as prisoners.

Colonization changed local societies in many ways. Partly, these changes were meant to control the local people; partly, they were carried out because Europeans believed their culture was superior to the local cultures. They felt they had a duty to "civilize" the local people. The Europeans acted in a cold and arrogant manner, imposing their rule on others.

GO TO www.worldbook.com/fun/aajourny/html/index.html

Click on From Africa to America, then click on The Slave Trade. Read about the Middle Passage. Identify two countries outside of North America that imported slaves from Africa.

> "*No one shall be held in slavery or servitude; slavery and the slave trade shall be prohibited in all their forms.*"
>
> **Article 4, Universal Declaration of Human Rights, 1948**

Figure 8.10

The triangular slave trade. Americans benefited from the captured labour force, while Europeans benefited from the products that they bought and sold in the trade.

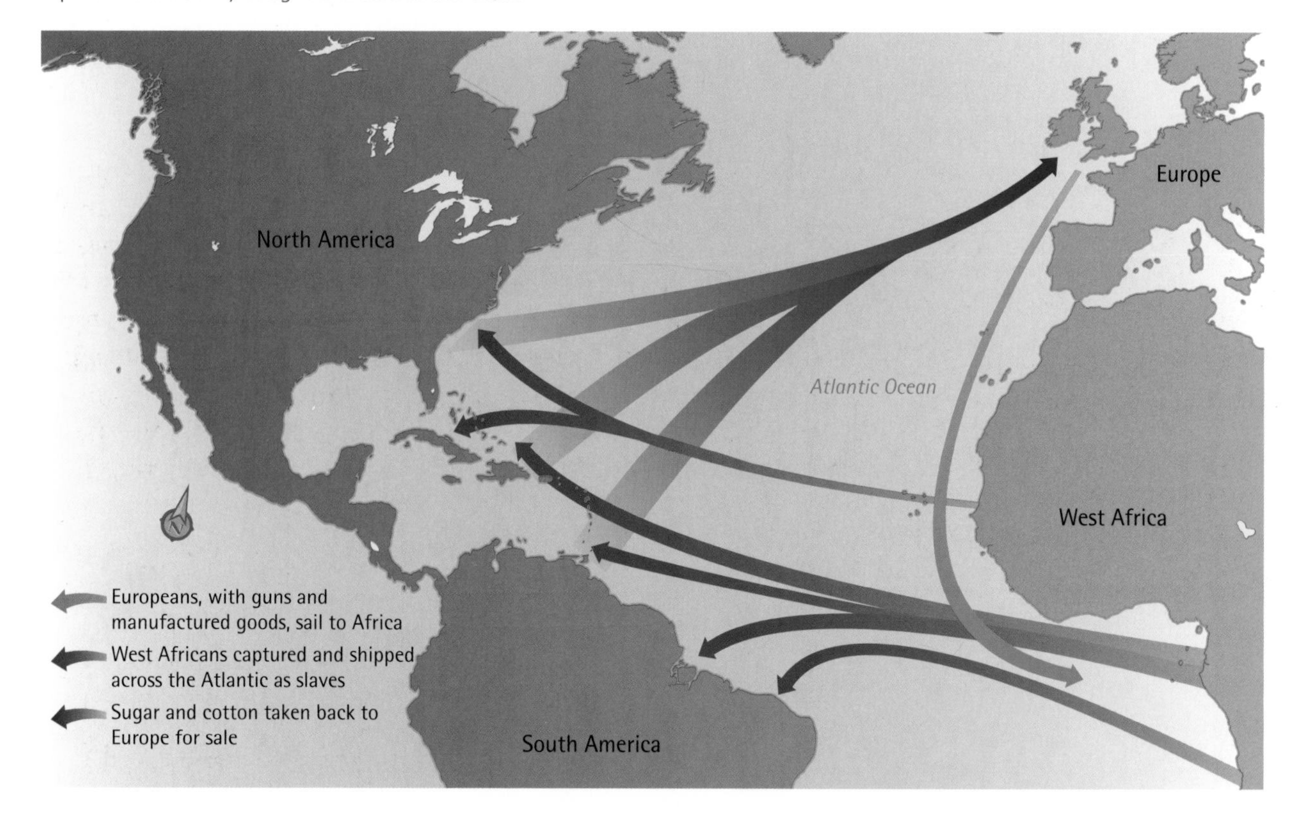

Figure 8.11

Why did the European powers work to change the local cultures of their colonies?

Area of Change	Type of Change	Reason for Change	Impact of Change
Leaders	Old leaders, or leaders who resisted European expansion, were replaced by co-operative leaders. Or, no local leaders were allowed.	This gave the European powers complete control of the people in the colonies, since local resistance was stopped.	The colonies were never able to develop skills in making political decisions. These skills were needed when they became independent.
Language	Business and government were carried on in the language of the European power.	This sent a signal that the local languages were not important.	Local languages and culture were reduced in importance, especially in economics and politics.
Religion	The European powers encouraged or enforced the spread of Christianity to the colonies.	This made the local religions seem weak. Religion built stronger connections to the European culture, which helped dis-courage rebellion.	Local religions and culture were seen as backward and weak.
Education	Education, when it was available, was based on European ideas and knowledge.	This undermined the local culture and reinforced European ideas.	Children were taught that the European way of life was better than the local way of life.

Fact File

An estimated 12 million African people were enslaved by western countries between 1500 and 1865.

GO TO

www.abcnews.go.com/

Scroll down to and click on Reference on the left side of your screen. Now click on Country Profiles. At the window, Select a Country, scroll down to Republic of Congo and click Go There. This site gives a profile of the Republic of Congo. What was the country's former name? What is its capital city? Report back to your class two reasons why the Congo's economy is so poor.

When the colonies finally became independent, they had to build new social and political structures from scratch. Some of their old ways had been destroyed. As a result, many newly independent countries have had difficulty organizing their means of production, especially capital (e.g., investing money in building new factories) and technology (e.g., applying new methods of farming to yield healthier crops).

Fact File

Thirty-three African colonies became independent countries between 1956 and 1966.

Weak Economies

European mother countries made no effort to build the economies of their colonies. Europeans felt that colonies had only two economic purposes:

- to be sources of cheap raw materials for industries of the mother country, including minerals, timber, spices, sugar, fish, and other foods
- to be buyers of goods manufactured in the mother country, such as the tools to extract raw materials, fabrics, farming equipment, and the like.

People in the colonies had to sell to and buy from the mother country. They were not allowed to establish their own trade connections or develop their own industries.

Fact File

Many developing countries are trying to improve their economies through tourism, but some people consider this another form of colonization. Hotels and beaches may be owned by multinational companies, and most of the profits leave the country without significantly benefiting the local people.

No Trade Base

As a result of **colonization**, the most important economic activity in many newly independent countries is extracting and selling natural resources such as sugar, timber, or minerals. Since many countries are selling these **commodities**, there is a lot of choice for the buyer. Competition is keen, and prices remain low. This is good for the buyers of the raw materials — industries in the richer countries of the world. In addition, demand for resource commodities varies widely, so prices are unstable. One month, prices might be high, but the very next they might be low. This makes long-term planning nearly impossible. Without industries and other economic activities to fall back on, former colonies face great difficulties in building stable economies.

Figure 8.12

Workers in the Philippines process sugar cane for juice, which will be refined for use in many food products consumed worldwide. Extracting natural resources is still very important to the economies of many developing countries.

No Manufacturing Base

When the colonies became new countries, they had trouble developing manufacturing activities. They often lacked the technical knowledge to compete with countries that were already industrialized, such as Canada. Without manufactured goods to sell, these countries have few trade ties to the rest of the world. As a result, their people earn lower wages; their governments collect less money in taxes and therefore have little to spend on social programs (e.g., to improve education, build hospitals, train workers, or construct power plants).

> "*Colonial powers laid the foundation of the present division of the world into industrial nations on the one hand, and hewers of wood and drawers of water on the other.*"
>
> **P. Donaldson, author**

GO TO www.icrc.ch

This is the Web site for the International Red Cross, an organization that works to improve the quality of life for people around the world. Click on operations by country. Choose a country on the map (e.g., Mexico) and click on it. Investigate one activity the Red Cross is doing in that country. Explain why you feel this activity is helpful.

Figure 8.13

Think of this chart as a world map. The area of each country is based on its share of world trade in exported goods. Those countries with a great amount of exports appear large on the map, and those with small amounts of exports might not even be shown. Which countries have more exports than Canada?

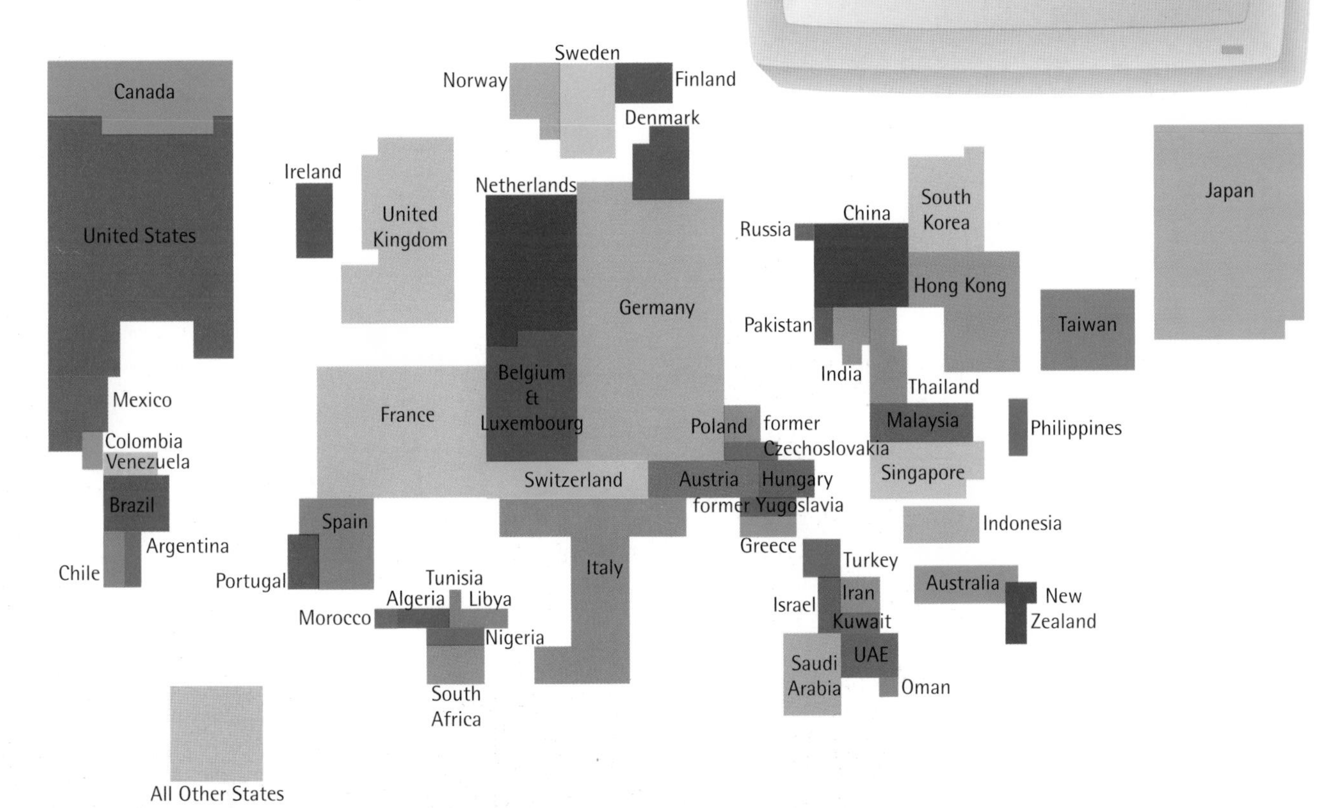

Exploding Populations

Most countries with low qualities of life have rapidly growing populations. This occurs for several reasons.

- Lack of education, especially for girls. Research studies in many countries have shown that educated women marry later and produce fewer children.
- Children often work to help the family meet its needs. Child labour may take place on the family farm, or perhaps in factories or on the streets of cities. Often, families survive because of their children's incomes. In these cases, there is little reason to limit the number of children in a family.

> *"Most of the population increase is taking place in the so-called Third World, where old traditions are strong, the social status of women is not very high, and the standard of living is already low.... Unfortunately, it is in the Third World that the increases cannot easily be absorbed."*
>
> Isaac Asimov, "The March of the Millennia"

Figure 8.14

In many parts of the world, children must work to help support their families, like these boys in El Salvador who sift through garbage looking for items that can be reused or resold. What impact do you think child labour has on children?

Figure 8.15

Population growth for the world, projected to 2020 (using 1999 figures). Why might the growth of developed countries be relatively slow for most of the time shown by the graph?

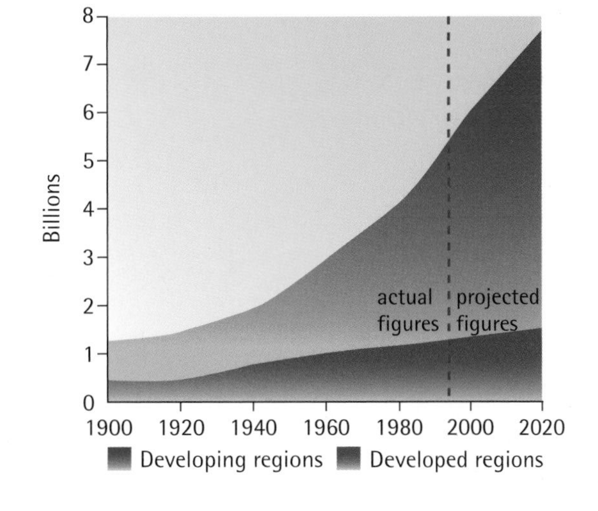

SEE PAGE 6

Fact File

Africa and the Middle East are the fastest growing parts of the world, with population growth rates of almost 3% per year.

- Health care in developing countries is often poor. As a result, there are high rates of infant mortality. Because families expect some children to die, they often have many children. This is because parents must rely on adult children to look after them in their old age.
- Birth control devices are often too expensive for couples in poorer countries. They may not even be available because of social or religious views.
- In some countries, religious views encourage large families. Traditions may also put a high value on having many children. In other cases, governments encourage people to have more children because it means a stronger military and a larger economy in the years to come.

GO TO **www.thehungersite.com**

Visit this site to make a donation of food to a child in a developing country. It is free for you, since the site's sponsors pay the bill. Write a letter to one of the sponsor companies asking why they support this charity. Address your letter to the manager of public relations of the company you choose.

Rapid population growth often means a lower quality of life. Resources must be shared among a greater number of people. Rapid population growth is a challenge for developing countries.

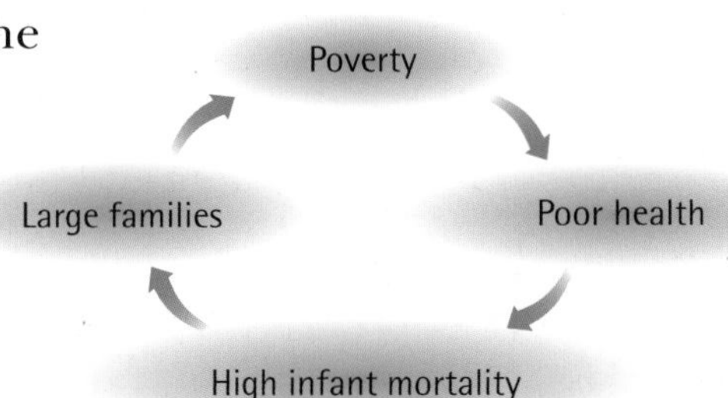

Figure 8.16

Poverty leads to large families, which in developing countries usually leads to more poverty. What is one idea that may help break this cycle?

CONNECTIONS TO Society

How does the debt that developing nations owe to developed nations affect those poorer countries? As these countries try to pay back their loans, they must cut social spending. That means:

- clinics close, so health care suffers;
- children, especially girls, are pulled out of school, damaging their future;
- adult literacy programs are cut, so retraining of workers stops;
- food and medicine prices soar, so poorer people have an even more difficult time living;
- wages are slashed and unemployment leaps, so poorer people have less money still (women are usually the first to lose their jobs);
- the country becomes poorer and has more trouble paying back the debt.

This seems to be a terrible cycle. How do you think it will affect your life?

Paying Off the Debt

After independence, many former colonies tried hard to improve conditions for their people: they built schools and hospitals, expanded electrical grids, developed factories, and improved roads. To do this, they borrowed large sums of money from wealthier countries. Everyone believed that these improvements would create new economic activity, and that the loans would be repaid in a few years. In some cases, money was borrowed for less constructive purposes, such as expansion of the military and construction of palaces for government leaders.

Unfortunately, many countries were unable to pay back their loans. In the 1970s and 1980s, world interest rates went up, and economic growth in the new countries was not as strong as had been predicted. In fact, some had to borrow even more money to keep their governments running. Many countries have paid much more in interest than their original loans.

It's Your World

Bolivia is typical of a developing country in debt. In 1984, the interest alone on its debt was worth more than half the money it made from trade with other countries.

Suppose you borrowed $150 for a bicycle that you needed for a weekend job delivering flyers. The job pays $30 a week. From this amount, you must repay your loan at a rate of $10 per week, plus $6 interest. How would repaying your loan affect your ability to buy lunch, school supplies, and other necessary items?

GO TO

www.mtv.com/mtv/news/gallery/u/u2990216.html

Visit this site to discover what rock stars like U2 and Prodigy are doing to help others. What do they suggest we do about the huge debt that many developing nations owe to developed countries? Report back to your class.

The banks and lending organizations pressure the borrowers to pay off their loans. As they struggle with their **foreign debts**, many countries have slashed spending on health and education — programs that would improve their quality of life. They have focussed on producing goods for export (such as minerals, food, and forest products) to earn money. These countries are struggling just to maintain their quality of life.

SEE PAGE 234

1. Copy the following chart into your notebook. Match the terms in Column A with those in Column B.

Column A	Column B
natural resources	poverty
mother country	colonies
few economic resources	foreign debt
source of raw materials	child labour
high interest rates	commodities
family farms	England

2. Summarize the four reasons for poor quality of life discussed in this chapter in a chart with these headings:

Reasons	Description of Conditions	Impact on Quality of Life
History		
Weak economies		
Population growth		
Debt		

3. You have just been hired by the Canadian government to make up programs to help improve economic activities in other countries. List two suggestions, and write a short paragraph in which you explain why your ideas would lead to better qualities of life in these countries.

CASE STUDY

Poverty in Sub-Saharan Africa

Most parts of the Sahara Desert receive less than 100 mm of rainfall each year. This is about one-eighth the amount Ontario gets.

As you travel southward from the Sahara Desert, rainfall increases. At first this would be noticeable by scattered clumps of grass and sparse shrubs. Soon the grass grows thicker, and scattered trees replace the shrubs. This vegetation zone is known as the **Sahel**, and this part of Africa is called **sub-Saharan Africa**.

Traditional Economic Activities

The Sahel region has a long history. In fact, civilizations existed in cities like Timbuktu (now in Mali) long before Europeans knew anything about the continent.

SEE PAGE 132

Early societies based their economic activities on the herding of goats, sheep, cattle, and camels. People obtained meat and milk from their animals and used the skins for housing and other needs. The animals grazed on grasses and small shrubs. Herds were moved throughout the year from one grazing area to another, influenced by the wet and dry seasonal cycles. This nomadic way of life ensured that no area was overgrazed. The vegetation in each area had time to renew itself before the herds returned. This sustainable way of life went on for thousands of years.

Because of their location on the edge of a great desert, the peoples of the sub-Saharan region became important traders. Camel caravans were formed in the communities for the long treks northward across the desert. The caravans depended on **oases** within the desert for water and food.

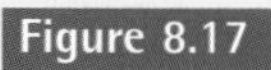

Figure 8.17

Traditional dwellings of the people of Ethiopia (left) and Senegal (above). Note the use of grasses in the construction of these homes. Although the two countries are on opposite ends of the continent, the houses look very similar. Why do you think this is so?

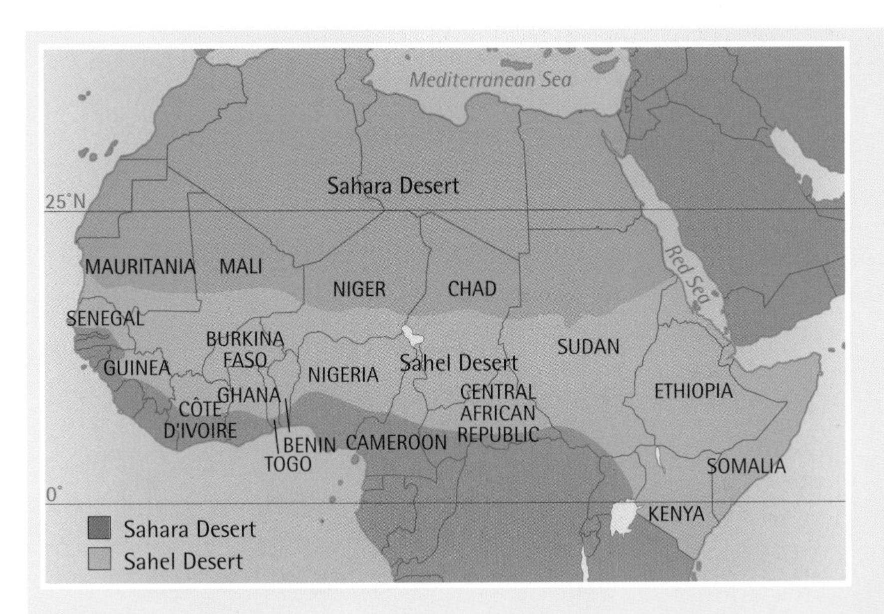

Figure 8.18

The countries of the sub-Saharan region. Which countries have you heard about in the news?

Fact File

Some governments have delayed action on desertification by arguing that the causes and solutions to the problem are someone else's responsibility. They blame the developed countries for their high output of greenhouse gases and burning of fossil fuels.

A New Way of Life

The traditional way of life in the region began to change with the arrival of Europeans in the late 1800s. To mark their land claims, the Europeans mapped out country boundaries. These boundaries prevented the nomadic people from travelling into neighbouring countries. The national boundaries also made long-distance trading much more difficult. In addition, the Europeans encouraged farming. Arable lands were divided into small farms and peanut and vegetable plantations. As a result, the way of life changed, and people became tied to particular locations. Herds began to overgraze this land and overuse water supplies. This resulted in shortages of food and water in times of drought.

Wells were drilled to help solve the problem of water shortages, sometimes paid for by aid agencies like the Red Cross or by the United Nations. With the improved water supply, people increased their herds so that they could increase their wealth. This led to more overgrazing.

Desertification

Overgrazing and the greater use of water from wells have resulted in **desertification**. With plants eaten by herds, winds can easily blow away the thin soil. The lack of roots means that soil is washed away when it does rain. In the end, there is less vegetation and more bare, infertile land that cannot grow crops or graze herds.

Figure 8.19

Aid agencies have helped to construct wells in the Sahel, like this one in Kenya, to make the water supply more reliable. What effects do you think this has had on the daily lives of the people?

Searching for Economic Opportunities

Many of the economic problems of this area come from how the land is used. Most people are subsistence farmers. The country of Chad illustrates this situation. Even though only 3% of the land of Chad is arable, 48% of the GDP comes from agriculture. There are few other economic opportunities. Without jobs in industries or services, workers must remain farmers, earning very little and barely getting by from one year to the next.

It is difficult to industrialize in this area because of the extremely low income levels. Families have little money to spend on goods and services. As a result, few industries develop. Corrupt governments and civil wars have also discouraged industries.

> *"For drought-stricken Africa, the cry that the climate is changing is ultimately ... an excuse for political inaction."*
>
> **Lloyd Timberlake, "Africa in Crisis"**

Looking to the Future

It is hard to be optimistic about the future of sub-Saharan Africa. The area desperately needs capital to invest in roads, electrical grids, schools, and health care — factors that will allow these countries to industrialize and develop their economies. However, foreign agencies don't want to invest much money because of the high level of debt and the political problems of the area. Sub-Saharan Africa is seen as a bad risk. In addition, governments in the richer countries around the world have cut back on their foreign assistance programs, so smaller amounts of aid are reaching African countries. This region faces a difficult future.

Figure 8.20

Some statistics give clues about the quality of life for the people of sub-Saharan Africa.

Population growth rate	2.9% per year
Population doubling rate	25 years
Infant mortality	124 deaths/1000 live births
Literacy rate	42%
Life expectancy	49 years
GDP per capita	US $1047
HDI score	0.312

Figure 8.21

This is a schoolroom in Mogadishu, the capital of Somalia. How would you describe conditions of life for the people of this city?

Fact File

Global aid for sub-Saharan Africa fell throughout the 1990s, a time when governments of industrialized countries were looking for ways to cut spending. In 1994, aid to sub-Saharan Africa stood at $18.9 billion. In 1996 this assistance had fallen to $16.7 billion. Between 1992 and 1997, Canadian aid to this region declined by 30.4%

Timbuktu once boasted a population of 100 000 people and was the major financial and trading centre for the sub-Saharan region. From about 1000 A.D., camel caravans left from this thriving city located on the northernmost loop of the Niger River. The camels were destined for the Mediterranean coast and were laden with gold, salt, ivory, kola nuts, and slaves. Timbuktu's importance came to an end in 1591 when Berber armies sacked the city. Today, only 15 000 people call Timbuktu their home. Tourism is fast becoming the most important industry.

Figure 8.22

The Tuareg, a nomadic people of the Sahel, are among the descendants of the great traders of ancient Timbuktu.

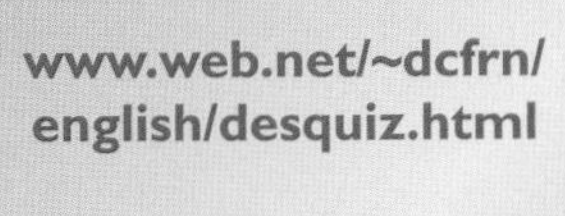

GO TO **www.web.net/~dcfrn/english/desquiz.html**

Take the desertification quiz. How well did you do? Do you feel it is important for students in a country like Canada to know about desertification? Explain your answer.

Figure 8.23

Watering livestock in Kenya

1. Identify two advantages and two disadvantages of living in the sub-Saharan region of Africa.
2. You have been asked by a local organization to give a speech on the reasons for the poor economy in sub-Saharan Africa. Write the speech that you will give, and provide facts to support your ideas.
3. The arrival of Europeans in North America resulted in many changes in the lives of First Nations peoples. How do these changes compare with the changes in the lives of the sub-Saharan nomads who were affected by European colonization?
4. "The people of sub-Saharan Africa shouldn't expect us to help them with their problems. They should be able to look after themselves and not depend on charity." This is a common opinion about giving assistance to other countries. Do you agree or disagree with this statement? Give facts and examples from the Case Study to support your opinion.

Understanding the Concepts

1. Make a sketch, or use cut-outs from magazines and newspapers, to show the features of Canadian life that give us a high quality of life compared to most other countries. Label your art piece and give it a title.

2. Suppose you could give up one material item that contributes to your high quality of life in order that people in sub-Saharan Africa could improve their economies and their quality of life. What would you give up? Explain your choice.

3. Write a paragraph about the reasons for poor economies and low quality of life in some parts of the world. Use this as your first sentence: "Events that occurred in the past have caused many people in developing countries to live economically poor lives."

Research and Communication Skills

4. Of the countries of the western hemisphere, Haiti has the lowest Human Development Index score. Prepare a poster to illustrate a simple economic change that could help some of the poorer people in a developing country such as Haiti.

5. Tourism is a growing industry in some parts of sub-Saharan Africa. Using the Internet and other sources of information, name and describe five places in the region that are important tourist destinations.

6. Suppose you were a United Nations aid official and were hiring Canadians to work in other countries around the world. Speaking a language that is commonly used in a destination country is important. Conduct research to find out which language would be best for an aid worker to know in order to be helpful in these countries.

Algeria
Belize
Haiti
Kenya
Niger
Papua New Guinea
Sri Lanka
Vietnam

Figure 8.24

Populations and areas of sub-Saharan countries.

Country	Population, 1998 (thousands)	Land Area (thousands km^2)
Benin	5 902	111
Burkina Faso	10 891	274
Central African Republic	3 342	623
Chad	7 166	1 259
Ethiopia	58 733	1 101
Ghana	18 100	228
Kenya	28 803	570
Mali	9 779	1 220
Niger	9 389	1 267
Nigeria	107 130	911
Senegal	9 404	193
Somalia	6 590	627
Sudan	32 594	2 376
Togo	4 736	54

Map and Globe Skills

7. a) Figure 8.24 contains some population data for sub-Saharan Africa. In your notebook, make a table showing their population densities. Remember that population density is the population of the country divided by the area of the country.
   b) Use the population densities you calculated to shade a map of sub-Saharan Africa. Start by separating the countries into three categories of density – high, medium, or low. Then, using an outline map of the region, shade each country according to your categories. Using only one coloured pencil, shade darkly for high density, use a medium shade for the middle category, and shade lightly for the lowest densities. Label your map appropriately.
   c) Describe the pattern that your map shows.

Figure 8.25
Tibetan refugee camp in India, 1993.

Applications

8. Figure 8.25 shows a Tibetan refugee camp in India in 1993. People fled here from Tibet when the Chinese invaded their country in the 1950s. Most of these children, like their parents, were born in the camp, and so have never even seen their homeland. Imagine that you are a United Nations official responsible for delivering food and medical help to this camp. Write a diary entry describing a typical day in the life of the camp.

9. A scale such as the Human Development Index, which is calculated using several factors, gives a more accurate picture of a situation than just one measurement. What measurements would you include if you wanted to determine a Students' Quality of Life Index for Canadian students? List five items that you would measure, and give reasons for choosing them.

10. Think about how material goods contribute to your quality of life. Suppose you did not have something as common as plastics in your life. Describe how your daily activities would change without these products.

11. Suppose you are an official in the government of Burkina Faso. What is the first action that you would take to improve the economy in your country? Give the reasons for your action.

12. One aid agency uses the slogan, "Give us the tools and we'll finish the job." Design an advertisement that would encourage Canadians to donate tools and money to sub-Saharan countries. Include an explanation for the symbols and images you use with your advertisement.

13. Why do you think poverty exists in North America? How can governments and ordinary citizens help solve the problem of homelessness in our own country? Identify some factors that contribute to the cycle of poverty, and list some possible solutions.

The Structure of Economies

EXPECTATIONS

- identify and give examples of the three major types of industries (i.e., primary/resource, secondary/manufacturing, tertiary/service), and describe how the distribution of these industries has changed over time
- describe the impact of a new industry on the economy of a region
- compare the characteristics of developed and developing countries

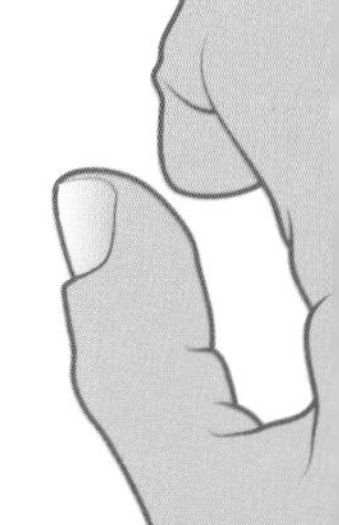

- Most people work processing natural resources (e.g., farming, mining, cutting trees).
- Most families are self-sufficient in food and buy only a few household items, such as sugar, tea, and cloth, at stores.
- There are few shops. My community has a general store, an inn, and a few other smaller shops.
- Most goods are made by craftspeople in small workshops. There is a blacksmith, a cooper (barrelmaker), and a cobbler (shoemaker) in this community.

The More Things Change...

Suppose you could travel back in time and see what your community was like in the past. You set the dial of your time machine for 125 years ago. When you emerge, you are immediately surprised by how different your community looks. People are dressed in old-fashioned clothes, buildings are smaller, and — this is most striking — there are no cars. After awhile you begin to focus on your mission. Your job is to record information about economic activities in and around your community. You record your observations on your high-tech wrist-band computer.

You return to the present and analyse your research data. Clearly, you need to understand the huge changes in economic activities that have occurred over the years. Questions come to your mind: What caused such changes? Have all communities and societies gone through changes like these? Which economic activities decline over time, and which become important? Answering these questions will take more research.

Figure 9.1

Economic activities 125 years ago were much different in Canada than at the present. What was the most important economic activity in your area 125 years ago?

Where Are Canadian Jobs?

It is often helpful to organize complex topics that you are studying into categories. **Economists** — people who do the kind of research you were doing with your time machine — have created categories of economic activities, or industries. They study **primary industries**, **secondary industries**, and **tertiary industries**.

Figure 9.2

Types of economic activities.

Category	Definition	Examples
Primary industries (resources)	Extract natural resources from the environment and make them into **semi-finished products**	Fishing, farming, forestry, mining
Secondary industries (manufacturing)	Take semi-finished products from primary industries and manufacture them into **finished goods** for consumers' use	Car manufacturing, furniture making, house construction
Tertiary industries (services)	Provide personal and business services to consumers	Hair styling, car repairs, teaching, government service, retail sales

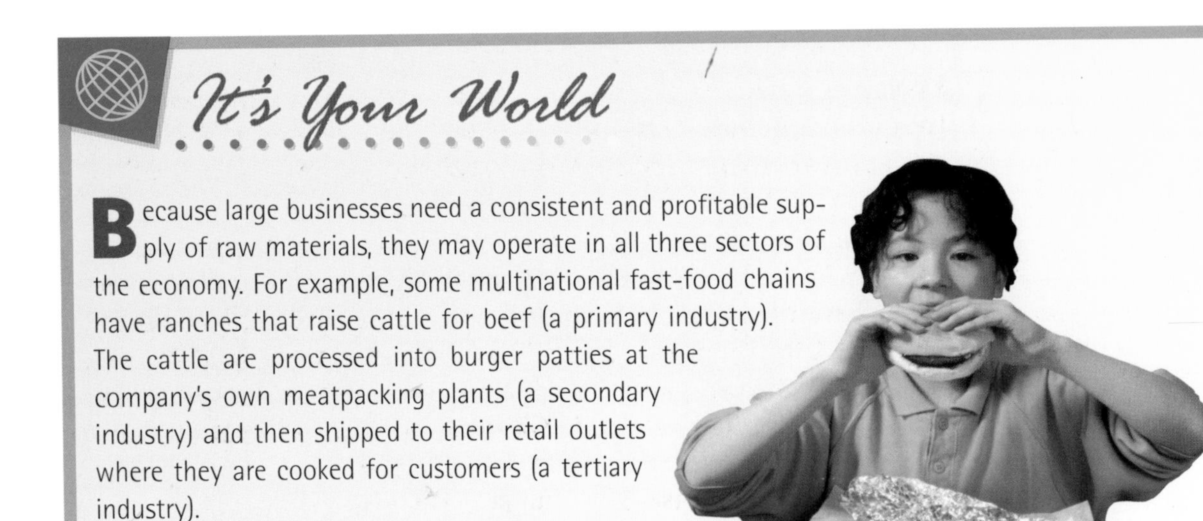

It's Your World

Because large businesses need a consistent and profitable supply of raw materials, they may operate in all three sectors of the economy. For example, some multinational fast-food chains have ranches that raise cattle for beef (a primary industry). The cattle are processed into burger patties at the company's own meatpacking plants (a secondary industry) and then shipped to their retail outlets where they are cooked for customers (a tertiary industry).

While these categories are helpful, some businesses or activities don't fit neatly into just one category. For instance, if you go to a greenhouse to buy flowers, you are dealing with both primary and tertiary industries: growing the flowers is a primary industry, while selling them is a tertiary economic activity. In spite of these problems, the category method does make analysing economic activities somewhat easier.

Fact File

Close to 60% of Canada's total exports are based on natural resources. These exports include minerals, pulp and paper, lumber, wheat, and pork.

Figure 9.3

The Ekati Diamond Mine in the Northwest Territories. Because the diamonds are located far from any large communities, workers are housed at the mill site.

Primary Industries: From the Earth to the Mill

Primary industries are the first step in making goods. All goods that we need and use must be made from raw materials found in the natural environment. All jobs related to getting and refining resources fall under the primary industries category.

Primary industries traditionally do not produce goods that are sold directly in stores. In steelmaking, for example, iron ore, coal, and limestone are brought together at a steel plant, such as Stelco in Hamilton, Ontario. The workers at the plant use these raw materials to make steel in a variety of forms — steel plates, sheets, bars, beams, and tubes. These are semi-finished products that must be worked on further (e.g., made into cars, tools, or buildings) before consumers can use them.

Most processing plants for primary industries are located far from populated areas but near sources of raw materials. This is because extracting natural resources from the environment usually produces a good deal of unusable material. Transporting this waste is expensive and would lower profits.

Fact File

Minerals such as iron and copper often make up only 1% to 5% of the ore dug from the ground. Profitable deposits of precious minerals, such as gold or diamonds, occur in even lower percentages.

Figure 9.4

Logging is an example of a primary industry. Where will these logs go from this location?

Figure 9.5

Before metals such as iron, nickel, and copper can be used in manufacturing, they must be smelted (treated at very high temperatures) to remove the metal from the raw ore.

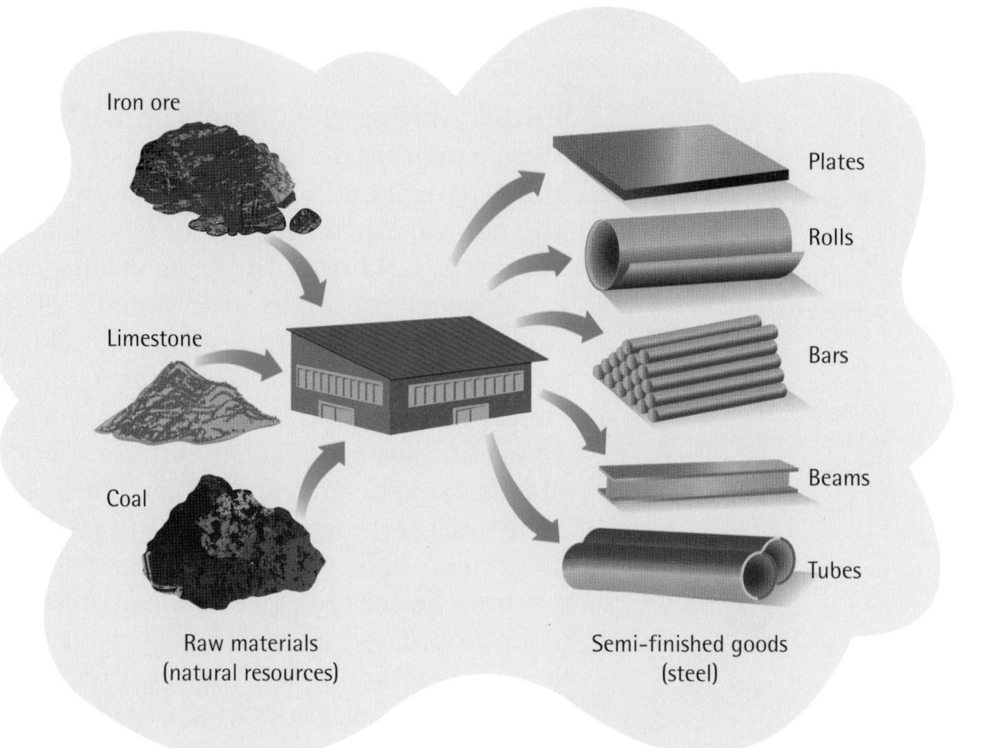

Figure 9.6

The processing of natural resources into semi-finished products almost always reduces the volume of the material being used.

SEE PAGE 208

In the 1800s, transcontinental railway lines in North America were built to supply factories in the industrialized east with raw materials. Powered by steam locomotives, the railways provided a steady stream of natural resources and also allowed manufactured goods to be sent back west to the interior of the continent. By 1910, about 10% of the wealth of the United States was invested in its railways.

Figure 9.7

Donald A. Smith, president of the Bank of Montreal, drove the last spike into the final rail of the new transcontinental Canadian Pacific Railroad at Craigellachie, B.C. on November 7, 1885. The photo does not show any of the immigrant Chinese labourers who worked under brutal conditions to complete the railway through the Rocky Mountains.

Secondary Industries: Making the Goods We Want and Need

The second step in manufacturing is to turn the semi-finished products of the primary industries into finished goods — e.g., making auto parts from the steel forms produced at Stelco.

For example, the desk you are sitting at went through many manufacturing processes before it arrived in your classroom. At the factory, semi-finished materials like steel, wood, and plastic were brought together for assembly. The metal legs were stamped out of rolls of steel, shaped, and welded onto desk bases. Chipboard (a semi-finished wood product) was delivered from a wood mill and cut to size. The plastic desktop was glued onto the chipboard and trimmed. Then, top and base were joined together using fasteners. The finished desk was packaged and shipped to a warehouse and then to your school.

Most secondary industries are located near the **market** where the finished products will be sold. Because the finished goods take up more space than the raw materials used in their manufacture (think about the shape of your desk if the materials were shipped flat versus the shape of your desk once it is assembled), transportation costs are higher to ship finished goods. Also, finished goods are more fragile and require more care in shipping than do semi-finished goods. So, to increase profits, manufacturing is traditionally located near large cities such as Vancouver, Winnipeg, Toronto, or Chicago.

Fact File

Manufacturing processes are varied and interesting and include:

- cutting
- shaping
- bending
- gluing
- polishing
- grinding
- welding
- assembling
- stamping
- drilling
- sanding
- packaging

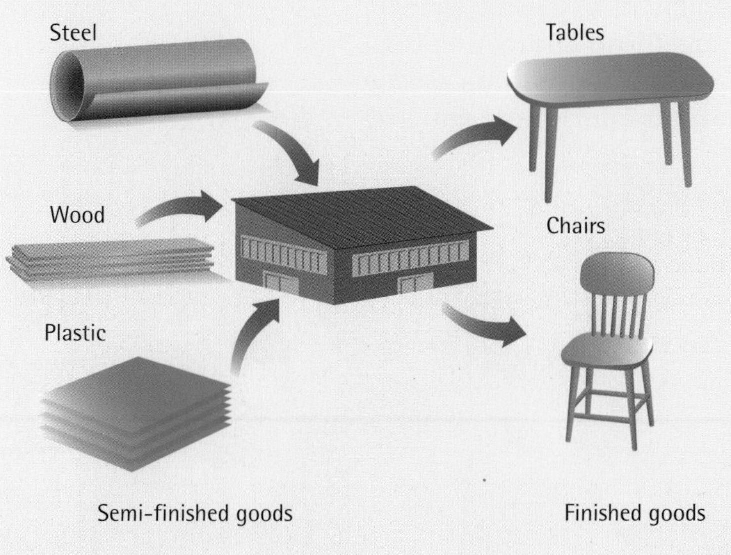

Figure 9.8

The processing of semi-finished products into finished products almost always changes the shape, and increases the value, of the materials being used.

Figure 9.9

Construction activities are also a secondary industry.

Tertiary Industries: Providing Services

Tertiary industries do not produce goods; rather, they provide services to help us use and enjoy the manufactured goods we buy.

An automobile dealership is a good example of tertiary industry. Before we can drive out of the showroom with our new car, we need a number of services:

- The dealer must order and display model cars.
- The dealer must get the car ready for sale (e.g., safety check, removal of transportation protection).
- We need to get a licence plate.
- A bank lends us the money to buy the car.
- We must obtain insurance through a broker.

SEE PAGE 74

Once we have the car, we need even more services:

- We need fuel.
- The car will need regular servicing and repairs.
- Often people buy accessories, such as sound systems, for their vehicles.
- Drivers buy auto club coverage for emergencies and breakdowns.

These are only some of the tertiary jobs needed just so we can buy and enjoy our car.

Tertiary industries are traditionally located near to their customers. Their services must be easily reached, or customers will go elsewhere. Exceptions to this rule are those companies that can supply their services electronically, such as those that operate on the Internet. In "cyberspace," it doesn't matter where you are.

Fact File

Some tertiary activities include:

clothing sales
banking
service stations
TV repair
food preparation
dry cleaning
accounting
entertainment

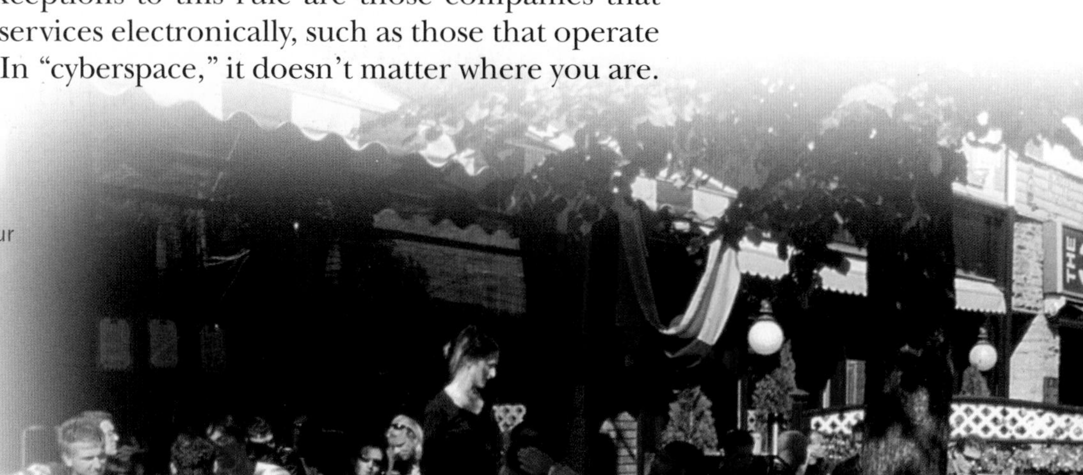

Figure 9.10
What services do you consume as part of your high quality of life?

It's Your World

You will probably work in tertiary industries when you finish school. Currently, about two-thirds of all Canadians are employed providing services to others. Think about your parents' jobs: are they primary, secondary, or tertiary activities? What jobs did your grandparents have? What do you think your children's jobs will be like?

Figure 9.11

Automobiles create a great deal of tertiary economic activity in the wealthier countries of the world, like Canada.

Fact File

Canada's industries break down roughly as follows:

Agriculture	3%
Primary/secondary	31%
Tertiary	66%

The tertiary industries category is very broad. It includes people who provide personal services like cutting hair, business services such as bankers and stockbrokers, doctors, teachers, prime ministers, and dogcatchers.

SEE PAGE 75

Some economists have argued that the tertiary category is *too* broad and should be divided into two subcategories. In this case, tertiary industries would include all those economic activities that are mainly concerned about *goods,* while a new category — **quaternary industries** — would include *services* that deal mostly with ideas and information. Under this system, bankers would be in the tertiary industries category because they help businesses operate, while teachers would be in the quaternary industries category because they deal with ideas. The quaternary category fits in with the notion that we are entering a new era — the Information Age.

> "*The fact that* TV Guide *makes a larger profit than all the major networks combined suggests that the value of information about information can be greater than the value of the information itself.*"
>
> **Nicholas Negroponte, "Being Digital"**

1. Copy the table below into your notebook and fill in the columns. Include examples of goods and services that you use in daily life.

Characteristics	Primary Industries	Secondary Industries	Tertiary Industries
Purpose			
Best location			
Examples			

2. Complete this sentence: "The most important reason that we discuss categories of economic activities is _____________."
3. Copy the word puzzle below into your notebook and complete it, using the clues below, to discover the hidden word.

Clues

1. The adjective that describes the output of secondary industries.
2. Semi-finished products are the raw materials of industries in this category.
3. This is the focus for economic activities in the quaternary industries category.
4. This is what secondary industries do.
5. In order to keep these costs low, natural resources are processed near to where they are found.
6 The word that describes how we get natural resources from the environment.
7. This is a secondary industry.
8. This is the category that includes fur trapping.
9. The category that includes services.
10. These are the users of products and services.

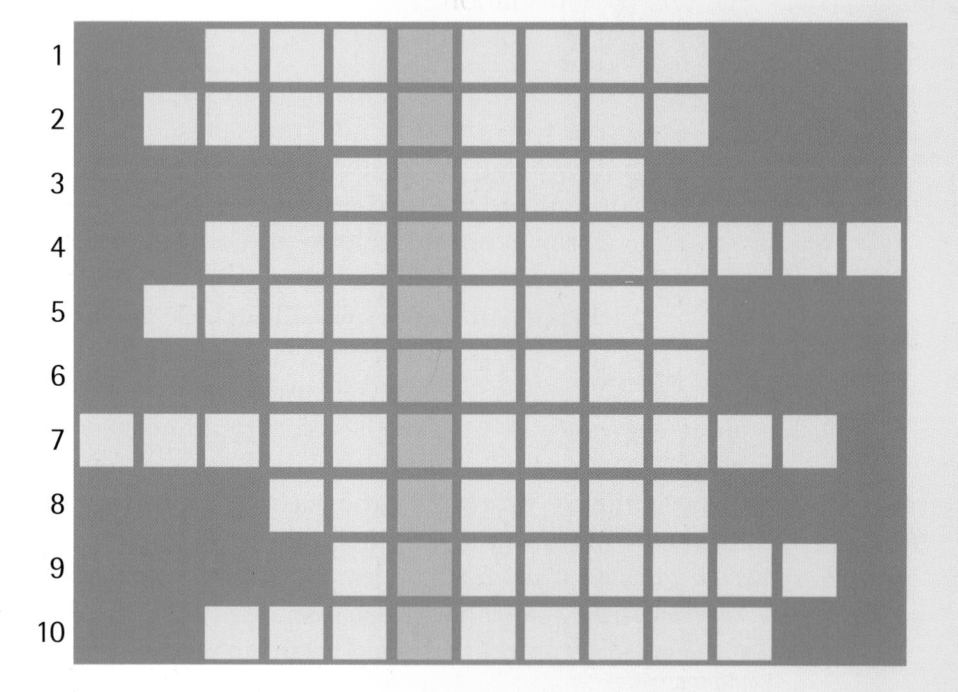

Economic Structure: Where Are the World's Jobs?

Fact File

Chad's score card, 1994:

World GNP rating	149th
GNP per capita	$180
Foreign debt	$91.7 million
Unemployment	Widespread

While all countries in the world have primary, secondary, and tertiary industries, these industries are not equally distributed throughout the world. We can learn a good deal about a country by looking at how many jobs it has in each economic category. There is a clear connection between the strength of the economic categories and people's quality of life.

LOCATION

Quality of Life

SEE PAGE 125

Data show us that countries with a high quality of life, such as Canada, earn only a small percentage of their gross domestic product from primary industries and a large percentage of their GDP from tertiary industries. Those places with poor scores on the Human Development Index — Chad, for example — earn most of their GDP from primary industries, while their tertiary industries account for only a small percentage of their GDP. In other words, a high quality of life seems to be linked to having many services available in a nation. Let's explore some reasons why this is the case.

Fact File

The word *data* is plural and means "facts." The singular form is *datum* ("fact").

Figure 9.12

Workers assemble televisions in Osaka, Japan; a boy tends goats in Kashgar, China. Are these primary, secondary, or tertiary activities?

Figure 9.13

A comparison of selected countries. An HDI score of 1.00 is perfect and means that the citizens have a very high quality of life.

Country	HDI Score	% of Gross Domestic Product from Primary Industries	Secondary Industries	Tertiary Industries
High Quality of Life				
Canada	0.960	3	30	67
France	0.946	3	29	68
New Zealand	0.939	7	26	67
Medium Quality of Life				
Ecuador	0.767	12	38	50
Syria	0.749	30	23	47
Sri Lanka	0.716	25	26	49
Low Quality of Life				
India	0.451	32	27	41
Haiti	0.340	39	16	45
Chad	0.318	44	22	34

Primary Industries

In many developing countries, there are not many jobs available. To feed themselves and their families, many workers are forced to remain in subsistence agriculture. European **colonization** left many developing countries dependent on the export of products from their primary industries, such as timber, minerals, or sugar cane. In richer countries, workers have a wider choice of jobs in other sectors of the economy.

Secondary Industries

Because they have more **capital** (money) to invest in manufacturing and construction, richer countries tend to have strong secondary industries. Countries with poor qualities of life have little capital to invest, and so they have difficulty establishing manufacturing industries that will be able to compete in the global market. On the other hand, the lower wages paid in Asian and African countries have in recent years attracted international corporations, who seek to keep labour costs low and profits high.

Figure 9.14

The data on primary, secondary, and tertiary industries are from Figure 9.13. Notice how the amount in each category varies for the countries. Which country has the lowest quality of life? How do you know this from the graph?

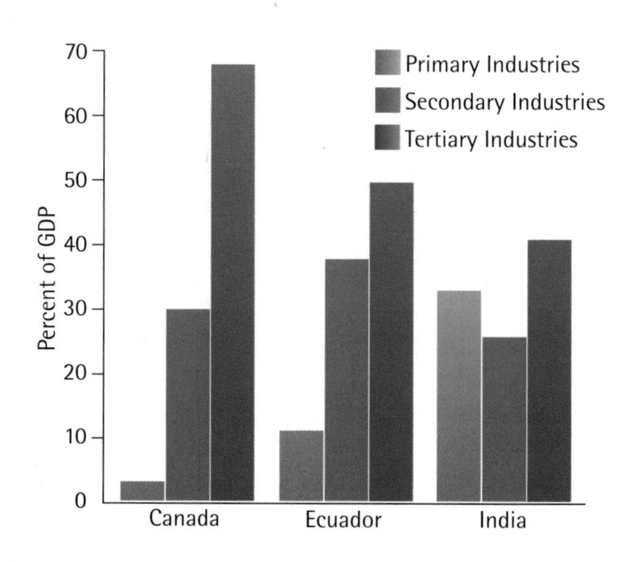

Figure 9.15

This scatter graph uses HDI score and percentage of GDP earned by primary industries. The data are from Figure 9.13. Using this graph as a model, draw a scatter graph to show HDI and tertiary industries.

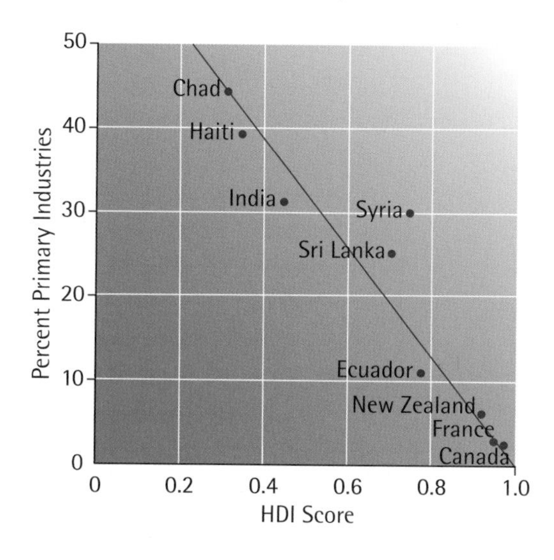

Tertiary Industries

The low income levels in countries with lower qualities of life mean that people do not have much money to spend on services. In wealthier countries, however, high incomes allow people to demand many types of services.

Fact File

Average hourly wages (in Can$) in selected cities around the world:

Tokyo, Japan	$27.99
Chicago, USA	$18.85
Toronto, Canada	$16.67
Sao Paulo, Brazil	$3.92
Bangkok, Thailand	$2.90
Bombay, India	$1.16
Lagos, Nigeria	$0.73

INTERACTION

GO TO **www.odci.gov/cia/publications/factbook/index.html**

Click on a country that interests you. Now, click on the Economy button on the left side of your screen. Find GDP by sector (agriculture, industry, services). Finally, go back and click on Canada. Find the same figures. Design a chart to compare the two countries.

Ways of Life

We have seen that quality of life varies with economic structure. Living conditions vary also. For example, since primary industries are traditionally located close to their natural resources, countries with a large number of primary jobs have fewer cities and more people living in small towns or villages. This is often true of developing countries. However, in industrialized countries where factories and jobs are plentiful, like Canada, most people live in cities. Tertiary industries also develop well in cities, since there are many customers demanding their services. Figure 9.17, on the next page, shows some other differences in employment and quality of life.

Figure 9.16

Manufacturing in developing countries – like this weaving co-operative in the Philippines – often starts small because there are few sources of investment capital. What are some advantages and disadvantages of starting small?

Figure 9.17

As countries develop, there are important changes in people's way of life. Why do you suppose that the number of children a family has declines as a country develops?

SEE PAGE 25

Low HDI Scores → High HDI Scores

Employment Structure
% employed in:
- Primary activities
- Secondary activities
- Tertiary activities

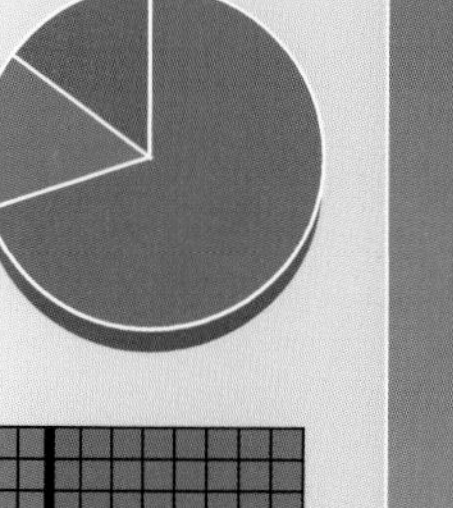

Level of Urbanization
- % living in towns and cities
- % living in the country

1 square = 1% of total

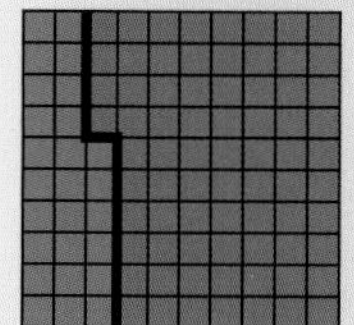
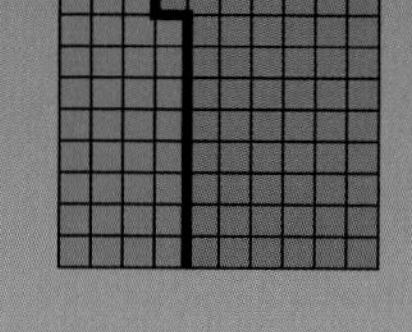
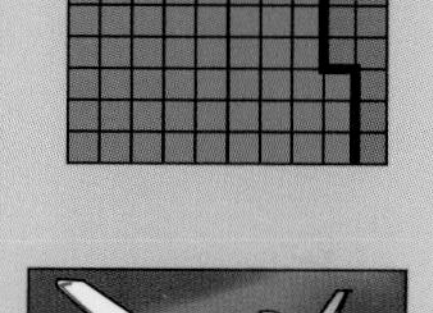

Levels of Technology

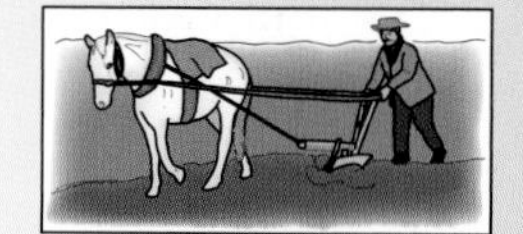
e.g., waterwheels, oxploughs, horse transport, pottery, hand-woven fabrics

e.g., tractors, fertilizers, electricity generation, simple electronics, mass production

e.g., advanced electronics, computers, scientific research and development

Size of Family

Spending on Food (as % of income)

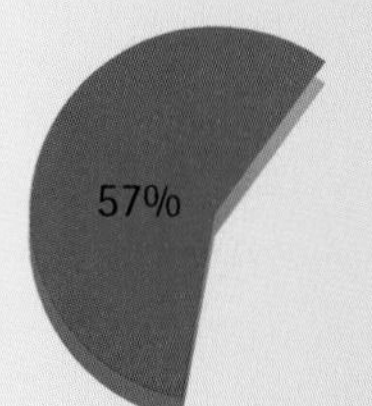

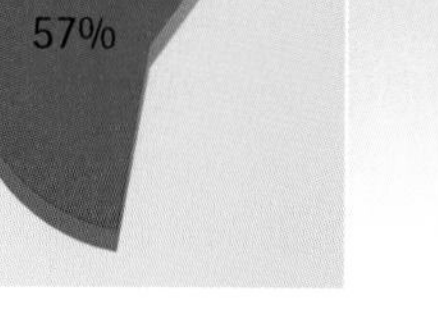
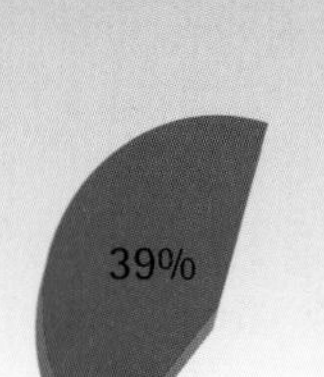

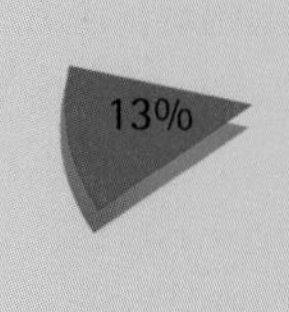

Fact File

The average person in a developed country consumes 3400 calories, 2400 g protein, and 130 g fat daily. The average person in a developing country consumes 2400 calories, 60 g protein, and 45 g fat.

SEE PAGE 76

It's Your World

More and more, high-tech jobs linked to computers are going to developing countries in Asia. In part, this is because wages are lower, but also, Asian workers' skills are increasing. Right now, China has 350 000 information technology engineers completing their degrees. This highly trained workforce is boosting China's ability to attract high-tech economic activity.

REGION

Figure 9.18

The influx of large numbers of skilled workers into China's workforce will dramatically improve its ability to compete in global markets.

Development

A century ago, Canada's economic structure and quality of life were more agrarian (agricultural). Most people were employed in primary industries and lived in rural areas. Over the years, as our economic conditions improved, our way of life changed, too. Our quality of life now ranks among the best in the world.

> *"It really doesn't matter where the work is done as long as quality, price, and service are right."*
> **Kenneth R. Short, businessperson**

We use the term "development" to describe the changes that take place in economic structure. Countries whose economies are becoming less dependent on primary industries and have growing secondary and tertiary industrial sectors are said to be **developing countries**. Many countries in Africa and Asia fit this category. Those countries that already have large proportions of their economies in tertiary industries are called **developed countries**. Canada is a developed country.

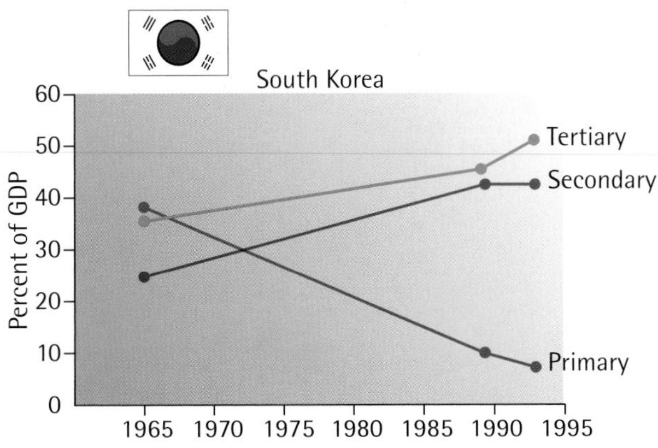

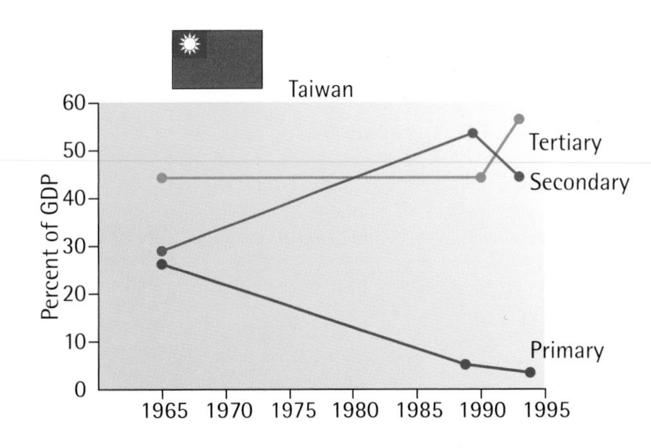

Figure 9.19

Changes in economic structure for (a) South Korea and (b) Taiwan, 1965–1993.

CONNECTIONS TO Environment

Manufacturing can cause serious problems for the environment. In the 1950s and 1960s, hundreds of people in Japan were killed or crippled because of mercury poisoning. A plastics company had been dumping waste mercury into Minamata Bay on the Japanese coast. Fish ate the plants and small animals that had been feeding on smaller life forms, all tainted with the deadly metal. By the time they reached the public, the fish were filled with mercury. While laws are now much more stringent, industries still have problems disposing of their waste products.

Fact File

China's shift from a command economy to a more mixed economy led to a growth in GDP of 10% per year during the 1980s and 1990s.

Development and Happiness

Living in a developed country with a very high quality of life can give Canadians a distorted attitude about happiness and contentment. It is easy to think that people in places with a lower quality of life must be unhappy and discontented. This is not true. We all find happiness in many forms, such as our family and friends, our jobs, patriotism, love, our personal accomplishments, and our spiritual beliefs. People living in countries whose economies are less developed than our own still live happy, contented, productive lives. Further, it is worth noting that even in Canada, surrounded by material wealth, there are many desperately unhappy people. Economic progress, development, and a high quality of life are no guarantee of happiness.

Figure 9.20

Two Tibetan exiles at prayer in a refugee camp in Leh, India. While material wealth is important to health and happiness, it does not guarantee these states of body and mind.

1. Explain why countries that depend on primary industries are also countries rated as having lower qualities of life.
2. Copy the chart below into your notebook. Complete the columns to compare countries with a low quality of life to those that have a high quality of life.

	Low Quality of Life	High Quality of Life
Economic structure • primary industries • secondary industries • tertiary industries		
Ways of living • urban living • level of technology • spending on food		

3. Suppose you are in charge of an agency that gives aid to a developing country. You have only a limited amount of money. What area of the country's economy would you invest in order to do the most good? Explain your answer.

CASE STUDY

E-Commerce

Tertiary economic activities include selling goods and services. These commercial services often take place in retail outlets, such as shopping malls or stores, or they can be done door-to-door or through the mail. A new method of selling that is growing quickly has been termed "e-commerce." E-commerce takes place using the Internet and computers.

> *"The Internet economy is reshaping the fortunes of business, countries, and people and driving the most significant economic shift since the Industrial Revolution."*
>
> **Mike Ansley, businessperson**

The Internet

The Internet links the computing power that exists in governments, universities, schools, factories, offices, and homes around the world through a high-speed telecommunications network. In 1994, three million people used the Internet. By 1998, 100 million people around the world were using it. Experts believe that one billion people will be connected to the Internet by 2005. With one billion potential customers, e-commerce is ready to explode into the business world.

Fact File

Computing power has been doubling every 18 months for the past 30 years. A computer bought today is over 2 million times faster and more powerful than one bought around 1970.

It's Your World

The Internet was adopted faster than any technology in history. Radio existed for 38 years before 50 million people tuned in to it; TV took 13 years to reach that number. Sixteen years after the first personal computers (PCs) appeared on the market, 50 million people were using them. After it was made available to the general public, the Internet reached the 50 million mark in just four years.

Fact File

A computer is switched on for the first time every 2 seconds in North America.

Figure 9.21 The home page of Chapters' Web site (www.chapters.ca). Why might someone buy books on the Internet instead of going to a bookstore?

Figure 9.22

Top 10 users of the Internet, July 1997.

Country	Number of Computers Connected
United States	15 646 597
United Kingdom	1 155 546
Japan	1 073 807
Germany	912 116
Canada	852 242
Australia	744 854
Finland	409 702
Netherlands	352 124
France	314 082
Sweden	305 890

Figure 9.23

Advantages of e-commerce for consumers.

Advantage	Explanation
Choice	Online customers can shop at stores anywhere in the world rather than be limited to stores within driving or walking distance.
Better information	Web consumers are often better informed than their offline counterparts. Product information can be provided in digital form.
Lower prices	Because consumers can access many more sources, competition is intense. Many Internet retailers offer discounts over regular sources to attract buyers. Booksellers have used this strategy to their advantage.
Customization	Some information products can be tailored to individual consumers. For example, readers of electronic magazines can receive just the news that they want to read.

Businesses began using the Internet for commercial transactions in the 1990s. People said it was faster, easier, and more convenient to buy or sell products and services on the Internet. By 2002, some experts predict that the Internet will be used for more than $300 billion worth of buying and selling. Most of this e-commerce will be in two forms: delivery of information and retail sale of goods.

Fact File

The Internet was developed in the 1970s by the U.S. army to speed up the transfer of research data. Commercial Internet service networks developed a decade later.

> *"To sell things online, you need to show people pictures. ... Whether there's gold out there or not, the Gold Rush is definitely happening."*
>
> **Charles Seiter, Internet consultant and author**

Delivery of Information and Goods

Digital information such as software programs, newspapers, and music no longer needs to be produced, packaged, and delivered to retail outlets. These formats can be delivered directly to customers electronically over the Internet. The Internet is also used to buy and sell goods and services that are not in digital forms, such as computers, cars, books, CDs, and flowers. Today, Internet sales are less than one percent of total retail sales, but sales are expanding rapidly.

MOVEMENT/PATTERN

Challenges of E-Commerce

E-commerce has raised some issues and problems, such as personal security and invasion of privacy. Transactions on the Internet usually involve the transfer of personal information — such as your credit card number — to unknown recipients. After that information has been sent, it can potentially be used in other ways that the customer may not know about. Canada is working to put in place laws to ensure fair trade practices in e-commerce, but the global scale of the Internet makes enforcement difficult.

Easy access to the Internet also has the potential to expose people to pornographic, violent, and hate materials.

Criminals are finding new and ingenious ways of using the Internet and e-commerce for personal gain. Each innovation in communications opens new opportunities for ordinary people, businesses, and criminals alike. Problems of this type will have to be solved before e-commerce gains universal acceptance in societies around the world.

Figure 9.24

People who continue to develop new skills throughout their lifespan will be able to make the best use of innovations like computers and the Internet, whether in the workplace or in the marketplace.

SEE PAGE 66

Connections to Careers The growing strength of e-commerce and other Internet-related economic activities means that you, as a worker of the future, will need to have solid computer skills. Programmers will be needed to design and set up e-commerce software. Retailers will need the skills to use the software to plan and run their operations. The rapidly changing nature of computers will require that workers be flexible, lifelong learners.

Check Back

1. Brainstorm three endings to the sentence beginning: "An important advantage that the Internet has for me as a consumer is..." Write each sentence in your notebook.
2. Suppose you work for a store owner who has asked for your advice about setting up a Web site to sell her goods. What would you identify as the advantages and disadvantages of e-commerce? Write a five-sentence paragraph giving your ideas.
3. Make up an advertisement to promote the use of the Internet to sell CDs. Think of an "e-commerce way" of getting the message across to the public. Or, your advertisement could take the form of a print ad, a poster, or a script for a TV commercial.
4. Should schools use e-commerce for buying supplies, getting resources for the library, or communicating? Give your views in a one-page written statement, using facts to back up your opinions.

Understanding the Concepts

1. You have been asked to give a speech about which one of primary, secondary, and tertiary industries you think is most important. Write an outline of the main points of the speech that you will give.

2. Write a paragraph in which you use the following words about economic structure and economic development:

natural resources	finished products
changes	quality of life
developing countries	material goods

3. Look at Figure 9.25, a picture taken in Yemen. What does this photograph tell you about the economic life of the people who live in this area?

Research and Communication Skills

4. Collect a variety of pictures about countries that have high percentages of their workforce involved in primary industries. Make a list of 10 descriptive terms that express the quality of life of the people in the pictures.

5. Conduct research on each of these countries to identify the single most important reason why each has not been able to improve its economic structure in the past few decades.
   a) Iraq
   b) Bosnia-Herzegovina
   c) Burma (Myanmar)

6. Conduct research on each of these countries to identify the single most important reason for optimism about their future in the next few years.
   a) Panama
   b) Chile
   c) South Africa

Figure 9.25

How do you think radio-phone and cell-phone technologies have affected people living in rural areas of less developed countries?

GO TO **www.odci.gov/cia/publications/factbook/index.html** to begin your research on these countries.

Map and Globe Skills

7. Using an atlas or an Internet source, draw a map of Brazil, a developing country that is changing its economic structure. Label important cities, rivers, and landforms on your map. Shade agricultural areas in green, and built-up areas in pink. The built-up areas will be the parts of the country where manufacturing and services are most concentrated. On the back of your map, write a paragraph describing the distribution of primary, secondary, and tertiary industries in Brazil.

GO TO

www.lib.utexas.edu/Libs/PCL/Map_collection/Map_collection.html

This Web site has a great collection of maps that you can download and print. See what their map is like for Brazil. Click on the map of Canada. Use that map to judge the reliability of the maps in this collection.

8. Percentages of GDP earned by each sector of the economy for three unnamed countries are given in Figure 9.26. Using an atlas and your knowledge of world patterns, identify two possible countries that each could be.

Applications

9. Here are some possible events that could happen in the future. Describe the impact on e-commerce of each of these events.

   a) A computer virus makes all computers break down.
   b) Innovations in manufacturing allow computers to be sold for $100.
   c) Computers become a required piece of equipment on every desk in every classroom.

10. You are a television interviewer who has been given a few minutes to talk to the leader of a developing country about economic conditions in that country. Make up five questions that you would like to ask.

Figure 9.26
GDP earned by sector of economy.

	Primary Industry	Secondary Industry	Tertiary Industry	HDI Score
Country A	50	14	36	0.347
Country B	8	41	51	0.735
Country C	2	33	65	0.932

Canada's Economy

EXPECTATIONS

- demonstrate an understanding of the manufacturing system (e.g., input, process, output, feedback), and describe how mechanization and technology have changed the Canadian economy
- identify the top trading countries of the world and the reasons for their success
- investigate and describe the advantages and disadvantages of economic associations such as the North American Free Trade Agreement and the European Union

Different Voices, Many Choices

Canadians have one of the highest qualities of life in the world. Yet, if you listen to the news or hear people talk, you get a bleak picture of how life is going in Canada. "Taxes are too high," some people complain. "More money should be spent on health care and education," others reply. "Our businesses are leaving to go to countries where wages are lower." "We need to work harder to compete with developing countries in Asia." "We aren't developing our high-tech skills fast enough." Everyone seems to criticize Canada's economy. But, criticism isn't necessarily a bad thing.

High taxes keep industries away

Canada's future bleak: Economic think tank report

Exports up, trade

Health care wo

Canadian brain drain: Professionals flock to U.S. job

Figure 10.1

There are many views on the economy. What do you think your future in Canada will be like? Why?

> *"In the past, an insatiable world appetite for raw materials and primary products allowed Canada to compete effectively in the global marketplace and develop robust manufacturing sectors. However, in recent years it has become clear that controlling unprocessed resources can no longer guarantee prosperity."*
>
> Stuart Corbridge, editor, "World Economy"

In Canada we have a **mixed economy**. That is, decisions about what business can and can't do, how we spend our taxes, and other marketplace issues are influenced by many different people. Voices are heard from government and business, from consumers, and from environmental groups and other organizations. Thus, every day many different voices are giving very different views about the economy and what we should do about it. This is a democratic process, and it is time-consuming and sometimes confusing. Also, not everyone will be happy with the economic system that results. But, this process does allow the greatest input for Canadians to shape their economy.

From Goods to Services

SEE PAGE 72

Figure 10.2

Canada's economic structure by percentage of workers in different sectors, 1951–1991. What trends do you notice in the data?

Year	Primary Industries (Resources)	Secondary Industries (Manufacturing)	Tertiary Industries (Services)
1951	22.8%	33.3%	43.9%
1961	14.2%	30.2%	55.6%
1971	9.1%	28.3%	62.6%
1981	6.2%	28.8%	65.0%
1991	5.5%	21.3%	73.2%

ure bright

ers to strike

Canadians lack high-tech skills:
More college programs needed

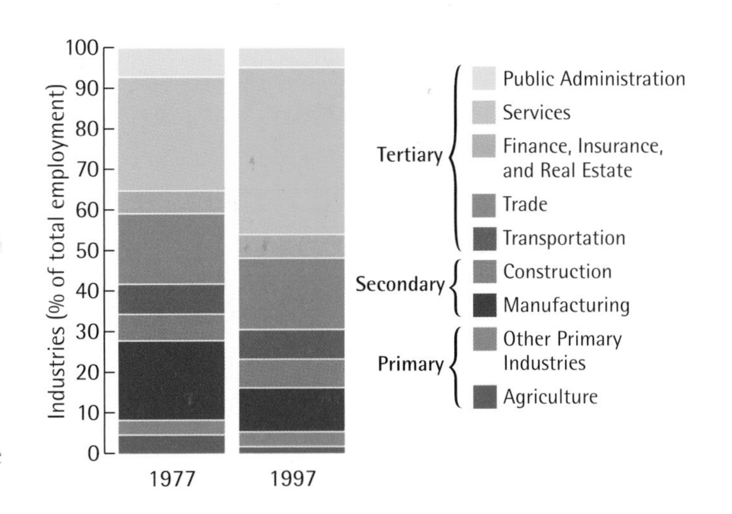

Figure 10.3

Canadian employment by industry, 1977 and 1997. What are the most significant changes in jobs over the 20 years shown in the graph?

Figure 10.4

Provincial employment by industry, 1997. Which regions have strong primary industries? Why do you think they developed where they did?

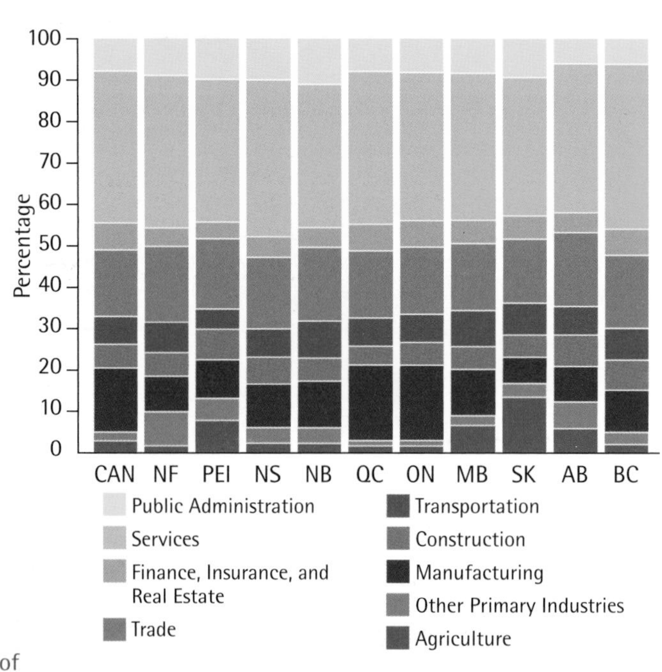

Fact File

Employment Insurance (EI) pays temporary benefits to people who are out of work. In 1997, EI payments for all of Canada totalled $12 018 601 000.

Figure 10.5

Unemployment rates in Canada by province, 1997. Which regions have the highest levels of unemployment? Which have the lowest levels? Why do you think this is so?

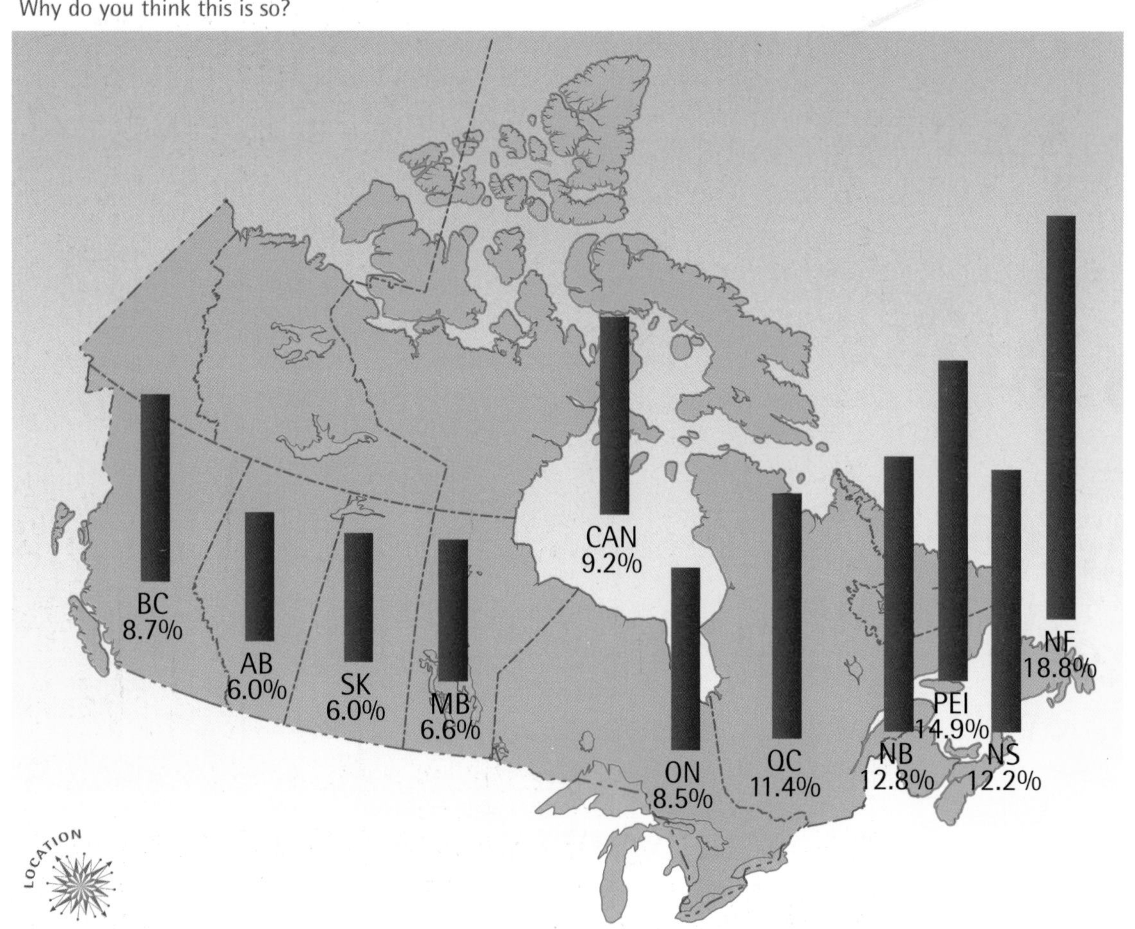

Canada's Imports and Exports

Figure 10.6

Canada's imports and exports over a 60-year period. What patterns do you see in the data? Why do you think these patterns developed?

	Exports			Imports		
Year	to USA	to U.K.	to others	from USA	from U.K.	from others
1937	36%	38%	26%	61%	18%	21%
1950	65%	15%	20%	67%	13%	20%
1975	66%	6%	28%	68%	4%	28%
1997	68%	2%	30%	82%	1%	17%

Figure 10.7

Imports to Canada, 1997. Why do you suppose we import so much from the United States?

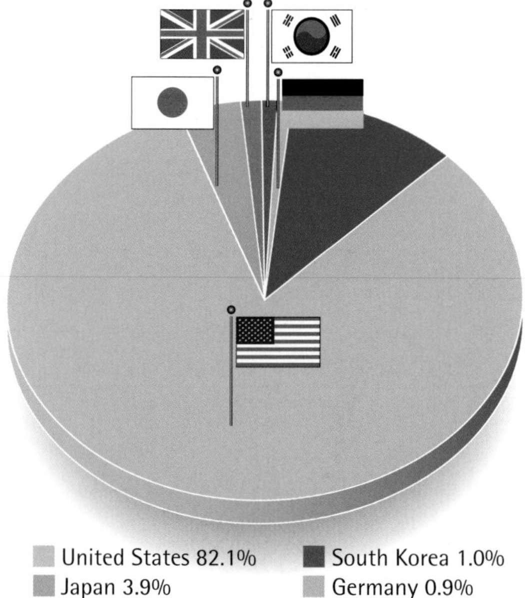

Figure 10.8

Exports from Canada, 1997. Which buyers of Canadian products do you think are becoming more important to our economy? Why do you think this is happening?

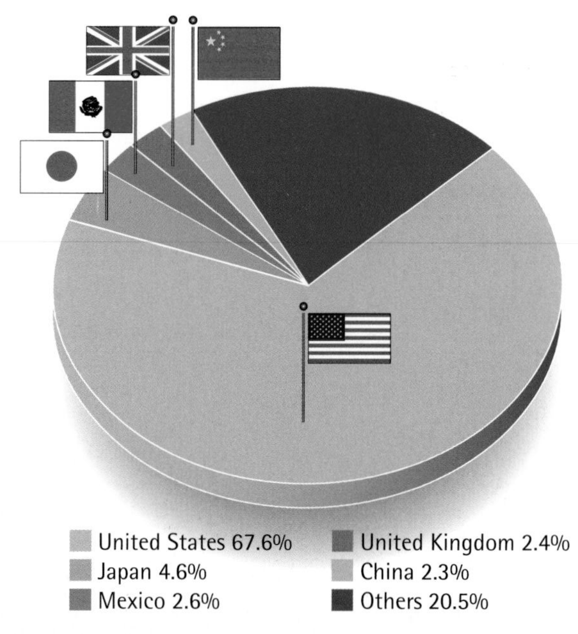

Figure 10.9

Canada's imports and exports by category, 1997. Why do you think we export and import machinery? Why don't we just make all the machinery that we need here in Canada?

Imports (billions)	Category	Exports (billions)
$39.7	Machinery and other equipment	$40.3
$17.7	Passenger autos and chassis	$36.6
$14.4	Metals and alloys	$20.0
$11.2	Agricultural and fishing products	$19.6
$34.4	Motor vehicle parts	$19.0
$19.5	Chemicals, plastics, and fertilizers	$17.0
$25.5	Industrial and agricultural machinery	$14.7
$8.6	Trucks and other motor vehicles	$14.5
$10.9	Aircraft and other transportation equipment	$12.9
$20.5	Industrial goods and materials	$12.9
$7.2	Crude petroleum	$10.0
$69.3	Other	$54.0

It's Your World

Quebec is the second largest producer of manufactured goods in the country. However, demands for separation from Canada and the political instability that goes with separatism have slowed the province's economic growth.

Figure 10.10

Commercial property for rent in Montreal. Since Quebec's 1980 referendum on sovereignty, many companies have moved their head offices and key manufacturing facilities to other provinces.

1. Using the data in this section of the chapter, make three true statements about the structure of Canada's economy.
2. Suppose you wanted to take three photographs, or draw three images, that would show the structure of the Canadian economy. What images would you choose? Explain your choices.
3. Based on the information in this chapter, what do you think is the most important problem facing the Canadian economy? Which facts led you to this conclusion?

Why is Our Economy Changing?

All economies change over time. Sometimes the changes are good and mean a better quality of life for people. In Canada, over the last 50 years, the growth of tertiary industries (i.e., personal and business services, software development, or retail sales) has been a good change that has created more jobs. However, changes in a country's economy can also have bad consequences. For example, in recent years Canada has lost many manufacturing jobs because companies have moved their factories to developing countries where wages are lower and profits will be higher.

Whether economic changes are good or bad, it is important to analyse what causes them, so that we can make the economy work better for Canadians. Two forces have been particularly important in recent

Fact File

After Mexico signed the North American Free Trade Agreement (NAFTA), automobile makers invested heavily in that country. The number of automobiles manufactured there increased from 1.2 million in 1995 to 2 million in 2000.

> *"The greatest error in economics is in seeing the economy as a stable, immutable structure."*
> **John Kenneth Galbraith, economist**

Figure 10.11

Canada has long been a trading nation, as these containers of trade goods in Vancouver's harbour demonstrate. Globalization of the world's economy has made our trade relations even more important. Why is world trade so important to Canadians?

years: globalization, and the creation of special **trade agreements** among countries to form trading blocs. A **trading bloc** is a partnership among countries that makes importing and exporting goods and services cheaper, easier, and more efficient.

One Big World

SEE PAGE 100

Globalization is a trend toward increasing trade among the world's countries. In the past, most countries protected their local industries by limiting competition from abroad. This is called **protectionism**, and was meant to ensure jobs and a good economic future for their citizens. Two ways of protecting local industry are:

- to reduce foreign imports (that is, don't let in goods made outside the country); and
- to impose taxes, or **tariffs**, on imported goods. Because tariffs make imported goods more expensive than domestic goods (items produced locally), they encourage consumers to buy products made in their own countries.

"Protectionism ... can only make industry less competitive. But free trade is not the answer ... . One answer is to form economic regions or blocs ... . This would give smaller economies the large region and market they need to create the 'critical mass' of production and the sales needed to be competitive."

Peter F. Drucker,
"The New Realities"

Protectionism can stimulate local industries and create jobs. But, it also reduces the competition that encourages businesses to stay productive. Reduced competition can result in poor-quality, expensive consumer goods, and industries that are inefficient and out of date.

In recent years, most countries have moved toward **free trade**. The "free" in free trade means there are no taxes or conditions. Tariffs and other rules about foreign goods have been reduced or eliminated. As a result, goods and services produced in one country can be sold in almost any other country around the world. Free trade means more competition worldwide.

GO TO

www.csl.ca/links.html

This site tells how ships carry and unload their cargoes. Click on Our Ships at the left of your screen. Choose How a Self-Unloader Works. Read through this set of pictures and explanations. Look up any words you are unsure of. Write a point-form report on how these new ships work.

Benefits of Globalization

People who support globalization and free trade claim that competition makes businesses and industries more efficient. In order to compete successfully with firms from around the world, a business must become very good at what it does. That is, it must reduce its costs, increase the quality of its products, and develop better production methods. Consumers benefit because they have access to cheaper, better-quality products and services.

MOVEMENT/PATTERN

> ***“We cannot survive as an island in a sea of change ... co-operation is in our own self-interest.”***
>
> **Rufus Yerxa, U.S. Ambassador**

With globalization, countries produce only those items that they are best at producing, and buy what is necessary to meet their needs and wants. Each country specializes in economic activities in which it has an advantage over other countries. For example, countries with highly educated populations, like Canada, focus on high-tech industries such as aerospace and telecommunications. Countries with low wage rates, like Mexico, produce lower-tech goods such as textiles and car parts.

Figure 10.12

Foreign-made vehicles for sale in Canada. What advantages are there for consumers in allowing imports of products like these without trade protections?

Connections to Business

Bombardier is a Canadian company that makes vehicles, including aircraft, trains, Sea-Doos, and Ski-Doos. Although the Ski-Doo was patented in 1959, Joseph-Armand Bombardier built his first “snow machine” in 1922, when he was only 15. This experimental model had four sleigh runners and was powered by a propeller and a four-cylinder Ford Model T engine.

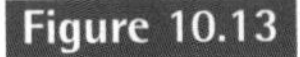

Figure 10.13

Joseph-Armand Bombardier’s first Ski-Doo, 1922.

Figure 10.14

The Canadarm was designed and built in Canada for the U.S. space shuttle. With free trade, countries specialize in those activities they do best. In what other industries, besides aerospace, do you think Canada has an advantage?

Fact File

Economic advantages may include a country's

- natural resources
- workforce skills
- technology
- location
- history
- traditions

Fact File

From 1950 to 2000, the richest 20% of the world's population increased their share of the world's wealth from 70% to 83%. The poorest 20% saw their share fall from 2.3% to 1.4%. The old saying that the rich get richer and the poor get poorer seems to be true.

Problems with Globalization

Not all countries have the economic advantages to compete successfully in the global marketplace. For example, the countries of sub-Saharan Africa have few natural resources, locations that don't encourage manufacturing, low literacy and skill levels, and a history of colonization that left them with poor economies and unstable political systems. Developing countries in Asia and the Americas face similar problems. The countries that are best able to compete are those that are already doing well, like Japan, the United States, and Canada. Globalization is widening the gap between rich and poor countries. The rich countries are making more money faster than ever before.

"The problem with the specialized division of labour between nations is that some nations specialize in winning and others in losing."

Eduardo Galeano, Uruguayan historian

Globalization also causes unemployment, even in industrialized countries like Canada. Increased competition means that inefficient industries are forced to shut down. Workers lose their jobs. Some workers may find new jobs with businesses that are successful and are growing. Often, however, these workers do not have the required skills, or cannot move to places where jobs are being created. The unemployment and closing of businesses that goes along with globalization is called **structural adjustment.**

"Fair trade, NOT free trade!"

Anti-free trade slogan used by opposition groups to the NAFTA proposal

Further, in a global marketplace, the need to keep costs low and profits high may mean that countries neglect the social benefits that improve people's quality of life. For example, a government may refuse to take a tough stand on environmental problems (which might increase the cost of production) or to protect the rights of its workers (which might increase the cost of labour). That means everyone may suffer because one company wants to make more money.

Fact File

Large multinational companies such as General Motors and Ford have sales larger than the GNPs of many countries, including South Africa and Norway.

Trading Blocs

Some countries get together to form a private trading club called a bloc. They make special rules to help them trade with each other more easily. A trading bloc links the economies of the countries together. This has two advantages:

- the linked economies of the countries are much larger and more powerful on the global scene
- the countries can exchange resources more easily and efficiently.

Figure 10.15

Workers protest outside a plant that has closed its Canadian branches and moved to Mexico. Should the Canadian government attempt to stop such closures?

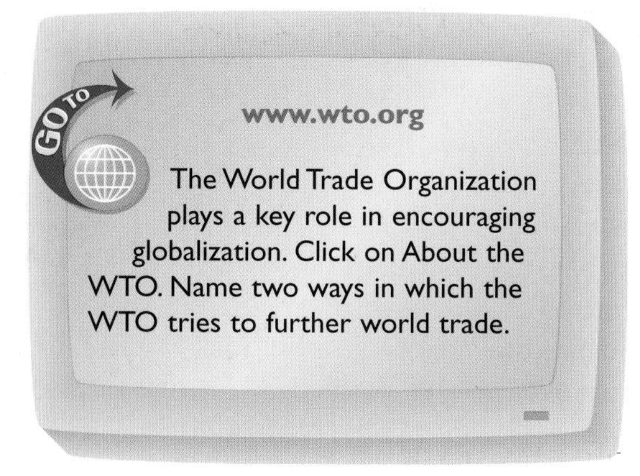

Figure 10.16

Important trading blocs of the world, 1998.

Name of Trading Bloc	Number of Members	Total Population (millions)
Andean Pact (Bolivia, Colombia, Ecuador, Peru, Venezuela)	5	105
Association of Caribbean States	25	199
European Union (EU)	15	372
North American Free Trade Agreement (NAFTA)	3	396
Southern Common Market (Argentina, Brazil, Paraguay, Uruguay)	4	209

The European Union

Of all free trade agreements, the European Union takes the idea of a trading bloc the farthest. Goods and services move freely among the 15 member countries, as does capital (money). A European Parliament makes rules about economic and political matters that apply to all countries. In addition, the EU countries use a common form of money (the "euro") to make business transactions even easier.

SEE PAGE 229

Figure 10.17

The member countries of the European Union. Can you think of two advantages that these countries enjoy by being part of this trading bloc?

The North American Free Trade Agreement

In 1994, the **North American Free Trade Agreement** (NAFTA) created a trading bloc among Canada, the United States, and Mexico. The agreement did not create the same close links as the European Union, but it did encourage greater economic co-operation among the three countries. The main points of the agreement are:

REGION

- to eliminate barriers to trade, and to speed the movement of goods across borders;
- to increase investment opportunities;
- to create procedures to resolve disputes quickly; and
- to look for ways to expand the benefits of the agreement, including bringing other countries into it.

SEE PAGE 37

Chile is being considered for membership in NAFTA. There has also been some discussion about a common currency for the trading bloc.

Fact File

The total value of all the goods and services produced by the three countries of NAFTA is valued at $6 trillion per year. Written with all the zeros, this is $6 000 000 000 000. If you counted at the rate of one number per second, you would have to count for almost 11.5 million years to get to 6 trillion.

1. What do you suppose the quote on page 192 means? What kinds of co-operation do you think the speaker is referring to?
2. Design a chart to compare three advantages and three disadvantages of globalization. Then make a similar chart comparing three advantages and three disadvantages of free trade. Include both developing and developed countries.
3. Suppose you were a member of Parliament at the time of the vote to accept or reject the North American Free Trade Agreement. Would you have voted in favour of it, or against it? Give reasons for your opinion.

CASE STUDY

Canada's Car Makers

The Canadian automobile manufacturing industry is one of the most successful and competitive in the world. Canada is the world's seventh largest producer of motor vehicles. Over 147 000 Canadians are directly employed in manufacturing cars and trucks. This figure represents 8.4% of Canadian manufacturing employment and 11.6% of Canadian manufacturing earnings.

Figure 10.18

Automobile workers on an assembly line. What are two advantages and two disadvantages for employees working in a large plant like this?

SEE PAGE 74

Fact File

Wages in automobile manufacturing are 23% higher than the average manufacturing wage in Canada.

Auto Manufacturing and NAFTA

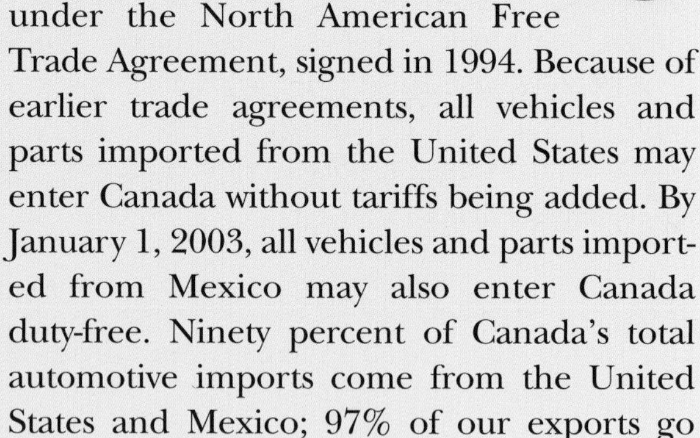

The Canadian auto industry is closely linked with the industries in the United States and Mexico under the North American Free Trade Agreement, signed in 1994. Because of earlier trade agreements, all vehicles and parts imported from the United States may enter Canada without tariffs being added. By January 1, 2003, all vehicles and parts imported from Mexico may also enter Canada duty-free. Ninety percent of Canada's total automotive imports come from the United States and Mexico; 97% of our exports go back to these two countries.

Many Canadians prefer to drive foreign-made vehicles. NAFTA helped the Canadian auto industry by requiring that foreign car companies set up manufacturing facilities in Canada if they wanted to have the tariffs removed. This created thousands of jobs for Canadians. Since the early 1990s, Japanese and European companies have increased their production in North America, and non-NAFTA imports (vehicles made outside North America) have declined.

Figure 10.19

World's top 10 auto manufacturers (thousands of vehicles). Which countries have changed their level of production most over the time period? Which have remained the most stable?

Position	Country	1965	1980	1996
1	United States	11 114	8 010	11 715
2	Japan	1 876	11 043	10 099
3	Germany	2 976	3 879	4 843
4	France	1 642	3 378	3 597
5	South Korea	0	123	2 812
6	Spain	229	1 182	2 421
7	Canada	846	1 374	2 367
8	United Kingdom	2 177	1 313	1 930
9	Brazil	185	1 165	1 819
10	Italy	1 176	1 612	1 211

Figure 10.20

New vehicles manufactured in Canada may be transported by ship, rail, or truck for sale in the United States or Mexico.

Fact File

In 1997, Canadians purchased about 1.4 million cars, vans, and pickup trucks, but produced almost double that number (2.5 million units).

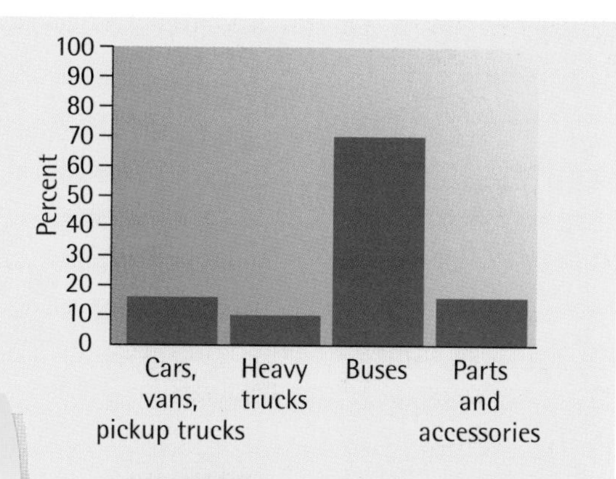

Figure 10.21

Percentage of North American motor vehicles made in Canada. Can you name one manufacturer or vehicle for each category?

Figure 10.22

The proportion of vehicles sold in Canada that are made overseas, 1983–1997. What are some factors that might influence the rate at which Canadians buy non-North American vehicles?

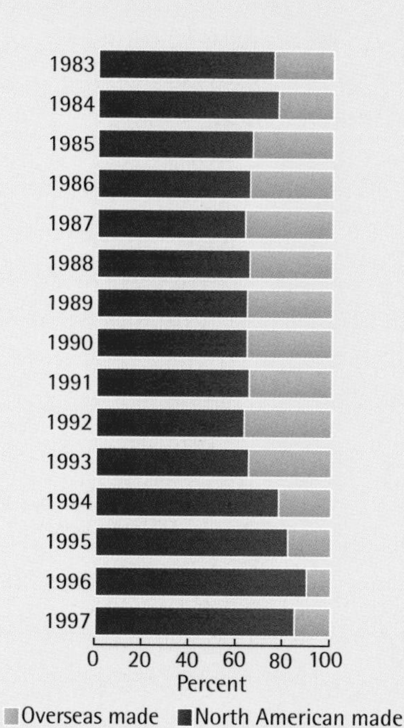

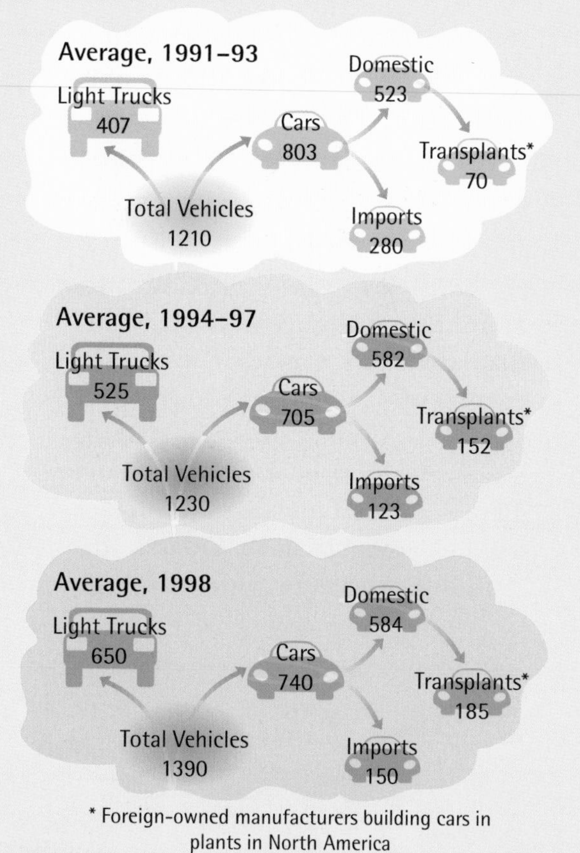

Figure 10.23

Automobile sales in Canada (thousands of vehicles). According to the data, what has been the impact of NAFTA since 1994?

Two pioneers in the Canadian automobile manufacturing industry were Sam and George McLaughlin. The McLaughlin company in Oshawa originally produced buggies. The McLaughlins saw that the "horseless carriage" was the way of the future, so they began to experiment with motors. By 1908, McLaughlin automobiles were travelling Canadian roadways. The firm became part of General Motors in 1918. Some of the many displays at the Canadian Automotive Museum in Oshawa show the role the McLaughlin family played in the car industry in Canada.

Figure 10.24

Robots spray and polish new auto bodies. What other types of jobs do you think robots would do better than human workers? What are some of the new skills that humans need in order to work with the robotic assembly line?

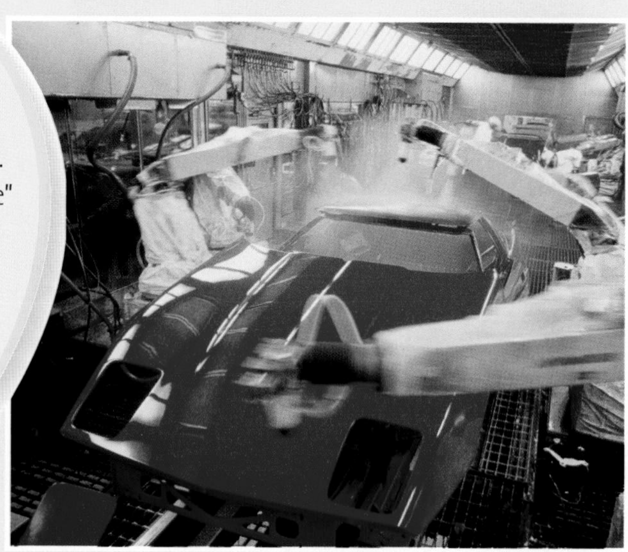

SEE PAGE 77

Reasons for Canada's Success

Canadian auto manufacturing has been successful largely because of three factors.

- *Competitive wage rates.* Taking into account the difference in the U.S. and Canadian dollars, Canadian wage rates are currently about 25% lower than those of U.S. auto workers, making auto plants north of the border more profitable. Although wages in Mexico are much lower than in Canada, the Mexican labour force right now lacks the technological skills that Canadian workers possess.
- *Better productivity.* **Productivity** is the efficiency with which *inputs* (labour, technology, capital) are used to produce *outputs* (vehicles). Largely because of a highly skilled workforce, Canadian automobile plants have consistently been more productive than U.S. and Mexican locations. We produce more, better, faster, and cheaper than the United States or Mexico.
- *Favourable business environment.* Canadian governments have encouraged manufacturing through trade policies that support innovation and investment. Companies that do research get lower taxes.

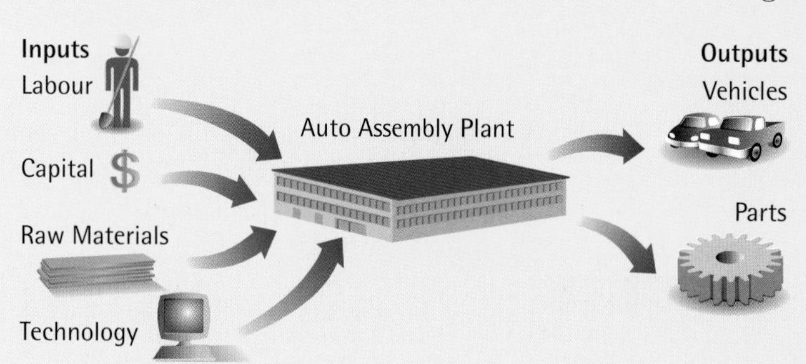

Figure 10.25

The manufacturing process.

How a Car is Made

Automobile manufacturing has two stages: parts and assembly. Thousands of factories scattered around the continent and overseas produce car parts. Magna International, a Canadian-owned firm, is one of the most successful car parts makers in the world. The car parts are shipped to a much smaller number of large auto assembly plants located at key sites. An auto assembly plant requires these locational advantages:

- near or in a large market;
- skilled labour force;
- excellent rail and road transportation;
- inexpensive building site; and
- available capital.

Figure 10.26

Automobile assembly plants in Canada. How would you describe the pattern of the plants' locations?

In Canada, these location characteristics are most often found in southern Ontario and southern Quebec, where most of the 14 assembly plants have been built. Because these plants employ thousands of workers, they have a great impact on the local economy.

U.S. corporations (such as the "Big Three" — Ford, General Motors, and Daimler-Chrysler) own most of the auto assembly plants in Canada. As large as these firms are, in order to remain competitive globally, they have had to develop partnerships with Japanese companies. For example, the General Motors–Suzuki assembly plant in Ingersoll, Ontario produces Suzuki vehicles under GM's Geo brand name. Partnerships allow the Japanese auto makers' products to be sold duty-free in NAFTA countries, and give the North American car makers access to Japanese technology and products. Some Japanese manufacturers, such as Honda (with a plant at Alliston, Ontario), have built their own facilities and are not involved in partnerships with the Big Three.

Fact File

Canada has over 550 plants involved in manufacturing car parts.

Given its recent success and the impacts of NAFTA, the Canadian auto manufacturing industry is optimistic about its future.

1. Make up a bumper sticker encouraging people to buy Canadian-made automobiles. Make sure that your bumper sticker gives a reason for "buying Canadian."
2. Make up a four-sentence paragraph in which you correctly use the following terms:
   NAFTA transplant
   Big Three productivity
3. Make up three endings for the sentence beginning: "The Canadian automobile manufacturing industry has been successful because..."
4. Would you, personally, like to be employed in a car manufacturing plant? Why or why not?

Understanding the Concepts

1. You have been asked to give a speech to foreign business people about the advantages of doing business in Canada. What would be the three most important points that you would make in your speech?

2. **a)** Give evidence to support the view that NAFTA has been good for the Canadian economy.
b) Explain why some people oppose NAFTA.

3. You have an opportunity to interview the president of one of the Big Three auto companies about the auto manufacturing industry in Canada. Make up five questions about the industry that you would like to have answered. Make sure that your questions demonstrate your understanding of the industry.

Research and Communication Skills

4. Collect at least five newspaper, magazine, or Internet articles about Canada's economy. For each one, summarize the main point of the article and write down one fact offered by the writer.

5. Choose one of Canada's important trading partners from those given in Figures 10.7 and 10.8 on page 189. Find out what goods Canadians buy from that country, and what goods we sell to them. Is our trade with this country changing? Describe any trends you see. Present your conclusions in a poster or in a PowerPoint presentation.

6. Conduct research to find out which other countries are being considered for entry into the North American Free Trade Agreement. Identify the three countries that you think are most likely to be accepted as partners. Give reasons for your choices.

Map and Globe Skills

7. Figure 10.19 on page 196 lists the top 10 auto-producing countries in the world. Using an outline map of the world, shade and label these countries.

   a) In a paragraph, describe the pattern that you see. What factors do you think created this pattern?
   b) In what ways do you think the pattern of auto production will change in 20 years? In what ways will it be the same?

8. Figure 10.27 shows Montreal's harbourfront. Place a piece of tracing paper over the photo and mark the areas that house the city's important economic activities, e.g., port facilities, older commercial areas, newer commercial areas, residential districts, and recreational areas.

Applications

9. Is globalization a good trend for Canadians and Canadian economic activity? Write a paragraph that answers this question, using facts to support your opinion. Compare your answer to a classmate's. Discuss any differences in your opinions.

GO TO

www.tourism-montreal.org/maps.htm

Click on the map at the right, Old Montreal/Old Port, to open this map. You can make it larger by clicking on the 20% button and selecting 75% in the pull-down window. This site gives a very good look at how the Port of Montreal works.

10 Read the newspaper article below.

a) What is meant by "outsourcing"?

b) How does outsourcing improve the competitiveness of the Canadian auto manufacturing industry?

c) Why are auto workers opposed to outsourcing?

11 You are the person responsible for hiring workers for an auto assembly plant in Canada. Make a list of the skills, experience, and attitudes that you want to see in people who apply for jobs. Organize your lists into a chart.

More Canadian Parts in Cars

Content doubles to $2000 for each vehicle: Report

SEOUL – The value of Canadian-made parts in North American-built cars has doubled since the mid-1980s to nearly $2000 in every vehicle, new industry figures show.

Most of that growth has come in the past seven years, as the Canadian auto parts industry outpaced that in the United States, according to the Canadian Auto Report released yesterday by Scotia Economics.

"Canadian auto parts suppliers are benefiting from increased outsourcing by auto makers," said Carlos Gomes, a Bank of Nova Scotia economist, who specializes in the auto industry.

But outsourcing, when companies contract out work to suppliers who can do it more cheaply, is also a tremendous source of contention between auto makers and their unionized workers, who protest the resulting loss of jobs.

Figure 10.27

Montreal's harbourfront.

UNIT 2 Economic Systems

PERFORMANCE TASK: Concepts, Skills, and Applications

New Industry: Economic Impacts

A great deal of economic activity takes place in a region when a new, large manufacturing plant opens. The new industry brings new economic opportunities, especially new jobs. The new workers at the plant will spend their pay cheques in the community on many different goods and services like food, entertainment, clothes, homes, banking, and car repairs. That spending creates even more jobs in the related stores and offices offering those goods and services to the new workers. New taxes flow into the community that is spent on improving and increasing the services to residents. This creates even more jobs. All of the economic activity that comes from that first new set of jobs is called the **multiplier effect**. The diagram below shows how one dollar from one worker moves through the community and multiplies as it goes.

The Multiplier Effect

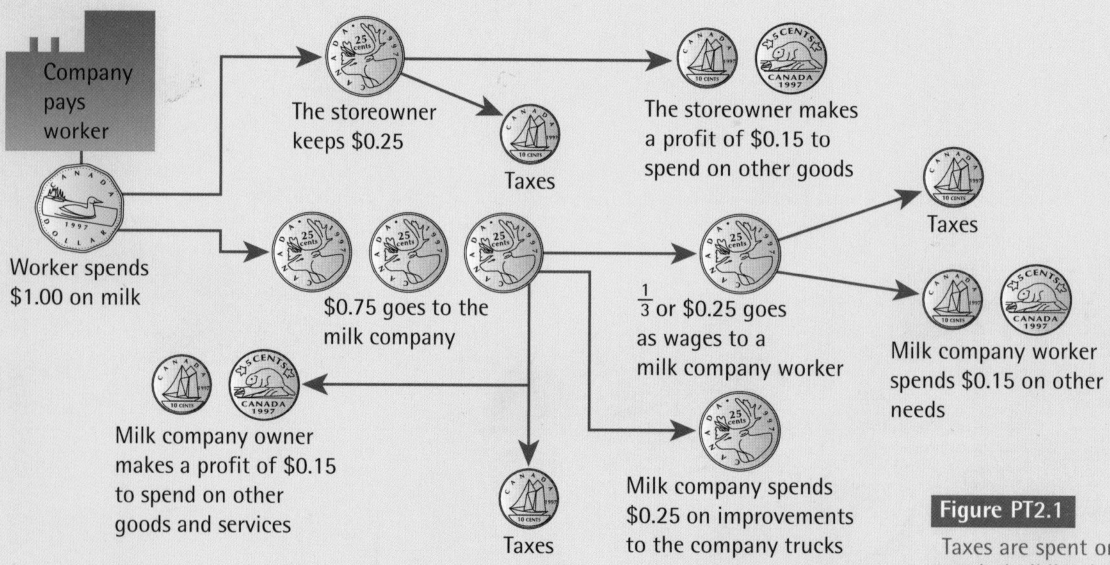

Company pays worker

Worker spends $1.00 on milk

The storeowner keeps $0.25

Taxes

The storeowner makes a profit of $0.15 to spend on other goods

$0.75 goes to the milk company

$\frac{1}{3}$ or $0.25 goes as wages to a milk company worker

Taxes

Milk company worker spends $0.15 on other needs

Milk company owner makes a profit of $0.15 to spend on other goods and services

Taxes

Milk company spends $0.25 on improvements to the company trucks

Figure PT2.1

Taxes are spent on fixing roads, building hospitals, running schools, and the many other goods and services needed by a community.

Often, new industries cause changes in the local area that not everyone agrees are good. They can have negative effects, like water and air pollution, dangerous by-products like heavy metals, waste scrap, and used chemicals, overcrowding of roadways and other facilities, and noise.

Unfortunately, the multiplier effect can work in reverse as well. Once an industry has been in business for a while, the community depends upon it. When it closes, workers are thrown out of jobs. Because there are no more wages going into the local economy, stores and businesses suffer and other workers loose their jobs. The economy of the whole area goes into a down turn.

Your Task

1. Here are some headlines that might appear in a local newspaper. Each one points out an aspect about growth from a new industry. In your notebook, draw a flow diagram like Figure PT2.2. Insert the headlines, shown below, into the most appropriate boxes.

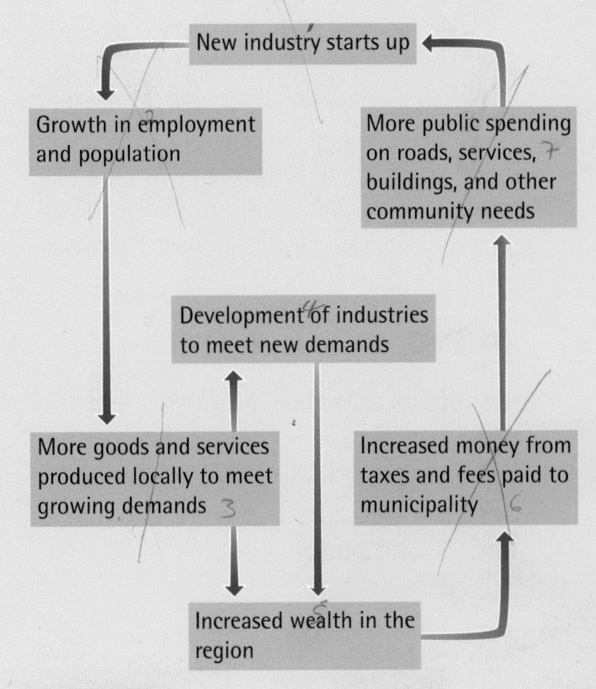

Figure PT2.2

The positive effects of a new, large industry on a community. Small businesses that start up or expand are important as well, but their impacts are harder to see.

Average income for town highest in province
— Statistics Canada report

City Council spending spree:
mayor claims meeting needs of community

Expressway construction plan approved

Prime Minister lays first brick at new auto assembly plant:
construction on schedule

Bargains galore:
shopping mall reports best year ever

Sports equipment company to manufacture here:
300 permanent jobs

Unemployment rate falls to lowest level in decade

2. In the flow diagram in Figure PT 2.2, the arrows show connections or effects. For each arrow in your flow diagram, explain what the connection or effect is and offer reasons why it occurs.
3. Use the flow diagram in Figure PT 2.2 to explain why "multiplier effect" is a good term to use to describe the effects of a new large industry in a community.
4. **a)** Brainstorm a list of five ways that business people may find opportunities when a new plant opens in a region.
   b) Identify five ways that workers may find opportunities.
5. Suppose a new automobile assembly plant was built in or near your community. What are three ways that your community would be affected? Explain which changes you think may be good and which ones may be bad.

UNIT 3

Migration

EXPECTATIONS

- identify factors that affect migration and mobility
- demonstrate an understanding of the ways in which cultures are affected by migration
- describe patterns and trends in migration and their effects on Canada

① Slavery was a blight on our culture. Research when Canada and the US outlawed slavery.

② Helping people in other cultures eventually helps us all. Why do you think this is so?

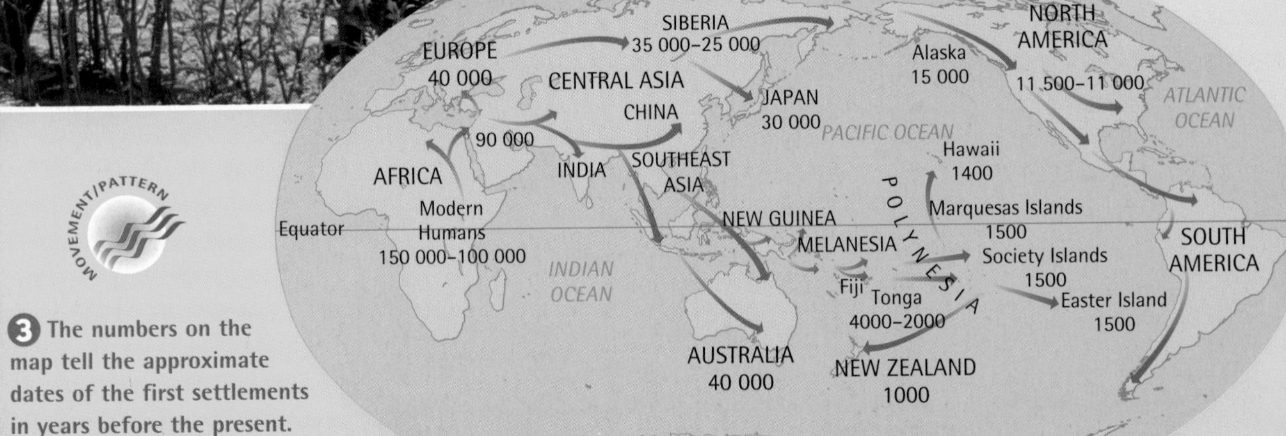

MOVEMENT/PATTERN

③ The numbers on the map tell the approximate dates of the first settlements in years before the present. How long ago was it that people moved across into North America?

❹ Much has changed for the Inuit. What changes do you think have taken place since this photo was taken?

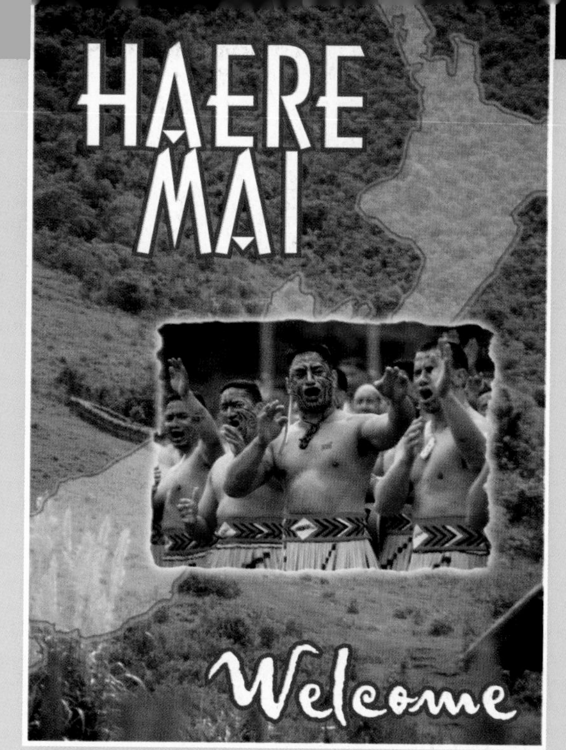

❺ This poster welcomed immigrants to New Zealand. What languages are on the poster?

❻ There are many cultural celebrations in Canada. What are some of the events that are celebrated in your community?

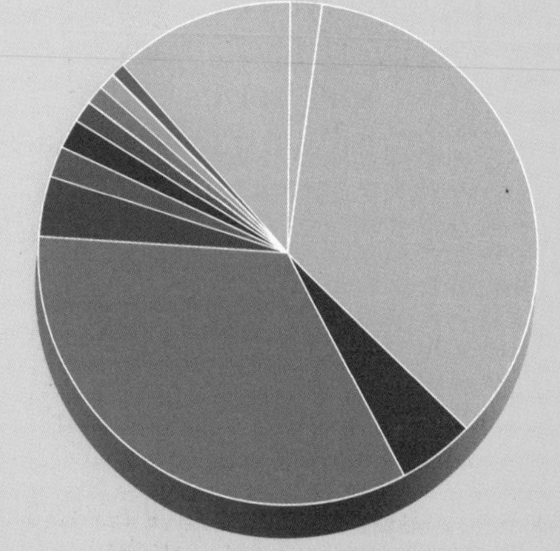

Ethnic make-up of Canada.

Italian 3.9%	Scandinavian 0.9%
Chinese 2.0%	Others 11.7%
Dutch 1.9%	First Nations 2.1%
Jewish 1.4%	British 35.0%
East Indian 1.2%	German 5.0%
Portuguese 1.1%	French 33.8%

❼ This graph shows the ethnic make-up of Canada. What group do you fall into?

❽ This is a classroom in London, Ontario. Do the children shown resemble classes in your school?

11 Migration

Figure 11.1
Aliens approach earth!

EXPECTATIONS

- identify factors that affect migration and mobility
- demonstrate an understanding that migration results from decisions people make about conditions and events around them
- identify factors that influence people to move to another place
- describe how technology has improved mobility

Earthlings Get Out!

North America has been taken over by aliens from outer space. They like it here. They want Canada all to themselves. They pass a law that all human life-forms must leave Canada within one week. The aliens are providing ships and planes. Each family will be allowed three bags of belongings, but the total weight must not exceed 150 kg. The aliens have taken control of the banks, the road systems, and all utilities. Suddenly, you have no country, no home, no money, and no clear future. Where in the world are you going to go? Which place would be best? What are you going to take with you?

Okay, this is not likely ever to happen. But each year, millions of people in the world do face similar situations and decisions. Geographers study these upheavals of people, called **migrations**. They look at the movements, their patterns, and the reasons why these migrations occurred.

What is Migration?

Migration is the movement of people, animals, or things from one place to another. There are a variety of reasons why migrations take place. Animals migrate at different seasons of the year to change their environments in order to have ample food, favourable weather, mate, and raise a family. In Canada, the Inuit and other First Nations peoples were nomadic or moved from

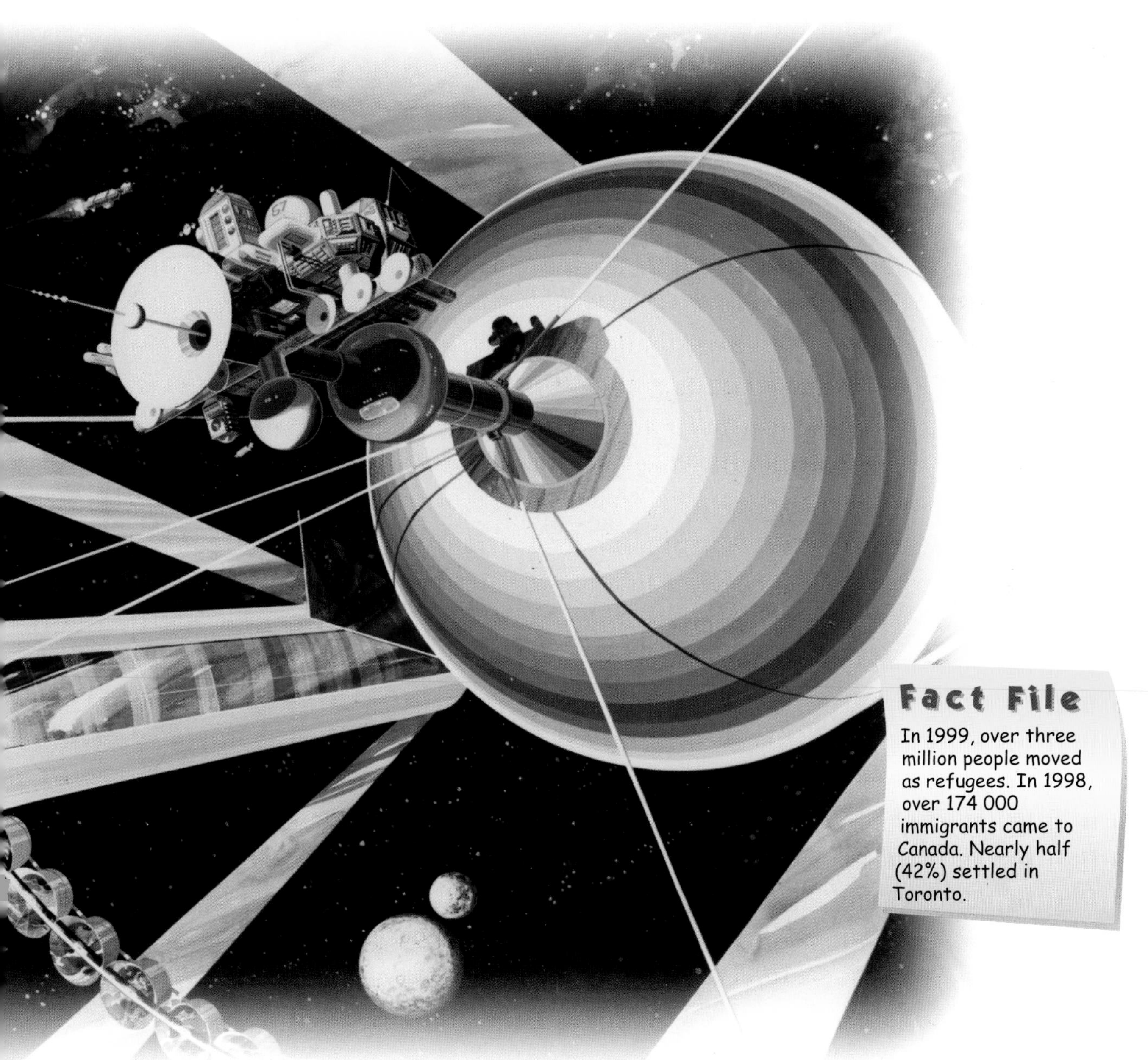

Fact File

In 1999, over three million people moved as refugees. In 1998, over 174 000 immigrants came to Canada. Nearly half (42%) settled in Toronto.

place to place, changing their environment with the changing seasons to ensure good hunting and gathering of food stuffs.

Today, people still move to change environments. For example, most adults and many children have lived in more than one house during their lifetime. People like to take trips on their vacations "for a change of scene." Sometimes entire industries migrate from one location to another in order to be closer to the source of their raw materials, their markets, or available workers. And in the 1950s, the whole town of Iroquois, Ontario had to be moved when the building of the St. Lawrence Seaway flooded the original town site under many metres of water.

Why Migrate?

So, people move for many reasons. For example, in the past, many moved to obtain free or cheap land. Others moved in answer to the lure of wealth. People have joined gold rushes in California, the Yukon, and Brazil. Sometimes, people moved to get a new start and better economic opportunities, like many of the Asian people who came to help build the CPR railway through the western mountains. Some groups moved to escape persecution and to find freedom to practise their religion, such as the Mennonites, Doukhobours, and Jews.

But moving has its price. Migration means dislocation. It means leaving somewhere familiar for a new and strange place. It means loss and gain, leaving and arriving, ending and beginning. As you examine migration, you must clearly keep in mind the turmoil and upheavals that migrants face.

Fact File

Before Canada acquired the great West, immigrants had to buy land for their houses or farms. But in 1872, Parliament passed the Homestead Act, which made land in Western Canada free to Europeans willing to settle there.

GO TO www.nfb.ca/

This is the Web site for the National Film Board, which rents and sells many videos and films about migration in Canada. If possible, watch the NFB video episode from the series "The National Dream" that tells about building this stretch of the CPR. Or, visit your local or school library to read Pierre Berton's book, *The Last Spike*.

Figure 11.2

Building the CPR in Western Canada. With machines still far in the future, railway ties were passed from the supply wagon over the shoulders of the tracklayers. What items in the photo help you to identify when the picture was taken?

Figure 11.3

This map shows the earliest movements of people, including approximate dates of first settlement (years before the present).

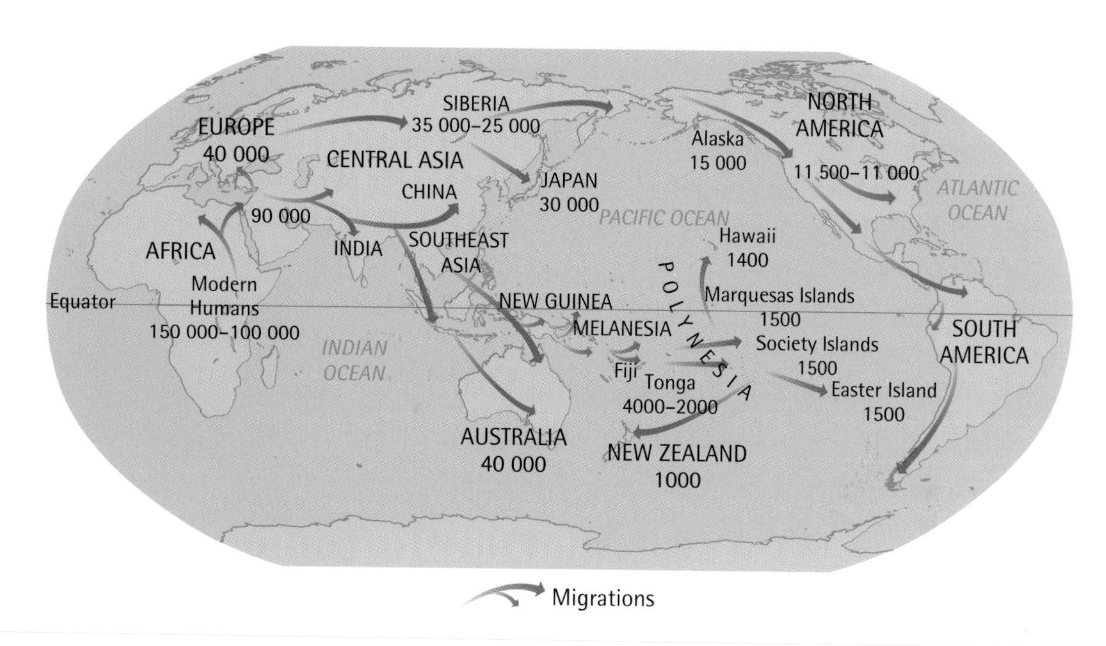

Fact File

While modern humans have existed for only about 150 000 years, fossils found in the Great Rift Valley suggest that our earliest ancestors flourished there between two and three million years ago.

The First Migrations

SEE PAGE 115

Our earliest ancestors moved to find food, shelter, fresh water, and security. Scientific evidence shows the first movements of people were out of central Africa. People followed natural valleys, like the Great Rift Valley in Africa, to move northward. Eventually, small groups of early humans found themselves in Asia and Europe and, lastly, the Americas. The spread of people around the earth took about a million years.

Building Empires

In more recent times, nations created migrations to satisfy many different national needs. Some countries wanted to reduce their populations at home, extend their power, create new wealth for themselves, or for the glory of conquest. Using sailing ships, the French and British moved people into eastern North America, Australia, India, and the South Pacific. The Spanish and Portuguese moved people into Central and South America; the Dutch established settlements and trade in all parts of the world.

"I do not like Canada so well as England; but in England there are too many men, and here there are not enough."

Anonymous British immigrant to Canada

Figure 11.4

World migrations since 1500 A.D.

SEE PAGE 152

	Migration	Dates
1	Slaves from Africa taken to the Americas	1500–1850
2	Russian settlement of Siberia	1850–1950
3	European settlement of North America	1820–1920
4	Settlement of southern Africa and Australasia by Europeans	1840–1960
5	Chinese migration to Indo-China	1880–1910
6	Migration of Chinese to the Americas	1860–1950
7	Movement of Indians to Africa	1860–1910
8	Japanese migration to North America	1870–1910
9	Jewish movement to Israel	1949–
10	Migration of Asians to Europe	1950–1970
11	Movement of Palestinian refugees out of Israel	1950–1970
12	Indo-Chinese refugees flee to southeast Asia and China	1970–1980
13	Afghans flee to Pakistan and Iran	1970–1980

Reaching the Ends of the Earth

By the start of the 1900s, there were few places left on earth untouched by immigration. Today, the pace of migration shows no signs of slowing down. With advances in transportation — trains and modern ocean liners, cars and planes — even larger numbers of people are able to move greater distances in shorter time periods. For example, migrants from countries far from the sea are able to travel by rail to reach ports and board ships to seek their fortunes in other countries.

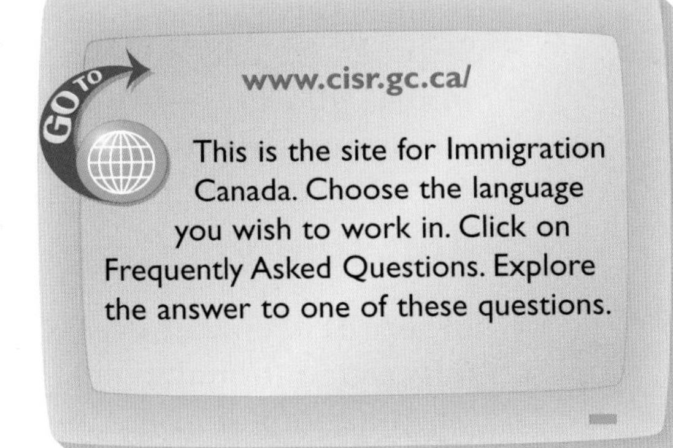

1. List three reasons why people have migrated. Underline the reason you think is most important today.
2. Which areas of the world were some of the last to have settlements? Why? (*Hint*: Think about harsh climates.)

Fact File

Canada's northernmost community is Alert, Nunavut, at 83°N.

Why Do People Move?

There have been many news stories about boatloads of people who have endured terrible travelling conditions in order to arrive on the shores of Canada or some other country. Why do people take such risks? Why are they so desperate to risk everything to find a new start? Why do they feel they have no choice except to leave their homes for a new country?

In general, people move because of social, economic, or political factors. Usually, more than one factor influences their decision.

Figure 11.5

A weather station in Canada's remote Far North. What are three difficulties that people living here year round might face?

Social Factors

Family ties are one of the most important ingredients in migration. During the war in Kosovo (formerly a part of Yugoslavia) in 1999, over one million people were displaced as **refugees**. They were usually lodged in refugee camps until they could be taken care of elsewhere. When opportunities came to move out of the camps to better conditions, many families were split up — children separated from parents, brothers and sisters from each other. Imagine how you would feel if, tomorrow, you were separated from your family with no idea where they had gone or whether you would ever see them again. When opportunities came for these refugees to move back to Kosovo, the hope of reuniting with loved ones was strong.

Figure 11.6

Difficult decisions face both those who decide to return home or stay to start a new life in Canada. This family decided to return to Kosovo. What problems might a refugee family face if they decided to stay in Canada?

Fact File

Over 6000 refugees were flown from Kosovo refugee camps to Canada, but every effort was made to ensure that family groups stayed together. They stayed at Canadian Armed Forces bases, such as those in Trenton and Camp Borden, Ontario.

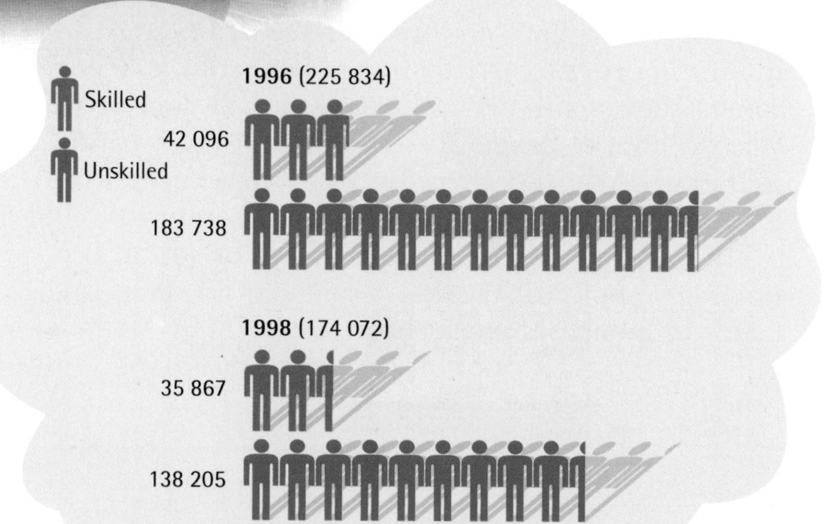

Figure 11.7

Number of skilled and unskilled workers arriving in Canada. Overall immigration dropped 23% from 1996 to 1998.

Figure 11.8

Refugee flows from Kosovo. What would you do if your family were shipped out but you were left behind? Would you wait for your relatives to come back? Perhaps you would try to track them down through the agencies and governments that help. Would you even be in any condition to start a search for your family? Millions of refugees face tough decisions like these every year.

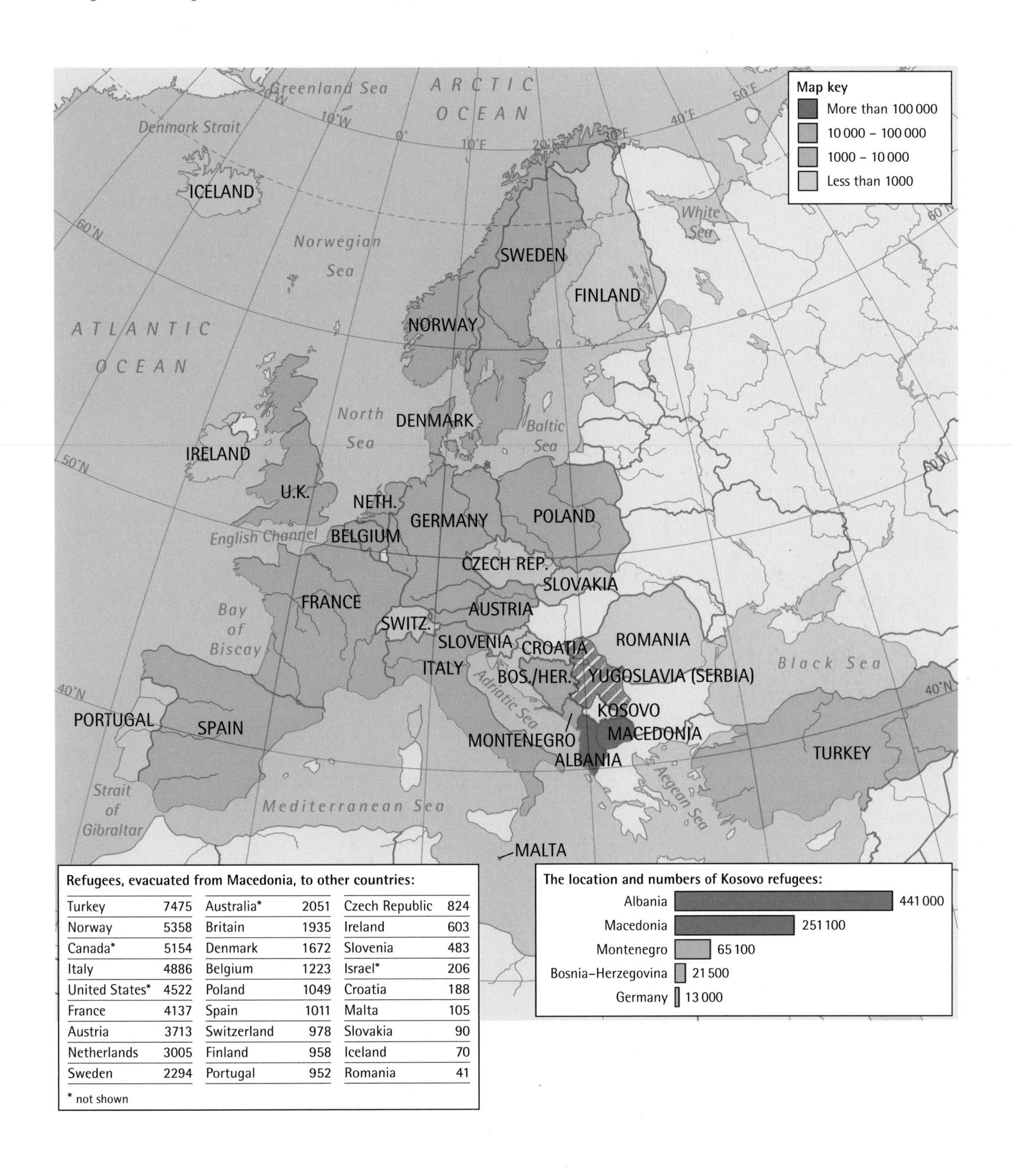

Refugees, evacuated from Macedonia, to other countries:

Turkey	7475	Australia*	2051	Czech Republic	824
Norway	5358	Britain	1935	Ireland	603
Canada*	5154	Denmark	1672	Slovenia	483
Italy	4886	Belgium	1223	Israel*	206
United States*	4522	Poland	1049	Croatia	188
France	4137	Spain	1011	Malta	105
Austria	3713	Switzerland	978	Slovakia	90
Netherlands	3005	Finland	958	Iceland	70
Sweden	2294	Portugal	952	Romania	41

* not shown

For the Sake of the Children

Whether people choose or are forced to migrate, they usually place the welfare and safety of their children above all else. Often, when a family decides to migrate, one parent will go first to get established and then send for the family.

Those who choose to migrate often select countries with high-quality education systems, like Canada, the United States, Japan, Australia, France, and Britain. Often we may take the quality of our schools and our education system for granted.

Your parents expect you to finish high school and perhaps go on to complete college or university. In many parts of the world, high numbers of children never complete elementary school. In some countries, like rural Brazil, for example, some of the teachers have only completed grade 5.

Figure 11.9

A classroom in Ethiopia. What do you think would be different from your classroom? The same? Why?

Figure 11.10

Secondary school enrolment by percentage, male/female, 1996. Over 25 African countries have less than 20% of both girls and boys enrolled in secondary school. Some countries don't allow girls to go to school past grade 3 or 4. Why do you think that is?

Country	Male	Female
Canada	98%	97%
Russia	84%	91%
Sweden	99%	100%
Bangladesh	25%	13%
India	59%	38%
Saudi Arabia	54%	43%
China	60%	51%
Japan	95%	97%
Venezuela	29%	41%
Malawi	6%	3%

World/Averages	Male	Female
N. America	99%	98%
Africa	36%	30%
Central/S. America	51%	52%
Asia	57%	45%
Europe	89%	94%

Figure 11.11

Some immigrants to Canada must pass the point system shown in this chart.

Age:
Applicants 21 to 44 earn top marks. A 45-year-old gets 8 points; people 49+ earn none.

Demographics:
This number is set by the government. Everyone gets 8 points.

Occupation and Education/Training:
Computer programmers earn the full 10 points; so do chefs, equipment mechanics, radiation technicians, and speech therapists. Education is recognized, too, whether or not it leads to a job. For example, if you're a historian or an astronomer, you earn 18 points for education, but only 1 for occupation.

Factor	Maximum points	Your score
1. Age	10	
2. Education	16	
3. Occupation	10	
4. Education/Training	18	
5. Arranged employment	10	
6. Work experience	8	
7. Language ability	15	
8. Demographics	8	8
9. Relative in Canada	5	
10. Personal suitability	10	
Total		

Personal suitability:
Points are awarded for such characteristics as adaptability, motivation, initiative, and resourcefulness.

It's Your World

When people try to migrate to another country, they are often given preference – preferred treatment – if they have family ties in their new country. The closer the family tie, the easier it is to migrate. So, a person joining a spouse would get higher preference than someone joining a second cousin.

Economic Factors

SEE PAGE 5

People most often move for economic reasons, such as employment and well-being. Demographers predict that, in the future, more people will move for employment reasons than for any others.

Jobs, Jobs, Jobs

SEE PAGE 281

People move to find and to keep jobs. Some jobs, by their very nature, cause people to migrate. For example, a miner may move many times from mining town to mining town, following the job opportunities. Sometimes a mine closes because it cannot make enough money to stay open. Sometimes, a mine just runs out of minerals. Some mining families, like the Drapers of Marathon, Ontario, have moved 14 times in 22 years. That means some of their children have lived in 14 different communities, have attended 14 new schools, and have had to make new friends 14 times.

Figure 11.12

These coal miners in Sydney, Nova Scotia held a mock funeral for their industry to protest the loss of jobs in their community. Why do you think coal mining may be in jeopardy today?

Figure 11.13

Finite resources like uranium eventually run out. Uranium City, Saskatchewan had no other means to keep itself alive after its mine closed. Nearly everyone moved away. It was a "ghost town" when this picture was taken in 1957. After a brief comeback in the 1970s, the town was finally closed for good in the early 1980s.

Figure 11.14

Since Canada has a worldwide reputation for talented, highly skilled, well-educated people, many Canadians are able to take advantage of contract work in countries in different parts of the world. What jobs do you think will be important worldwide when you are ready to enter the job market?

People's attitudes toward jobs and the reasons they take them differ greatly. Many of the people who migrate do so to take up better jobs that require high education, special skills, or both. These high-paying jobs are often in professions like medicine, computer science, and engineering, or in special trades like tool-and-die making, business management, and high-end technology and communications.

SEE PAGE 66

Globalization is causing an increasing amount of executive and contract migration. That is, business executives move around the world as part of their career training. Many such families may spend a few years in each of several different countries over their careers. Other professionals, skilled technicians, and managers also gain contracts to go to other countries.

SEE PAGE 191

GO TO www.statcan.ca/english

Choose Canadian statistics. Now click on Labour, Employment, and Unemployment. Then choose Earnings. Click on Level of schooling, census of metropolitan areas. From the window, select a city such as Toronto, Hamilton, or St. Catherines. Note the relationship between level of education and earning power. How do you think these statistics affect migration?

Fact File

The cities of Calcutta and Bombay in India each have over one million homeless people living on their streets. Many spend their entire lives in such conditions.

The biggest migration in history was, and continues to be, the flood of people moving from rural to urban areas. This **mass migration** began in the 1800s with the Industrial Revolution. Fewer jobs were available on farms, so people left for the towns and cities to get work in the new factories that were opening. This flow continues today, and in many countries, it is creating massive problems. As millions of people move into a city, governments cannot keep up with the demand for services. There is often not enough affordable housing. Sanitation systems can't be built fast enough or at all because of lack of money. Basic human needs such as clean water are just not available. Slums and **squatter settlements** of makeshift shacks grow up in these circumstances, creating an environment for diseases to spread.

SEE PAGE 116

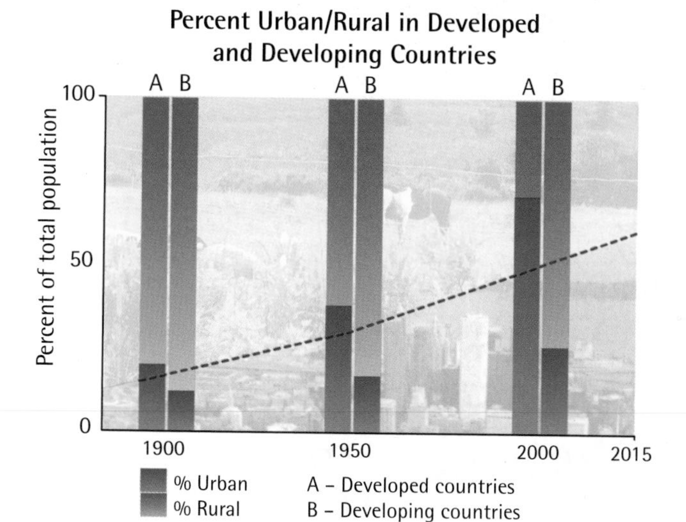

Figure 11.15

The move to urban areas, showing world change from 1900 to 2015 (estimated). Since so much of our world is rural, the average is closer to rural than urban. Is your community more urban or more rural? Is it changing?

Fact File

Squatter towns have different names around the world. They are called "bustees" in India, "favelas" in Brazil, and "barrios" in the rest of Central and South America. This is a very complicated problem that no one has been able to solve. Can you think of one thing that a government might do to start a solution?

Figure 11.16

A squatter settlement in Corinto, Colombia. Living conditions are poor. The houses are made of wood and plastic, with zinc roofs and dirt floors.

Many of the world's major religions are hundreds, even thousands of years old. Christianity started during the time of the Roman Empire. At that same time, Hinduism, Judaism, and Buddhism were already well established. The religion of Islam developed in what is now Saudi Arabia during the 700s AD. At times, their followers have been persecuted for their beliefs. This has resulted in many groups having to defend their faith or seek new and safer homes.

Political Factors

In some countries, the government denies certain citizens their rights. The politicians make new laws that reduce or eliminate the freedoms that we take for granted in Canada.

Persecution

For centuries, people have migrated to escape persecution because of their religion, their skin colour, their nationality, or even the language they speak. Persecution has often forced people to flee to find freedom, peace, and acceptance. Religious persecution and conflict are long-standing problems. Many devastating examples have occurred in recent times. Some of the major ones that have caused significant migration include

- the movement of Jewish people to Israel
- the movement of "break-away" Christian groups like the Mennonites and Quakers
- the conflict between Hindus and Muslims, which led to the partition of India in 1948 and the migration of over 11 million people.

Figure 11.17

Jewish immigrants arriving in Israel, 1949.

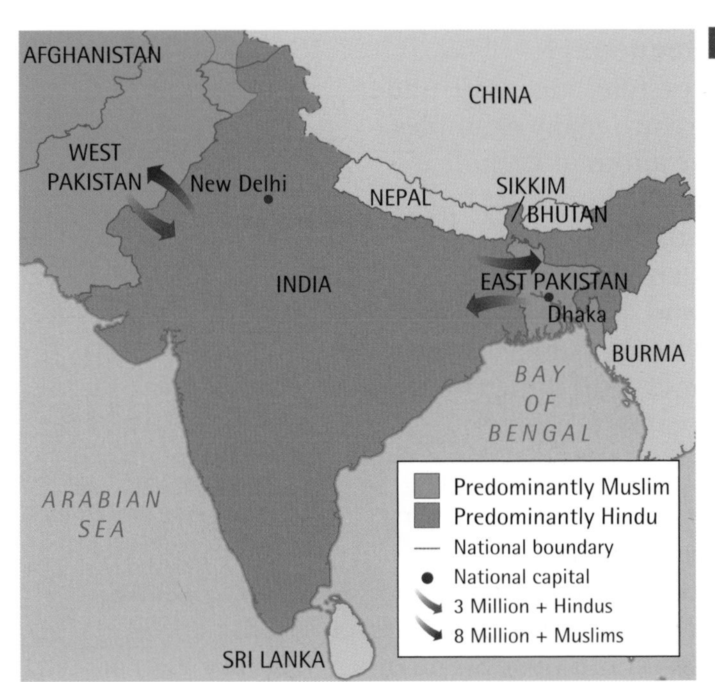

Figure 11.18

In 1948, India was divided into three countries – India, and East and West Pakistan. Hindus moved to stay in India and Muslims moved to be in the Pakistans. Today, East and West Pakistan exist with different names. Check your atlas and find out what they are called now.

LOCATION

Fact File

India is 83% Hindu, 11% Muslim, 2% Christian, 2% Sikh, and 2% other. Pakistan is 97% Muslim, with non-Muslims making up 3% of the population.

"Like a sunbeam from a clouded sky came permission for us to come to Canada, a free country."

Marianne Echt, immigrant
Arrived on the ship Andania from the Free State of Danzig, March 7, 1939

SEE PAGE 123

1911; The government orders all African-Americans entering Alberta from the US to be turned back.
1914; 350 East Indians arriving in Canada at Vancouver harbour are refused entry and forced to leave.
1923; The government passes the Chinese Immigration Act banning almost all Chinese from entering Canada.
1938; The government declares that all Jewish refugees must have at least $20 000 in cash before being allowed into Canada.
1946; Canada welcomes over 22 000 orphan children from Europe.
1947; The Chinese Immigration Act is repealed.
1956; Canada accepts 37 000 Hungarian refugees.
1967; The Immigration Appeal board is set up to give immigrants the right to fight government deportation orders.
1990; Canada opens its doors to 220 000 immigrants a year for five years.
1998; Canada increases the number of immigrants allowed to enter the country.

Human Rights and Migration

The 1950 United Nations Declaration of Human Rights identified the key rights and protections that everyone in the world should have, such as

- freedom of speech
- freedom from wrongful imprisonment and
- freedom from mistreatment and torture.

Unfortunately, some world leaders still do not follow this Bill of Human Rights. They continue to violate the rights of many of their citizens, forcing some to flee their country. They go wherever they feel safety can be found. Eventually, if they cannot safely return to their homes, they try to gain **refugee status** in some other country. While there have been times when Canada was not open to immigrants, today it has an excellent record of being "humanitarian" and taking in many refugees.

Have the U.N. Declaration's Aims Been Met?

There is a great need in our world for tolerance and understanding among peoples. But still, there are many examples each year of people's inhumanity to one another. Prejudice of all kinds continues to haunt the world's cultures. No one should be discriminated against because of his or her race, religion, language, social class, or gender. There should be no room for these acts of violence and intolerance. Even though it may take time for all governments to meet the aims of the Declaration of Human Rights, there is something you can do. You can start by practising equity, fair treatment, and respect to all in your community.

> *"Since I am of the world, when I change myself, I change the world."*
> Cree saying

Fact File

Of the 12 million slaves transported to the Americas between 1500 and 1850, an estimated two million did not survive the voyage.

SEE PAGE 180

Forced Migration

What you have been reading about are examples of forced migration – people leaving their homelands against their will. Whatever the causes, though, the result is almost always the same: danger, hardship, unhappiness, and economic loss for the migrants.

SEE PAGE 152

Figure 11.19

Slaves were sold at auctions and were treated as the property of the landowners who bought them. Some slaves from the southern U.S. states escaped to freedom via the "underground railroad," a secret network of safe havens that provided food and shelter along the way.

Slavery

Perhaps the most brutal example of **forced migration** in history is the millions of black Africans who were captured, herded onto ships, and transported to the Americas. They were stripped of all their social, human, and political rights. Families were split apart. Living conditions were inhuman. Their cultural heritages and languages were suppressed. Yet, through pride, music, religion, and storytelling, many of the black African cultures were kept alive through these terrible years of slavery.

SEE PAGE 151

GO TO http://collections.ic.gc.ca/acadian/intro

There have been other forced migrations in North America. Visit this Web site to learn about the Acadian forced migration. Explore the Acadian story.

Forced Dislocations

In North America, many bands and tribes of First Nations people were forced by European settlers to move from their lands to reserves. These were lands that were of little value for farming and contained few natural resources. They were lands that no settlers wanted. What the settlers did want, how-ever, was the rich farmlands and forests that were the homes of the First Nations peoples. As more and more Europeans moved into North America, greater numbers of First Nations peoples were forced onto reserves. This type of forced migration has created many social and economic issues for societies today. Can you identify some of the problems reported in the news that the First Nations people face today stemming from these forced migrations?

Early in 1942, when Japan had joined World War II, the Canadian government moved to dispossess and relocate all British Columbians of Japanese descent, even those who were Canadian citizens. Families were split up, and whatever property they could not carry was disposed of by the government. This was the culmination of decades of anti-Asiatic feeling on the Pacific Coast.

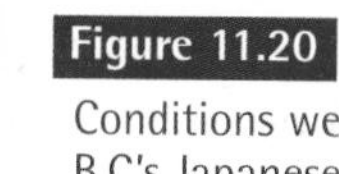

Figure 11.20

Conditions were harsh in B.C.'s Japanese internment camps. Some families lived in flimsy shacks, while others were split up into separate dormitories for males and females.

The Poem on the Emigrants' Monument, La Coruna, NW Spain
(translated from Gallego, the language of Galicia, by Russell King)

Goodbye rivers, goodbye springs
Goodbye little streams
Goodbye view from my eyes
I don't know when we will see each other again

Goodbye glory, goodbye happiness
I leave the house where I was born
I leave the village that I know so well
For a world I have not seen
Goodbye also my loved ones
Goodbye forever, perhaps
I say this goodbye with tears in my eyes
Whenever I am overseas
Do not forget me, my love
If I die of solitude
So many leagues across the ocean
O for my little house my home

These same emotions flow through the hearts and minds of immigrants today.

The gap in wealth between the richest and poorest groups is widening. In 1965, the richest 20% of the world's people consumed far more than the rest and controlled 70% of the world's income. Today, the richest 20% of the world controls 86% of the world's money, and this number is still increasing.

Figure 11.21

Share of total world income owned by the richest 20% of the population.

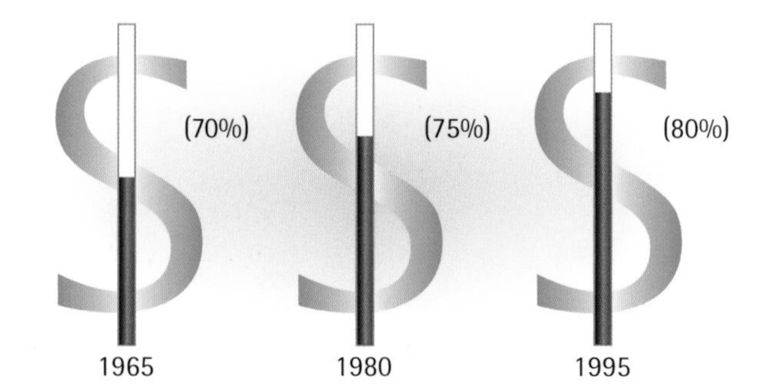

The Going Gets Faster

Migration in our world shows no signs of slowing down. The pressures people face that encourage migration, such as drought and starvation, political conflicts, resource and environmental loss, lack of jobs, and social and economic problems continue to plague us. And where do people migrate to? They are pulled to the more developed countries, like Canada, where they are attracted to our lifestyle and the things we have. Television and the Internet have brought people closer together. We all get glimpses of how our neighbours live — even when those neighbours live very far away.

It is natural for people to want to look after their basic needs and to have some pleasures in their lives. Unless people's problems are solved in their own countries, they will continue to migrate.

Fact File

An average Canadian consumes 10 to 15 times more than an average person in Argentina, the Philippines, or Egypt (and produces much more waste, too)! The average Canadian household has 10 000 "things," yet of these, only about 200 are basic necessities.

1. Suggest reasons that explain why having family ties in a country would be very important for a new immigrant.
2. What kinds of jobs are available to young people aged 15 to 18 in your community? Considering these jobs, pick from the following list the terms that best describe them:

resource-oriented	manufacturing-oriented		service-oriented
low-paying	high-paying	skilled	non-skilled
part-time	full-time	short-term	long-term

3. Look at Figure 11.11 on page 215. Develop your own point system that you think Canada should use to qualify people wanting to immigrate here. Give reasons for your choices.
4. Immigration refers to the people who come into your country. Emigration refers to those leaving. Work out an easy way to remember which term is which and how to spell them.

CASE STUDY

Migrant Workers to the Persian Gulf

A new form of migration has recently emerged in the poorer countries of the world. **Migrant workers** from these less developed countries trek each year to richer and more industrialized countries for seasonal or even longer work periods. These workers provide a pool of labour used by many people and companies for jobs that are considered low-level.

For example, migrant workers come to Ontario from areas like the Caribbean to help with the tobacco or apple harvests. However most workers go to Europe, the United States, and Japan. They often feel that any job is far better than being unemployed in their own country. Sometimes, though, when it is difficult for them to enter other countries because of strict immigration restrictions, they try other, perhaps illegal, ways of entering in order to get a job. These illegal immigrants are often taken advantage of by some employers who pay them very low wages.

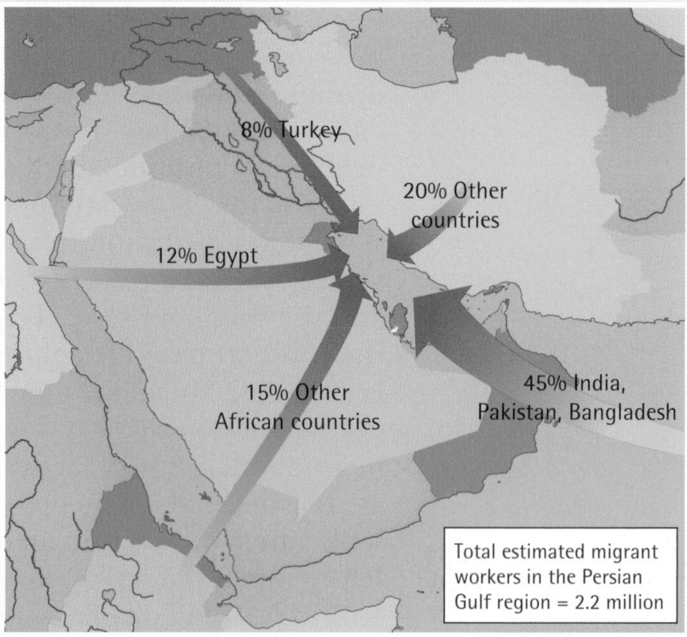

Figure 11.22

Thousands of people leave less wealthy countries each year to work elsewhere. The oil-rich countries around the Persian Gulf are one of the biggest attractions. How must it feel to be away from your friends and family for so long each year?

Fact File

Over 35 million people are migrant workers. The fastest growing category of foreign workers in the world is Asian women, increasing by 800 000 annually.

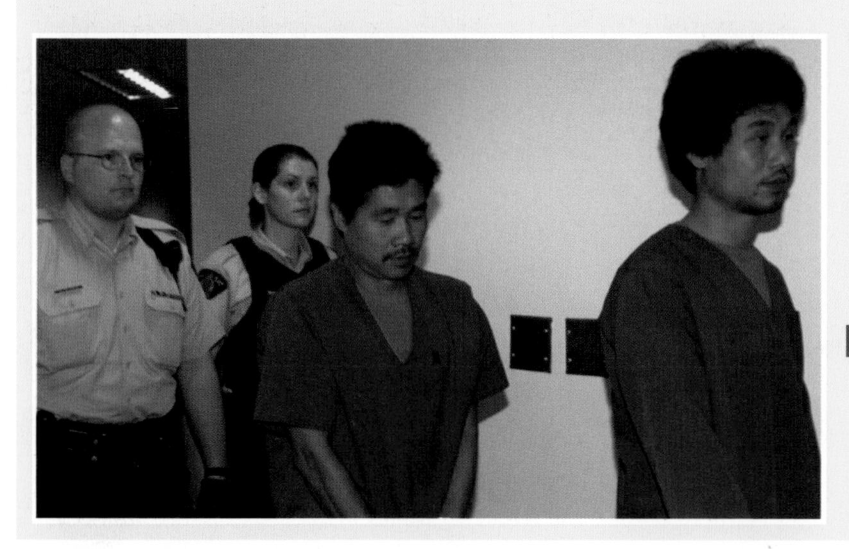

Figure 11.23

In 1999, hundreds of Chinese risked their lives in crowded, often leaky boats, trying to enter Canada illegally along the coast of British Columbia. How would you monitor such a long coastline?

Persian Gulf Migrant Workers

Amin Sharif, age 30, and his brother Ahmed, age 24, live in Lahore, Pakistan. Each year for the last three years, they have worked 11 months a year in the oilfields of Saudi Arabia. They live in a compound with over 500 other workers from countries around this region like India, Bangladesh, and Egypt.

Amin and Ahmed help install oil pumping equipment. They work around the oil shipment centre on the shore of the Persian Gulf. For them, the $500U.S. they receive each month is high pay. Their accommodation and meals are provided. They spend very little money on themselves. Instead, they send most of what they earn back to their families in Pakistan. This money sent back is called **migrant's remittance**. It is an invisible gain to Pakistan's wealth, since it is money added to their economy from outside their country.

Amin is married. He and his wife have two little girls, ages five and three. His wife and children live in his parents' home in Lahore with his two younger sisters.

Amin and Ahmed work long, 10- to 15-hour days. Yet, jobs like these are essential to the well-being of their families back home.

Figure 11.24
Workers on an oil rig in the Persian Gulf. Around the world, migrant workers obtain jobs to meet basic needs for themselves and others in their homelands. How does their working abroad help their own countries?

SEE PAGE 259

1. Identify three reasons that might lead people to leave their homeland to work in distant countries.
2. Migrant workers come to Ontario mainly from the Caribbean. Compare their travelling distance to that of Amin and Ahmed.
3. Explain what an "invisible benefit" might be in terms of the migrant's remittance.
4. Make a list of the things you think are absolute basic human needs. Don't forget emotional needs.

Understanding the Concepts

1. There are several key pressures on people to migrate: drought/starvation, political conflict, resource/environmental loss, and social/economic conditions. Copy the organizer below into your notebook to help understand these pressures. For each pressure, identify an event of that type and where it happened.

Pressure	Event	Location
Drought/starvation		
Political conflict		
Resource/environmental loss		
Social/economic conditions		

2. Turn to the poem on page 222. What are the key things the writer cares about in the poem? Write your own poem about an immigrant's excitement upon reaching a new country.

Figure 11.25

A Canadian from Doctors Without Borders treats a young cholera patient in a refugee camp in Goma, Zaire, where thousands of Rwandans fled after a civil war in their own country.

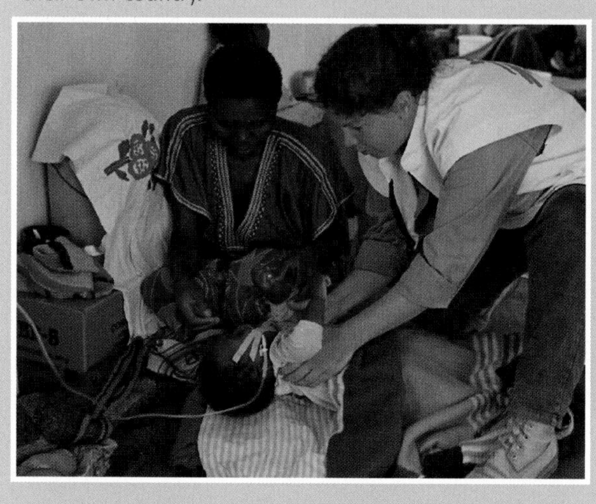

3. What do you consider to be five important human rights for all children? Create your five, and then combine them with other students' lists to make a "Charter of the Human Rights for Children." Compare this list to CREDO, the efforts of our government to involve young people in this area.

GO TO

www.pch.gc/ca/credo/

Choose the language you want. Click on "The votes are in! It's your CREDO! Click here." Compare your charter with that of CREDO.

4. Governments often complain about losing their best people because they emigrate to other countries. These are citizens that the country has educated and trained. This loss is called "brain drain." Give three reasons why a government would want to stop brain drain.

Research and Communication Skills

5. Use PC Globe, other similar software, or an atlas to research data on two countries in Asia, two in Africa, two in South or Central America, and Canada. Find the levels of education attained, level of health care (such as the number of hospitals and doctors per 1000 people), and one other category. Compare the data and explain how the data could relate to migration. Your data can be collected in a chart like the one below.

	Asia		Africa		Central/South America		Canada
Category	Country 1	Country 2	Country 1	Country 2	Country 1	Country 2	
% Completing high school							
Doctors/1000 people							
Other							

Map and Globe Skills

6 **a)** Survey your class to find out about peoples' origins. Ask each student where and when her/his family came from. Some may have arrived fairly recently. Others may have been here for several generations. Every Canadian family has a migration history. Compile a list of the countries and times.

b) Plot the countries on a world outline map and calculate the percentage of arrivals from each continent.

c) Draw proportional arrows from the continents to Canada to show the flows.

d) Using the data in Figure 11.26, compare the "source regions" of your class to the most recent flows of immigrants to Canada.

Applications

7 Contact your local federal immigration office to invite a representative to speak to your class regarding current immigration issues and concerns.

8 Develop a diary for one week in the life of a family coming to Canada from a war zone in another country. Tell about the family. Describe the conditions of their country and why they left; their feelings about leaving, and their emotions about coming to Canada.

Where Immigrants Settle, 1998

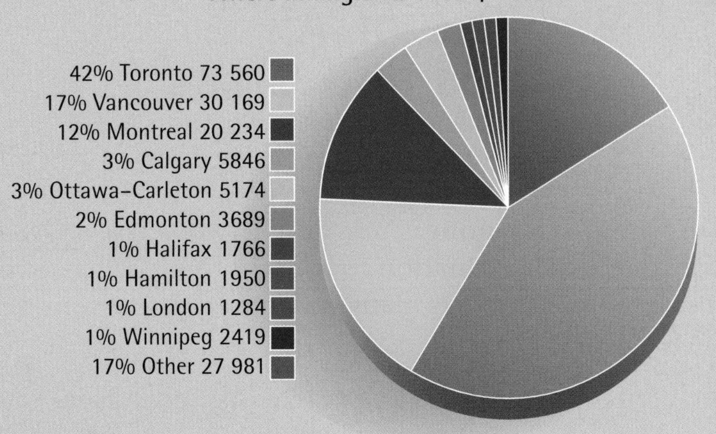

Figure 11.26

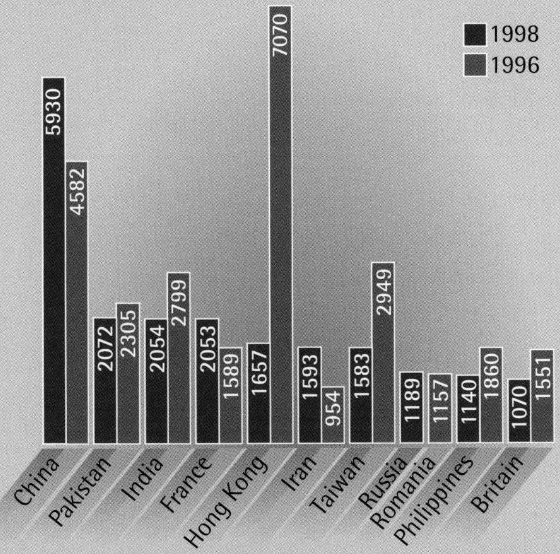

Who the Skilled Workers Are, Top 10 Source Countries

The number of skilled immigrants coming to Canada fell 15% from 1996 to 1998.

Barriers to Migration

EXPECTATIONS

- identify factors that affect migration and mobility
- demonstrate an understanding that migration results from decisions people make about conditions and events around them
- identify barriers to migration

Barriers of All Shapes and Sizes

Imagine: you want to leave your country, but everywhere you turn there are people stopping you. Frustrating? Yes, and it will take a great deal of determination to overcome these barriers.

There are many barriers that prevent people from migrating

- physical barriers like distance, oceans, or mountains
- economic barriers, like not having enough money to move
- political barriers, like laws prohibiting emigration
- legal barriers, like limits to the number of people the new country will let in and
- procedural barriers, like getting passports and visas.

MOVEMENT/PATTERN

Is migration a fundamental human right? Most people have no trouble supporting a person's right to **emigrate** (leave a country), but the right to **immigrate** (enter a country) seems debatable to some. Many people want the flow of immigrants into their countries controlled.

Figure 12.1

Some people, like this young woman in Kosovo, have spent much of their lives in the midst of conflict and war. If they want to leave the country of their birth, what could stop them?

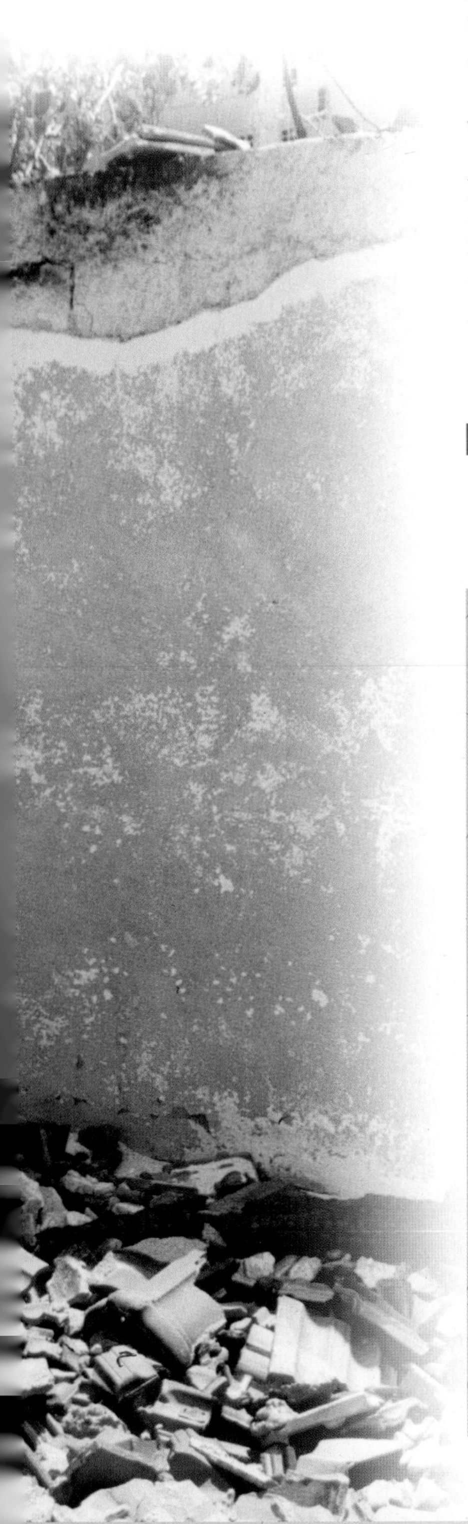

Political Barriers

Governments may set up different ways to stop people from leaving. Sometimes nations make it difficult for their citizens to emigrate by making them pay large sums of money to leave. These fees are known as **exit taxes**. Some countries close their borders completely, allowing only trusted people in or out.

When the Iron Curtain Fell

After World War II, the communist-controlled countries in Europe closed their borders. It became illegal to emigrate. In fact, those who tried were often shot or imprisoned. In what was then East Germany, the authorities built a wall — the **Berlin Wall** — to keep their citizens in and foreigners out.

LOCATION

Figure 12.2

Europe as it was divided in 1950. This map has changed dramatically since then. Using your atlas, identify which countries of Europe are the same, and which have new names or borders.

The Berlin Wall and the heavily guarded border between East and West Europe became the focal point for many Hollywood movies, such as *The Spy Who Came In From the Cold*. Many thrillers were written about the exploits of spies from both sides of the Iron Curtain, by such authors as Len Deighton and John Le Carré.

Fact File

Sir Winston Churchill, a former British prime minister, gave the sealed borders between the East and West its name — the **Iron Curtain** — a hard, cold barrier between the two worlds.

Figure 12.3

An East German soldier leaps to freedom over a checkpoint at the Berlin Wall.

Figure 12.4

Some people cheered, but others cried as this monument to conflict fell in 1989. Why do you think some people would be upset by the Berlin Wall coming down?

Connections to History

In 1989, the Berlin Wall was knocked down following the collapse of the East German government. People were amazed, because it was so unexpected. One night, people were virtually prisoners in their own country; the next, they could freely move to visit families and friends or rejoin relatives. If the Wall could come down, they thought, what else was possible? Following the opening of the borders between East and West Germany, huge numbers of people moved from the East to the West. What had been two separate countries for nearly 50 years rejoined to become one unified Germany again.

> ***"There is no reason to celebrate ... . There is still a long way to go."***
>
> **Andreas Steiner, lawyer and East Berlin resident**

It's Your World

During the Iron Curtain years, many Eastern Europeans did defect (escape) to the West. Hockey players, musicians, and dancers slipped away from their teams and groups while on special visits here. They sought asylum (freedom from political persecution) in the West, particularly in the United States. Famous defectors included ballet dancer Mikhail Baryshnikov, who defected while on tour in Toronto.

Physical Barriers

At one time, physical barriers were very significant in blocking migration. Mountains effectively stopped people's movements. Deserts forced people to go long distances out of their way to get around them, or prevented migration completely. Large bodies of water were barriers as well. People did not want to risk long trips on open water, so they only followed coastlines.

Such physical barriers slowed the pace of migration. But, advances in technology changed all this. Modern transportation systems easily and safely took people over mountains, across deserts, and over oceans. Communities even sprang up in mountain and desert regions. Continents such as the Americas and Australia were populated by millions of immigrants who had crossed the ocean.

Fact File

There are 25 million **environmental migrants** in the world today — one for every 225 people. There are another 135 million people whose land is under threat of becoming a desert.

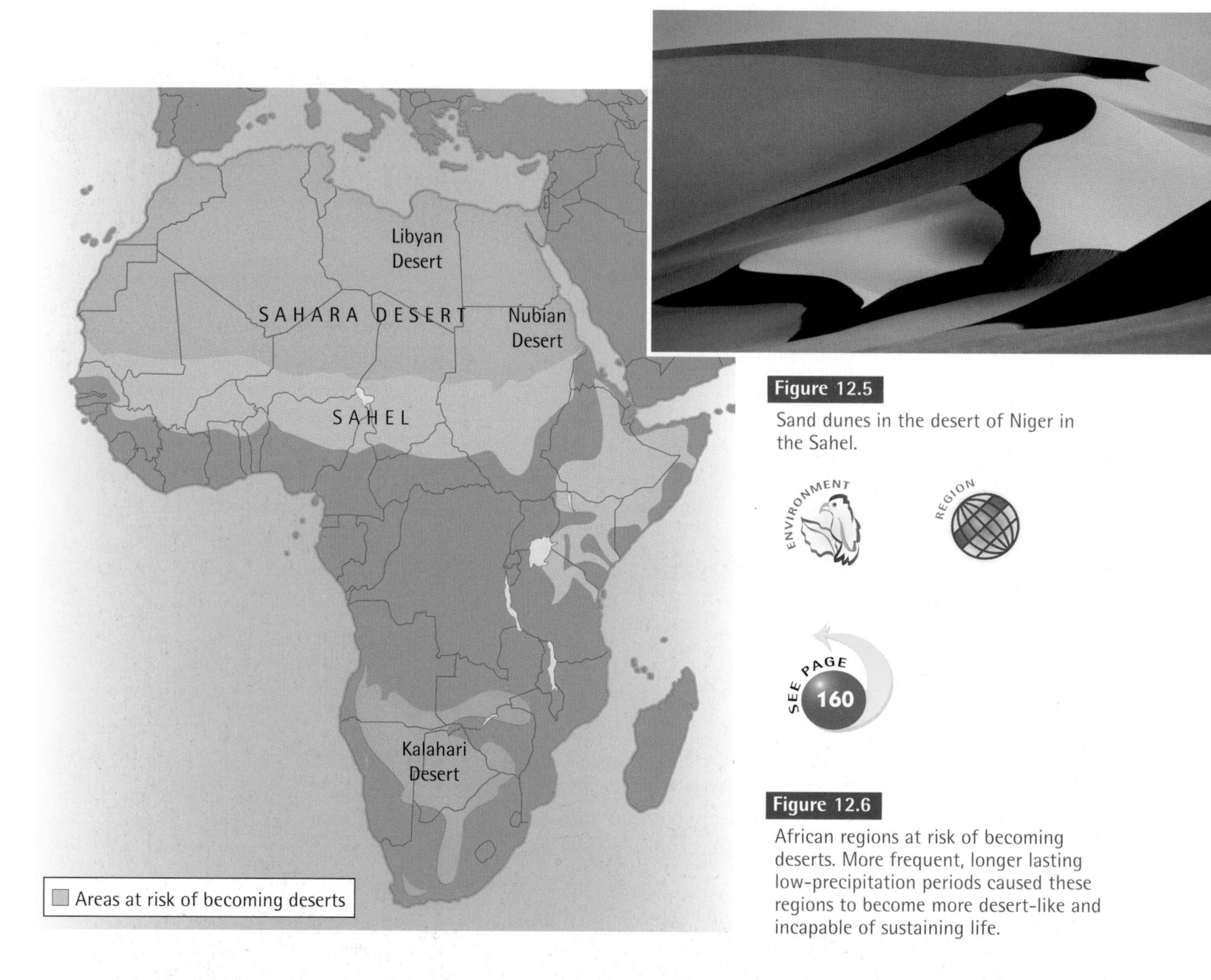

Figure 12.5

Sand dunes in the desert of Niger in the Sahel.

SEE PAGE 160

Figure 12.6

African regions at risk of becoming deserts. More frequent, longer lasting low-precipitation periods caused these regions to become more desert-like and incapable of sustaining life.

It's a Long Walk!

In the 1970s, several million people died from starvation in the **Sahel**. Others packed up their few belongings and began treks to distant cities, sometimes hundreds of kilometres away — like walking from Windsor to Kingston, Ontario. Many died along the way. They had no money to buy food. Their local governments couldn't help.

Many people worldwide contributed much to help peoples in such situations. Food, shelter, equipment, and people were sent by the United Nations and humanitarian groups such as World Vision, Oxfam, and the Red Cross.

Unfortunately, for most of these migrants, help came too late. Hundreds of thousands of children and adults died from starvation and disease. Those who survived did not see their lives improve. They continue to live in and around towns and cities, mainly living off the support of others. Even though their living conditions are horrible, few find ways to leave. In order to emigrate, people need some money to get started.

Fact File

Although we think mainly of international migration, 1997 saw 30 million people internally displaced around the world — forced to move from one place to another within their own countries.

Figure 12.7

When people move under such conditions, they have to live on what they can find along the way, and that is usually very little. Why do you think their governments cannot do more to help them?

LiveAid Goes WWW

(OTTAWA)—October 18, 1999

Over one billion people tuned into the NetAid benefit concert last night via the World Wide Web, radio, and TV. Millions of dollars flowed in from online donations. This United Nations–sponsored event received endorsements from U.S. President Bill Clinton and British Prime Minister Tony Blair, and featured acts like Sting, Jewel, David Bowie, and Puff Daddy. This was a follow-up to the 1985 LiveAid benefit concert for hunger relief, which raised over $120 million.

Figure 12.8

Bob Geldorf performing at the original LiveAid concert in 1985.

It's Your World

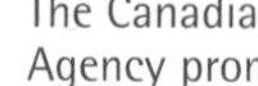

Your neighbourhood, their neighbourhood! Almost 900 million of the world's poorest people, existing on less than one dollar a day, live in areas vulnerable to soil erosion, droughts, and floods. Canada's aid organizations are trying to help them.

GO TO **www.acdi-cida.gc.ca** to find out how young Canadians are helping people in developing countries.

SEE PAGE 151

Figure 12.9

The Canadian International Development Agency promotes programs, like this one in India, that reduce erosion by interplanting soil-saving crops.

1. Ask some older adults about their memories of the Iron Curtain and how they felt when it came down. Record their comments.
2. Using a relief wall map or atlas, identify the main physical barriers facing migrants when they moved across North America.
3. **a)** Identify the countries in Figure 12.6 (page 232) that share a risk for desertification.
   b) Using a climate map from an atlas, compare the living conditions in this zone to those areas in southern North America that receive 10 to 50 mm of precipitation. Why don't these areas in North America face major migration problems?

Environmental Migration: A Problem in the Making

Figure 12.10

A Venice police officer directs foot traffic over temporary scaffolding after canals flooded St. Mark's Square. Rising sea levels have caused widespread damage in places like Venice, Italy. Are our lifestyles part of the problem? Explain.

Fact File

An October, 1999 report in the *London Free Press* stated that the Antarctic ice cap could melt very quickly under some conditions. Places like Bangladesh, the Netherlands, and New York City would be in the most danger from rising sea levels.

Severe environmental change usually causes terrible hardship for the people in the area. Floods, desertification, drought, storms, and other environmental disasters will always happen, and they will force people to migrate. Some experts feel that environmental migrations are likely to get worse because of global warming.

ENVIRONMENT

- Sea levels have been rising. Coastal areas could disappear under the oceans. It is predicted that 200 million people will be forced to move to higher ground by 2010.

- Today, half a billion people live with chronic water shortages. Three billion people are expected to live in countries without enough water by 2025. Many millions will be forced to move.
- It is likely that climate change will cause the migration of 50 million people from famine by 2050.

Imagine the problems that will erupt with such huge numbers of people on the move. Just think of what would be involved if everyone living in Ontario were forced to leave — and we only have 11 million people.

GO TO

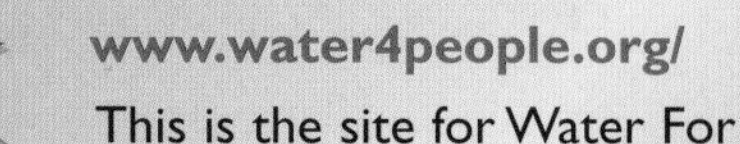

www.water4people.org/

This is the site for Water For People, a non-profit, charitable organization in the United States and Canada that helps people in developing countries obtain safe drinking water. Water For People works with local partner organizations to provide financial and technical assistance to communities, depending on their needs. They are committed to helping people help themselves. You can learn more about safe water and what scientists are doing about it by visiting this Web site.

Figure 12.11

This map shows areas where drought and flooding are most likely to occur. Which parts of Canada are affected?

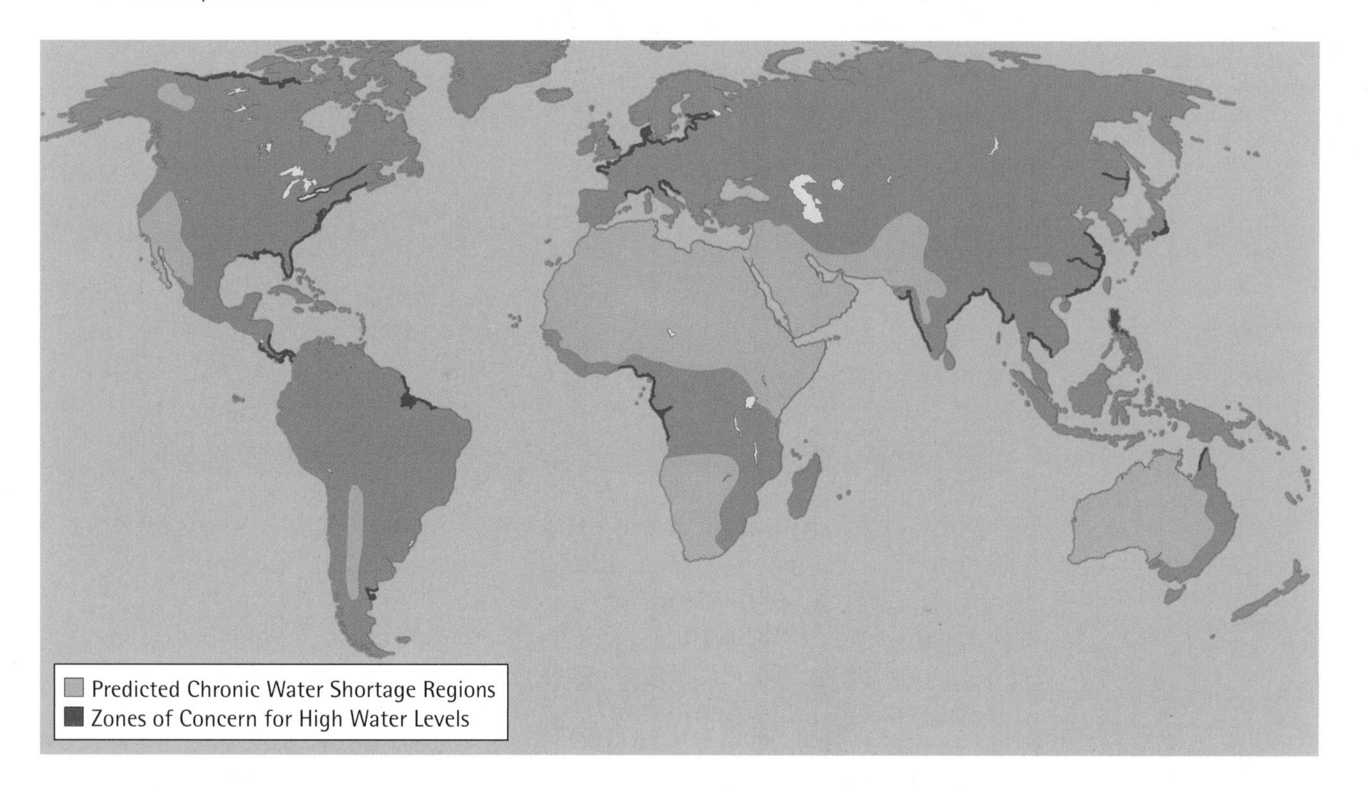

Figure 12.12

In many parts of the world where people lack clean drinking water, vendors walk though market areas selling fresh water from kettles or jugs.

GO TO

www.worldbank.org/depweb/english/modules/environm/water/map.htm

Click on Explore the Map at the botton of your screen. Try the Explore the Map test. Look back at the map. Choose a region where fewer than 50% of the people have access to safe water. How many countries are in the region? Find their names in an atlas.

Fact File

- 2 000 000 000 people lack clean drinking water.
- 30 000 children die every day from water-related diseases.
- 340 L of water are used each day by the average Canadian.
- 8 L of water per day are all that is available to many people in developing countries.

Practical Barriers to Migrations

There are many practical problems when so many people move into one country. No matter where people are, they still need food, housing, clean water, clothing, health care, and other basic services.

SEE PAGE 13

Services for Everyone

When masses of people migrate to one area, tremendous stress is placed on that area. Where will the doctors, nurses, social agencies, and other services come from? Will there be enough jobs available for the immigrants to earn a living to buy the necessities of life? What about sewer systems, schools for all the new students, language teachers to help the newcomers adjust to their new language? When you consider all the requirements, the list seems endless.

Fact File

In the former USSR, people wishing to migrate had to pay nearly $50 000 U.S. to move. Since virtually no one had that much money, the "exit tax" stopped emigration.

A Place to Live for Everyone

When the migration occurs quickly because of war or natural disasters, serious social problems arise. Houses must be built quickly. The money to provide these accommodations, even if only tents, also must be provided. Space for the houses — in what is usually a crowded area to begin with — must be located and serviced. A sudden inflow of refugees creates difficulties and problems for local communities, and often requires outside help. International organizations and governments are then asked to send tents and other supplies to assist the host country in helping the immigrants.

Figure 12.13

Top six desirable immigrant destinations, showing main source nations, 1995. Canada and the United States accept more immigrants each year than the whole of Europe. Why do you think that is?

UNITED STATES

Countries of origin	Numbers of immigrants
Mexico	89 900
Ex-Soviet Union	54 500
Philippines	51 000
Vietnam	41 800
Dom. Republic	38 500
China	35 500

FRANCE

Countries of origin	Numbers of immigrants
Algeria	8 400
Morocco	6 600
Turkey	3 600
USA	2 400
Tunisia	1 900
Ex-Yugoslavia	1 600

CANADA

Countries of origin	Numbers of immigrants
Hong Kong	31 700
India	16 200
Philippines	15 100
China	13 300
Sri Lanka	8 900
Taiwan	7 700

JAPAN

Countries of origin	Numbers of immigrants
China	38 000
Philippines	30 300
USA	27 000
South Korea	18 800
Brazil	11 900
Thailand	6 500

BRITAIN

Countries of origin	Numbers of immigrants
Pakistan	6 300
India	4 900
USA	4 000
Bangladesh	3 300
Nigeria	3 300
Australia	2 000

AUSTRALIA

Countries of origin	Numbers of immigrants
New Zealand	12 300
Britain	11 300
China	11 200
Ex-Yugoslavia	7 700
Hong Kong	4 450
India	3 700

"We joined with Europe to have free movement of goods. ... I did not join Europe to have free movement of terrorists, criminals, drugs, plant and animal diseases, and illegal immigrants."

Margaret Thatcher, former prime minister of Great Britain, May 1989

Political Barriers

So, it is unlikely that many countries are going to welcome large-scale arrivals of immigrants. Governments will pass new laws to regulate the flow of immigrants. Political barriers will be raised to keep people out, such as new restrictions, border closings, and tight quotas. Some countries though, like Canada, encourage different groups to live peacefully together through policies supporting multiculturalism. Canada believes a person's heritage should be remembered. Most Canadians applaud the contributions made to our country by our immigrants.

Quotas as Barriers

SEE PAGE 264

Setting quotas is one way governments set limits on immigration. A **quota** on immigrants is the maximum number allowed to enter the country. Under a quota system, a source nation is allocated only so many immigration spots. If more than that number apply to enter, they are refused. For many years, some countries used quota systems to support racist policies. Australia at one time had a "whites-only" immigration policy. It is still almost impossible for any immigrant to Japan to become a citizen there. Japan's policy is to keep Japan "Japanese." Canada also once had quotas on the number of non-whites entering. World opinion and world problems have helped to alter many of these policies for the better.

"I believe a constitution can permit the co-existence of several cultures and ethnic groups within a single state."

Pierre Trudeau, former prime minister of Canada, September 1965

Figure 12.14

Caravan is a yearly celebration of Toronto's ethnic communities. For the price of a "passport," anyone can visit the many pavillions and enjoy the music, dance, and cuisine of a variety of cultures.

Procedures as Barriers

When people apply through one of our international embassies to come to Canada, they must complete application forms and be measured on our **point system**. These procedures are time-consuming and often frightening and frustrating for the individuals. Yet, they establish the person's suitability for entry according to our rules. With 100 million migrants and 20 million refugees around our world, governments feel there have to be ways to handle them. There are many arguments both for tightening our controls and for loosening them.

SEE PAGE 215

Figure 12.15

In 1956, many Hungarian refugees applied for permission to immigrate to Canada following a revolution against the communist government. In recent years, dealing with immigration concerns has become the main function of many embassies. Immigrants bring fresh ideas, new views, and many talents to Canada.

Illegal Migration

INTERACTION

When people are desperate, they may resort to illegal actions. Families forced out of one region and not allowed into others often have no choice but to try and sneak into another country. This has led to a world problem with illegal migration. Thousands of "illegals" pay people thousands of dollars to be taken to other countries. In the late 1980s, Canada had several boatloads of illegal immigrants left on its shores. Each year, the United States tries to prevent hundreds of thousands of people from entering illegally, especially along its southern borders and coasts.

Figure 12.16

In 1999, one Korean and four Chinese ships brought illegal human cargo to British Columbia. Most of these people were refused entry.

In 1997, the U.S. government spent $495 million keeping illegal migrants in jail.

1. Could population growth ever be a cause for migration? Explain your answer.
2. If our climate warms 2° to 5° Celsius, where will people tend to move in Canada? What might stop them?
3. Using an atlas, find three highly populated areas in the world that could be greatly affected by rising sea levels. List three ways in which they would be affected.
4. Why do you think any country would want to keep some immigrants out? Do you think it is right? Why or why not?

CASE STUDY

Controlling the Flow — Many Kosovo Refugees Go Home Again

After a bitter war, peace was achieved in Kosovo in July, 1999. Now, those who were airlifted out as refugees to Canada had a choice to make: should they stay in Canada and start a new life, or return home? By July 9, 300 of the 6500 Kosovars brought to Canada decided to leave. They boarded buses at their shelters in different Canadian Forces bases to go to airports. Some of their comments showed how they felt.

> *"Thank you, Canada. I have made many new friends here. Even if Canada is my second motherland, I have to go back to Kosovo... . I have my land there, I have my friends there, I have everybody there. When I left Kosovo, I promised the others I would be back on the first plane."*
>
> **Ali Pilana, refugee**

Figure 12.17

Tough choices have to be made — do we go home or stay here and start anew? What would you do?

The Canadian government warned the returning refugees that their houses may be booby-trapped or that there may be land mines. Canadian immigration official Rene Mercier said, "They are going home contrary to the advice given to them, but it is their choice." To help them on their return to their war-torn country, the Canadian government gave each single refugee $500 and each family $2000. Many of those returning were the heads of families. They were leaving women and children here in safety while they determined conditions in Kosovo. What would it be like? Could they live side by side with the Serbs, with whom they had so recently been at war?

Fact File

In the first year, Canada's Kosovo refugee aid worked out to about $20 000 per refugee, including their flights home.

> ***"I was born there; it is my duty to go back to rebuild a new Kosovo. Life is a battle — a fight to rebuild our homes, to rebuild our businesses."***
>
> **Bislim Ramusa, refugee**

Choosing to Settle in Canada

Other Kosovars made the choice for a new start here in Canada. These people were given a choice of possible "refugee resettlement" sites in Canada to go to. At each site, they were provided with a sponsoring family to help them adjust to life in Canada. If they chose not to live in a selected refugee resettlement city or town, they would be on their own. The sites chosen were based on the availability of local services and job opportunities. Sudbury, Thunder Bay, and London were three of the cities chosen as refugee resettlement sites.

People's lives and futures are at stake in such decisions. Canada has provided a good model of helping people in distress around the world.

GO TO www.iom.ch/

This is the Web site of the International Organization for Migration. Click on About IOM. What is the main idea of their mission statement? Explore this site. View the many photos and examples of the organization's involvement.

1. Many Canadians complain about the costs of aiding others. What would you say to those people?
2. What do you think are the three most important considerations for refugee families who decide to stay in Canada and live in a resettlement site?
3. Write a list of "feeling" words that might describe an immigrant teenager's emotions when he or she
   a) leaves his or her country
   b) arrives at the airport in Canada
   c) enters your classroom for the first time
   d) reads stories about the continuing problems in his or her homeland.

Understanding the Concepts

1. Summarize, in point form, the barriers that some people face in trying to migrate. Use these headings to organize your points
   - political barriers
   - physical barriers
   - practical barriers.
2. For people forced to migrate, how do you think their view of the meaning of "place" changes?
3. Explain how the geographic theme of interaction relates to barriers to migration.

Research and Communication Skills

4. Name one country whose borders have been closed and whose people cannot leave, at least not without great difficulty and years of waiting. Why do you think they are restricted?
5. Debate, in your class, the following proposition: "Canada should place fewer restrictions on refugees and immigrants entering Canada."
6. Using the population/immigration data in a current atlas, calculate the ratio of new immigrants to the total Canadian population, e.g., 1:139. Explain what this ratio means.

$$\frac{\text{Total population, 1997}}{\text{Immigrants admitted, 1997}} = \frac{30\ 004\ 000}{216\ 044} = 138.8 \text{ (or 139, rounded)}$$

Map and Globe Skills

7. Ask your parents or caregivers where your family came from. Try to get information about the countries or cities that they started from, the routes that they took to arrive in North America, and the locations where they lived once they arrived here. Draw a map showing the routes that they took.
8. Read, watch, or listen to the news for one week. Note the trouble spots around the world that are or may become sources of refugees. Locate these places and mark them on an outline map of the world. Indicate, by each place on the map:

   a) what the main problem is in that spot

   b) why this problem has caused (or will cause) people to become refugees

   c) where the refugees are going, or will likely go.

Applications

9. Read the newspaper article on the next page. Write a letter to the editor of the newspaper expressing your feelings about the situation.
10. List what you think are the top four qualities immigrants should have to enter Canada. Give a reason for each one.

11. Look back at the photographs of the young woman from Kosovo on page 228 and the soldier at the Berlin Wall on page 230. Suppose you could interview one of these people about his or her life and feelings about conditions in his or her homeland. Make up six questions that you would ask. Some of your questions should deal with feelings about migrating and why or why not that is something that he or she would do.

12. Notice in Figure 12.11 on page 235 that some parts of Canada could face high water levels from global warming if scientists' predictions are accurate.

    a) Which parts of the country are at risk of flooding?

    b) Which of these areas have high population densities (see the map of population densities on page 290 in the map appendix)?

    c) Develop a plan of action that the government of Canada might use to make sure that people's lives are not at risk of flooding. Your plan, which can be done in point form, should include ways to deal with the environmental migrants who will be forced to move to new, higher locations.

13. Visit this Web site. **http://geography.about.com/education/geography/msub24.htm** Click on Countries with the Largest Populations. Look at Figure 12.13 on page 237. Decide if there is a correlation between where immigrants come from and the countries with high populations. Explain your decision.

Illegal Migrants Rescued From Container Hospitalized

Four young people were rescued from a frigid cargo container last night as it sat on a Vancouver loading dock. All four suffered from hunger and cold. Their banging and yelling had attracted a security guard who called immigration authorities.

The four young people, three males and a female, all in their early twenties, are believed to be of Chinese origin. Immigration officers are questioning them to determine where they got into the cargo container and how it arrived in Vancouver. One officer speculated that the migrants might have paid human smugglers to transport them to North America.

The food the young migrants had taken into the container had been eaten days ago and the blankets and sleeping bags that they were huddled in could not protect them from the recent cold temperatures. It is unlikely that they could have survived another night in those conditions.

Jean Lalonde, the security guard who rescued the quartet, was baffled by the incident. "Why would anyone risk their life in that way to come here?" she wondered. "They must have been desperate to have tried such a thing."

All four of the young people have asked to be allowed to stay in Canada as refugees. Officials at Immigration Canada took them into custody pending a hearing to decide their status.

How Culture is Affected by Migration

EXPECTATIONS

- demonstrate an understanding of the ways in which cultures are affected by migration
- identify global distribution patterns of various cultures
- identify the components of culture that can be affected by migration
- demonstrate an understanding that migration results from decisions people make about conditions and events around them

What is Culture?

What is a culture? A **culture** is a way of life shared by a group of people and is composed of a number of things, such as the way people obtain their food, the way they bring up their children, and the values they believe in. Cultures change over time. Imagine the way things were when your grandparents were your age. Think about how your culture has changed since then.

Culture gives us our identity and helps us sustain it. It has many elements: language, religion, social practices, shared experiences and activities, forms of shelter, economic activities, education systems, art, music, and dance. Often, culture is connected to a specific place. This location becomes a symbol for people of their "belongingness" within a particular group. For example, many people of Irish descent who live in North America still feel a strong bond with Ireland.

LOCATION

"Our memory of the past must be faithful to the future if it is to act as stimulus for the present."

Naim Kattan, author

Figure 13.1

Cultures change, as these two photographs of Toronto's skyline show. What changes can you see that have occurred since the top photo was taken 100 years ago?

Figure 13.2

The world's **cultural realms**. Each realm has economic, political, linguistic, religious, and ethnic similarities that distinguish it from others. How does Canada fit into this picture? What is your cultural realm? Do you have only one?

Language

Language is often considered the most important element of a culture. When you share a language with others you can communicate and at least understand, if not share, their values. That is why, through history, forcing a people to stop using their language has been a powerful way to control them.

There are many examples of a language being forced on other groups. The British forced the use of English in Ireland and the original language, Gaelic, almost died out. It is making a strong comeback in Ireland today. The people in the former Republics of the Soviet Union were forced to learn Russian in their schools. In Canada, First Nations people who attended residential schools were discouraged from speaking their native languages and forced to use English or French.

Fact File

First Nations languages are spoken throughout Canada, but the number of people who speak them is decreasing. In the 1990s, some 60 000 people nationwide spoke Cree. Languages most in danger of extiction are Cayuga (360 speakers), Oneida (200 speakers), and Onandaga (fewer than 100 speakers).

Figure 13.3

World language families. A language family is a group of similar languages that have developed from a common parent language. Are you surprised to see that many areas of the world are in the same language group as you? Compare this map to Figure 13.2 on the previous page. What similarities do you see?

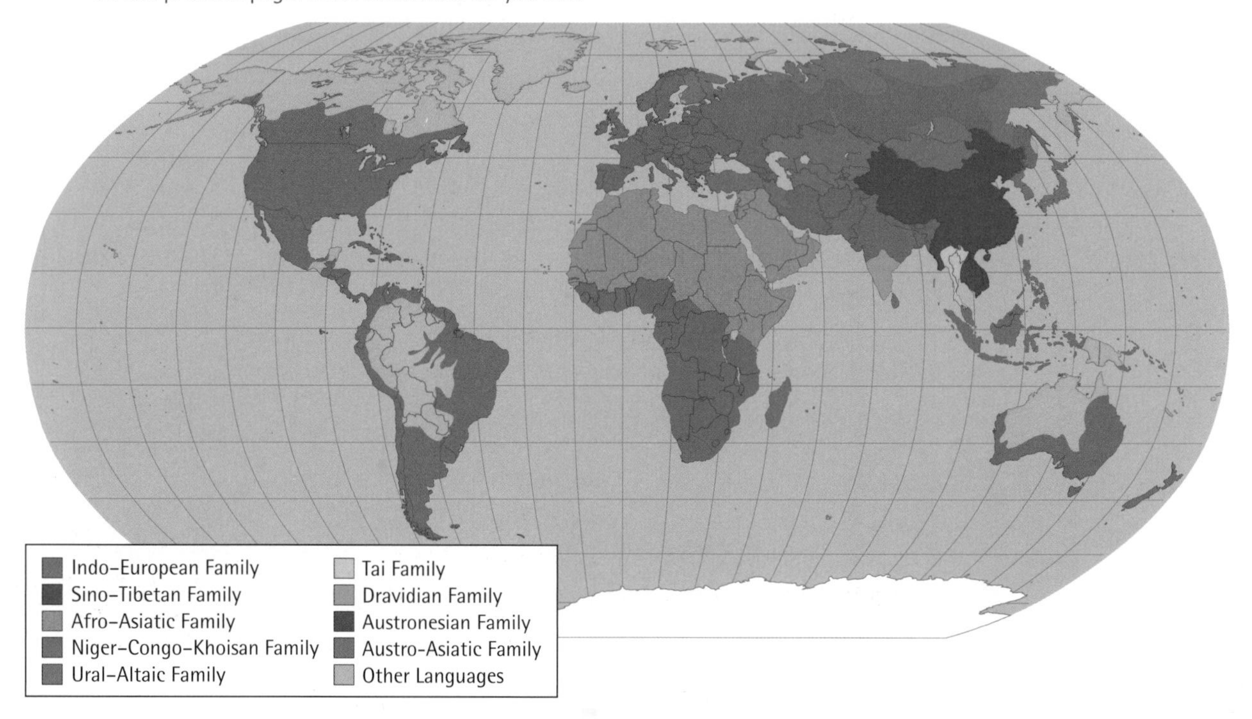

Figure 13.4

The Muslim community is part of the Canadian religious mosaic, and is culturally very diverse. Muslim immigrants have come from the Arab world and from Pakistan, Bangladesh, Turkey, Iran, Eastern Europe, East Africa, and the Caribbean.

Religion

Like language, religious systems are powerful cultural elements. Religious beliefs often influence people's decision to migrate, the time that they choose to move, and their destination. Religion has been a major force in migrations and the spread of cultures. Some migrations were caused by religious persecution, others by people's desire to live among a larger community of those who share their religious views.

When Cultures Meet

Since the 1500s, the cultural map of our world has been changing quickly. Migration and mobility have had a tremendous influence on cultural change, bringing together large groups of people from different cultures.

As explorers and conquerors moved into the Americas, Africa, and elsewhere, they made contact with the local cultural groups. As cultures blended, there was an explosive spread of people, ideas, and information. Very different cultures were thrown together suddenly. This interaction altered and destroyed many long-established cultures.

Fact File

Between 1850 and 1914, over 50 million people left Europe. Seventy percent of them went to North America, 12% to South America, and 9% to South Africa, Australia, and New Zealand.

Figure 13.5

European voluntary migrations, 1815–1914.

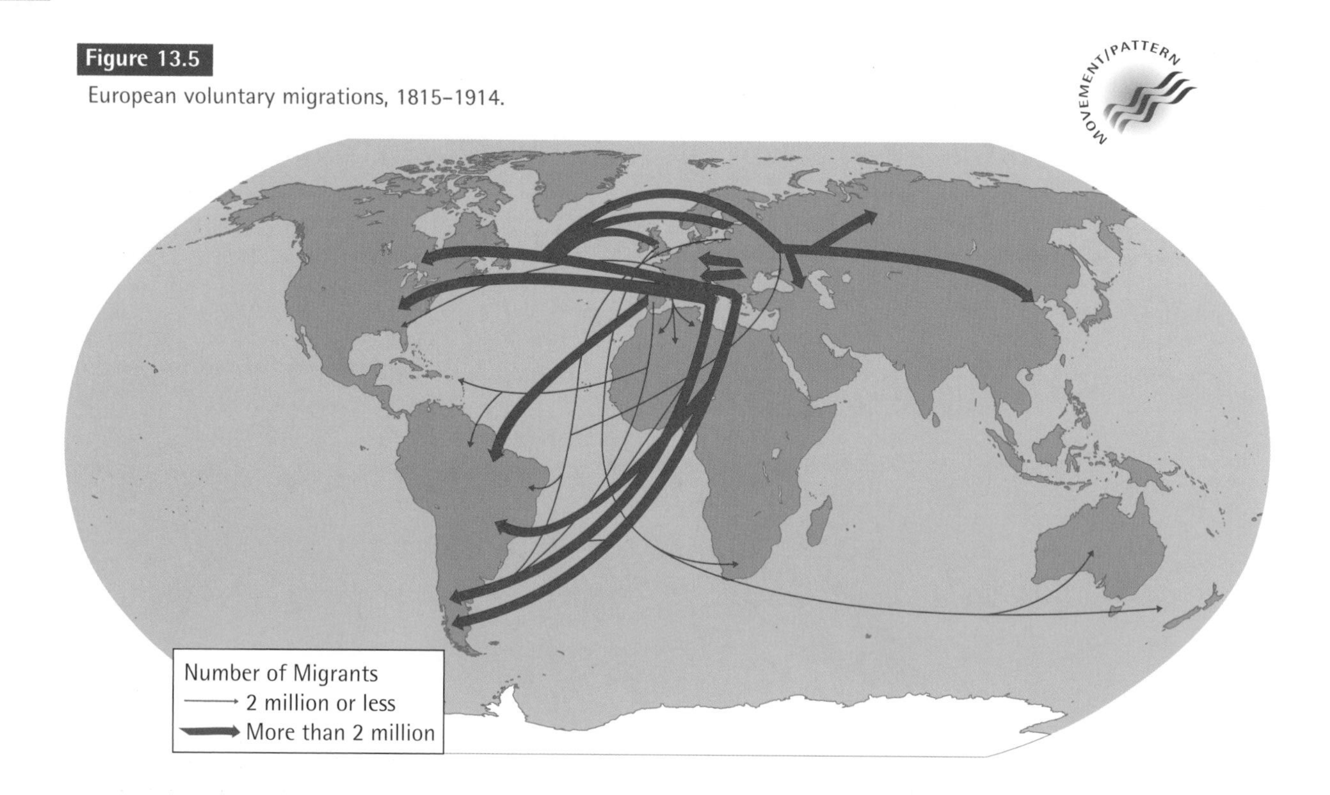

Cultural Isolation

For many reasons, some cultures — like those of Japan, Korea, China, and Mongolia — were not greatly influenced by outside groups until more recent times. These countries had official policies designed to keep foreigners out. Contact with outsiders was infrequent and unwelcome. These countries were able to remain isolated, and to protect their cultures, largely because of the great distance between them and Europe or the Americas. Westerners who wanted to reach these Eastern countries had to face a long journey over land or a dangerous ocean voyage.

> ***"Drinking Coca-Cola does not make Russians think like Americans any more than eating sushi makes Americans think like Japanese. The heart of a culture involves language, religion, values, traditions, and customs."***
>
> **Samuel P. Huntingdon, "The Clash of Civilizations and the New World Order"**

Why Cultures Change

Cultures change for many reasons. Sometimes the living conditions of a group change. For example, when the Bantu people of Africa moved south, they forced the people who were already there, the !Kung, to move toward the Kalahari Desert. To survive, the !Kung had to change their way of life. They needed new tools, new methods of getting food, and new survival skills. Their culture changed to match their new living conditions.

Figure 13.6

The !Kung once lived throughout a large area of South Africa, but were pushed into the Kalahari Desert by the Bantu. Think how difficult it would be for you to have to start life anew in the Arctic. The fact that the !Kung developed new skills to survive in their new desert habitat shows how creative and adaptable their culture is.

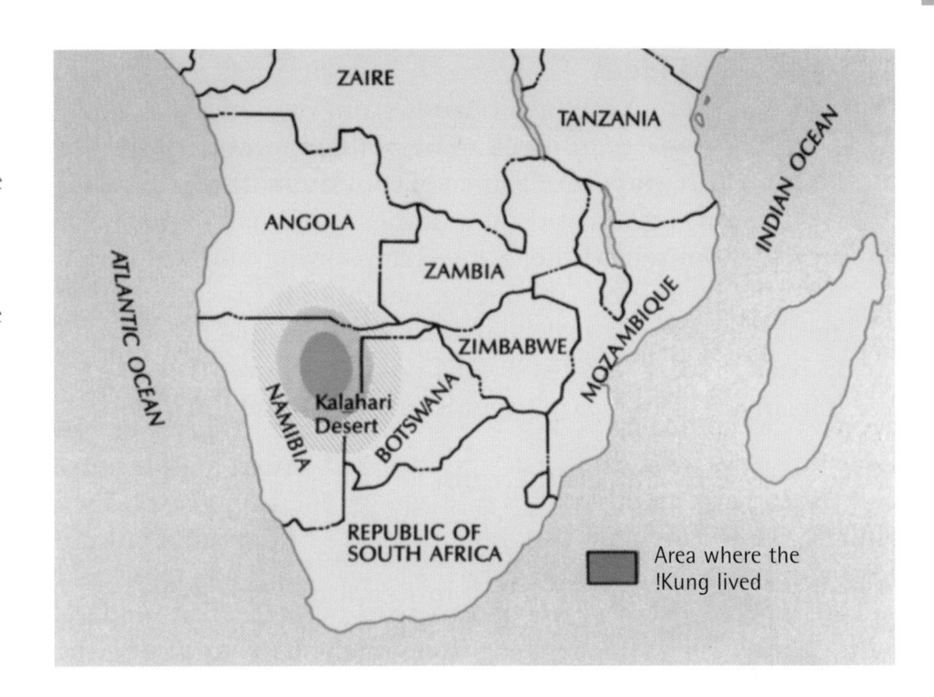

Figure 13.7

A !Kung hunter in the Kalahari Desert (right); Cape Province, the original home of the !Kung (below). Notice the difference between the two landscapes.

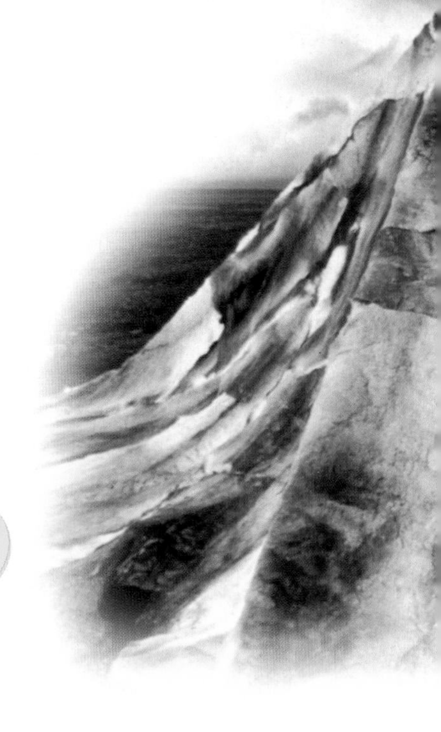

The Spread of Ideas

INTERACTION

Sometimes different cultures borrow from one another. The early Lapps of Norway were hunters. Some of them moved south and met other groups who were farmers. From them, the Lapps learned how to grow grain and raise domestic animals. They began to live a more settled life. Some Lapps living along the seacoast learned from their Norwegian neighbours how to build boats. They became such excellent boat builders that they even sold many back to their teachers! This peaceful movement of cultural ideas from one group to another is called **cultural diffusion.**

Destruction of Cultural Groups

SEE PAGE 151

Throughout history, cultures have been destroyed, lost, forgotten, or become unimportant. Cultures that were more technologically advanced in weaponry often simply overran another culture, destroying it. This was especially true of the Europeans who, in their wild quest for riches, tried to control or destroy most cultural groups they encountered.

As well, the minor diseases of one group can become deadly killers of another. When the first Europeans came to Amazonia, the area drained by the Amazon River and its tributaries, they brought diseases with them against which the native people had no resistance: smallpox, tuberculosis, measles, and even the common cold. Thousands of Amazon Indians died of these diseases. Today, there are few surviving Indians of Amazonia, and those live mainly on reserves.

SEE PAGE 32

Figure 13.8

The Trans-Amazonas Highway opened the Amazon Basin to settlement and Western-style development. It went right through the natives' reserve lands, and has meant drastic, damaging cultural changes to the rainforest and to the people living there. What are some of the changes that these people might be forced to accept?

Figure 13.9

What evidence do you see of outside cultural influences (cultural diffusion) in this Inuit community?

It's Your World

As the demand for Arctic oil and gas increased through the 1970s, large companies moved their drilling rigs into the Canadian North. This had a great impact on the culture of the Inuit people. Many Inuit left their traditional ways of living to work on the oil rigs. They learned the skills needed for their new life and began the change to fit into modern North American society. When oil prices dropped and oil companies stopped most of the drilling in the Arctic, many Inuit lost their jobs. They had little money to look after their needs, and very poor hopes of a job in the North in the near future. Also, they had sometimes lost the skills needed to live off the land. What responsibility should large companies have to the northern people whose lives have been changed so severely?

Fact File

The United States' immigration policy encourages all arrivals to assimilate into the dominant culture. They call this the "melting pot." Canada's policy of ethnic diversity has been likened to a "mosaic," that is, different cultural groups are encouraged to hold on to their traditions.

Toward Assimilation

Overpowering or dominant cultures often leave little room for the original culture to survive. The new, more modern culture makes the older way of doing things seem less important. Many of the young people in the less dominant culture turn away from their traditional lives in order to try to join the more modern culture. This changing to fit into another culture is called **assimilation**. It is not always very successful. Young people from the older culture seldom have the skills required to get good jobs in the new culture. Even when they do have the skills, they often face strong resistance in the form of prejudice and **racism**.

1. Copy the chart below into your notebook and complete it, showing what you think is the main expression for each element of *your* culture.

Cultural Element	Main Expression
Language	English
Religion	
Place	
Music	
Stories	

2. What is meant by the term "melting pot," as it is used in the Fact File on the previous page? How does this differ from a "mosaic"?
3. Outline three ways in which cultural change occurs.

This short, satirical poem by Jamaican poet Louise Bennet talks about how Jamaican immigrants to England are changing British culture. Bennet uses the poem to highlight some of the problems immigrants face. While it is presented in a humorous way, there is sadness in the poem, too.

"Wat a joyful news, Miss Mattie
I feel like me heart gwine burs'
Jamaican people colonizin'
England in reverse ...
Wat a devillment a Englan'!
Dem face war an' brave de worse
But I'm wonderin' how dem gwine stan'
Colonizin' in reverse."

From Roots to Routes

The greatest force influencing the choice of destination for a migrant is the strength of the cultural connection to that destination. Are the people there like me? What language do they speak? Will I be able to practise my religion there? The answers to these and other similar questions play a major role in a person's decision on where to emigrate. Often, the connections between the two places may date back to colonial times. Or, there may be more modern ties.

Figure 13.10

Britain's ethnic minorities account for less than 5% of the total population. The ethnic population is concentrated in the inner cities, where poverty and social problems persist despite progress over the last 25 years.

GO TO

http://cicnet.ci.gc.ca

This is the site for Immigration Canada. Choose the language you wish to work in. Click on Applications on the left side of your screen. Now click on Immigrating to Canada. What are the four categories of immigrants accepted by Canada?

Coming to Canada

MOVEMENT/PATTERN

When you travel to a strange city or community, there are things that can make you feel more comfortable, like seeing signs in your own language, hearing music with which you're familiar, or visiting stores similar to those you find at home. Many Canadians who travel a great deal remark that they feel best when their airplane touches down in Canada or when they cross back over our border. It is your comfort with your cultural identity, and the place where that identity is welcomed, that gives you a feeling of relief upon returning home.

Most immigrants look for that same level of comfort. They try to go to countries that share some of the things they are familiar with, such as language, religion, music, or history. For example, when people move to Canada from the countries of West Africa, they generally go to Montreal because the language of colonialism in Western Africa was predominantly French. In Montreal, West Africans will be able to communicate more easily with Canadians. Similarly, most migrants from the Caribbean Islands, like Jamaica, who move to Canada settle in Toronto, a city whose English roots make life more comfortable for them.

Within many large cities, there are clusters of people who come from the same cultural background. Immigrants new to a country often tend to move near these cultural clusters, or **enclaves**. They can find personal support, eat familiar foods, and acquire friends more easily within the districts where these groups live.

REGION

Figure 13.11

Not only do these ethnic neighbourhoods provide support to immigrants, they also become attractive to the broader community for ideas and celebrations. What are some of the ways in which immigrants enrich Canadian culture?

Changing Times, Changing Migrants

Today, there are new types of migrants. An increasing number are professionals — including musicians and athletes like Jaromir Jagr, the hockey star; Orlando Hernandez, the baseball pitcher; and Ricky Martin, the singer. These are high-profile people who change countries to further their careers.

Modern, fast transportation systems, such as those in Europe, have given us the "commuting migrant." This is someone who may work one or more days each week in a neighbouring country, returning home at day's or week's end. These workers have not given up their country. They merely work in another land.

Figure 13.12

For many professionals like Pedro Martinez, their talents are a way for them to migrate out of poor economic conditions. Their salaries often help their families in their homelands. Do you think high-profile professionals should get special treatment upon entering Canada?

Women as Migrants

Before 1980, most migrants were men. These were the long-distance migrants, often pioneers in new areas. Women used to be short-range migrants, moving to low-risk areas along well-established routes. This has all changed. More women now move more often. For example, women have become the majority of migrants from many Asian lands.

SEE PAGE 277

Fact File

The U.S. Bureau of Census reported on February 1, 1999 that over 40 counties in the coastal western states had over 5000 people from Asia and the Pacific Islands in the population. The largest was in Los Angeles County, with 1 187 392 Asian people.

1. Name three high-profile migrants. Tell where they came from, where they went, and what their professions are (or were).
2. Why do you think there are more women migrants now?

In the Mainstream

The major cultural group in a society is called the **mainstream population**. In Canada, outside of Quebec, the mainstream population for nearly all of our country's history has been white, Anglo-Saxon, and Protestant. In Quebec it has been white, European, and Catholic. When newcomers arrive, they bring both social and economic changes to their new country. Most people in the mainstream group react to these changes. In some instances, the reactions are favourable; in others, they are not.

Using Immigration to Foster Racism

When cultures are threatened by changes stemming from migration, some people resist. Many don't want their culture to be changed. Some cultural groups mistrust strangers — people who look and act differently. This fear is called **xenophobia** and often gives rise to racism.

GO TO http://collections.ic.gc.ca/obho/

This site talks about black history. Click on People and then Historical. Now scroll down to #16 in the Human + Civil Rights list on the right side of your screen. Click on Harriet Tubman. She was one of the many "conductors" on the Underground Railroad. Read her story. What was her connection to Canada?

There are groups who foster racism. Some use immigration and its problems to gain supporters. For instance, within some countries, the idea of "racial purity" continues to influence many laws, making it very difficult for immigrants to become citizens. Some immigrant families have lived in some countries for over 200 years, but still are not citizens.

LOCATION

SEE PAGE 220

Some groups throughout the world foster racism by misusing religious teachings. They argue that for their culture to stay intact, all citizens must strictly adhere to the teachings of their faith. Allowing others with different beliefs and values into their country, they think, would unfavourably affect their identity.

Figure 13.13

Two hundred marchers from the Hungarian National Front demonstrate in Budapest. Do you think racist organizations like this one should be allowed? Why or why not?

Closing Cultures

In some countries, there has been a revival of nationalism. Some small groups within a nation may want to be independent. They wish to have their own land, with their own cultural identity. This is happening in Quebec, in many parts of the former Soviet Union, and with native groups in Central America, Mexico, and Central Africa. They want to be able to protect their cultures from outside influences. This thinking seems to go against the major trends in the world today. Most nations are trying to encourage global connections through freer trade, travel, and communications.

CONNECTIONS TO

The Basque separatist group ETA has been blamed for causing 800 deaths in its 30-year fight for independence from Spain. In fact, the Basques – who live in northern Spain, mainly around the Pyrenees Mountains – have maintained their distinct culture, including their unique language, since the time of the early Romans. Modern DNA testing of blood groups has shown that the Basque people probably had very different ancestors from other Europeans.

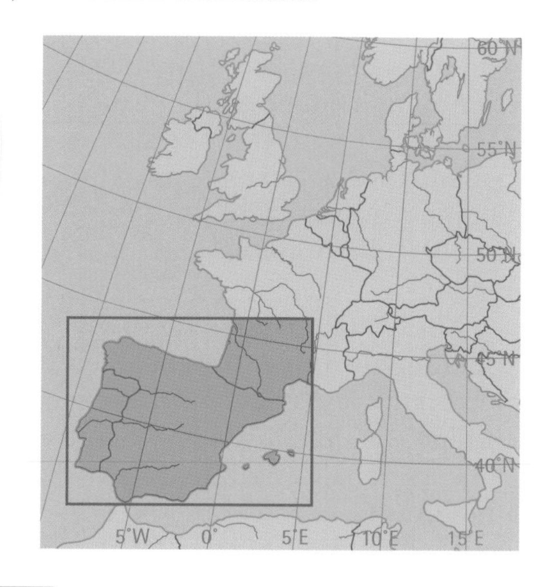

Figure 13.14

Basque separatists demonstrate in Spain. Keeping an identity and heritage strong is a difficult task for many minority groups. Why do some groups feel it is important to have their own country in order to maintain a strong heritage?

Gatekeeping

Fact File

In 1994, France established a special police force aimed only at finding the one million illegal immigrants in the country and deporting them. The French government acknowledged that they were targeting North Africans and blacks.

Governments have always been active in restricting the flow of migrants to protect their country's culture. Many countries set up systems that favoured one race, culture, or religion over others. When whole countries agree to barriers like this, it is national racism.

Immigration Helps

For many, immigration is a positive force. Our government encourages immigration because the contributions made by immigrants to our culture and economy increase the vibrancy of Canadian life.

"*I feel like I've won the lottery!*"

Canadian expression of good fortune

"*I feel like I've won a ticket to Canada!*"

Polish expression of good fortune

Worldwide Good Will

Canada has a policy of openness to immigrants and refugees. The world sees Canada as a leader in humanitarian aid. Canadians benefit from this point of view. Our improved international stature helps us when we travel abroad. For example, our businesspeople establish themselves more easily overseas because of Canada's good reputation.

Figure 13.15

Many travellers — even non-Canadians — wear the maple leaf because it seems to gain them acceptance more easily.

How Does Immigration Create Wealth?

The addition of many skilled workers and professionals helps countries' economies grow. When immigrants arrive in their adopted homelands, they need all sorts of new products — stoves, refrigerators, clothing, furniture, TVs, and toys. Factories have to make more of these items, thus creating new jobs. The newly arrived immigrants also start new businesses and hire many workers.

SEE PAGE 80

SEE PAGE 276

Immigrants also increase the number of workers that are available to work in every sector of the economy — skilled, unskilled, and professional. Studies show that over the long term, immigrants increase a nation's wealth.

Fact File

One of every 12 jobs in Germany is held by a **Gastarbeiter** ("guest worker"), or foreign migrant worker. There are 1.8 million Turkish migrant workers in Germany.

Immigrants Add to Our Culture

Immigration adds new vibrancy to a country's cultural life. Celebrations such as Caribana in Toronto or Mardi Gras in Rio de Janeiro add excitement to a community. Immigrants bring wealth, new foods, music, literature, dance, and ideas with them. This sharing and appreciation of other people and their history add to world understanding and co-operation.

Figure 13.16

Caribana, Toronto's celebration of Caribbean music and dance, draws one million people annually from all over North America.

1. Write your definition of racism.
2. List three ways that racism hurts people.
3. Give four examples of how immigration helps Canada.

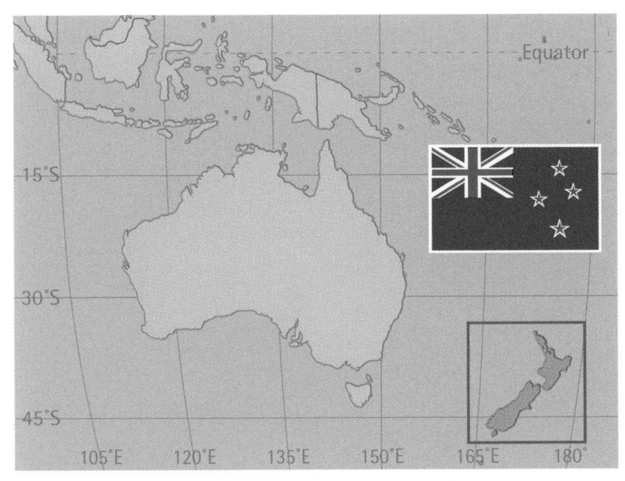

Figure 13.17

Location of New Zealand.

New Zealand – Tricking Immigrants

In 1990, New Zealand decided to try to strengthen its trade ties with other Asian–Pacific countries. Part of the plan they developed was to advertise a new, more liberal, immigration policy. The New Zealand government hoped that immigrants would provide ties that would help to open trade with other nations.

When the new policy began, immigration grew rapidly. Between 1991 and 1996, 173 000 Asian immigrants entered New Zealand.

The 33 000 immigrants that arrived in 1994 brought $355 million with them, or an average of over $10 000 per migrant. They were ready and eager to start their lives in their adopted country. But for the many that headed to New Zealand with great hopes, they soon found a reality that said "we don't really want you here." For example, immigrants could not get high-paying jobs. Of half the Chinese who said they were in business before they went to New Zealand, only 20% were able to start a business there. Many official roadblocks were put in their way.

SEE PAGE 276

Some doctors and dentists were restricted from practising by a system of qualification points set up by the government. If they did not pass a very difficult English language test, they had to pay nearly $10 000 to start work. Professionals in other fields also found their qualifications and degrees were not accepted.

Figure 13.18

"Haere mai" means "welcome" in Maori, the language of New Zealand's indigenous people. For many newcomers, the welcome was false and soon over.

Figure 13.19

New Zealand is a country of migrants, beginning with the first Maori settlements 1200 years ago. Today's population is 88% descended from European migrants. Recent arrivals include Asians from Hong Kong and Malaysia, and refugees from Bosnia and Kosovo.

Some immigrants couldn't find work at all. Families had to split up to find work on nearby Pacific islands. One couple, both doctors, said, "Back in Sri Lanka we had a good home and land. It's hard not to get depressed." Their new home in New Zealand was a humble place, with six broken-down chairs making up their living room furniture.

These immigrants were deceived about life in New Zealand. Many suffered social problems, such as family break-up and mental illness. Social assistance was not available until a new arrival had been in New Zealand for two years. That meant many were forced to take any job they could find to get by for at least two years. One couple from Egypt who scored high points on entering New Zealand could not get work in their fields. They had over 75 job refusals. They sadly commented, "If the country did not need us, why did their government invite us here? We have lost so much. We want to work. It is humiliating to be on welfare. I am so frustrated."

Connections to Society

Complaints of racial discrimination toward immigrants were reported in a survey called "Beyond 2000," undertaken by the *Toronto Star*. Of all ethnic groups polled, blacks reported the highest incidence of discrimination. Ninety-one percent felt the discrimination was based on skin colour (*Toronto Star*, July 4, 1999). While Canada has a better record of human rights than many countries, racial discrimination is still a serious problem.

Check Back

1. What are three hardships that any immigrant might face arriving in a new country?
2. Could New Zealand's immigration system be considered national racism? Why or why not?

Fact File

Between 1991 and 1996, while all other provinces increased in population, Newfoundland's dropped by over 27 000.

When Countries Lose Their Young

Many of the countries that are losing people to migration have populations with a very high percentage of people under 20 years of age. They choose to migrate because they have few prospects locally. Sometimes, young people migrate for adventure, change, challenge, and excitement.

SEE PAGE 31

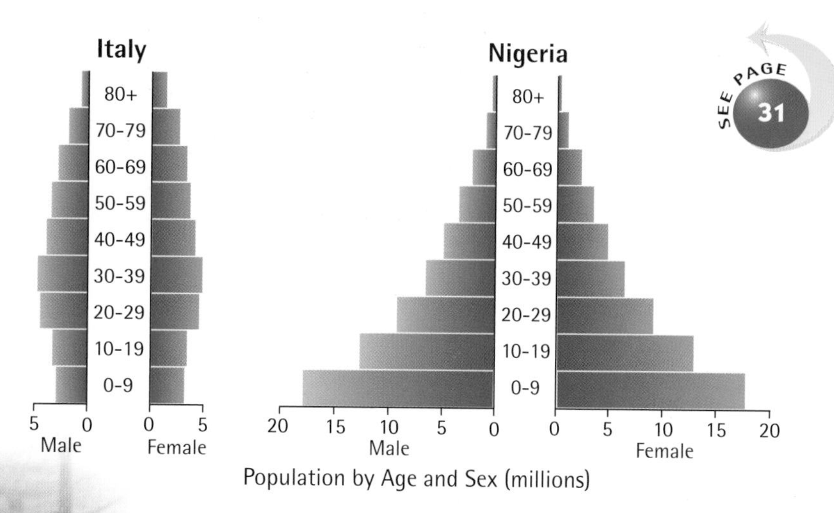

Figure 13.20

Population pyramids for Italy and Nigeria. The high percentage of youth under 20 will create many economic and social problems for some developing countries in the future. What might some of these problems be?

Figure 13.21

In 1996, over 8000 people left Newfoundland for other provinces – up from 6000 in 1994 and 2500 in 1992. Why do you think the numbers have increased so dramatically over this time?

REGION

As parents see their children migrate, they are glad their young ones will have a chance for a better future. But parents also see a generational loss to their local community. When most of a small rural community's youth migrate, either to big cities or to other countries, the character of the communities is changed. Some regions see such a big decline in their population that whole villages disappear, leaving only a few elderly behind. The traditions of these communities — possibly even their language — will die with the elders.

1. As prime minister of Canada, you must make a case for opening the nation's doors to more immigrants. Write a paragraph to show Canadians why this would be beneficial.
2. Why do many people want to keep their culture from changing?
3. Suggest three ways to reduce discrimination toward immigrants.
4. Would you like to migrate? Explain.

CASE STUDY

Recent Migration to Greece

Greek culture and history date back over 5000 years. Greece has always attracted immigrants. Today, it faces many difficult problems stemming from immigration.

Greece is a small country by Canadian standards. While its population is nearly 11 million, about the same as Ontario, Greece is only one-sixth of Ontario's size. The country has a very long coastline — 59 200 km, including its many islands. It is also quite mountainous. These conditions make it hard for Greek authorities to stop the illegal flow of people into the country.

REGION

Figure 13.22

Location of Greece.

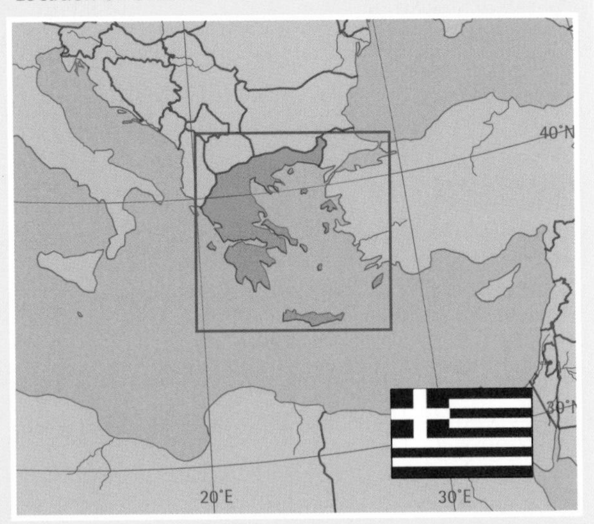

Where Do They Come From?

MOVEMENT/PATTERN

Since the collapse of communism in the Soviet Union and Yugoslavia at the end of the 1980s, Greece has experienced a flood of immigration from these countries. By the end of 1999, Greece had received over one million refugees. Most were from nearby Albania and Kosovo, but large numbers also came from Iran, Iraq, Turkey, Ethiopia, and Somalia. Hundreds of thousands of Albanians and Kosovars trekked over the mountains to reach the Greek border. There have been so many that Greece established reception centres for the refugees along its northern frontier.

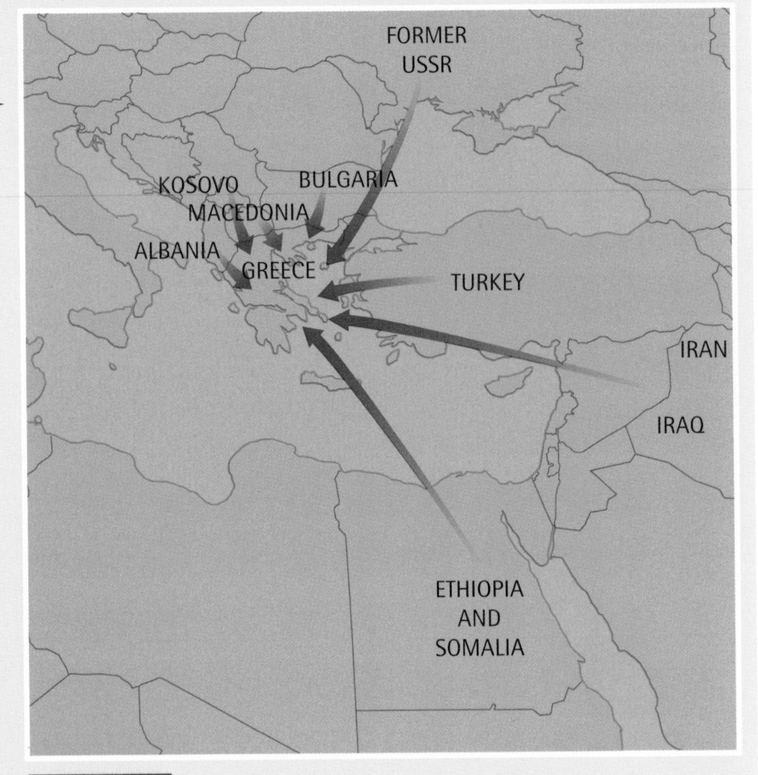

Figure 13.23

Main flows of migrants to Greece, 1989–1999 (total, one million +).

Public Concern

Greece's economy did not grow much during the 1990s. This made it difficult for the country to provide for the great numbers of people flowing in. Jobs were difficult to find. Some in the mainstream population were upset by all the arrivals. Many Greeks encouraged the government to "shut the door" — to stop the flow of migrants.

To complicate matters, there was a big problem with "drop-offs". There are people traffickers (human smugglers) who charge immigrants over $5000 to be dumped illegally on the shore of some Greek island. A big international incident occurred in 1993 when the Greek government stopped a Turkish ship filled with illegal Iraqi immigrants. The ship was trying to enter Greek waters. It was held at sea for 18 days while the governments of Greece and Turkey argued over a solution. Eventually, the Turkish government agreed to let the Iraqis enter Turkey.

GO TO

www.iom.ch

Click on About IOM. Then, click on Trafficking in Migrants. Choose Overview. Scroll toward the end of the Overview and note the seven key summary points about the people-trafficking problem.

Figure 13.24

Visitors to Greece seldom fail to visit the Parthenon, one of the historic sites of Greek greatness.

1. Refer to Figure 13.23. For one source region shown, research the reasons why people leave – for example, civil war, poor economy, or an environmental disaster.
2. No one has yet figured out how to stop human smuggling. Suggest a way of looking at the problem that may help find a solution.

Understanding the Concepts

1. Explain how immigrants can alter the character of a place. Think of the impact of Italians settling in Canada, Algerians settling in France, or Vietnamese settling in the United States.
2. How could a movie theatre in a community cause cultural change or influence migration?
3. List three ways in which immigration is visible in your community.
4. List, in point form, how TV could influence immigration decisions, such as "Should I leave?" and "Where should I go?"
5. Some governments are passing laws to limit the number of American movies that will be allowed into their countries. Why do you think this is so? Do you agree with such laws? Explain.

GO TO

http://deil.lang.uiuc.edu/exchange

This is a site mainly for foreign students who are studying English as a Second Language (ESL) in the United States. Students contribute personal essays about their home countries and also about their experiences in North America. Click on World Cultures to explore some of their observations. You can also find a pen pal at this site.

Research and Communication Skills

6. Use books, videos, and other aids you find at your school or local library. Compare how children live in different regions of the world. Consider such things as what boys and girls are allowed to do, their work responsibilities, material goods, and other cultural factors.
7. Visit your school or local library. Read narratives about people's migration to other regions, such as the move to the American or Canadian West, Japanese or Chinese people going to California or Vancouver, or people moving out of Europe after the world wars. List the reasons these people gave for moving.

Map and Globe Skills

8. Prepare a display of maps showing cultural themes (such as ethnic origins, food preferences, and language spoken at home) that reflect the many cultures in your school or community. You may have to interview your friends, other students, or neighbours to get information.

Applications

9. Use maps and pictures to show two big changes due to migration in London, England, New Delhi, India, or Toronto.

10. Contact a local federal immigration office to arrange for a representative to speak to your class regarding current immigration issues and concerns.

11. How does the spread of cultural traits, such as U.S.-based fast-food franchises, the popularity of Chinese foods, or the use of English as a business language in many world regions assist the process of cultures coming together? Does spreading material goods and trends from our society to others around the world really change other people's cultures? Explain your answer.

12. "Whatever may come after multiculturalism will aim not at preserving differences, but at blending them into a new vision of Canadianness ... where every individual is Canadian, undiluted and undivided." Do you agree or disagree with this statement? Explain your answer.

13. Write a set of postcards to your friends and family telling them about your life as an immigrant to Canada. Send seven postcards, each dated a month apart.

Figure 13.25

A Baskin-Robbins outlet in Tokyo, Japan. What looks similar to, or different from, Baskin-Robbins outlets in your community? Do any of these similarities or differences surprise you? Explain.

14 How Migration Affects Canada

EXPECTATIONS

- describe patterns and trends in migration and their effects on Canada
- demonstrate an understanding that migration results from decisions people make about conditions and events around them
- identify the components of culture that can be affected by migration
- demonstrate an understanding of the effects that migration has had on the development of Canada
- identify patterns in migration, using thematic maps

A Country of Immigrants

Canada is a land of immigrants. Everyone's ancestors got here one way or another. Our original settlers walked across a land bridge between Asia and North America over 20 000 years ago. New settlers arrived from Britain or France to farm Lower and Upper Canada starting around 1600. Migrants from Europe came here after the two world wars. Refugees from human and environmental disasters in other lands arrived in Canada throughout the 1900s.

> *"Instead of being welcomed to our new home, we were tagged like surplus merchandise at a bargain-basement sale and herded into large cages."*
>
> **Peter C. Newman, author, immigrant to Canada**

Many different cultural groups entered Canada after 1850. They settled either in and around already established places, or in frontier areas (the Canadian West was just being settled by Europeans at this time). Often, these groups settled in parts of Canada that were much like their homelands in appearance. People from the steppes of the Ukraine settled on the prairie grasslands. Swedes and Finns settled on the Canadian Shield lake country west of Lake Superior. Settling in a familiar landscape meant that newcomers could keep some of their lifestyle practices, and that their memories of home would stay with them.

Figure 14.1

Immigrants to Canada, then and now. While our earliest migrants came mainly from Europe, most of today's immigrants come from Asia. The man taking Canadian citizenship in this photo was born in Hong Kong; his daughter is 100% "made in Canada"!

GO TO

www.ednet.ns.ca/educ/heritage/pier21/

Click on Stories. Click on one of the pictures and read about the experiences of those people in coming to Canada.

Fact File

Between 1928 and 1971, over one million immigrants entered Canada through Halifax. All were processed at Pier 21, which has been restored as a museum of immigration.

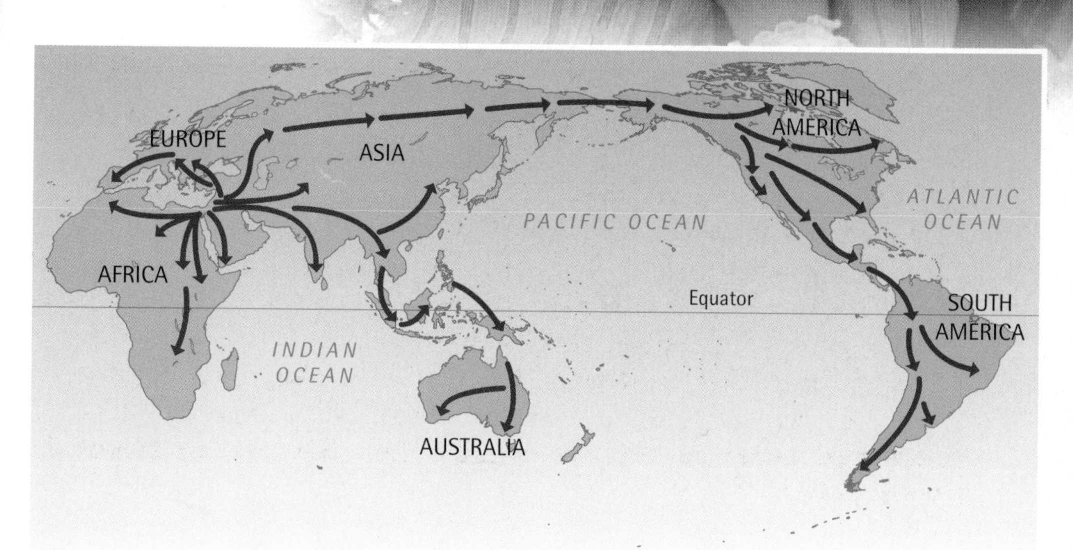

Figure 14.2

The original settlers into North America probably arrived some 20 000 years ago when they crossed from Asia at the end of the last Ice Age. At that time, sea levels were lower.

Connections to Demographics

Births, deaths, and net migration (immigration minus emigration) can have both long- and short-term effects on society. These numbers alter the demand for schools, housing, health care, and age-related recreational items (such as rock CDs or golf clubs). Estimates of these changes help economic and social planners calculate how many workers, consumers, and taxpayers will be active in coming years.

SEE PAGE 5

SEE PAGE 32

Love It or Hate It?

Canadian culture has been built over time and has been in a continuous process of change. Migration continues to influence Canada. Many people have strong feelings about its effects on our society and economy.

There is much prejudice and discrimination regarding the topic of migration. Some attitudes are based on mistaken ideas that have little evidence to support them. A newcomer can be rejected because of these false ideas. For example, language differences or appearances can create barriers to acceptance of newcomers.

Figure 14.3

Can you think of two ways your school helps to eliminate prejudice and discrimination?

GO TO www.tulipfestival.ca/history/

This site tells about a very famous immigrant to Canada. Visit it and discover who she was.

Fact File

Net migration of a country is calculated by subtracting the number of people who emigrate from the number of people who immigrate. It is a positive number when more come in than leave. Canada has had a positive net migration for most years.

SEE PAGE 27

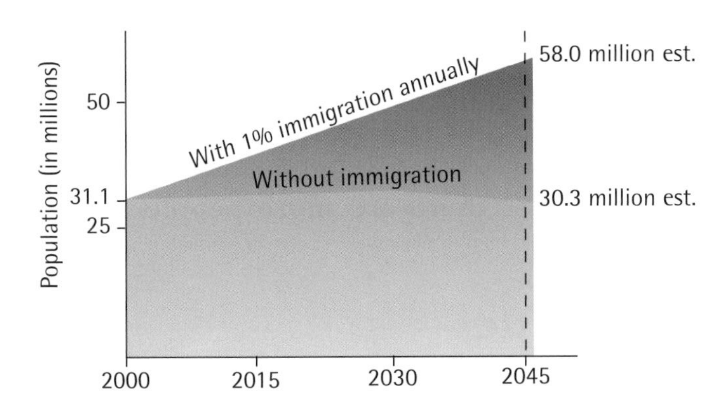

Figure 14.4

Canada's future population, with and without immigration. Without immigration, our population growth in 2000 (0.6%) could fall to 0.0% by 2030.

How Many is Enough?

Do you think Canada has too many people? In 1999, Canada's population was nearing 31 000 000. Our population density was 3.35 people/km^2. As a comparison, France has nearly twice our population in only about 10% of the space we have.

In 1999, Canada's rate of natural population increase was 0.6%. At that rate, it would take Canada's population 116 years to double. But, demographers predict that our natural rate of increase will drop to zero by the year 2030. Our population would then actually start to decrease. The hidden factor in all these numbers is immigration.

SEE PAGE 26

Fact File

In the 1980s, 14% of immigrants to Canada who became Canadian citizens migrated to the U.S. within five years.

Figure 14.5

Population growth components for Canada, 1851–1997 (thousands of persons).

	Total Population Growth	Natural Increase		Net Migration		Census (population at end of period)
		Births	Deaths	Immigration	Emigration	
1851–61	793	1281	670	352	170	3 230
1861–71	459	1370	760	260	411	3 689
1871–81	636	1480	790	350	404	4 325
1881–91	508	1524	870	680	826	4 833
1891–1901	538	1548	880	250	380	5 371
1901–11	1836	1925	900	1550	739	7 207
1911–21	1581	2340	1070	1400	1089	8 788
1921–31	1589	2415	1055	1200	971	10 377
1931–41	1130	2294	1072	149	241	11 507
1941–51	2141	3186	1214	548	379	13 648
1951–56	2072	2106	633	783	184	16 081
1956–61	2157	2362	687	760	278	18 238
1961–66	1777	2249	731	539	280	20 015
1966–71	1553	1856	766	890	427	21 568
1971–76	1492	1755	824	1053	492	23 518
1976–81	1382	1820	843	771	366	24 900
1981–86	1304	1872	885	677	360	26 204
1986–91	1907	1933	946	1199	279	28 111
1991–96	1848	1935	1027	1170	230	29 959
1997	317	365	217	219	50	30 276

As our population grows, changes happen around us, but it often takes time for these changes to be realized. You may notice that the town population signs on the highways change, or that there are a lot of new housing projects or more traffic around the community, or simply that there are more people in the streets and shops.

Figure 14.6

Source regions for Canadian immigrants over an 85-year period. What changes do you notice? What effects do you think these changes have had on Canadian society today?

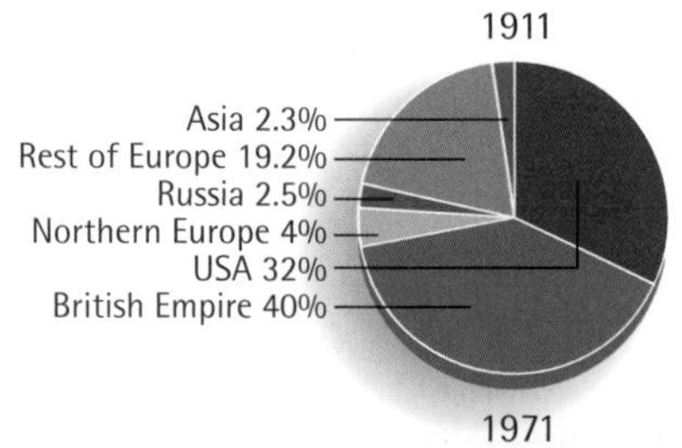

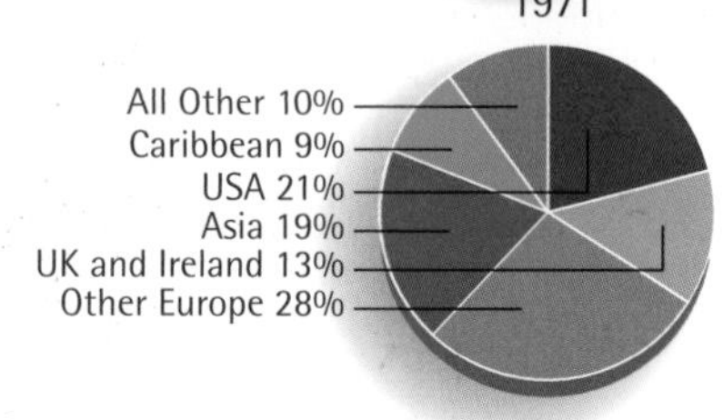

Visible Minorities

A **visible minority** is a group of people who stand out from the mainstream population because of a clearly seen physical characteristic. People of colour are visible minorities in most Canadian cities. Our population is changing, not only in number but also by race and cultural background, especially in the last 40 years. As a result, when many Canadians see people who look visibly different than the mainstream population, they take more notice of migration.

Until the 1960s, white European immigrants made up the majority of new Canadians. Canada now receives significant numbers of people from Hong Kong, the Philippines, China, India, the Caribbean, South and Central America, and Africa. The effects of these non-European immigrants have been tremendous and can be seen most vividly in our large urban centres.

It's Your World

Like many other countries, Canada sets a quota on the number of immigrants and refugees allowed to enter each year. It is usually a little less than 1% of our total population, or about 200 000. In some years, we have not even reached our quota.

Figure 14.7

Immigration has changed, and continues to change, the way we view our country, its connections to other countries, and our basic values.

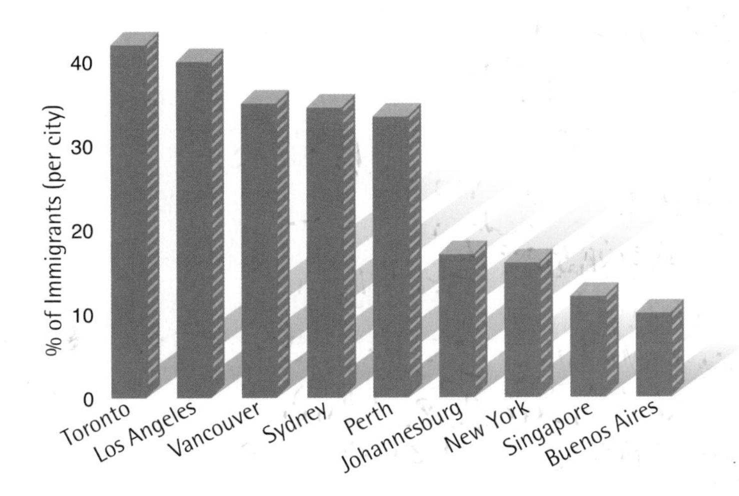

Figure 14.8

The world's most cosmopolitan cities (Toronto and Vancouver rank first and third, respectively). Migrants are lured to big cities by jobs, families, friends, and the city's reputation for tolerance and diversity.

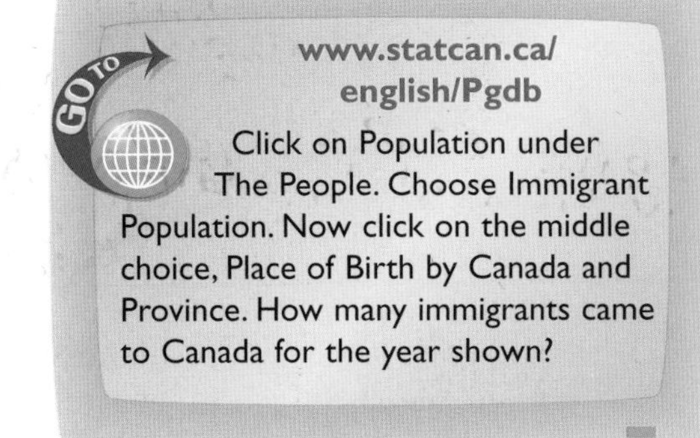

Figure 14.9

Ethnic composition of Canada in the 1990s.

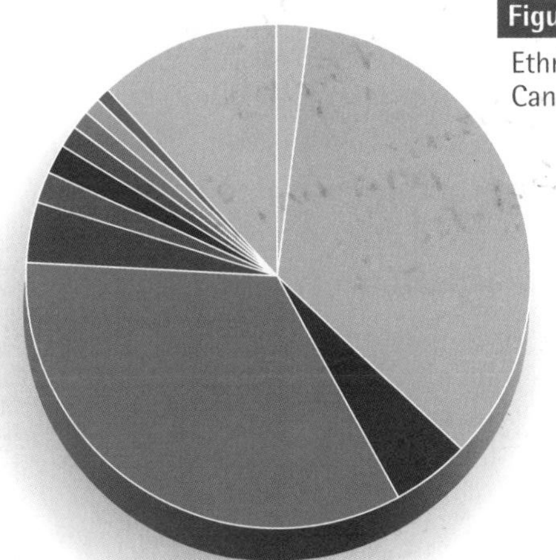

- Italian 3.9%
- Chinese 2.0%
- Dutch 1.9%
- Jewish 1.4%
- East Indian 1.2%
- Portuguese 1.1%
- Scandinavian 0.9%
- Others 11.7%
- First Nations 2.1%
- British 35.0%
- German 5.0%
- French 33.8%

Cosmopolitan Canada

In Canada, migration has created an ethnically diverse society. Our population is nearly 20% foreign-born. Some of our cities are among the world's most **cosmopolitan**, that is, they have many different ethnic groups living together. It is not just the big cities that are changing; many smaller communities see change as well. While it has not affected all communities equally, it has affected *all* communities.

1. Use Figure 14.5 on page 271 to answer the following questions. Describe the trend for each column of data.
   a) Has our population been consistently rising?
   b) Have the birth and death rates been rising/falling?
   c) Has immigration been growing steadily?
   d) Has emigration been increasing?
2. Summarize how the cultural makeup of immigrants to Canada has changed in recent decades.

CASE STUDY

Changing Population, Changing Schools

London, Ontario has witnessed major changes in its population mix over the past 50 years.

Figure 14.10

Location of Lord Elgin School, London, Ontario. This map shows concentrations of non-Europeans by place of birth (1996 data). Fifty years ago, London's population was less than 2% non-European.

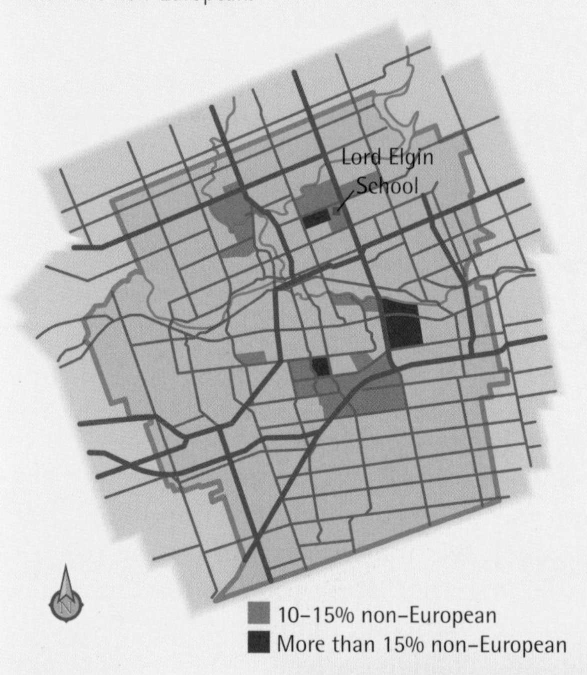

London is a centre for migration, both for refugees and for immigrants. This has many effects on the community. Schools have greater cultural diversity, and there is a high need for teachers of English as a second language (ESL). Of the approximately 32 000 students in London's schools, about 5%, or 1300, are in an ESL program.

Lord Elgin School: A "Mini" United Nations

In northeast London, Lord Elgin School has seen its population change from nearly all English-speaking to one using 21 different first languages. In 1998, 261 of its 320 students spoke another first language. For many of the children, Lord Elgin is their first school experience in their new homeland. The 18 teachers have exciting days supporting and educating students from so many backgrounds. Communicating with parents, though, is a big challenge, as English is the major barrier.

SEE PAGE 83

Figure 14.11

When Lord Elgin School was built in the 1960s, it was the centre of a new, homogeneous suburb. If you visited this community now, what changes would you expect to see? Think of stores and food as well as people.

Students from other lands bring cultural diversity, a wide array of new experiences, different customs, and exciting ideas to share with their Canadian classmates. The immigrants learn about Canada; the Canadian students learn about the world.

In other world regions, as in Canada, there are individuals who want to put up obstacles to cultural diversity, continued immigration, and education. These people should visit Lord Elgin School to see a happy, safe, and nurturing environment where students get along and support one another. Perhaps London, Ontario is a model for the future.

Fact File

In 1997, students in ESL at Lord Elgin School were from:

Vietnam	Poland
Cambodia	Philippines
Iraq	Afghanistan
India	Thailand
El Salvador	Japan
United Arab Emirates	Iran
	Saudi Arabia
Bosnia	Burma
Ethiopia	Romania
Syria	Czech Republic
Somalia	China

Figure 14.12

Grade 5 students at Lord Elgin School.

1. Is your community cosmopolitan? What signs are there to show this diversity?
2. Describe two important steps communities can take to help newcomers feel welcome.
3. Using a blank world outline map, shade in the countries listed in the Fact File above for the students from other lands attending Lord Elgin School. Compare this map to Figure 13.2 on page 247. Identify which cultural realms, by number of countries shaded having immigrants to Canada, are the four leading areas.

Myth Busting

In many countries, including ours, there is a notion that migrants harm their host countries. Some believe they take jobs from the locals and place a strain on social services such as welfare, children's programs, education, health care, and police. In fact, the opposite is the case! Immigrants increase economic growth and actually create employment. They buy products (furniture, clothes, vehicles, food), which increases business. They invest money and use services like banks, go to restaurants, and get their cars repaired. They also add skills, knowledge, new ideas, and labour to the workforce. All these activities contribute directly to the local economy. And, like all Canadians, immigrants pay taxes.

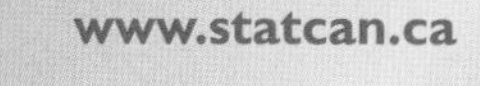

GO TO: Click on English or French, and then on Canadian Statistics. Scroll to The People. Click on Population, and then on Mobility and Migration. Finally, click on Immigrants: Population by Place of Birth, 1996 Census, the Provinces and Territories. From the chart, calculate the percentage of immigrants from each world region. Which regions are the top three?

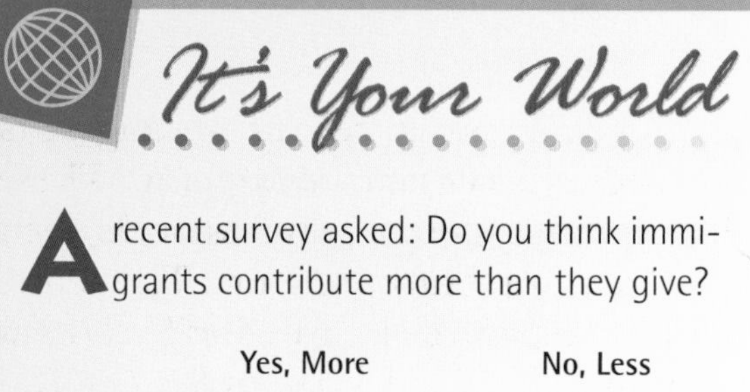

It's Your World

A recent survey asked: Do you think immigrants contribute more than they give?

	Yes, More	No, Less
1994	36%	64%
1998	48%	39% (13% not sure)

What does this suggest about North American attitudes toward immigrants?

The Nature of Our Immigrants

Immigrants to Canada are usually well-educated and prepared for life in this country. According to the 1996 census, an overwhelming majority of immigrants could carry on a conversation in English or French. As well, newcomers in the 1990s had, on average, higher levels of education than Canadian-born people in the same age groups. For example, in 1996, immigrants had more university degrees than their Canadian-born counterparts.

Fact File

In 1999, 34% of 25- to 44-year-old immigrant men had university degrees, compared to 19% for Canadian men.

The Supreme Court has ruled that Sikh police officers in Canada can wear a turban, as required by their faith, rather than a hat. How does this reflect Canada's acceptance of new ideas?

It's Your World

Many nations give foreign aid to help other countries. The countries receiving this aid are often source countries for migrant workers. Migrant workers also send money back to their home countries. In 1991, migrant workers sent $71 billion home – more than all the money that all countries together gave in foreign aid!

SEE PAGE 225

SEE PAGE 256

Most of our recent immigrants are classed as *economic immigrants*. These are skilled tradespeople, professionals, technical workers, and entrepreneurs. The remainder of our immigrants are *family class*, whose entrance is based on family reunification, and *refugees*.

SEE PAGE 215

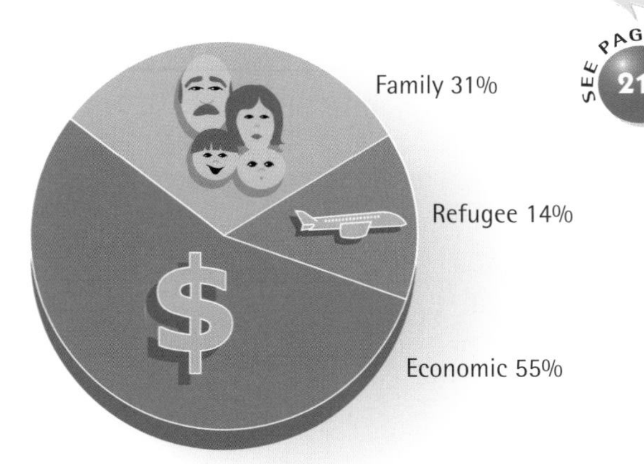

Figure 14.15
Types of immigrants to Canada in 1998.

Figure 14.14
In the last two decades, Asian women have become the majority of migrant workers in Canada. By opening our borders to a migrant worker, it seems we help more than just that one worker.

1. Do you think immigrants contribute more to our society than they take? Poll the class and discuss reasons for your views.
2. Should Canada be increasing the amount of international aid we give? Why or why not?

The Richness of Multiculturalism

There are many reasons why immigrants choose Canada. They include

- job opportunities
- environmental factors
- political stability and
- democratic elections.

There are two other important reasons. The Canadian Charter of Rights and Freedoms protects the rights of individuals, and our government has a policy of **multiculturalism**. In many other countries, such basic rights and freedoms do not exist. Often, we take these rights for granted.

Our multicultural policy supports people of different races, religions, and ethnic groups that settle in Canada. This government policy speaks to all Canadians, promoting tolerance and acceptance. Our laws protect everyone from racial prejudice and hate. It takes more than laws, though, to make these ideas real. We must all practise them each day — on the street, in our classrooms, in our offices, and in our hearts.

> *"The cult of ethnicity exaggerates differences, intensifies resentments and antagonisms, drives ever deeper the awful wedges between races and nationalities. The endgame is self-pity and self-ghettoization."*
>
> Arthur Schlesinger Jr., "The Disuniting of America"

> *"It is hereby declared to be the policy of the Government of Canada to recognize and promote the understanding that multiculturalism reflects the cultural and racial diversity of Canadian society and acknowledges the freedom of all members of Canadian society to preserve, enhance, and share their cultural heritage."*
>
> Canadian Multiculturalism Act, 1971

Fact File

There are over 4000 Web sites dedicated to human rights. Enter the words "human rights" in a search engine such as Alta Vista or Lycos, and explore what different groups around the world are doing to help improve the rights of others.

Figure 14.16

A Moroccan family at a citizenship ceremony in Montreal. Citizenship, whether through birth or naturalization, is an important part of feeling that you "belong" in a society.

Cultural Identity

When people move, they don't forget their roots and traditions. These are important to identity and well-being. Although our first impressions of other cultural groups are usually through their food, celebrations, and entertainment, having a variety of cultural groups also opens the doors to cross-cultural understanding. Our lives can be enriched by their presence.

In the last 30 years, Canadian communities have witnessed a major cultural change marked by the new buildings of our immigrants: mosques, synagogues, temples, shops, and ethnic community centres.

Figure 14.17

Nearly all Canadian towns and cities now have cultural indicators such as these buildings. Which cultural groups are in your community?

Cultural Celebrations

Across Canada, there are cultural events and celebrations that honour the past of many cultures and bring people closer together in understanding. Such events include Pier 21 celebrations of immigrant arrival in Canada; Oktoberfest, the German harvest festival; Dreamspeakers, the First Nations arts and film festival in Edmonton; Chinese New Year celebrations in Vancouver, Toronto, and Montreal; Caribana, the Caribbean celebration in Toronto; or Sunfest, the International Celebration of Cultures in London.

SEE PAGE 210

GO TO **www.ednet.ns.ca/educ/heritage/pier21/** and see much of our European immigration of the 20th century recounted. Click on Interaction. Go to the Photo Gallery and examine the photos. Then, take a Guided Tour, or go back and read the Stories, or go to the Library.

Figure 14.18

Oktoberfest in Kitchener, Chinese New Year celebrations in Montreal, and Sunfest in London: all contribute to the constantly changing Canadian cultural identity and to a blending of all our cultures.

1. Select three of your community's celebrations. Describe the celebrations you have chosen and complete a chart like the one below to show how cultural traditions are remembered and expressed.

Type	Nature of Event
Religion	
Nation-building	
Traditional practice	
Music-based	
Food-based	
Community-contributor	
Other	

2. Identify buildings in your local community that show other cultural groups are present besides the mainstream group.

The Effects of Migration Within Canada

Although international migration greatly affects our society, so, too, does **interprovincial migration**. This is migration from one province or territory to another. Over time, every country experiences changes due to the movement of people within their own borders.

Economic Migration

Many of the causes of internal migration are economically based. In Canada, the post-war industrial boom in Southern Ontario and Quebec caused a major movement of people from other provinces to those areas. During the boom in the oil business in the late 1970s through the '80s , people flocked to the West, particularly Calgary and Edmonton. With the loss of the east coast fishery and the slow growth of the Maritime economy, many people, particularly youth, have left the Atlantic provinces for other parts of Canada.

Figure 14.19

The oil boom in Alberta fuelled migration to that province and boosted the local economies of the oil towns.

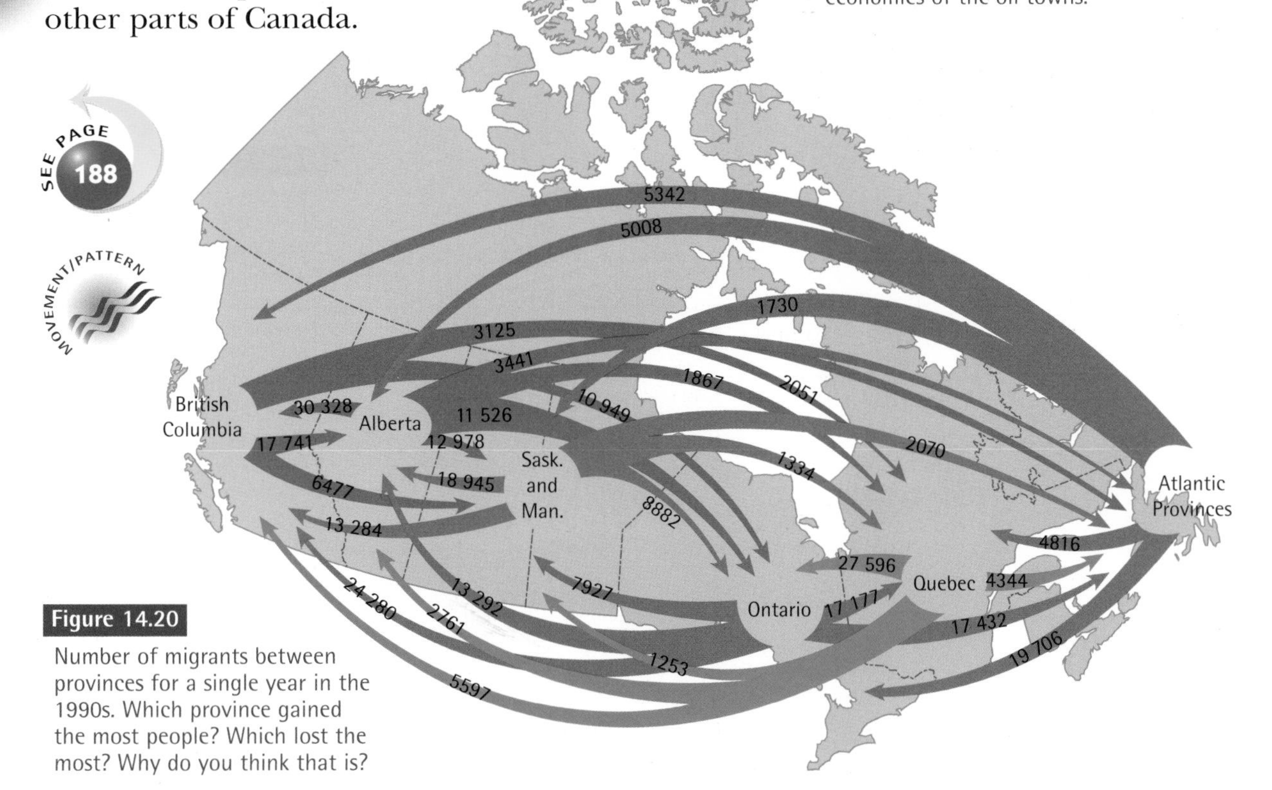

Figure 14.20

Number of migrants between provinces for a single year in the 1990s. Which province gained the most people? Which lost the most? Why do you think that is?

Regions Losing People

It is predicted that some parts of Canada will continue to lose population. The most significant is Newfoundland. Its population could fall from over 550 000 in 1998 to 425 000 in the next 25 years — a 22% drop. This "emptying of the Rock" reflects the current lack of economic opportunity there. Perhaps the hope of jobs from offshore oil and gas development may change things.

This ongoing loss of population will have cultural effects for Newfoundland as well. More and more properties in many communities have "for sale" signs. People see their neighbours leave with no one moving in to take their place. Some communities may even die out altogether. It is depressing for many to witness such changes, to see their futures and their children's futures become so limited. Their identity — which has always been linked to the fishery — and their traditional ways might be lost.

Fact File

In the 1990s, an average of 5440 people per year left Newfoundland for other provinces in Canada.

Regions Gaining People

British Columbia and Ontario are two of the regions in Canada that are gaining people. This is altering the culture in various provincial communities. With new immigrants, urban densities continue to rise. Higher population density in cities gradually modifies how people interact and get along. Population density is also reflected in urban congestion and a more impersonal society. Many migrants feel isolated from the mainstream population and need help getting re-established.

Figure 14.21

When the government closed the northern cod fishery because of dwindling supply, these fishers in Bonavista, Newfoundland, were able to survive by catching crab instead. However, many young men and women have had to leave Newfoundland in order to make a living.

The Homeless Canadians

Figure 14.22

The problem of homelessness in Toronto became so bad that, during one severe winter, the city opened its Moss Park Armoury to keep people from freezing on the streets. Since homeless people find it hard to get jobs, some try to make a living by panhandling or cleaning windshields. Few people know what to do about this complex social problem. What is one thing you feel we should do?

Homelessness also causes people to migrate. The numbers of homeless men, women, and youth who live on city streets significantly affect communities. Residents daily encounter street people asking for help or money. Few cities have come to grips with solving the complex problems faced by the homeless.

Fact File

Toronto has 10 000 homeless wandering its streets, San Francisco has 400 000, and Saõ Paulo, Brazil over 1 000 000.

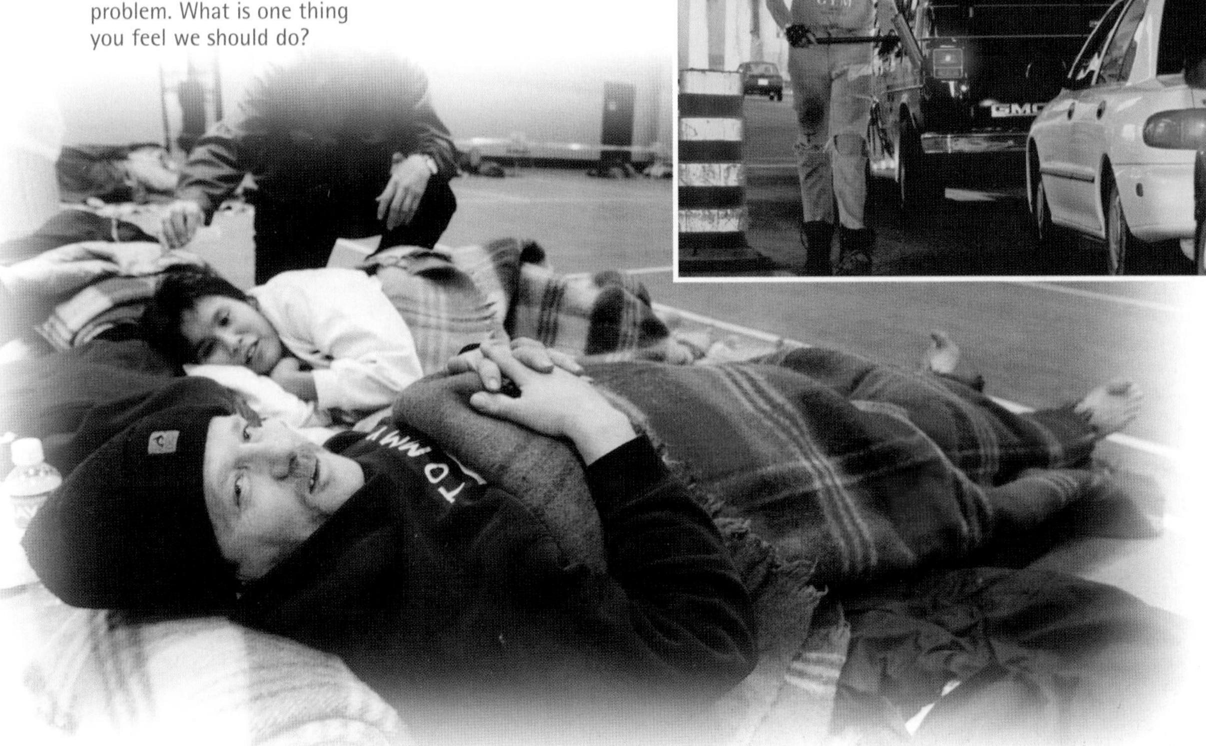

1. Do you think that high-density living, as in large apartment buildings, makes people's interactions less or more impersonal? Why? Give two examples of how high-density living might change people's interactions. (*Hint:* Think of privacy fences versus shared courtyards.)
2. Why might governments spend money to have industries locate in areas of the country experiencing population loss?

Understanding the Concepts

1. Compile a list of the ways that movement of people can change the character of a community.

2. Identify two ways in which human migration patterns are currently evident in urban service industries in Canada and the United States. Explain why many of these migrants have jobs in these areas.

Research and Communication Skills

3. Research records of the earliest settlement or migration into your community and report back to your class. What types of records were you able to find? What cultural groups can you identify?

4. Research emigration from Canada since 1990. Report on the number by province, the trends in emigration, and information about the types of migrants.

5. **a)** Identify and list, with the help of any new Canadians in your class, English language words or phrases that were misleading or puzzling to them when they first heard them spoken.

   b) For each word or phrase, explain its meaning and why it was misleading or confusing. For example, slang words like "cool" or idioms like "you're barking up the wrong tree" might be taken literally.

GO TO

http://atlas.gc.ca/legacy/schoolnet/issues/home.html

This is the site for the National Map Project. Click on Languages in Canada. After reading the first page, click on Next Page at the bottom of your screen. Now, click on Highlights at the bottom of this page. Bring back three facts about the languages spoken in Canada and share them with your classmates.

Map and Globe Skills

6. **a)** Survey your class and find out about people's origins by asking each student where his or her family came from. Compile a list of the countries. Some students may have migrated recently with their families, while for others migration may have occurred several generations ago. Every Canadian family has a migration history. Compile a list of the countries.

   b) Plot the countries on a world outline map.

   c) Calculate the percentage of arrivals from each continent. Draw proportional arrows from the continents to Canada to show the flows.

   d) Using a current atlas, compare the source regions of your class to the most recent flows of immigrants to Canada.

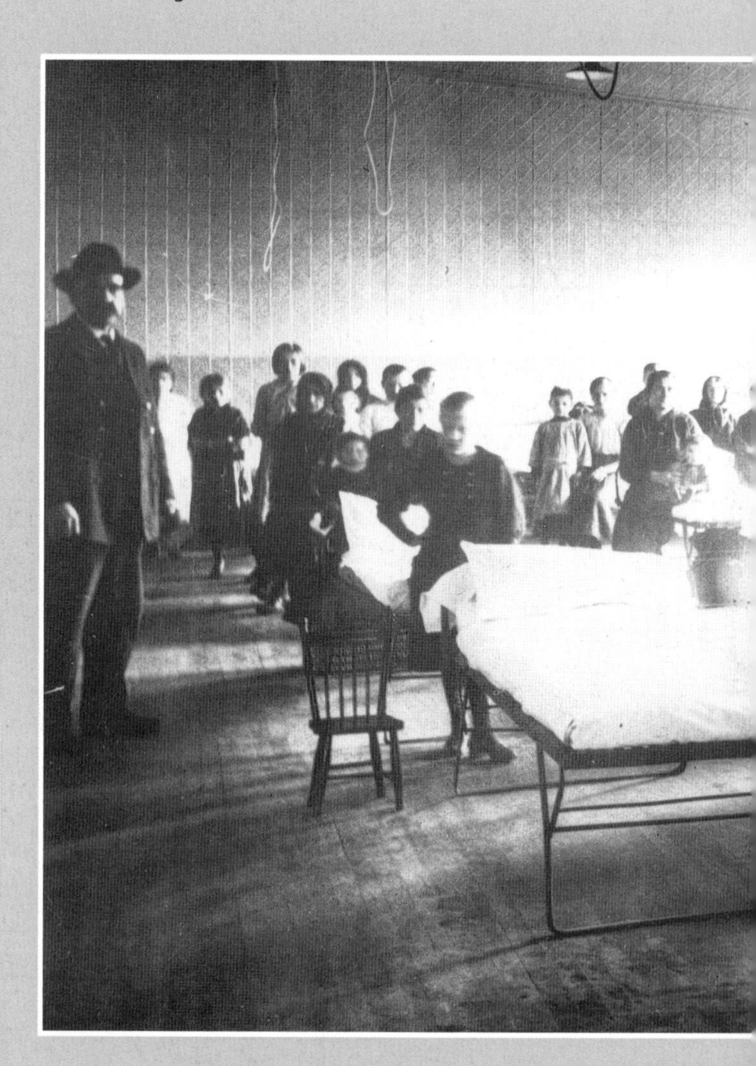

Applications

7. Using an Ontario road map (or any provincial road map), find individual or groups of place names that represent cultural groups other than English. For example, Neustadt = Dutch, Belle River = French.

8. What is your local district school board, town, or city council doing to advance race relations? Does your community have a race relations policy? Identify any local initiatives to advance race relations in which your class might participate.

9. Create a photo display of buildings in your community that reflect cultural differences. Write an account of how migration has affected your community.

10. Consider the ways in which we organize and mark our living spaces (e.g., property boundaries). Identify two ways that indicate either openness or closedness to others.

Figure 14.23

This was the women's dormitory at the Immigration Building in St. John, New Brunswick, around 1920. How would you feel if you spent your first night in Canada in these surroundings?

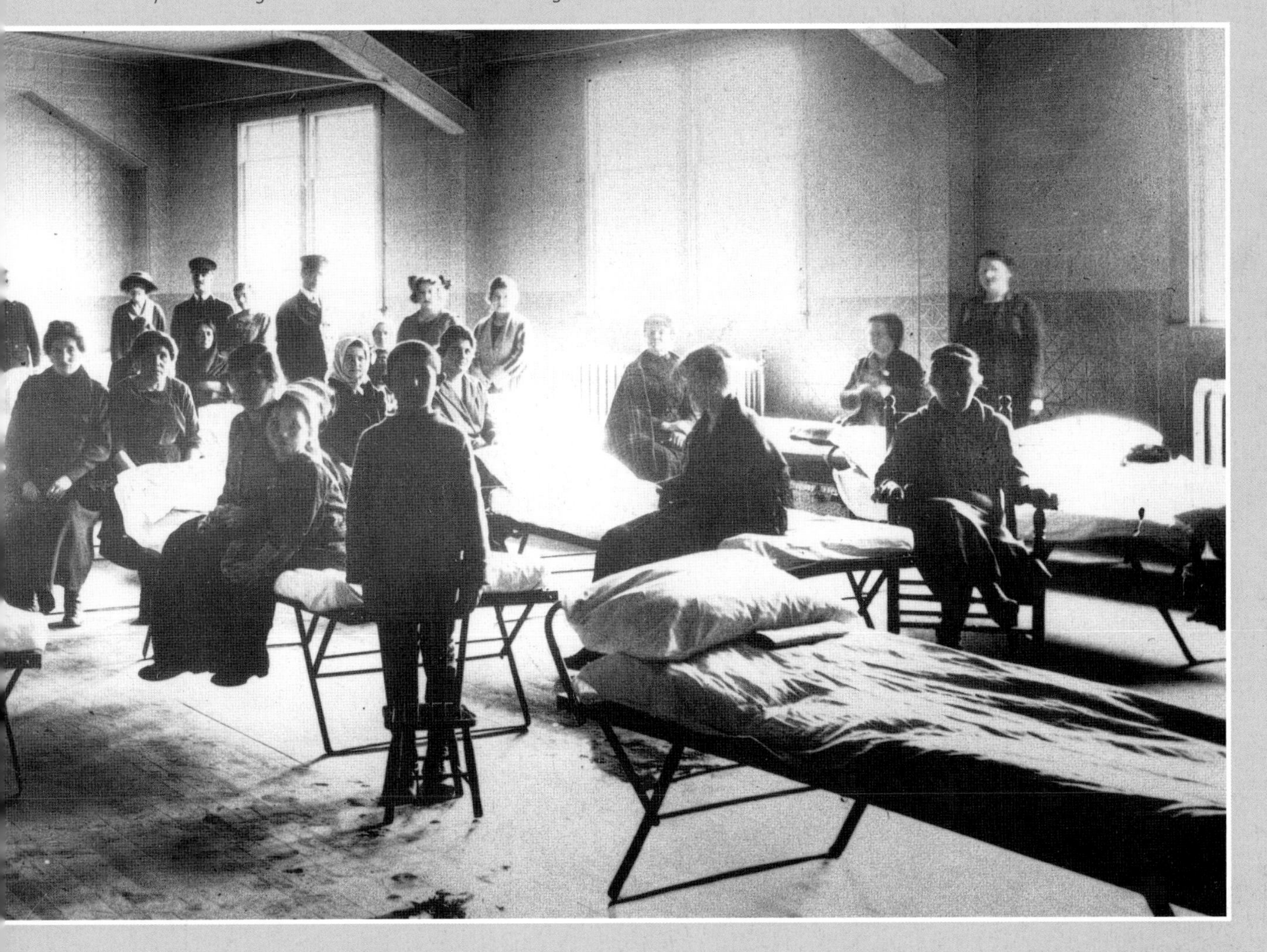

UNIT 3 Migration

PERFORMANCE TASK: Concepts, Skills, and Applications

Decision of a Lifetime

Remember at the opening of Chapter 11, aliens had decided that they wanted Canada and you had no choice in the matter. Well, perhaps it's not aliens, but let's imagine that some form of crisis in your family's life is forcing you and your family to emigrate and whatever your problem is it's limiting your choices and timing.

Where to Go?

You and your family have three days to decide where in the world you are going to live other than Canada or the US. You have the task of helping to determine the country you'll go to. You explain to your family that there are certain factors that should be considered in order to increase your chances of success in your new country. You must think about such things as the language spoken, the health care system, available education, job opportunities, the political system, the stability of the environment.

Your family asks you to investigate these factors for different countries to help make the emigration decision a good one.

Your Task

1. Conduct a survey of your family to help decide what the most important things or "criteria" for success, health, and happiness in the new country are for them. Aim for about seven to ten criteria.
2. Pick the three countries that would be at the top of your list of choices. At this point, your country choices are only "educated-guesses" of where you might want to move.
3. Collect data on each of the criteria you have chosen. You will have to find "indicators" of the criteria (e.g., for education, an indicator would be "literacy rate"). Record your data in an organizer like the one shown on page 226, which will help make your decision of where to go clearer. This organizer has some examples of possible criteria. You are to use the criteria you and your family have picked.

Some of the data you may want to use can be found in the map appendix at the back of the book, at the Web sites shown, or on a database software program like PC Globe.

http://plasma.nationalgeographic.com/mapmachine/index.html

This Web site provides maps and other data on various countries.

Sample Organizer

Criteria (examples)	Country 1 (you choose)	Country 2 (you choose)	Country 3 (you choose)
Language(s) spoken			
Quality of health care (e.g. doctors per 1000 people)			
Growing economy (e.g. economic growth rate in %)			
Political stability (e.g. number of riots or revolutions)			
Quality of education (e.g. teachers per 1000 students)			
Job availability (e.g. unemployment rate)			
Standard of living (e.g. TVs per 1000 people)			
Environmental quality (e.g. pollution data)			
Opportunities for culture/entertainment (e.g. museums per 1000 people)			

Maps to check in the Map Appendix

- ❑ World Population Density
- ❑ Life Expectancy
- ❑ Literacy
- ❑ Health Care
- ❑ Population Growth
- ❑ Family Size
- ❑ Gross National Product per Person
- ❑ Food Availability
- ❑ Employment in Manufacturing
- ❑ Employment in Services
- ❑ Employment in Agriculture
- ❑ Access to Safe Water

4. Transfer the data in your organizer to a piece of poster paper. Decide from examining the data which country you would recommend to your family.

Here are some steps that you can take when using a decision-making matrix:

- choose the three most important criteria and make them worth five points
- pick your next three most important and make them worth three points each
- make each remaining criteria one point each
- now look at each of the criteria for all three countries. If country 1 is the best in a high-ranked category, give it five points, and so on.
- when you have filled in the numbers, sum them for each of the three countries. Now you have numerical evidence for your decision.

5. Write a one page description of your decision-making process that shows how you chose your criteria and the various factors/conditions that influenced your moving choice. Include a paragraph that considers how you and your family may influence the culture of the country you are moving to. Edit your description. Transfer it to your poster.

6. Create a map of your chosen country showing its major physical features and cities. Add your map and any photos or information you find in newspapers or magazines about your new country to the poster.

7. Put your poster up in class with your classmates'. When your turn comes, explain your decision-making process. Best of luck in your new home!

The World — Political

30°W
0°
30°E
60°E
90°E
120°E
150°E
ARCTIC
OCEAN
EENLAND
ENMARK)
ICELAND
Reykjavik
RUSSIA
60°N
SCOTLAND
UNITED KINGDOM
DENMARK
NORTHERN IRELAND
IRELAND
London
NORWAY
SWEDEN
FINLAND
ESTONIA
LATVIA
LITHUANIA
RUS.
NETH.
BELG.
GERM.
POLAND
BELARUS
LUX.
CZECH REP.
SLOVAK REP.
UKRAINE
LIECH.
AUS.
HUN.
MOLDOVA
SWITZ.
FRANCE
ROM.
ITALY
BULGARIA
BOS. & HER.
YUG.
MAC.
ALB.
GREECE
PORTUGAL
SPAIN
KAZAKHSTAN
AZERBAIJAN
GEORGIA
ARMENIA
UZBEKISTAN
TURKMENISTAN
KYRGYZSTAN
TAJIKISTAN
MONGOLIA
NORTH KOREA
SOUTH KOREA
JAPAN
Tokyo
CHINA
TURKEY
CYPRUS
LEBANON
SYRIA
ISRAEL
JORDAN
IRAQ
Tehran
IRAN
AFGHANISTAN
PAKISTAN
KUWAIT
TUNISIA
Algiers
MOROCCO
Canary Islands
ALGERIA
LIBYA
Cairo
EGYPT
SAUDI ARABIA
QATAR
U. A. E.
OMAN
NEPAL
BHUTAN
BANGLADESH
INDIA
MYANMAR
LAOS
VIETNAM
THAILAND
KAMPUCHEA
Taipei
TAIWAN
PACIFIC
Tropic of Cancer
30°N
International Date Line
WESTERN SAHARA
MAURITANIA
MALI
NIGER
CHAD
SUDAN
ERITREA
YEMEN
DJIBOUTI
SENEGAL
GAMBIA
GUINEA-BISSAU
GUINEA
BURKINA FASO
NIGERIA
SIERRA LEONE
LIBERIA
IVORY COAST
GHANA
TOGO
BENIN
CAMEROON
CENTRAL AFRICAN REPUBLIC
ETHIOPIA
SOMALIA
SRI LANKA
Manila
PHILIPPINES
BRUNEI
MALAYSIA
Singapore
Equator
0°
EQUATORIAL GUINEA
GABON
CONGO
DEMOCRATIC REPUBLIC OF THE CONGO
UGANDA
KENYA
RWANDA
BURUNDI
TANZANIA
SAO TOME & PRINCIPE
OCEAN
INDIAN
INDONESIA
Jakarta
EAST TIMOR
PAPUA NEW GUINEA
OCEAN
MALAWI
ANGOLA
ZAMBIA
ZIMBABWE
MOZAMBIQUE
MADAGASCAR
NAMIBIA
BOTSWANA
Tropic of Capricorn
FIJI
NEW CALEDONIA
AUSTRALIA
SWAZILAND
SOUTH AFRICA
LESOTHO
30°S
Cape Town
OCEAN
NEW ZEALAND
Prime Meridian
60°S
ANTARCTICA
30°W
0°
30°E
60°E
90°E
120°E
150°E

World Population Density

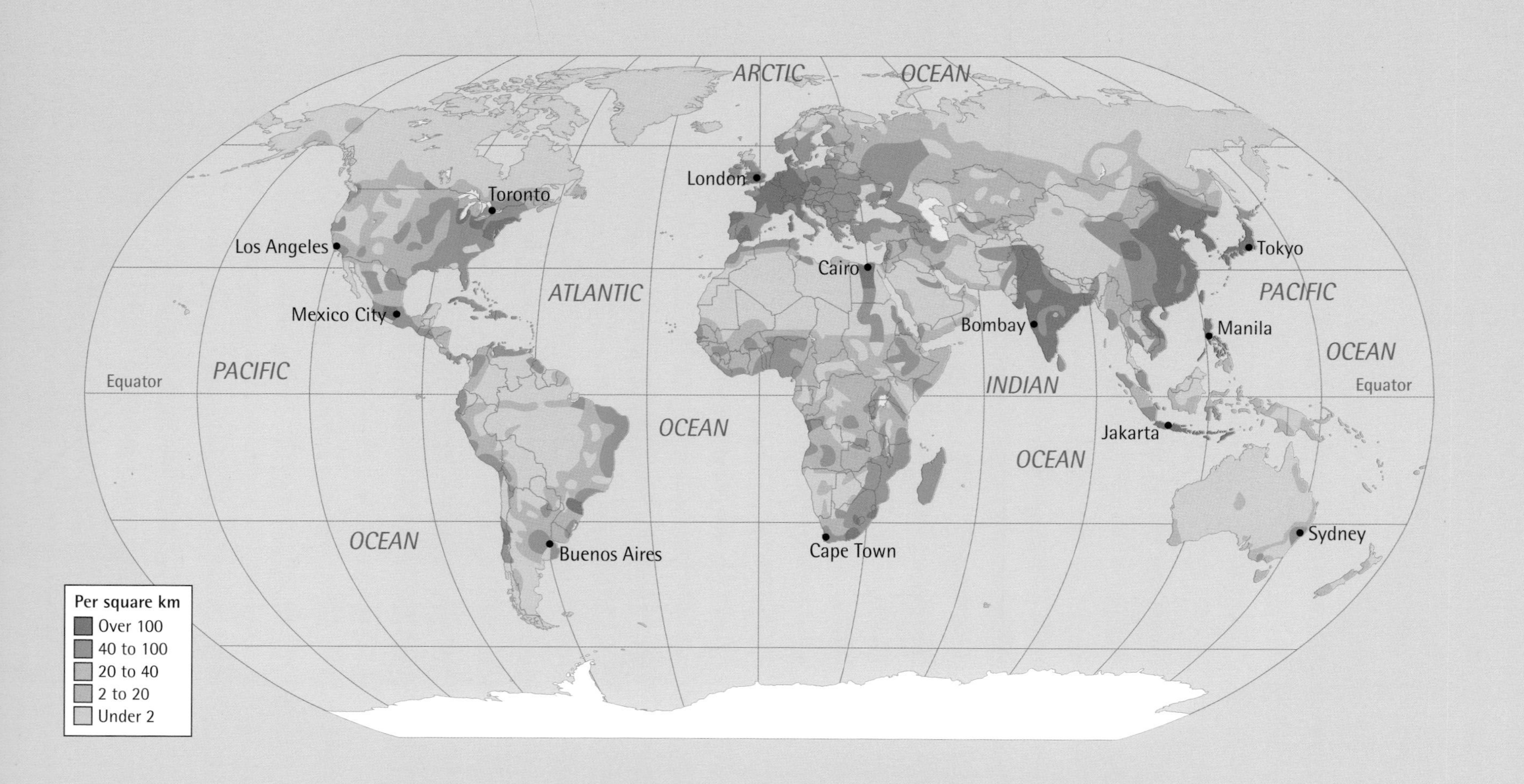

Time Zones

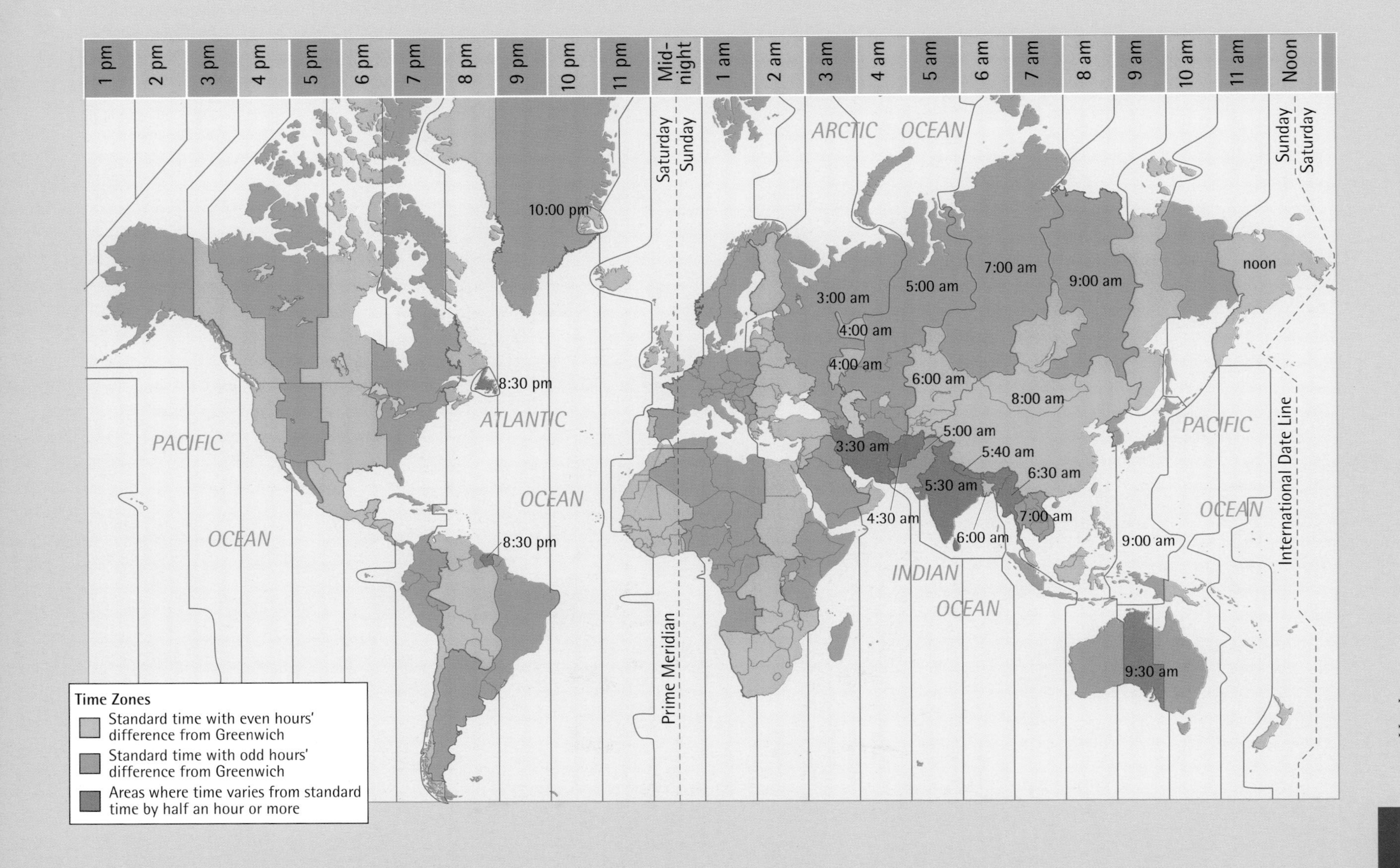
1 pm
2 pm
3 pm
4 pm
5 pm
6 pm
7 pm
8 pm
9 pm
10 pm
11 pm
Mid-night
1 am
2 am
3 am
4 am
5 am
6 am
7 am
8 am
9 am
10 am
11 am
Noon
Saturday
Sunday
Sunday
Saturday
ARCTIC OCEAN
10:00 pm
noon
7:00 am
9:00 am
5:00 am
3:00 am
4:00 am
4:00 am
6:00 am
8:30 pm
8:00 am
ATLANTIC
PACIFIC
PACIFIC
International Date Line
5:00 am
3:30 am
5:40 am
6:30 am
5:30 am
OCEAN
OCEAN
4:30 am
7:00 am
OCEAN
6:00 am
9:00 am
8:30 pm
INDIAN
OCEAN
Prime Meridian
9:30 am
Time Zones
Standard time with even hours' difference from Greenwich
Standard time with odd hours' difference from Greenwich
Areas where time varies from standard time by half an hour or more

Land Use

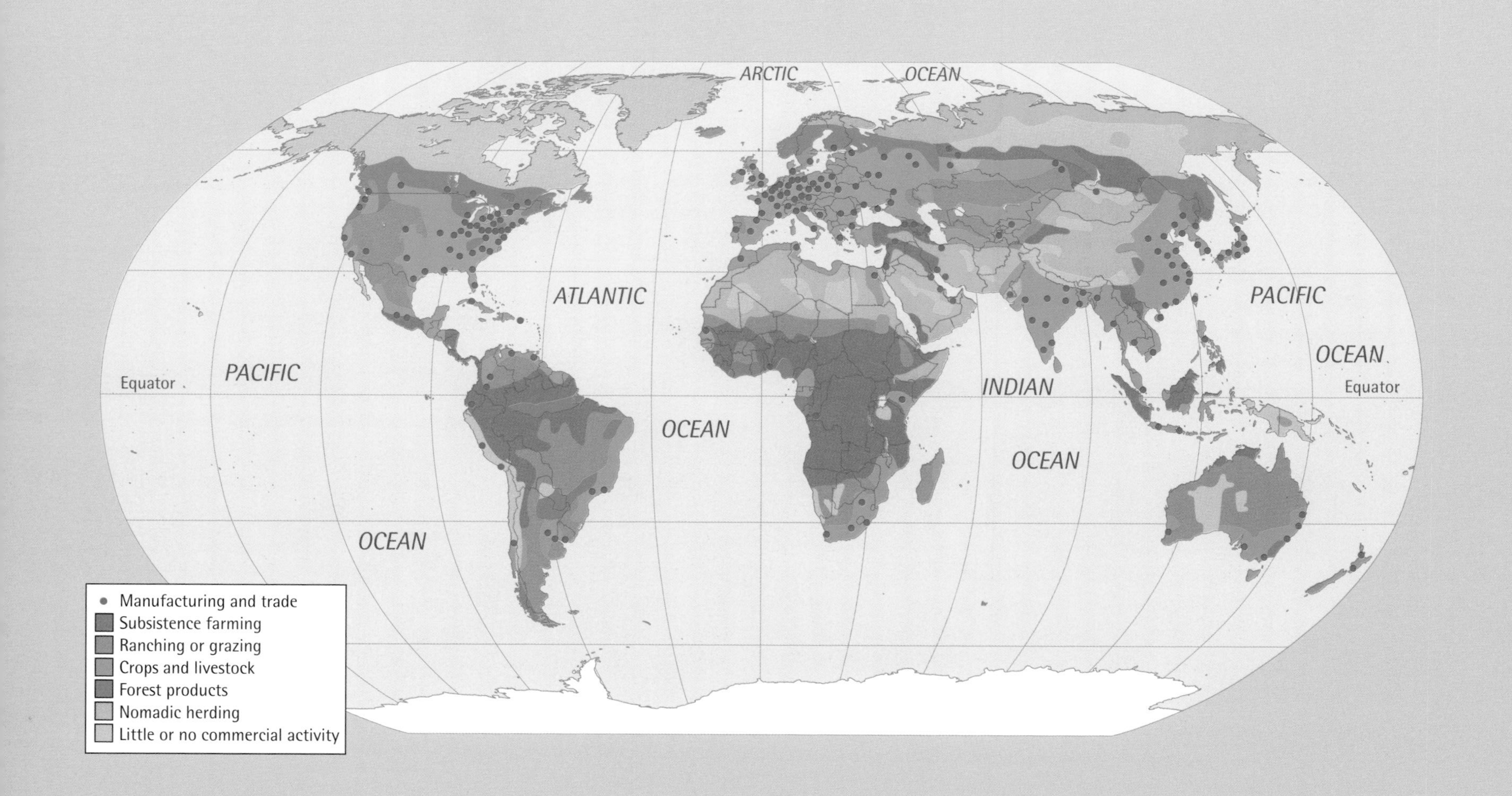
ARCTIC
OCEAN
ATLANTIC
PACIFIC
OCEAN
Equator
PACIFIC
OCEAN
INDIAN
OCEAN
OCEAN
Equator
OCEAN
Manufacturing and trade
Subsistence farming
Ranching or grazing
Crops and livestock
Forest products
Nomadic herding
Little or no commercial activity

World Agriculture and Fishing

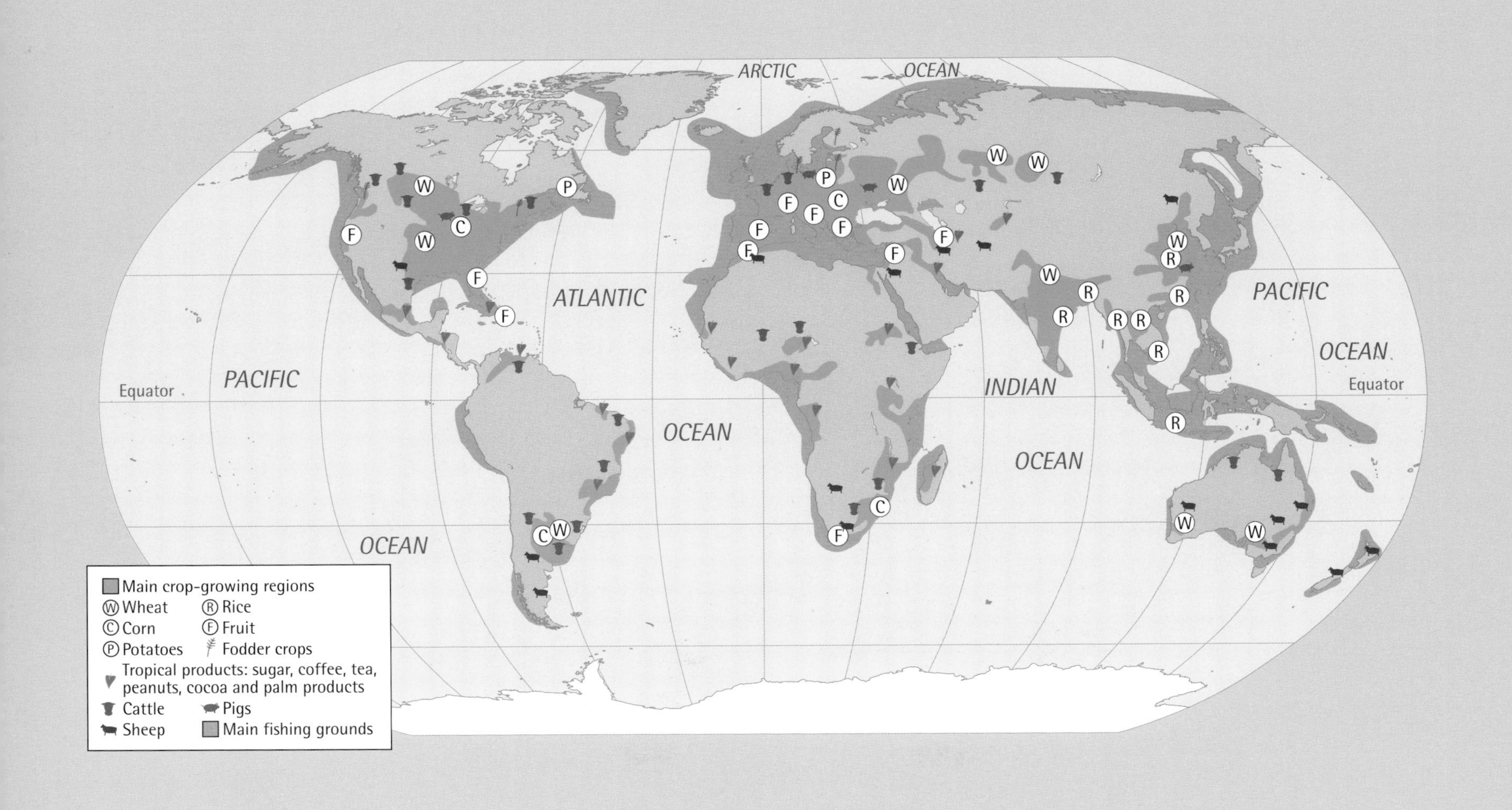

The World's Big Cities

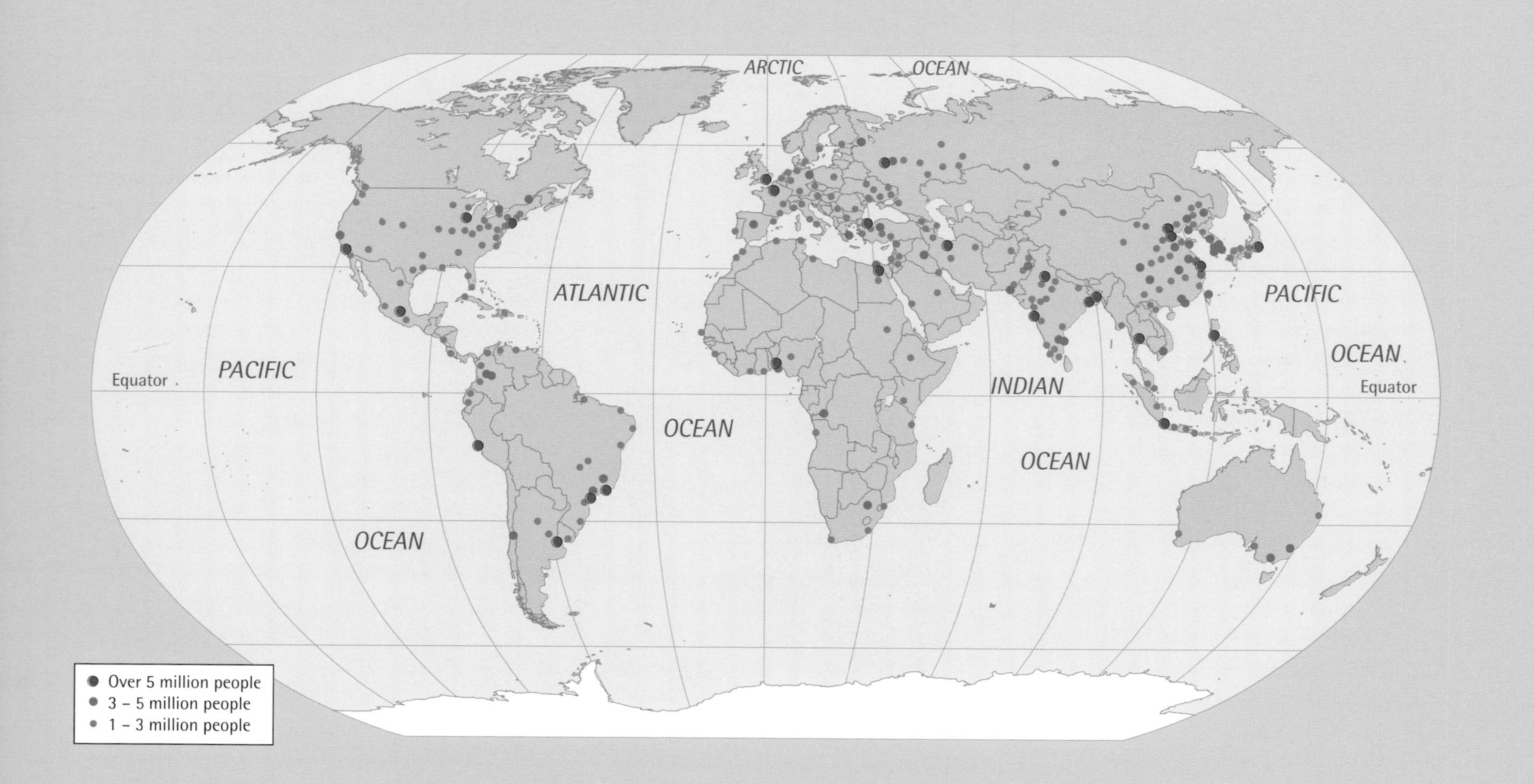

Population Growth

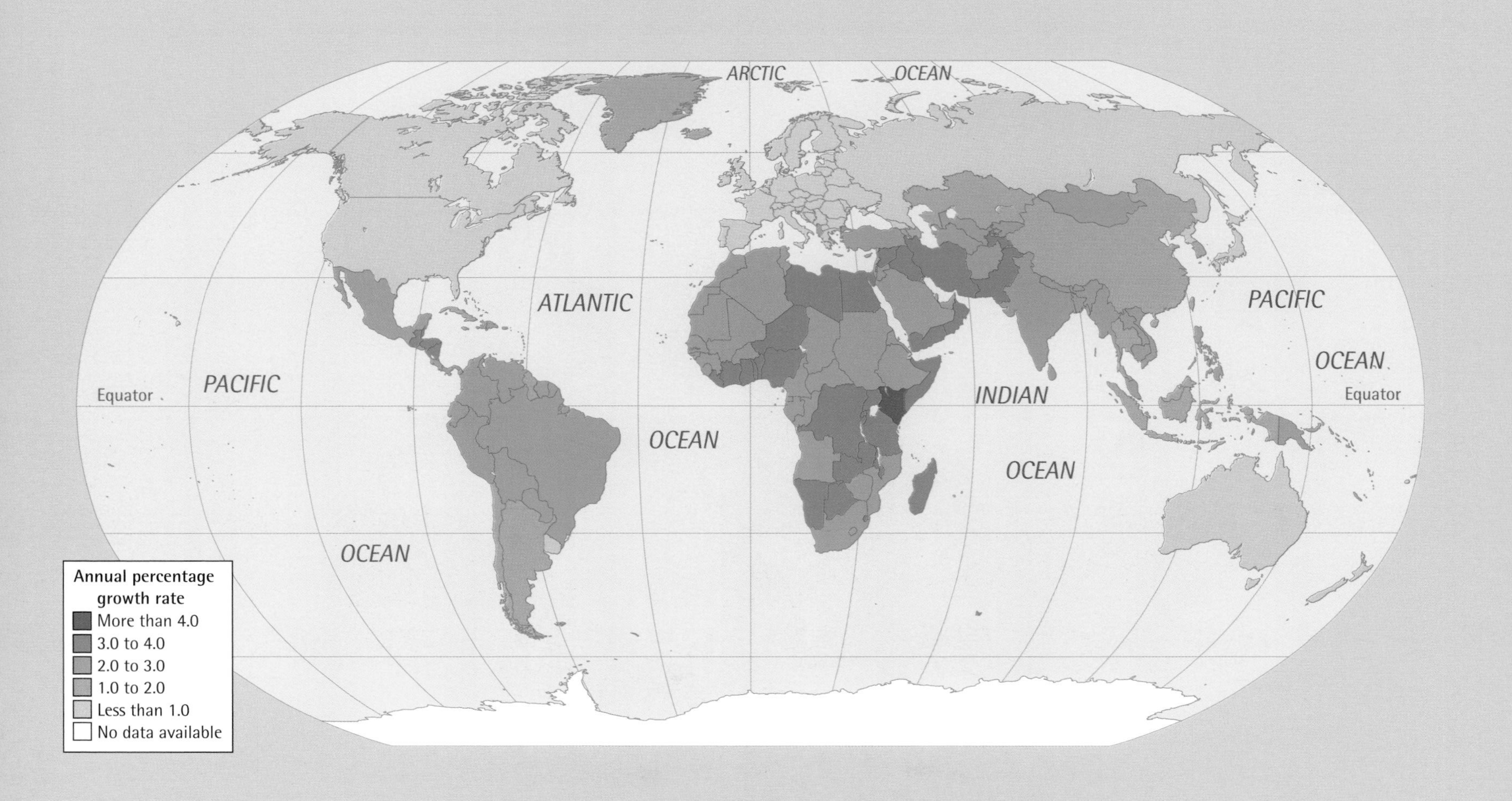

Life Expectancy

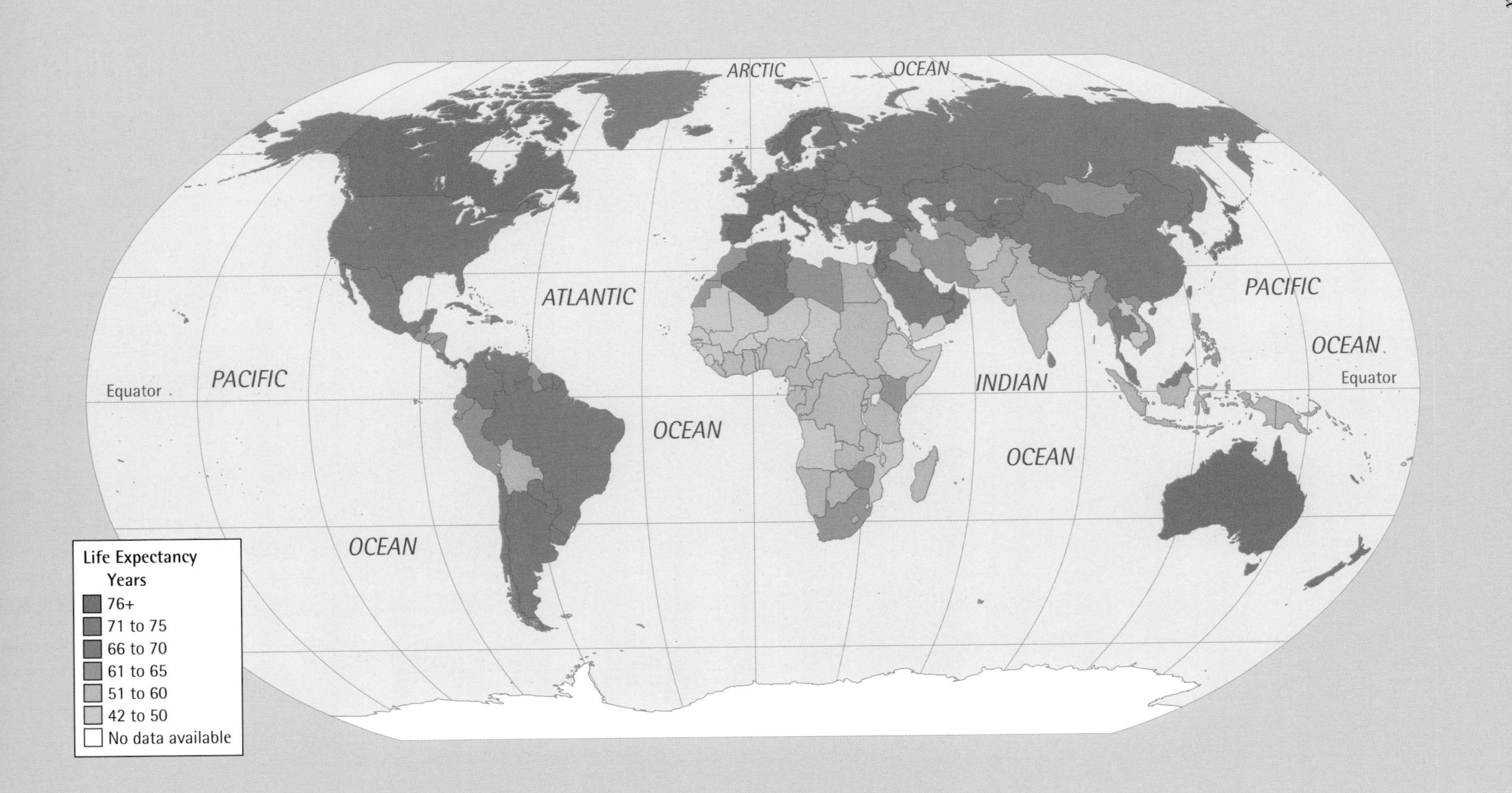

Family Size

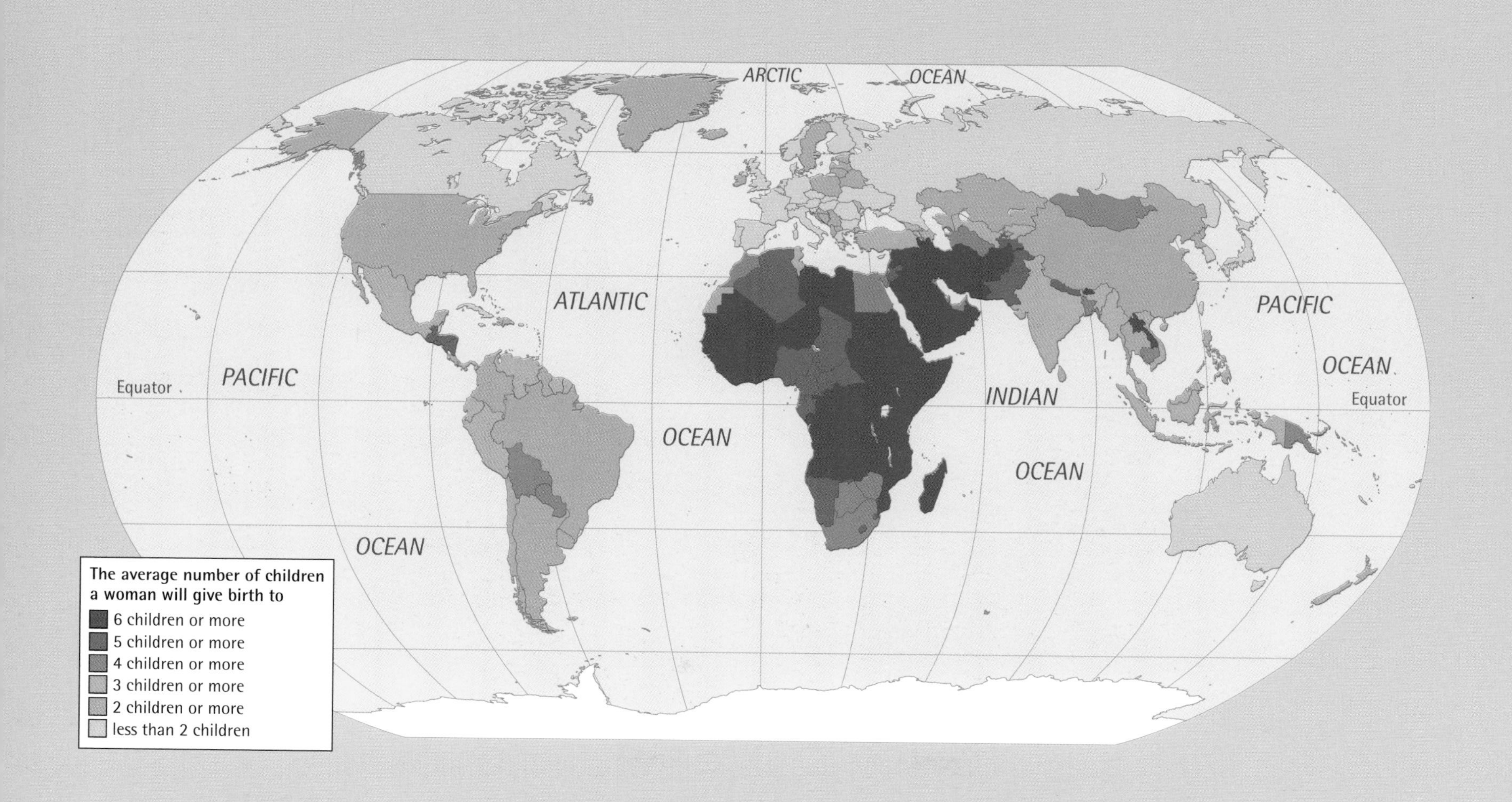

ARCTIC OCEAN
ATLANTIC
OCEAN
Equator
PACIFIC
OCEAN
INDIAN
OCEAN
PACIFIC
OCEAN
Equator
The average number of children a woman will give birth to
6 children or more
5 children or more
4 children or more
3 children or more
2 children or more
less than 2 children

Literacy

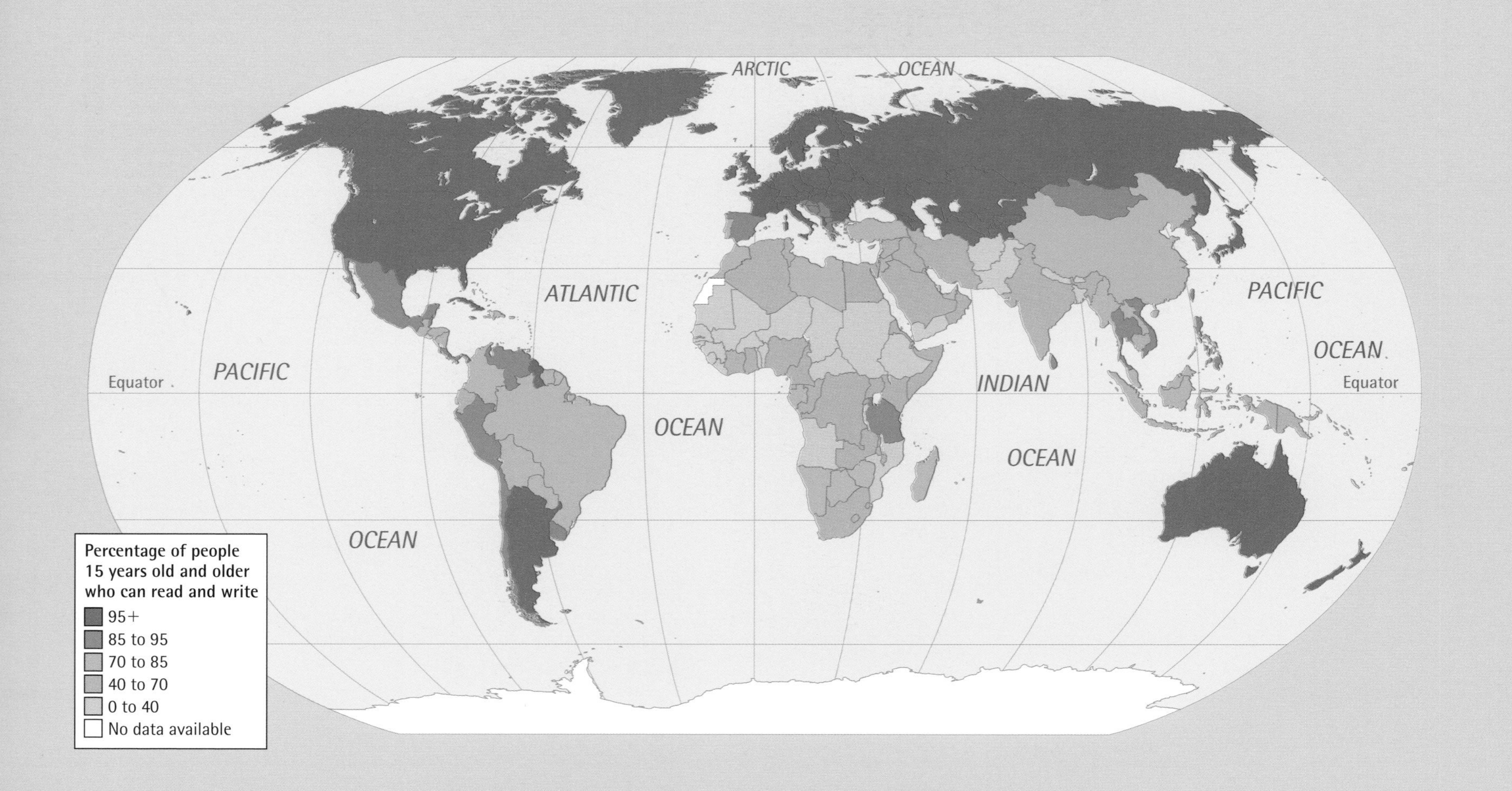

ARCTIC OCEAN
ATLANTIC
OCEAN
PACIFIC
OCEAN
Equator
INDIAN
OCEAN
PACIFIC
OCEAN
Equator
Percentage of people 15 years old and older who can read and write
95+
85 to 95
70 to 85
40 to 70
0 to 40
No data available

Gross National Product per Person

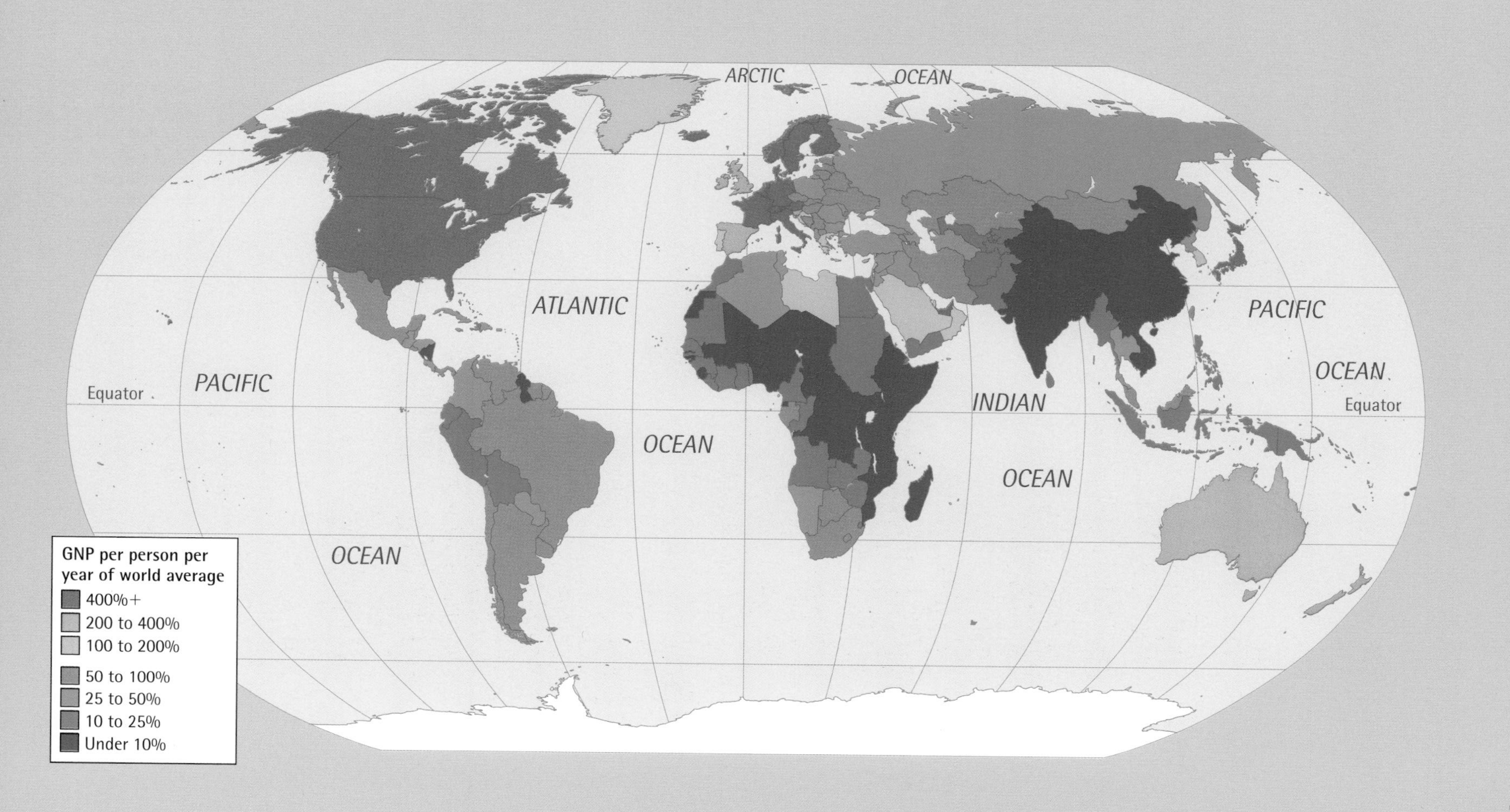

Health Care

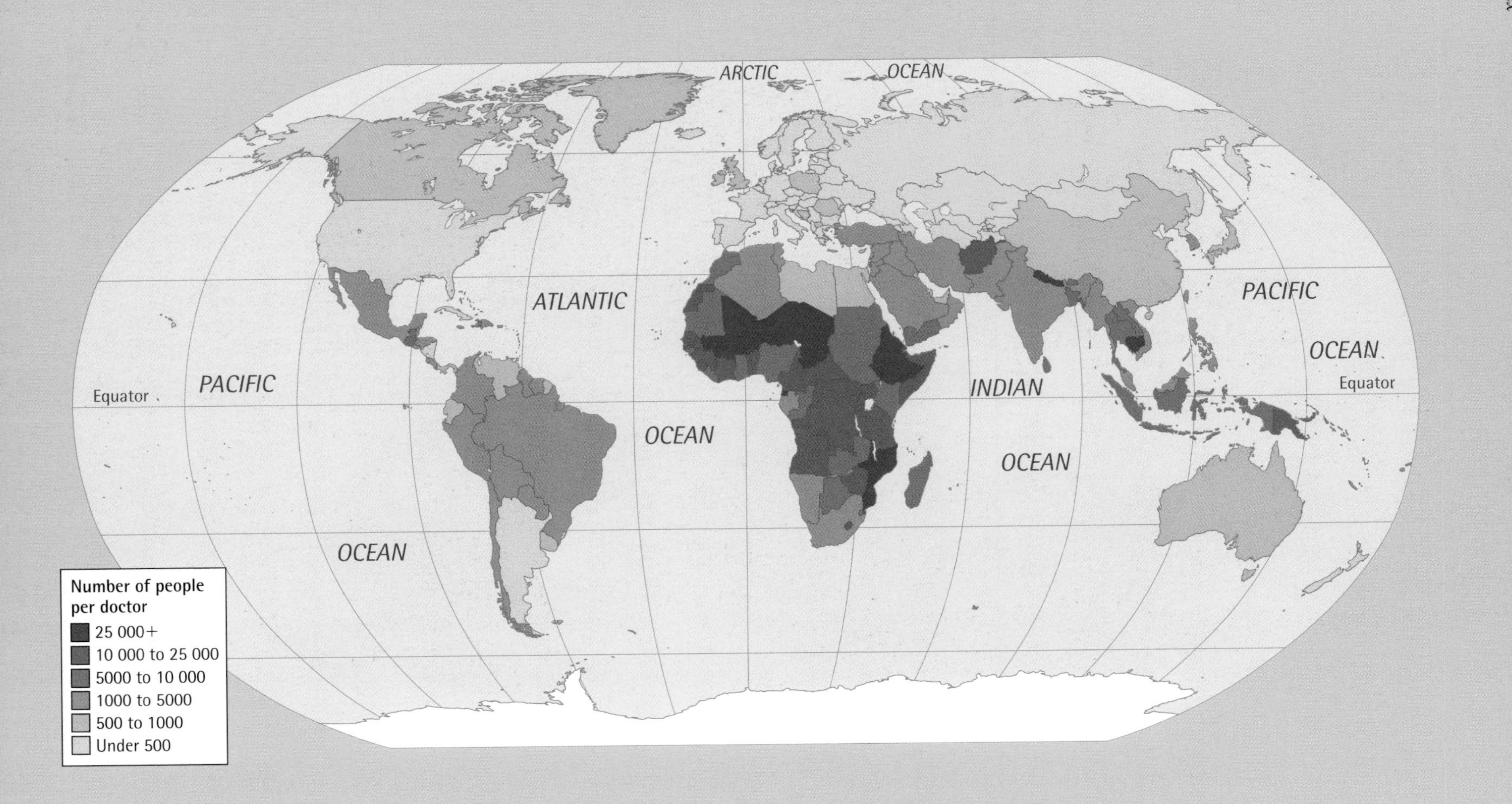
ARCTIC
OCEAN
ATLANTIC
OCEAN
PACIFIC
OCEAN
Equator
INDIAN
OCEAN
PACIFIC
OCEAN
Equator
Number of people per doctor
25 000+
10 000 to 25 000
5000 to 10 000
1000 to 5000
500 to 1000
Under 500

Food Availability

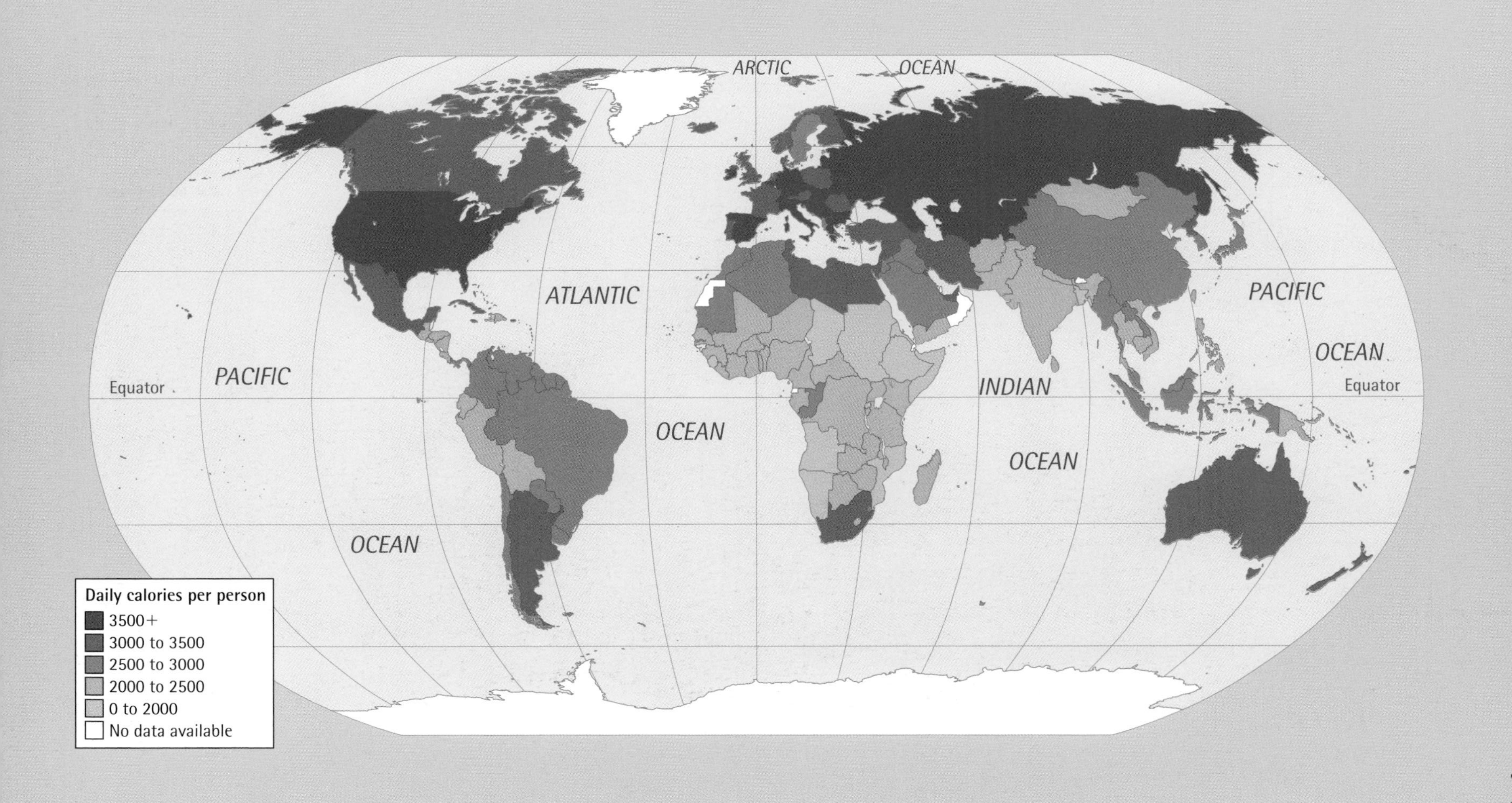

Access to Safe Water

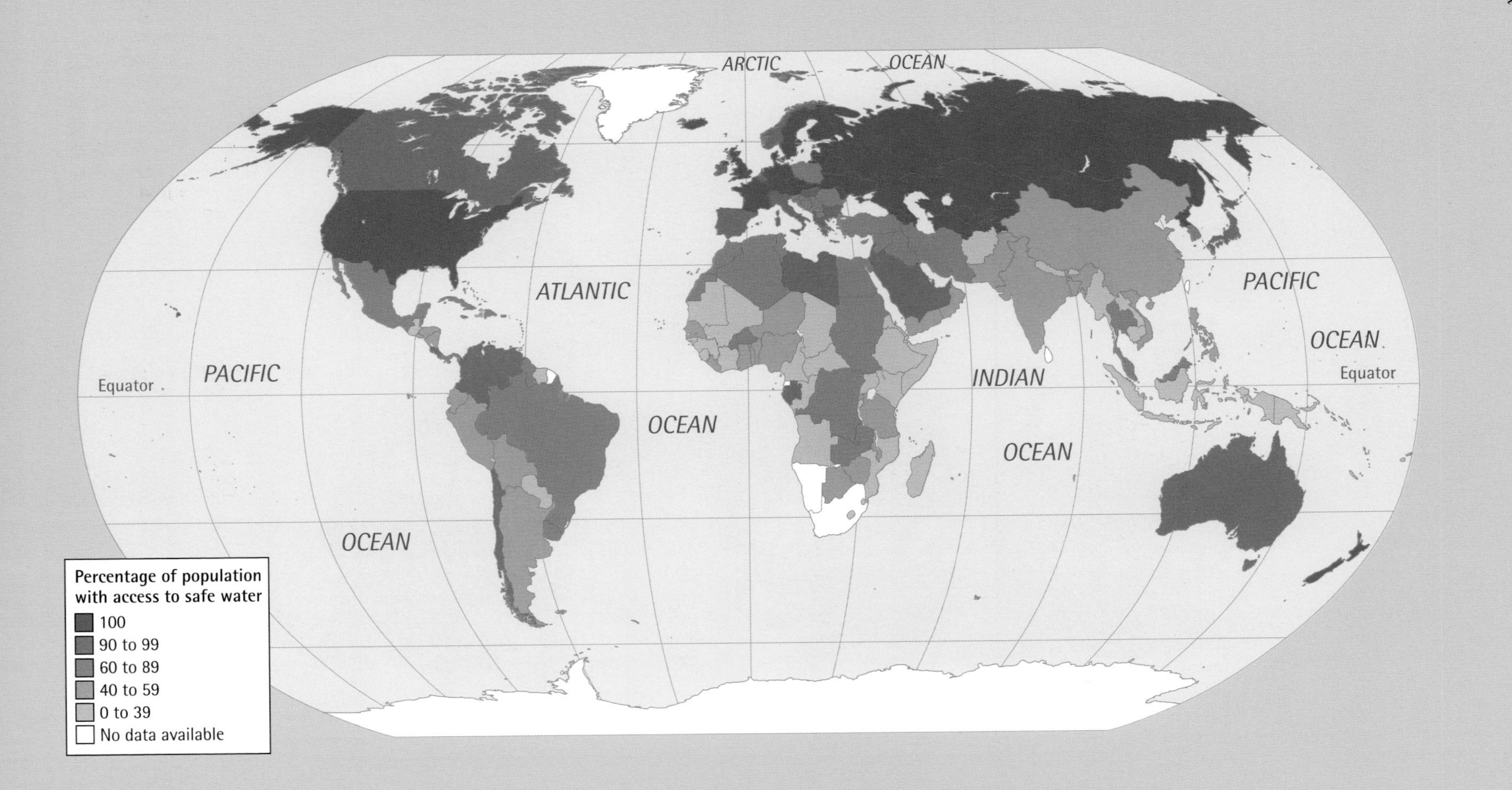

Employment in Agriculture

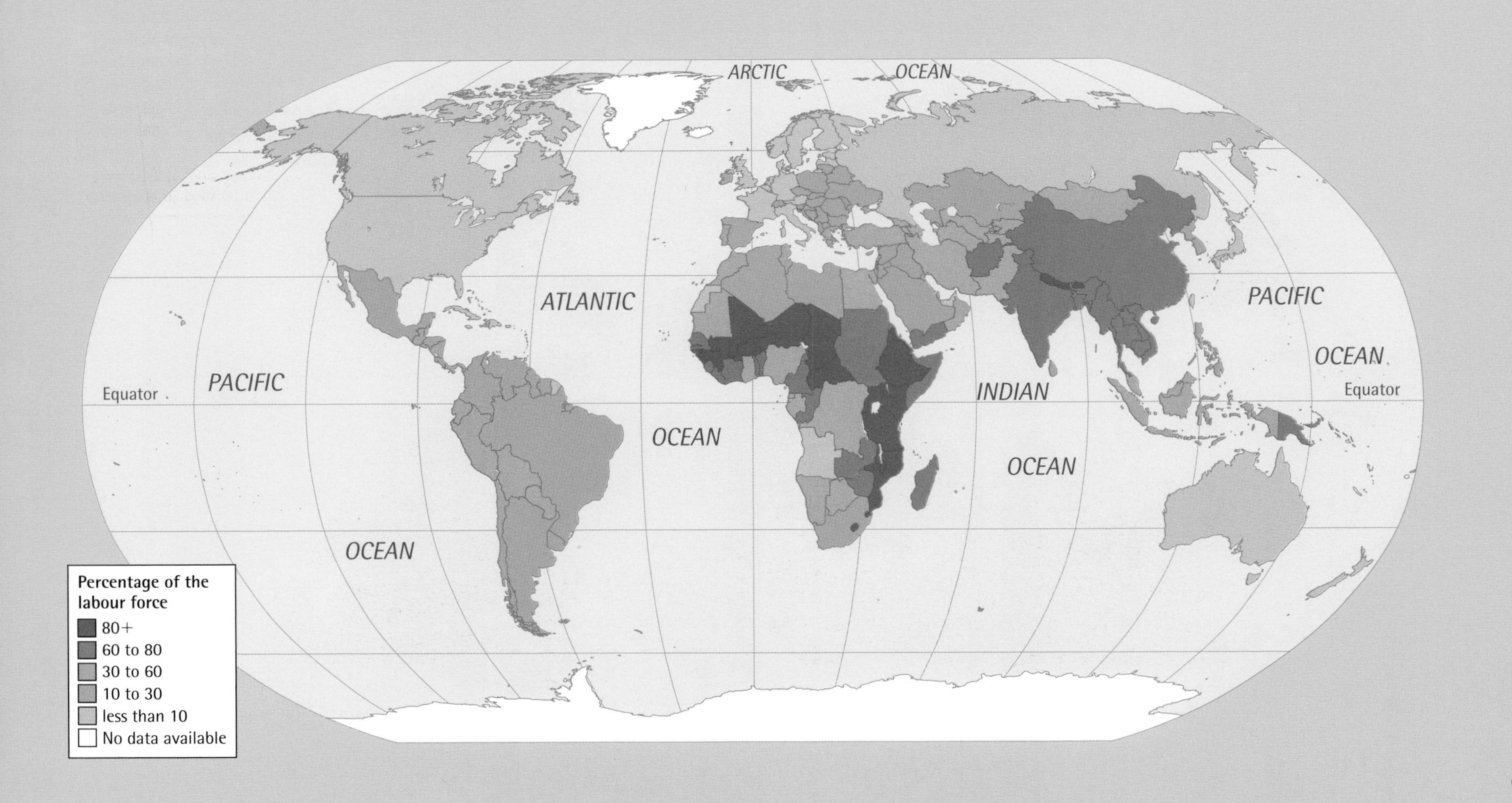

Employment in Manufacturing

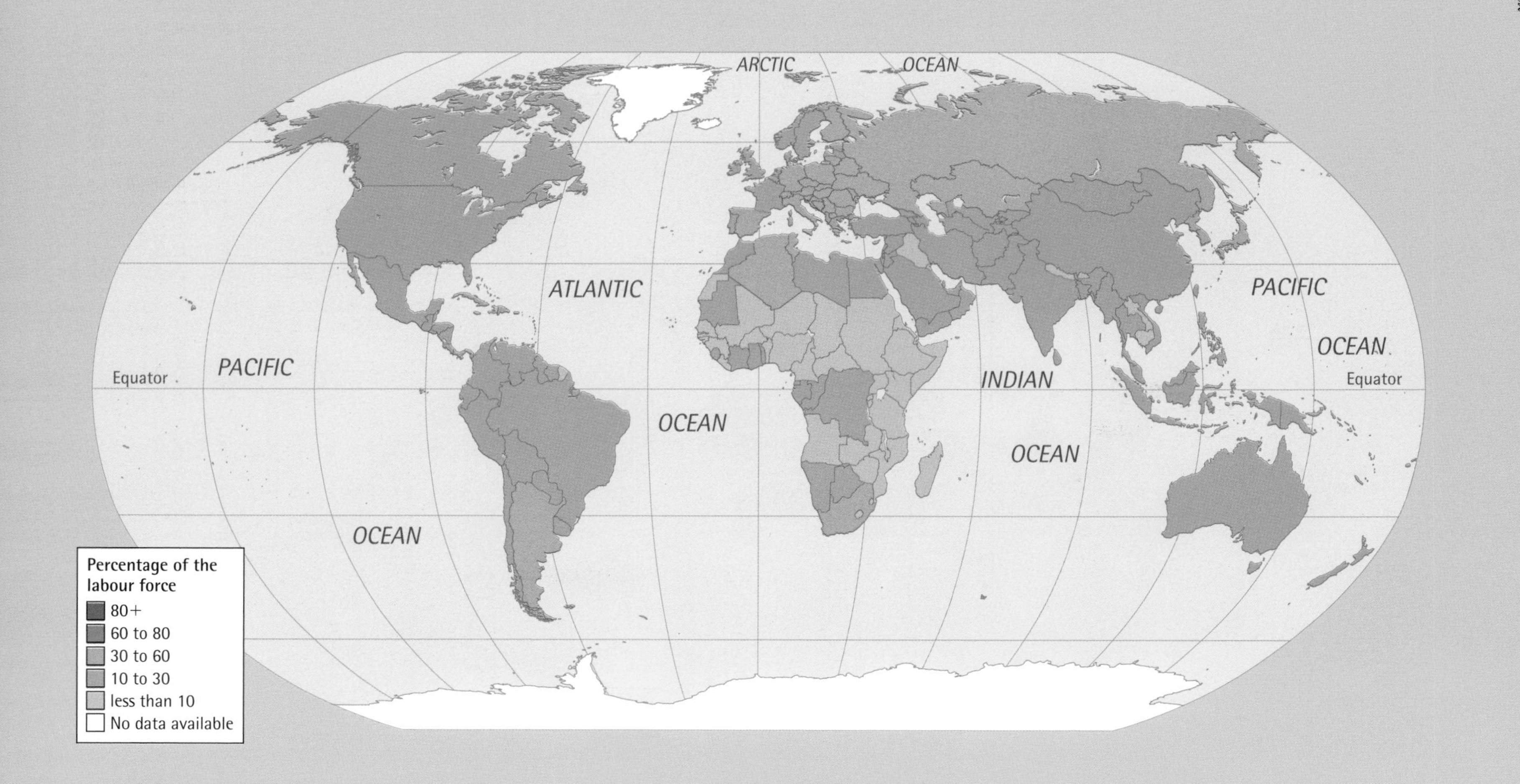

Employment in Services

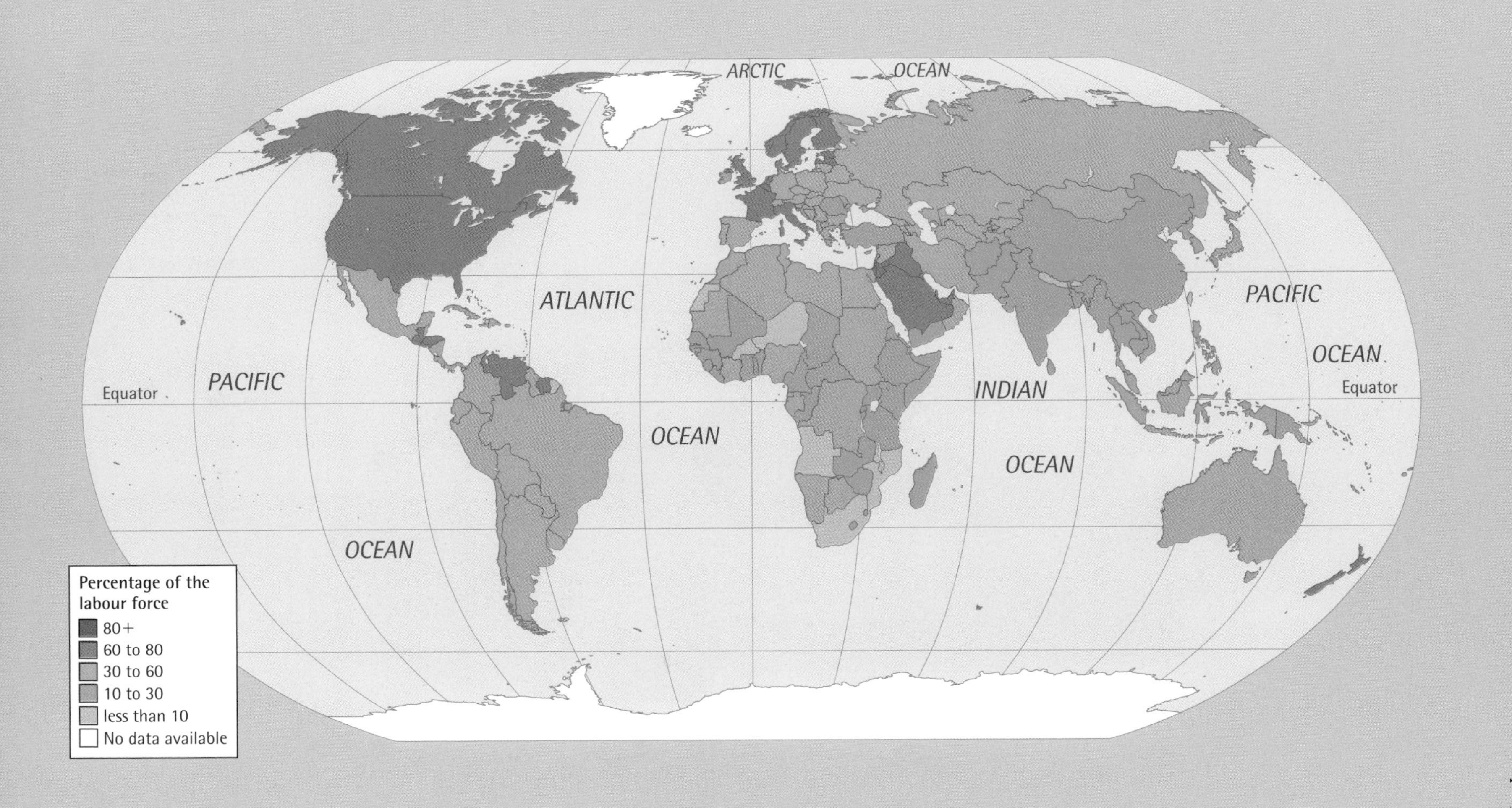

Energy Production

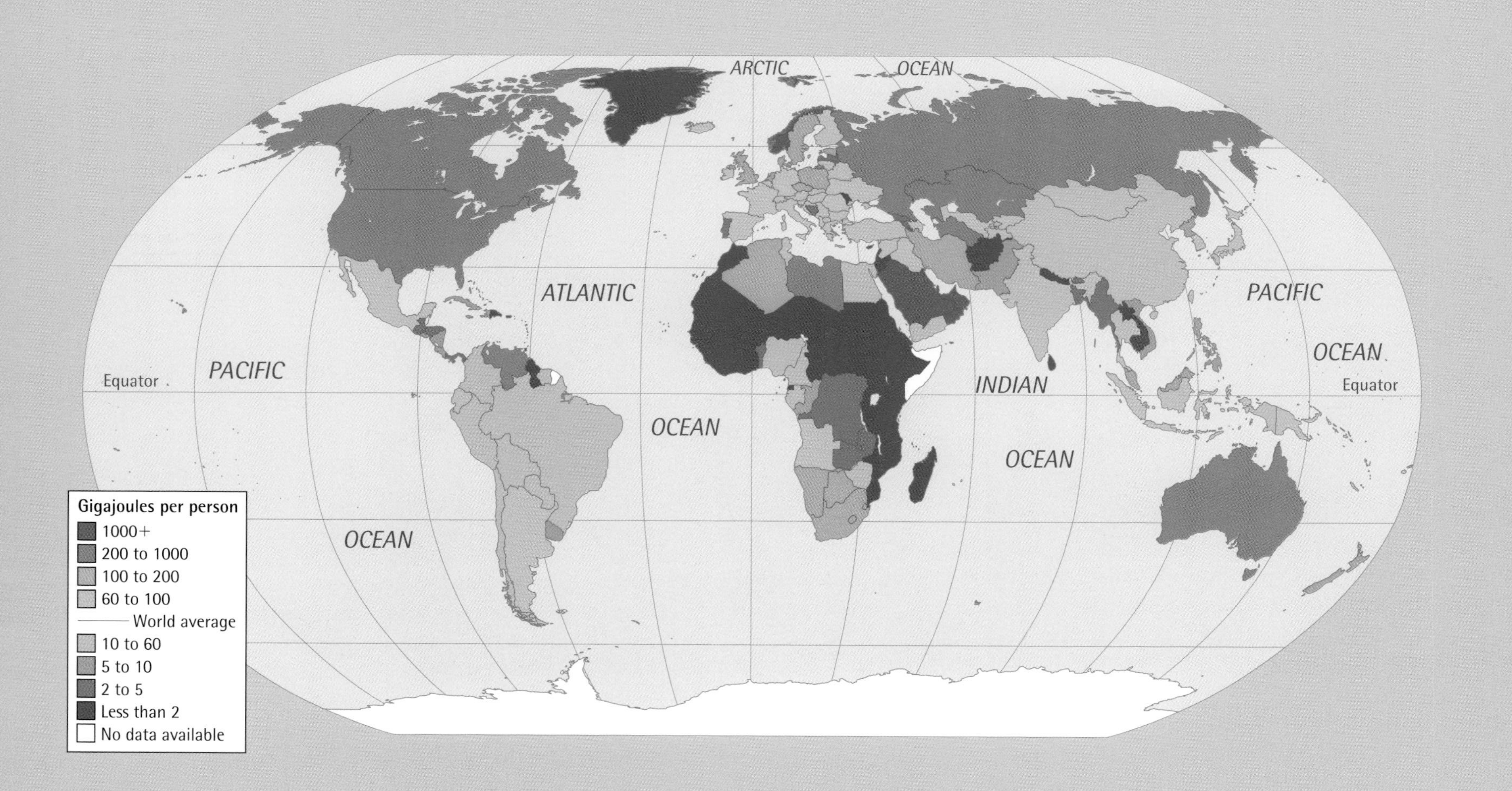

Energy Consumption

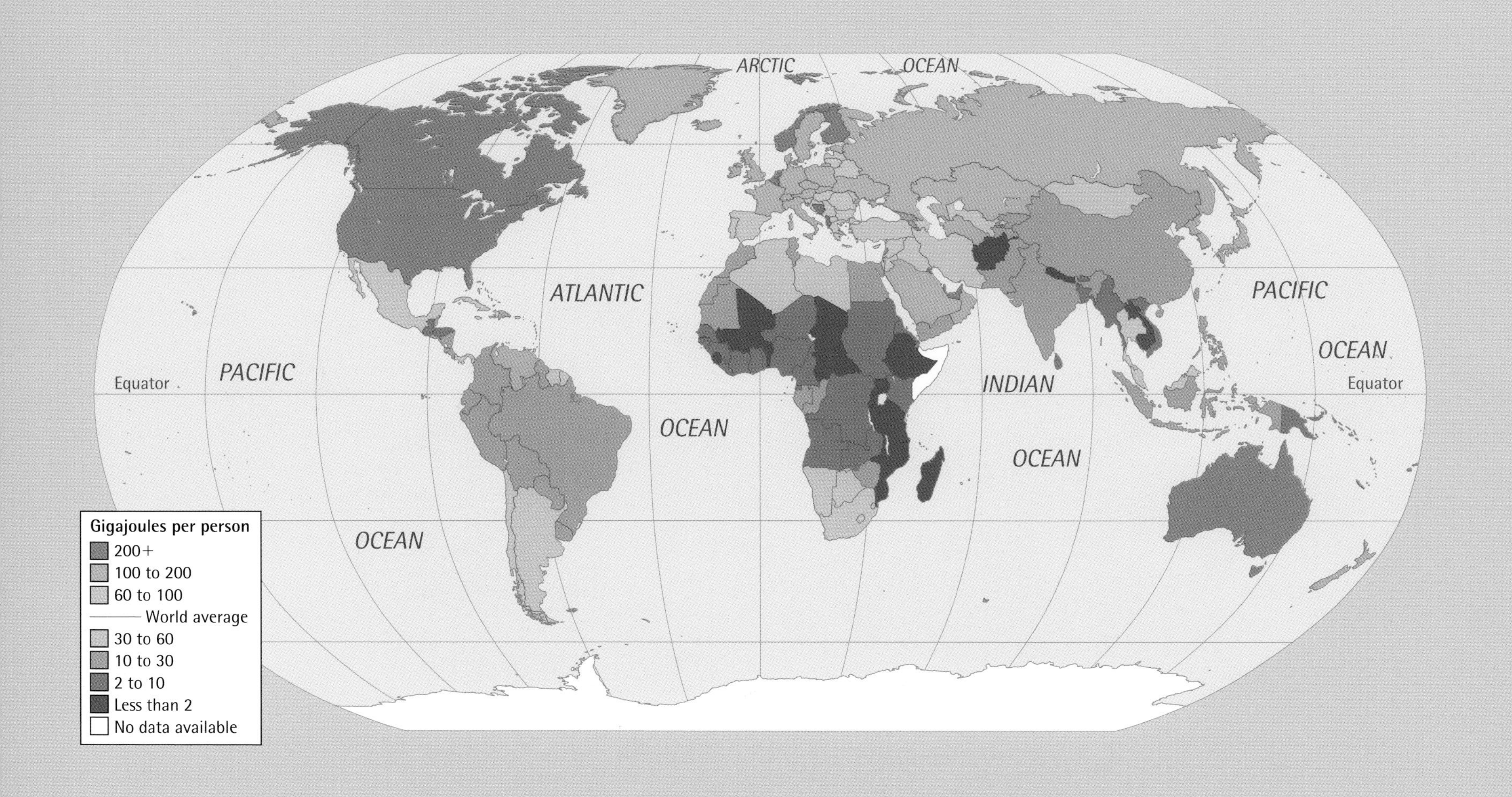

Balance of Trade

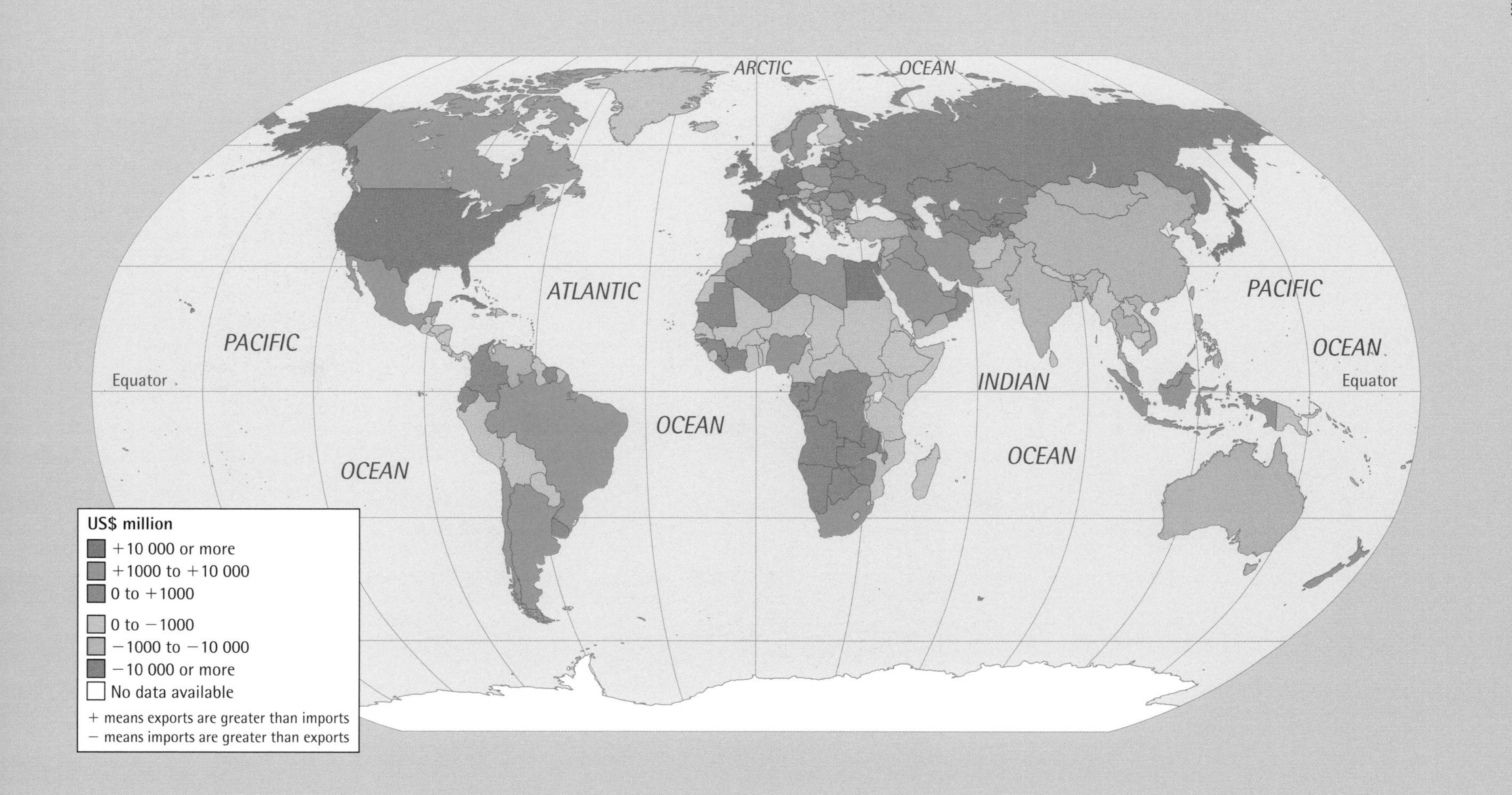

Canada — Political

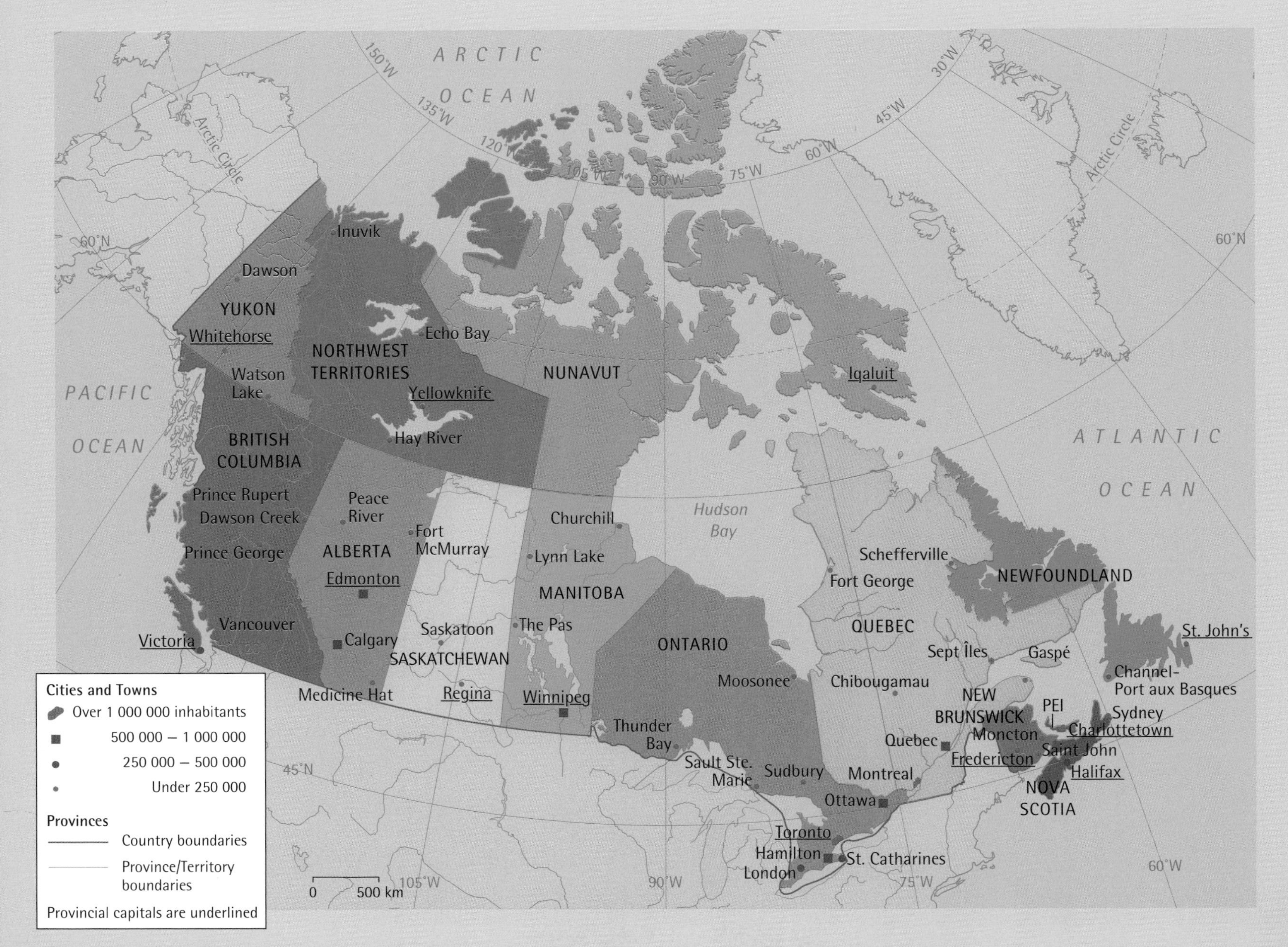

North America — Population Density

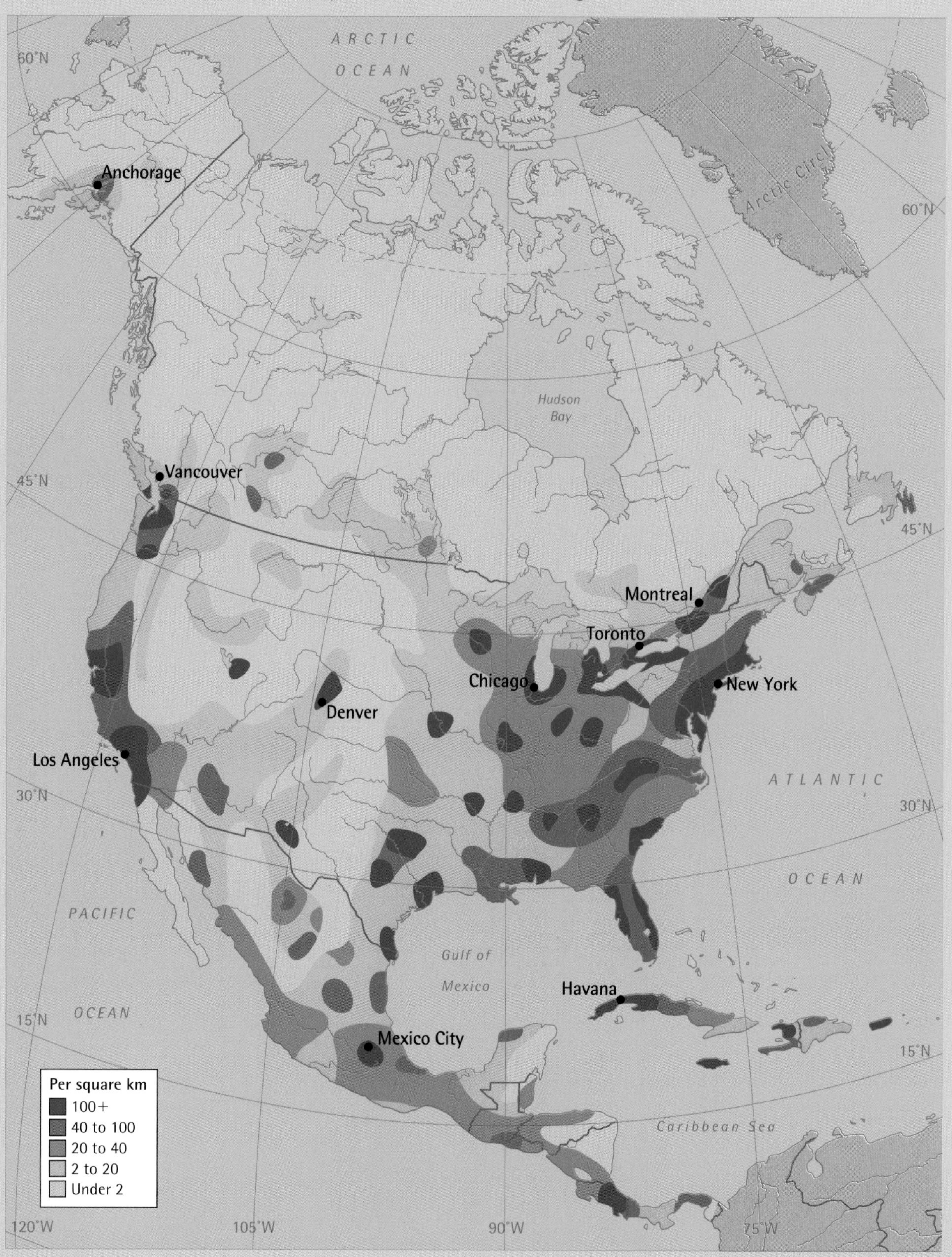

Appendix 2: Skills

Drawing a Comparative Bar Graph

Step1: Draw the axes.

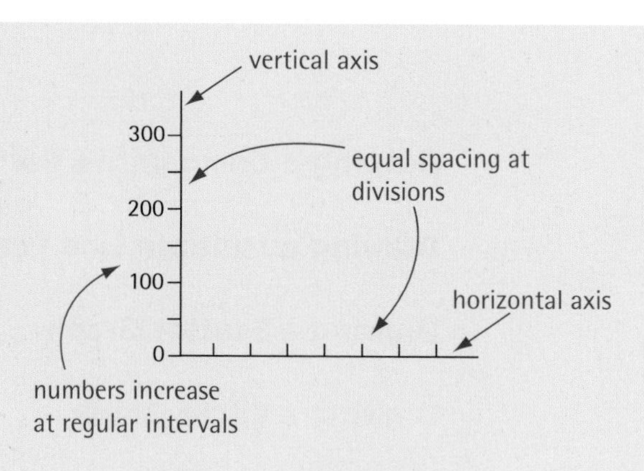

Step 2: Plot the data.

Populations of North American Countries (millions)

Country	1990	1998
Canada	26.4	30.3
Mexico	88.3	97.6
United States	250.4	268.0

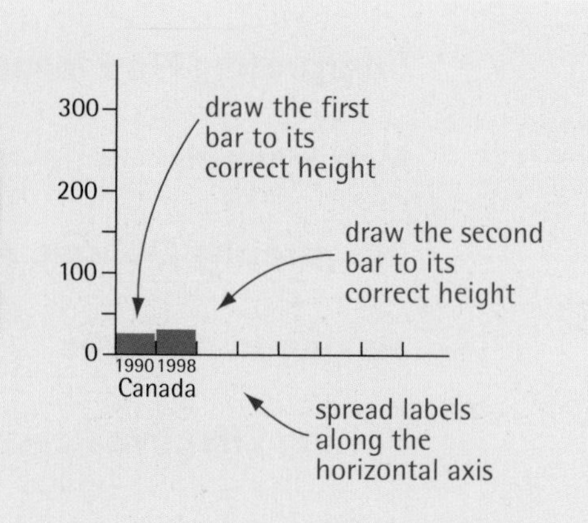

Step 3: Finish the graph.

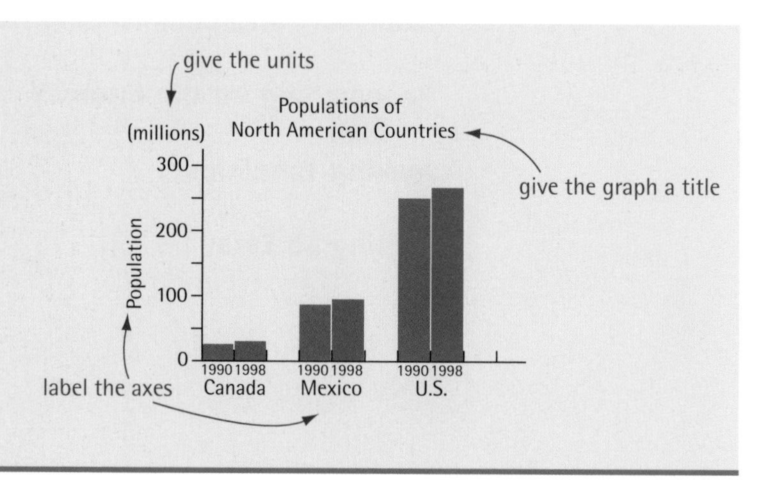

Drawing a Multiple Line Graph

Step 1: Draw the axes.

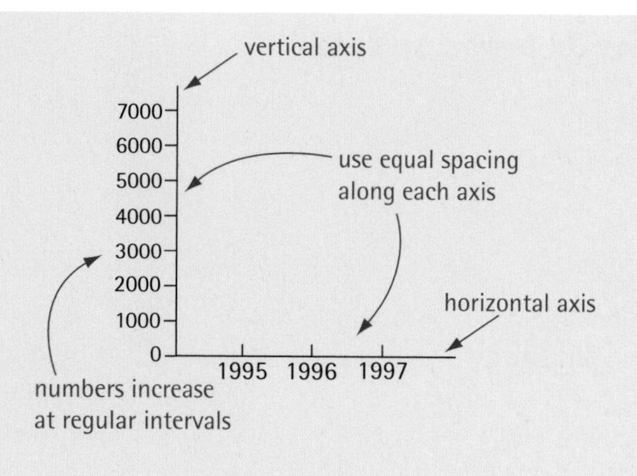

Step 2: Plot the data.

Domestic Production of Energy (petajoules)

Energy Source	1995	1996	1997
Oil	5033	5283	5449
Natural gas	5592	5890	6319
Hydro-electricity	1190	1214	1242
Nuclear	1108	1115	956
Coal	1799	1817	1855

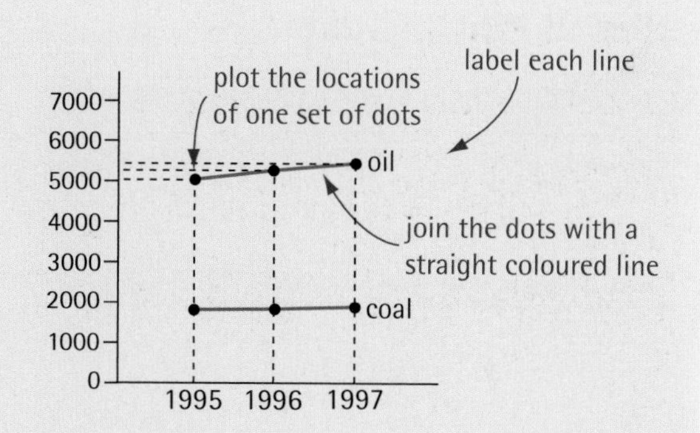

Step 3: Finish the graph.

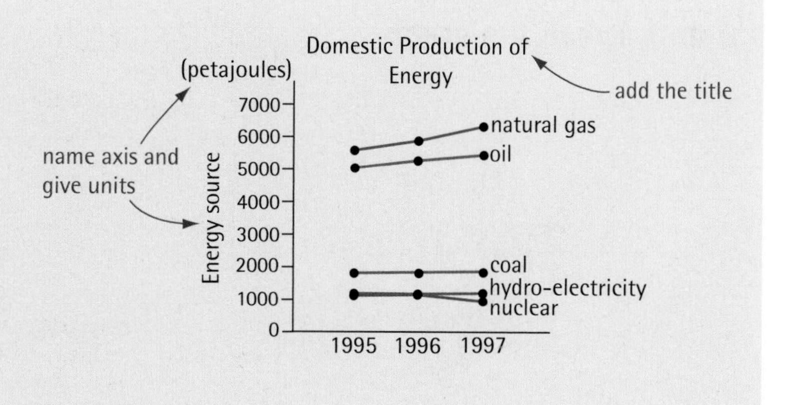

Drawing a Scatter Graph

Step 1: Draw the axes.

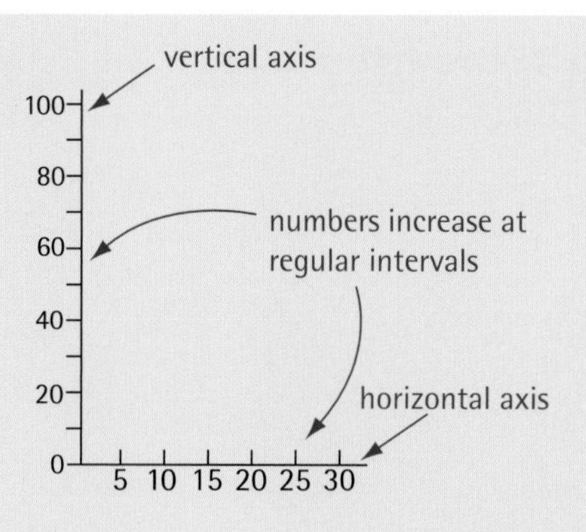

Step 2: Plot the data.

Country	Life Expectancy of Females	Doctors per 10 000 People
Brazil	66	9
Canada	82	22
India	63	4
France	83	28
Kenya	55	1
Vietnam	69	4

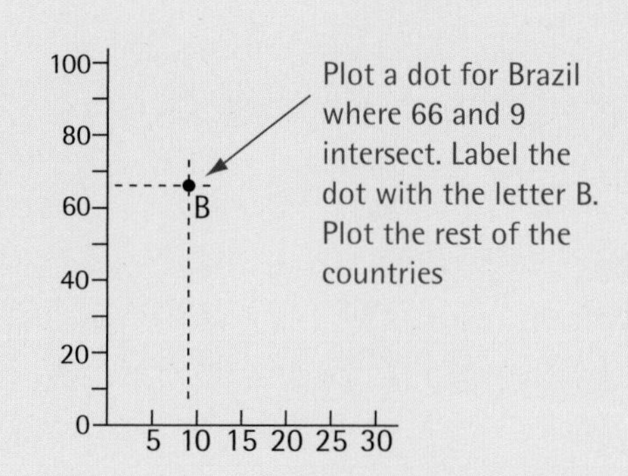

Step 3: Finish the graph.

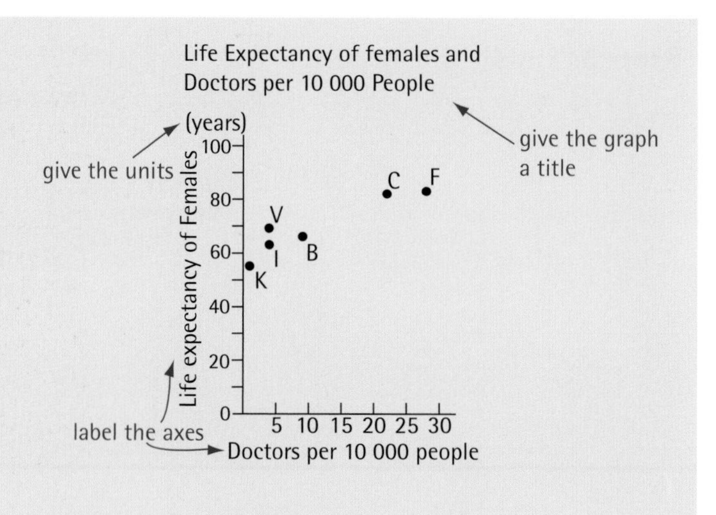

Drawing a Circle Graph

Step 1: Draw a circle.

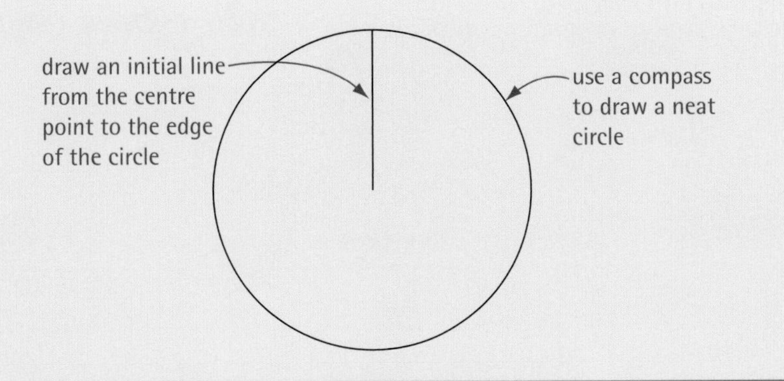

Step 2: Plot the data.

World Grain Production for 2020

Grain	2020 (estimate)
Maize (corn)	31%
Wheat	31%
Rice	20%
Other	18%

Calculate the number of degrees of the circle for each item. Multiply the number of percents by 3.6 to calculate the number of degrees

Circle = 360° = 100%
Therefore 3.6° = 1%

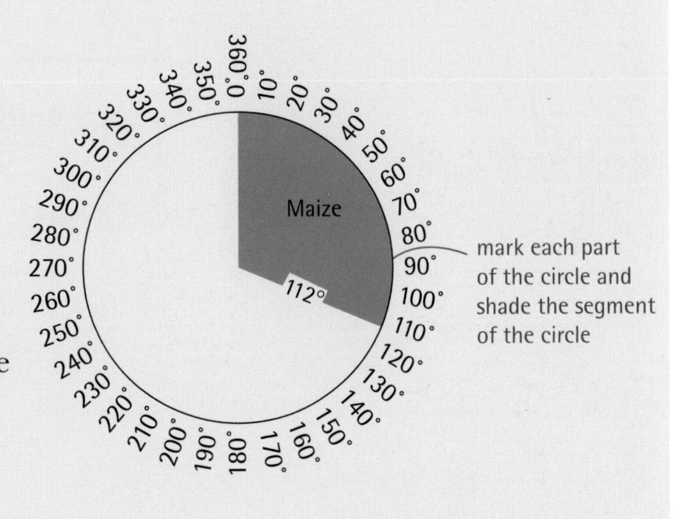

Step 3: Finish the graph.

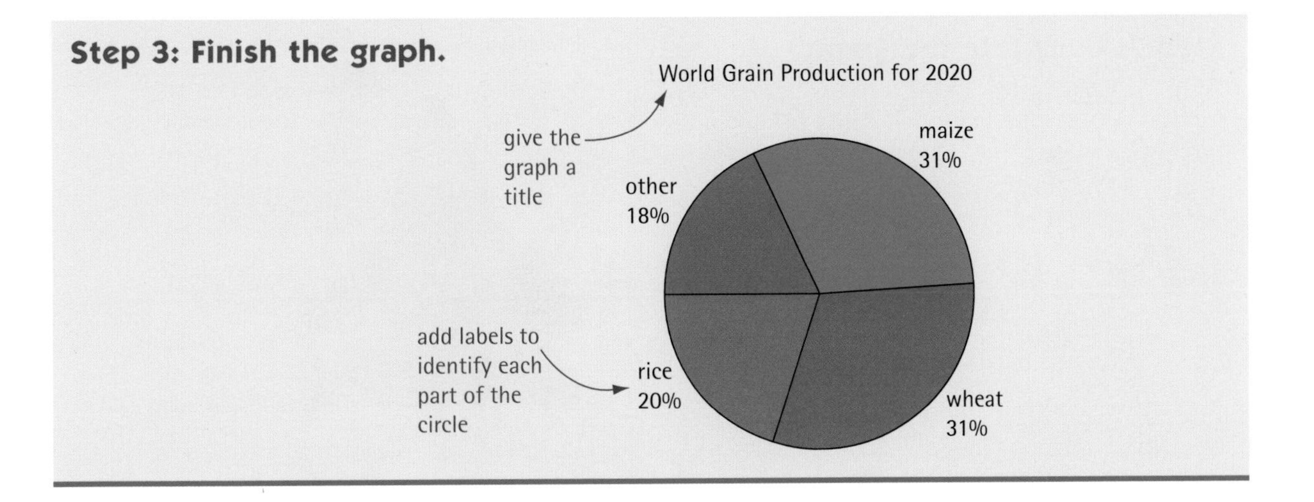

Drawing Population Pyramids

Population for China

Age Group	Males (%)	Females (%)
80+	0.3	0.5
75 – 79	0.5	0.6
70 – 74	0.9	1.0
65 – 69	1.3	1.3
60 – 64	1.7	1.6
55 – 59	1.9	1.7
50 – 54	2.1	1.9
45 – 49	2.7	2.5
40 – 44	3.6	3.4
35 – 39	3.6	3.3
30 – 34	4.5	4.1
25 – 29	5.3	5.0
20 – 24	5.1	4.9
15 – 19	4.0	3.8
10 – 14	4.3	4.0
5 – 9	4.8	4.5
0 – 4	5.0	4.7

Step 1: Draw the axes.

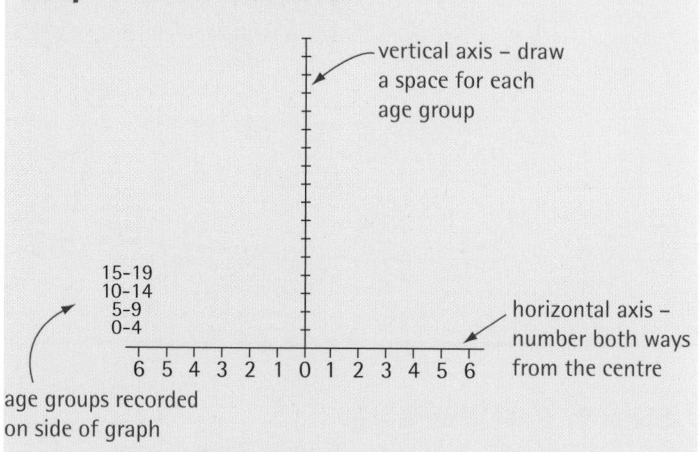

Step 2: Plot the data.

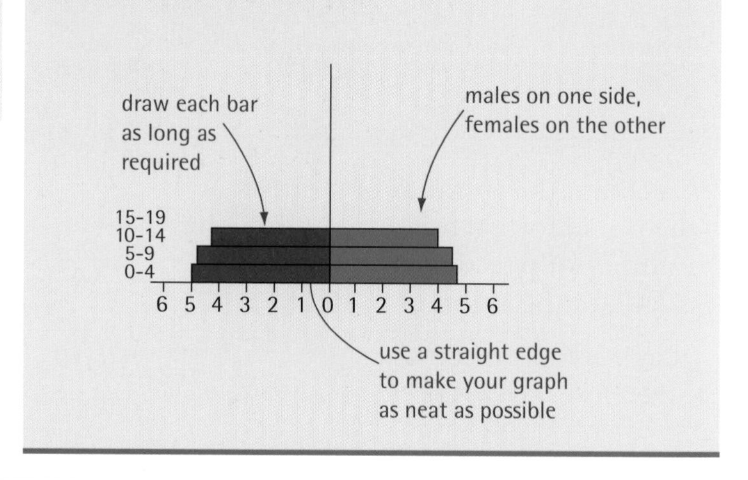

Step 3: Complete the graph.

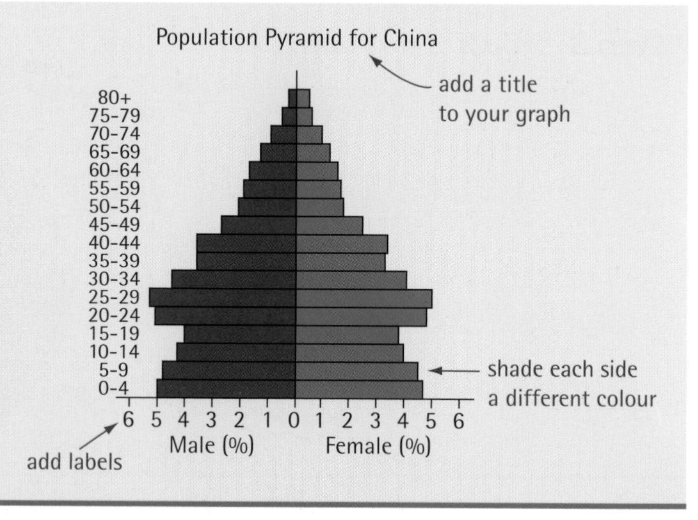

Drawing Choropleth Maps

Choropleth maps show the amount of something in an area. They are commonly used to show population density. This type of map uses colouring or shading to show information.

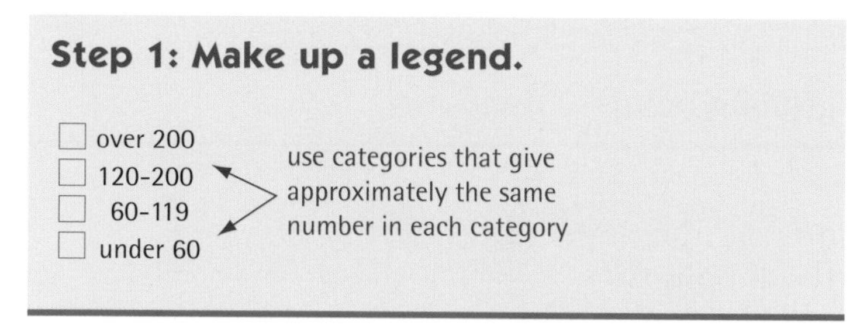

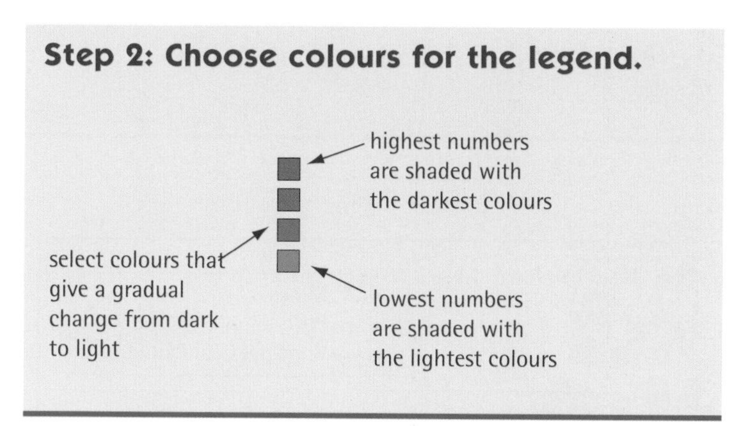

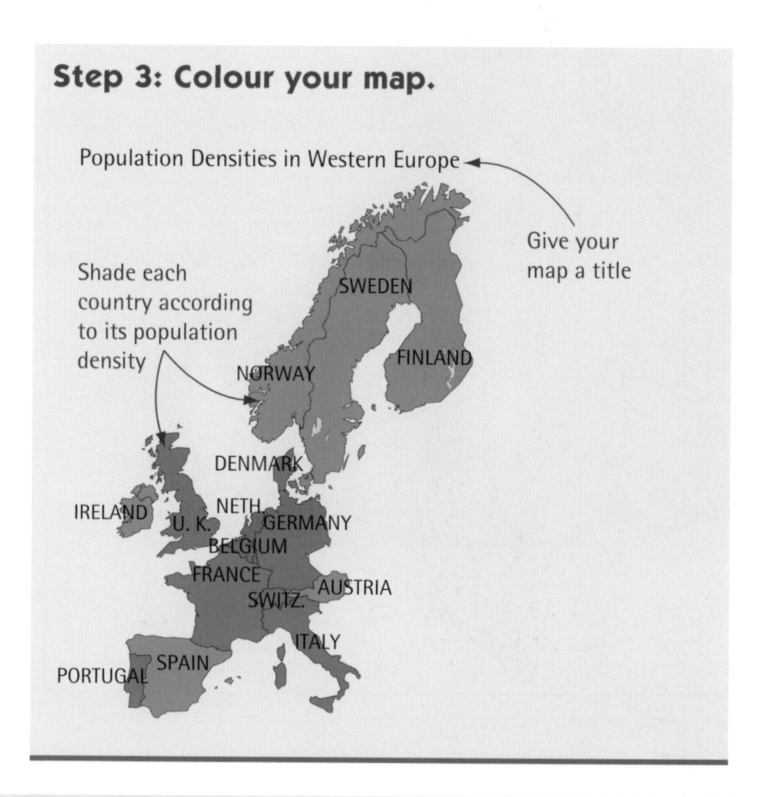

Population Densities in Western Europe

Country	Population Density People/km^2
Austria	94
Belgium	331
Denmark	122
Finland	16
France	104
Germany	231
Ireland	50
Italy	197
Netherlands	450
Norway	14
Portugal	107
Spain	78
Sweden	21
Switzerland	172
United Kingdom	239

Interpreting Flow Maps

Flow maps show the direction and distance of a movement of people or goods using lines or arrows. The arrows (or lines) begin at the source of the movement and end at the destination.

Step 1: Identify the source.
Use the legend to determine the beginning points of the flows.

Step 2: Identify the destinations.
The destinations are the end points of the lows (lines or arrows). Use the legend to identify these points.

Step 3: Identify the flows.
Flows are shown by lines or arrows that follow the paths taken by the people or goods.

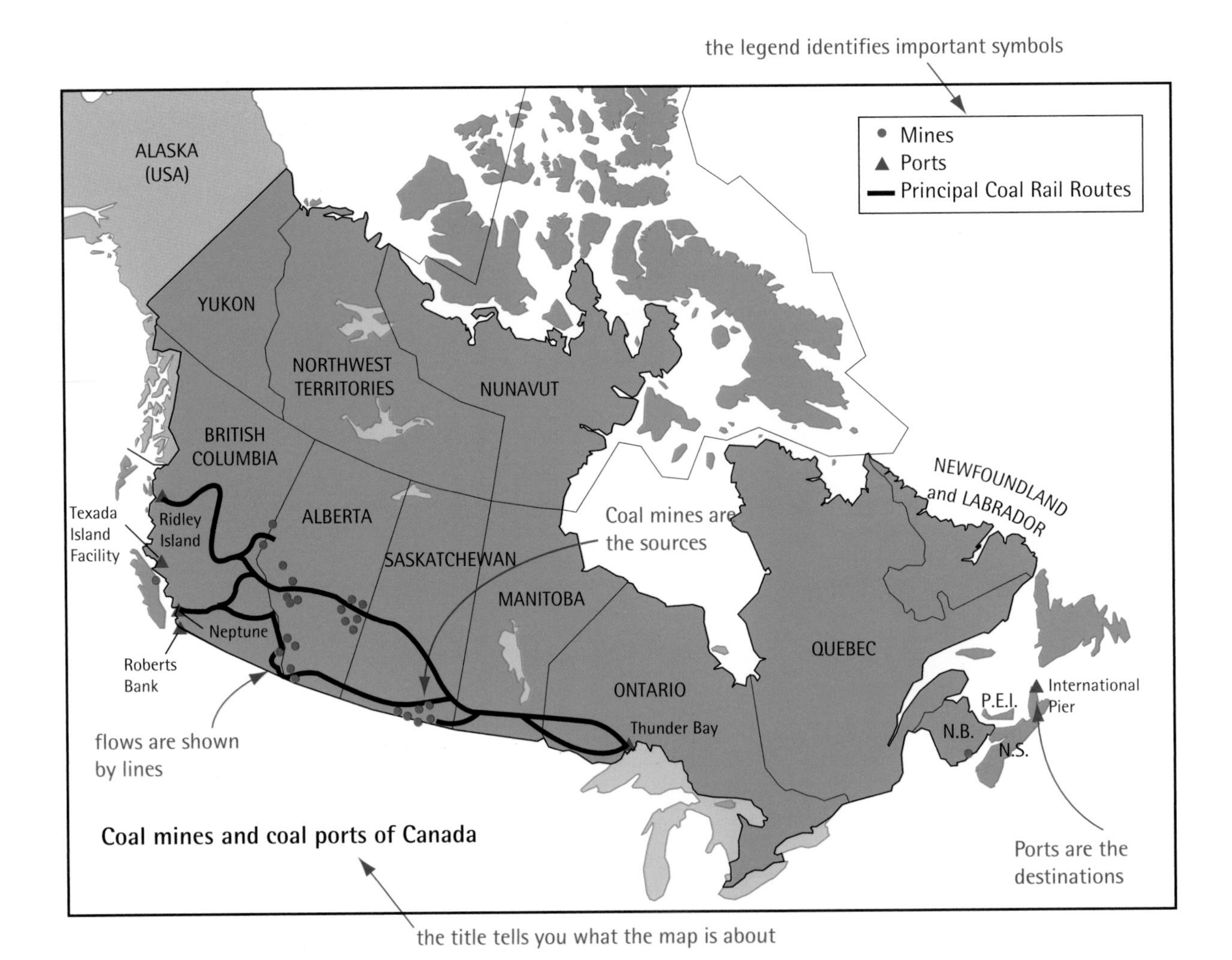

Map Symbols

Major cities

Capital cities

Regional capital cities

Other cities

Towns and villages

International boundaries

State/Provincial boundaries

Undefined boundaries

Highways

Railroads

Major roads

Tunnels

Passes

Other roads

Seasonal roads

Canals

Pipelines

Shipping routes

Air routes

Airports

National/Regional parks

Elevations:

Metres above sea level

5000
4000
3000
2000
1500
1000
500
0

Metres below sea level

-1000
-2000
-3000

Streams

Spot heights in metres

849

Lakes

Swamps

Abbreviations:

mm	Millimetres
m	Metres
km	Kilometres
°C	Degrees Celsius
mb	Millibars

Interpreting Oblique Aerial Photos

Aerial photographs are pictures of places on the surface of the earth taken from airplanes. Vertical photos are taken when the camera points straight down. These photos resemble maps. Oblique air photos are taken when the camera is tilted at an angle. The horizon may or may not be visible in oblique air photos.

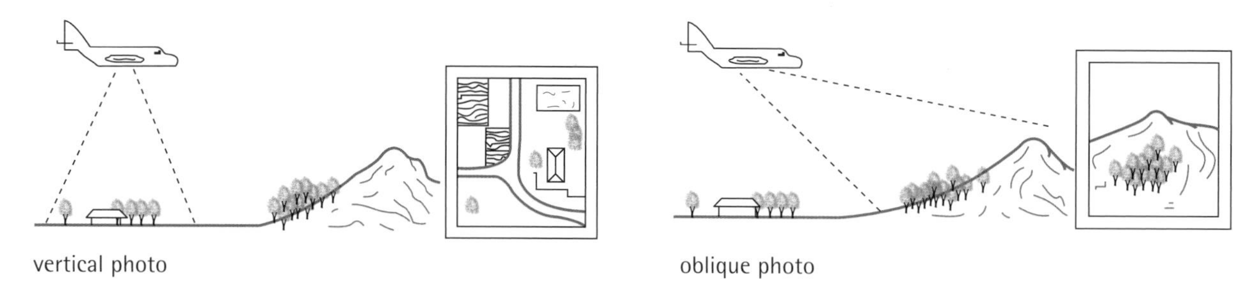

Step 1: Get a general impression.
Figure out generally what what is being shown in the photo. For example, is the photo showing part of a city or is it in the countryside? Is it a mountainous area or a flat landscape?

Step 2: Look at the background.
Note information from the background, including if the horizon is showing or not.

Step 3: Find details in the foreground.
Note details in the foreground, including:

- physical features
- transportation routes
- buildings
- water bodies
- vegetation

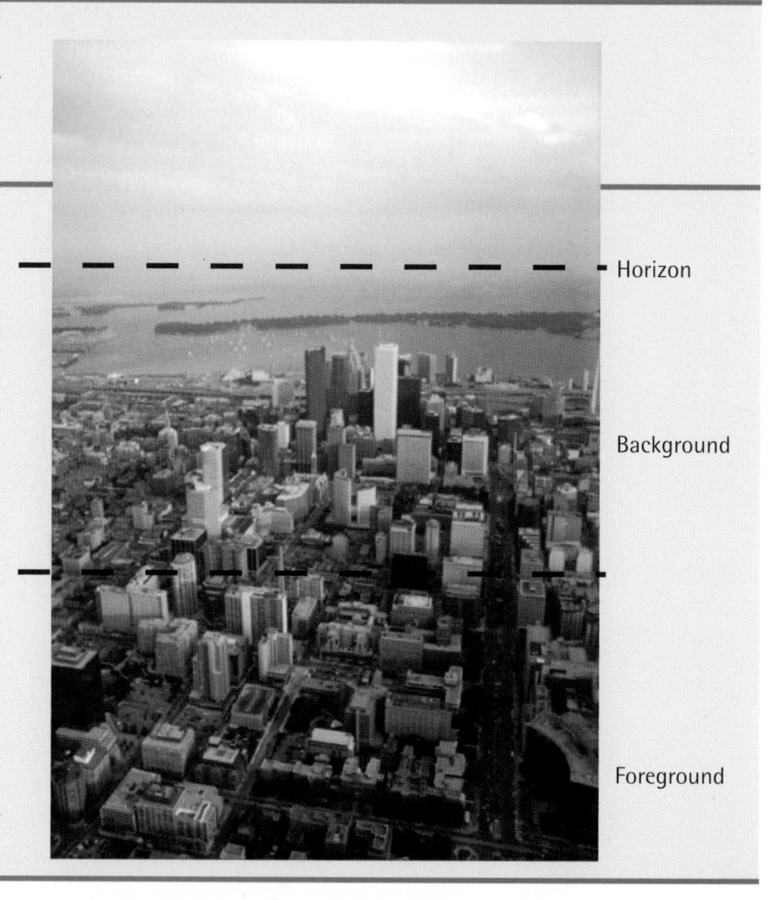

Making Ideas Webs

An ideas web is a visual way to show the connections among ideas.

Step 1: Begin with the most general idea.

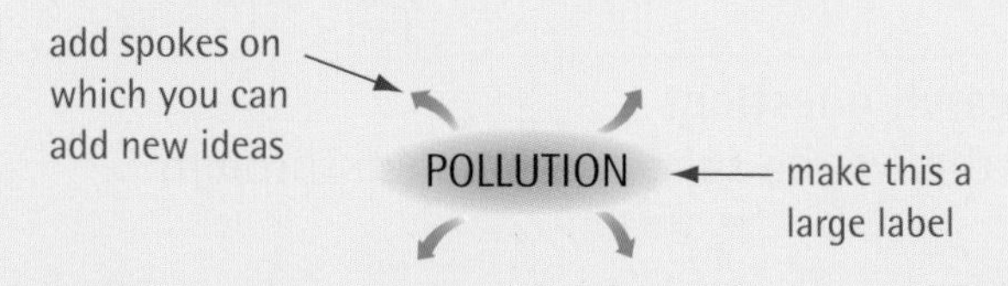

Step 2: Add connecting ideas to your web.

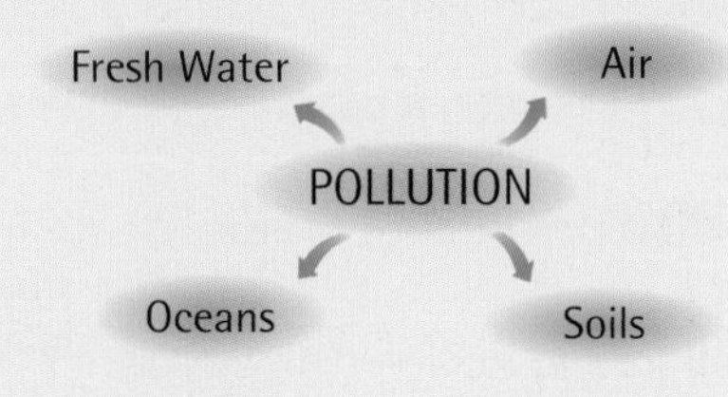

Step 3: Keep adding more specific ideas.

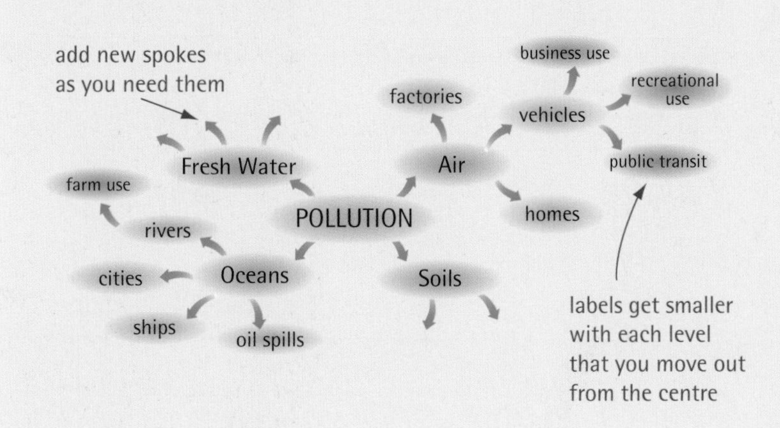

Writing Effective Research Questions

Before you can begin an investigation, you need a research question. The research question directs and limits the information that you gather about the investigation. You can ask different types of research questions. The type you use depends on the problem being considered.

Purpose of a research question:
to focus or point the way to solving a problem through investigation

Question Type	Explanation	Example
Factual	Identifies details that you need to know about the problem	In which countries are rainforests being cut down most quickly?
Definitional	Clarifies the meanings of the terms that are important to understanding and solving the problem	What are the characteristics of a tropical rain-forest?
Comparative	Gets at differences or similarities related to the problem	In what ways are tropical rainforests similar to temperate rainforests?
Cause and effect	Looks at reasons why a problem is occurring	Why are tropical rainforests being cut down so quickly?
Decision making	Explores actions that could be taken to deal with the problem	What would be one very effective way of stopping the destruction of the tropical rain-forests?
Speculative	Considers what might be an outcome or a conclusion	What would happen if Canadians stopped buying lumber products made from wood from the rainforests?
Ethical	Explores the rights and wrongs of a problem	Do Canadians have the right to stop people in other countries from cutting down their own rainforests?

Solving Problems

Problems can be solved most effectively if you use an organized and systematic approach.

Problem Solving Model

Stage	Action
1. Identify the problem	Define a problem or issue for further investigation. Write a question that has to be answered.
2. Establish a tentative answer (a hypothesis)	Using the knowledge you already have about a topic, think up a possible answer to the question you set. This possible solution is your hypothesis.
3. Gather more information	In order to test your hypothesis (to prove it is either true or false), you need more information. You get these data (information) through research.
4. Analyse the data	Carefully examine the information you have gathered. Look for patterns and relationships that are connected to the problem you are investigating.
5. Arrive at a conclusion	You use the data you gathered to either prove or disprove your hypothesis. At this point, you can change your hypothesis to come up with an even better possible solution or answer. You may wish to start gathering more data to add to your research after you change your hypothesis.

Analysing and Summarizing News Articles

You get a great deal of your information about the world from newspaper articles. Learning to analyse the news helps you understand the news that much more.

MEXICAN DAM THREATENED BY FLOOD WATERS

Officials open dam gates to relieve pressure

Weeks of torrential rain have forced authorities to open the floodgates of the Las Penitas dam on the Grijalva River. The dam was filled to capacity and in danger of breaking.

The opened gates released four times the normal amount of water through the dam. Downstream, residents of Villahermosa, a city of about 460 000 people, watched anxiously as the water in the river began to rise. Already it was waist high. In some places floodwaters reached to the rooftops of flooded homes and businesses.

Soldiers and volunteers worked frantically around the clock to raise a 1.5 m high dike that surrounds the city. The dike has protected the business district of the city from flooding, but no one knows how high the water will get and how long the dike will hold it back.

"If the waters get over the dike, half of the businesses in the city will be swept away," said Jose Fernandez, a local municipal official.

A month of steady rain has left more than 227 000 people in the region without homes. At least 400 deaths have been blamed on the flood. Since some bodies have not been recovered, the death toll could go much higher.

National Water Commission officials said that they opened the floodgates because the weight of the water was threatening to collapse the dam. If heavy rains continue, they add, they may be forced to open the floodgates of other dams upstream of Villahermosa.

News Article Analysis

What happened to cause the article to be written?

What is the main or general idea of the article?

What evidence is given in the article?

What sources of information are given in the article?

Are all sides in the story treated fairly?

What do I think about the story?

Researching on the Internet

Step 1: Brainstorm key words and ideas.

What are **Canada's economic ties** to **China?**
Canada
China
Wheat sales
Nuclear power generators
Trade
imports
exports
agreements

Step 2: Use combinations of terms in a search engine. Since China and Canada are central to your search, you should include them.

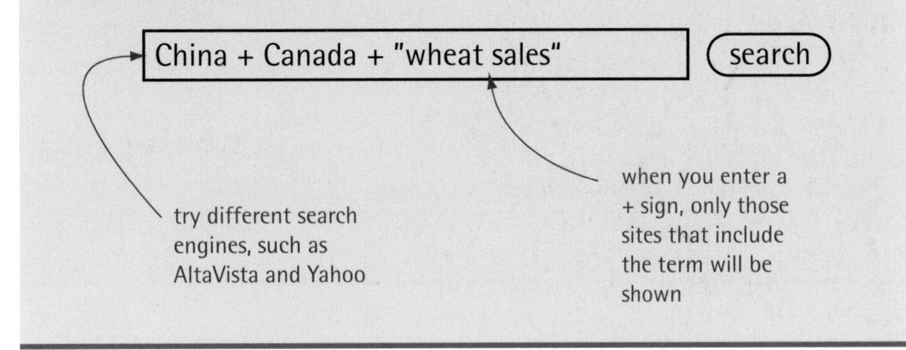

Step 3: Try different terms or combinations of terms if you are not finding useful sites.

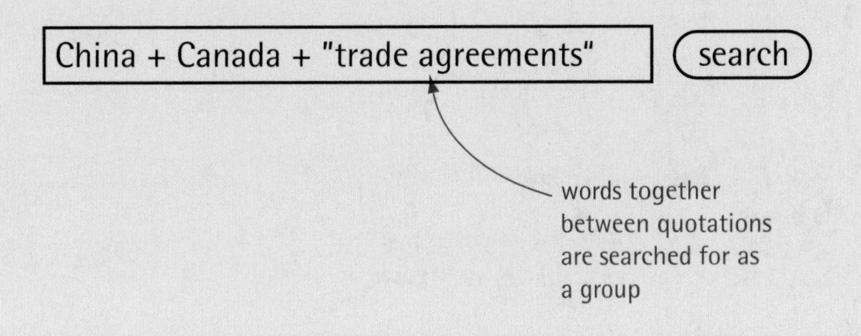

Making Timelines

Step 1: Draw a line.

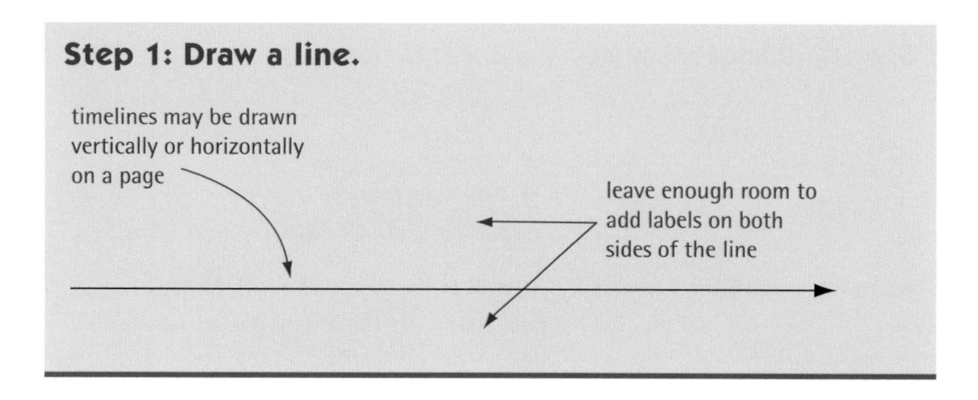

Step 2: Add the year labels to the line.

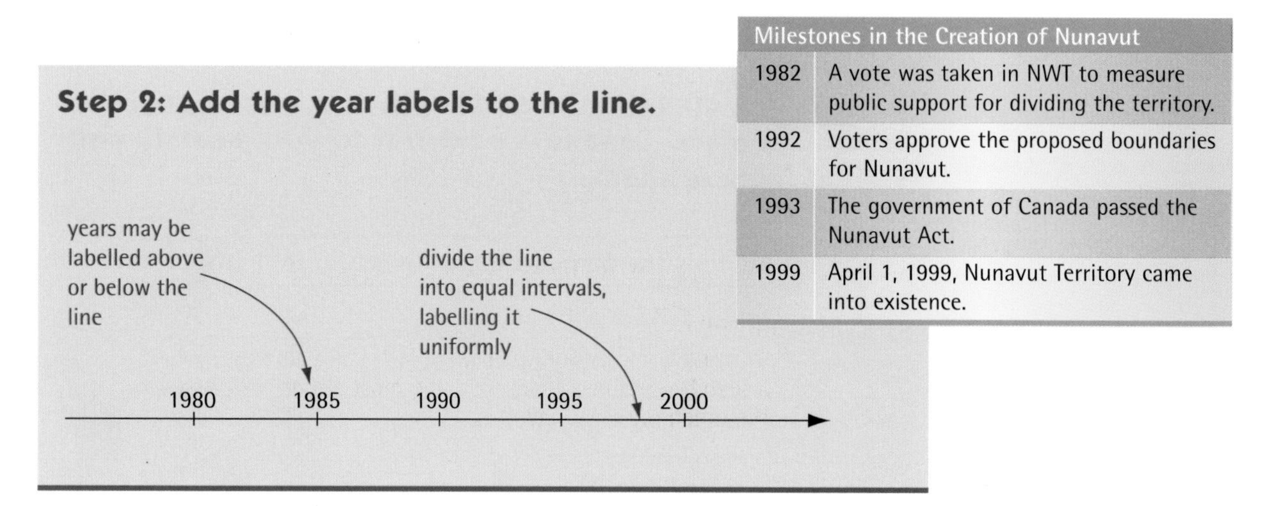

Milestones in the Creation of Nunavut	
1982	A vote was taken in NWT to measure public support for dividing the territory.
1992	Voters approve the proposed boundaries for Nunavut.
1993	The government of Canada passed the Nunavut Act.
1999	April 1, 1999, Nunavut Territory came into existence.

Step 3: Add events to the timeline.

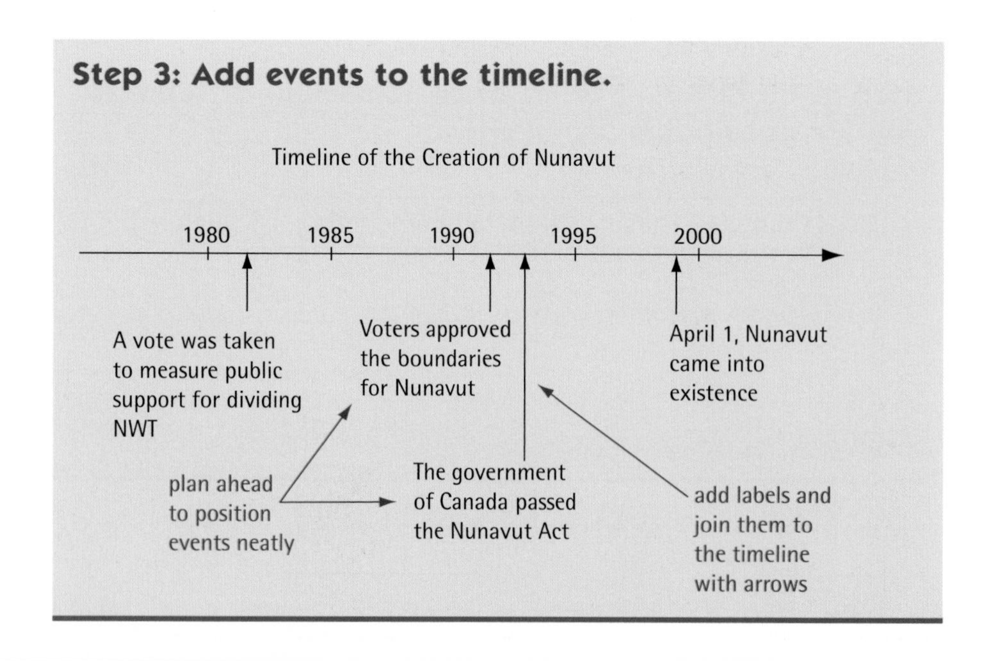

Writing an Essay

Step 1: Plan your essay.

An essay should have three parts:

Introduction	• sets the tone for the essay • states the purpose • identifies the research question (the thesis)
Body	• this is the largest part of the essay • presents the information you have found to answer your research question (hypothesis)
Conclusion	• reminds the reader of the purpose of the essay • sums up the evidence that was produced in the body of the essay

Step 2: Outline your essay.

The Causes of the Greenhouse Effect

INTRODUCTION
- to identify the important causes of the greenhouse effect
- research question: What are three most important causes of the greenhouse effect?

BODY

Cause #1
- burning fossil fuels
- identify fossil fuels (coal, oil, natural gas)
- identify the impact on the environment of burning them (produces carbon dioxide)

Cause #2
- burning tropical forests

Cause #3
- releasing freon into the air (spray cans, air conditioners, refrigerators)
- harmful gas
- other types of appliances that are not harmful

Step 3: Write your essay.

You need to make a first draft that you carefully edit and improve. In the first draft you edit for spelling or grammatical errors, statements that aren't supported by facts, clarity, and completeness. Then, write the final good draft.

Glossary

Agricultural revolution: Advances in technology that dramatically change our ability to grow, process, and distribute foods. The first agricultural revolution occurred when people domesticated plants and animals 12 000 years ago. In the 1700s A.D., farmers applied scientific ideas and new machines to produce more food.

Arable land: Land that can be used to grow crops.

Assimilation: One culture's changing to fit, or be more like, another.

Baby boom cohort: The group of babies born between 1947 and 1960.

Bartering: An informal economic activity in which goods and services, but not cash, are exchanged. Trading car repairs for bookkeeping services is an example.

Berlin Wall: A patrolled, high wall built through the city of Berlin in the 1950s to prevent movement of people between the East and West.

Birth rate: The number of babies born each year for every 1000 people in the country.

Capital: Money used to promote economic activities, for example, to build machines or to construct buildings.

Census: The survey of a population to gather particular facts.

Collectivize: The pooling of resources so that all members of the group can use them and there is no longer private ownership. In farming, collectivization means that farmers do not own the land.

Colonies: Places that are controlled by a more powerful country. From the 1400s through the 1800s, European countries kept colonies in the Americas, Africa, Asia, and Australia.

Colonization: The establishing of colonies in other parts of the world, often by force.

Command economy: An economic system in which decisions are made by an individual or a small group of people for everyone else.

Commodities: Anything that is bought or sold. The term is most often used to refer to products made from natural resources.

Conglomerate: A large corporation that owns many different companies.

Co-operative farming: A system in which farmers work together, sharing the labour and the output of a farm. No one person owns the farm or its equipment.

Correlation: The relationship between two variables.

Cosmopolitan: Ethnically and culturally diverse.

Cultural diffusion: The movement of parts of one culture into another.

Cultural realm: A large region of the world sharing significant cultural similarities.

Culture: A way of life shared by a group of people, including the way they obtain food, the way they bring up their children, their values, beliefs, language, customs, and religion.

Death rate: The number of people who die each year for every 1000 people in the country.

Demographic trends: Factors that describe changes in the general population.

Demography: The study of human populations.

Dense population: A high population in relation to the area that contains it (high ratio of people to land area).

Desertification: The expansion of deserts into surrounding areas.

Developed countries: Countries that have a high proportion of their workforce in tertiary industries, with small percentages in primary industries. Incomes in these countries are usually high. Canada is a developed country.

Developing countries: Countries that have a high proportion of their workforce engaged in primary industries and a small proportion working in the tertiary sector. Incomes in these countries are usually quite low. India is a developing country.

Doubling time: The time it takes for a country's population to double in number.

Downsizing: A massive lay off of workers by a company.

Economic activity: All those things that people do to try to make their lives better and more comfortable.

Economic systems: The ways that societies make economic decisions about what to produce and how to distribute it.

Economically diversified: Having many different ways to generate jobs and money. For example, a city has factories, stores, restaurants, etc.

Economists: People who study the way economies work, often collecting data about how people make economic decisions.

Emigrant: A person who moves out of a country.

Emigrate: To leave your country for another.

Enclaves: Areas, often within large cities, that are concentrations of a particular cultural group.

Entrepôt: A transportation centre where goods are shipped to be prepared for transportation in larger loads to destinations around the world. Halifax is an entrepôt in Canada.

Environmental migration: Movements of people or animals in response to an environmental trigger, such as an earthquake or a long-term drought.

Epidemic: A sudden outbreak of illness that causes the death rate to go up sharply.

Exit tax: A high fee that people had to pay in the USSR to leave during the 1950s to the 1980s.

Fertility rate: The average number of babies born throughout a woman's lifetime in a country.

Fibre optics: A technology used to send electronic data over specially designed cables.

Finished goods: Goods produced by secondary industries that consumers can use, such as automobiles, furniture, or food products.

Forced migration: A mass movement of people who must leave their homes against their will.

Foreign debt: Money that a country owes to banks and lending agencies in other countries. Such loans are usually taken in order to make improvements in people's quality of life.

Formal economic activities: Work for which wages are paid and records are kept.

Free trade: Trade between countries that takes place without tariffs or other barriers. Canada has a free trade agreement with Mexico and the United States.

Frontier areas: Regions that are just being opened up to human settlement.

Gastarbeiter: A foreign migrant worker ("guest worker") in Germany.

Globalization: The increasing trend to do business on an international level. Trading countries must take into account all the forces that are at work around the world in order to compete.

Gross domestic product (GDP): The total value of all the goods and services produced within a country in a year. It is often expressed as **GDP per capita**, which is the GDP divided by the population.

Gross national product (GNP): The sum of all the economic activities of the citizens of a country in one year, regardless of where the money was earned. It may be expressed as **GNP per capita,** which is the average per person earnings.

Habitation: A place where people live.

Human Development Index (HDI): A set of living conditions, such as literacy rate, death rate, and life expectancy, that give a general picture of what life is like in a given country.

Immigrant: A person who moves into a country.

Immigrate: To move into another country.

Industrial Revolution: The period in the 1700s and 1800s that saw the changeover from a mainly farm-oriented society to a mainly industrial society.

Industrialization: The rapid development of manufacturing in a society. Workers usually move out of a declining agricultural sector into an expanding industrial sector.

Informal economic activities: Work that people do that is not reported as an economic activity to avoid records being kept and taxes paid. Garage and yard sales are examples of informal economic activities.

Infrastructure: Structures and systems built to enable a society to work well, such as roads, hospitals, electricity, clean water systems, schools, etc.

Interprovincial migration: The movement of people from one province or territory in Canada to another.

Iron Curtain: The name given to the borders separating Communist- controlled countries from the West. This was a very controlled border that prevented people from crossing from the 1950s through the 1980s.

Knowledge worker: A person working in one of the information industries, such as computer software development.

Labour: The human effort that goes into producing goods and services.

Land: All the natural resources that people have available for economic activities. Forests, minerals, and water fit this economic category.

Land use: The different ways that people use land, for example, for farms, houses, roads, etc.

Life expectancy: The number of years that a baby born in a certain year in a country can be expected to live.

Literacy rate: The percentage of people over age 15 in a country that can read.

Mainstream population: The major cultural group in a society. In Ontario, the mainstream population has been white, Anglo-Saxon, and Protestant.

Market: The consumers who buy a good or purchase a service.

Market economy: An economic system in which decisions are made by everyone acting on his or her own. There is no form of central control on people's economic decisions.

Mass migration: The movement of large numbers of people over a fairly short time period (for example, the flow of people out of Europe after the world wars).

Material wealth: Goods and services that we can see and touch that make our lives better, such as refrigerators and haircuts.

Megalopolis: A "super city."

Migrant workers: People who travel from one country to another for seasonal or even longer periods of employment.

Migrants' remittance: The money sent home by migrant workers to their families which becomes an "invisible" gain for their country.

Migration: The movement of people (or animals or things) from one place to another for political, economic, or environmental reasons.

Mixed economy: An economic system in which decisions are made by a combination of consumers, businesses, and governments. Canada has a mixed economy.

Moderate population density: A medium level of population in relation to the area that contains it (medium ratio of people to land area).

Monoculture: Growing only one crop on a farm.

Multicultural policy: Canada's official government policy of encouraging groups representing many different cultures to keep their identities and heritage alive while participating in mainstream Canadian society.

Natural increase: A rise in population because the birth rate is higher than the death rate.

Net immigration: The difference between the number of people who leave a country (emigrate) and the number who enter the country (immigrate).

Non-governmental organizations (NGOs): Groups that are not connected to any government and that work to solve social problems.

Non-material wealth: Those factors that improve our lives but are difficult to touch or describe, such as human rights and the freedom to worship as we wish.

North American Free Trade Agreement (NAFTA): An agreement currently among Canada, Mexico, and the United States to allow tariff-free trade of goods and services.

Oases: Locations where water is available in a desert, usually marked by trees. The singular form of the word is **oasis**.

Organic farming: Growing food without using any chemical fertilizers or pesticides.

Outsourcing: The hiring of outside, independent workers to do some part of a company's work.

Per capita income: The average amount of money earned in a certain year by a person in a country.

Point system: A method used by governments to assess a potential immigrant's suitability using different measures such as family ties, language, and work skills.

Population characteristics: Factors that describe how a group of people is doing or changing in a given country, for example, natural increase, literacy rate, infant mortality rate, etc.

Population density: The ratio of the number of people living in an area to the size of the area.

Population distribution: The patterns of where people live.

Population pyramid: A graph that shows the number of males and females in a country at each age division at a specific time.

Primary industry: Economic activities that extract natural resources from the environment and make them into semi-finished products.

Processed: Materials that are changed in some way before we use them. For example, wood is processed to make paper; some foods are processed by changing their colour or texture.

Productivity: The amount of work done related to the time, effort, energy, and money that was needed to produce it. More efficient ways of doing things usually result in greater productivity.

Protectionism: Actions taken on the part of a country to isolate itself from the rest of the world. Tariffs are one way that countries try to protect themselves from industries in other countries.

Quality of life: The amount of satisfaction we have with our lives, taking into account both material and non-material wealth.

Quaternary industry: A category of economic activities that mostly provides services dealing with ideas rather than with material goods.

Quota: The maximum number of immigrants allowed to enter a country per year.

Racism: Discrimination against people because of their skin colour or appearance.

Refugee status: A level of recognition given to people who claim to be refugees on entering a country. After government officials hear their case, a decision is made to grant or not grant refugee status.

Refugees: People who are displaced or who flee from their country for social, economic, political, or environmental reasons.

Replacement level: The fertility rate required for a population to replace itself. Usually, a fertility rate of at least 2.1 is needed, taking into account infant mortality rates.

Revolution: A period of rapid change when people adopt new ways of doing things. An **agricultural revolution** occurred when early humans first domesticated plants and animals; in the 1800s, the **industrial Revolution** saw the development of manufacturing and industries. Today, computers and the Internet can be described as a **technological revolution**.

Sahel: The region along the southern fringe of the Sahara Desert across Africa, where long-term drought and desertification have occurred.

Scatter graph: A graph of plotted points that shows the relationship (or lack of relationship) between two sets of data.

Secondary industry: Economic activities that take semi-finished products from the primary industries and manufacture them into finished consumer goods.

Semi-finished product: The goods produced by primary industries. These products are not refined enough to be used by consumers. A roll of steel produced by the steel industry is an example. The steel needs to be manufactured into goods like pots and pans before consumers can use it.

Settlement patterns: The ways in which people organize the places in which they live.

Site: The physical features of an area.

Situation: The relationship between a site and its surroundings, such as available natural resources, transportation routes, etc.

Sparse population: A low population density in relation to the area that contains it (low ratio of people to land area).

Squatter settlement: A makeshift community in or around large cities where people gather and live in poor conditions.

Statistics: Information given in the form of numbers.

Stone Age: An early time of human history when technology was not well advanced. Tools were often made of stone or bones.

Structural adjustment: Changes in employment patterns that occur as a country tries to change its economy to compete in a global market. Often, unemployment is a result of structural adjustment.

Sub-Saharan Africa: The Sahel region of Africa, south of the Sahara Desert, where mainly grasses and shrubs grow.

Subsistence farming: Farming that meets the needs of the farm family, with little left over to sell.

Tariffs: Taxes charged on goods imported into a country. Tariffs make imported goods more expensive than locally made products.

Technology: Resources used in economic activities that are not natural resources, such as machinery and knowledge.

Tertiary industry: Economic activities that provide services to consumers, such as auto repairs, book-keeping, and dry cleaning.

Third World: The developing countries of the world, especially those that became independent in Africa and Asia after World War II. This term is now considered old-fashioned.

Trade agreements: Arrangements in which countries agree to regulate the exchange of goods and services among themselves. The first **North American Free Trade Agreement** was a trade agreement among Canada, Mexico, and the United States.

Trading bloc: A group of nations that have agreed to treat the goods and services of fellow members in a special fashion, giving them preference over goods and services from non-member countries.

Urban sprawl: The growth of cities out into surrounding rural areas.

Urbanization: A shift of population from the rural areas to the cities, with the resulting changes in people's lifestyle.

Visible minorities: Groups that, because of their skin colour or dress, are easily recognized as appearing different from the mainstream population.

Xenophobia: Fear of strangers; particularly, a mistrust of people who look and act differently.

Yield: The amount of food grown on a specific amount of land.

Index

Acknowledgments

Care has been taken to trace ownership of copyright material contained in this text. The publishers will gladly take any information that will enable them to rectify any reference or credit in subsequent editions.

1.1 Health & Welfare Canada; p. 5 Chicago Tribune; 1.5 The Japan Foundation, Toronto; 1.6 Tony Stone Images; 1.7 Ontario Ministry of Natural Resources; 1.9 Australian Tourist Commission; 1.10 Ontario Ministry of Agriculture & Food; 1.11 Ontario Ministry of Tourism & Recreation; 1.12 Ontario Ministry of Natural Resources; 1.14 The Japan Foundation, Toronto; 1.15 Francine Geraci; 1.17, Australian Tourist Commission; 1.19 Victor Last; 1.21, 1.24 Australian Tourist Commission

2.1 Robert Waldock (p. 22), Ontario Ministry of Tourism & Recreation (p. 23); 2.3 CP Picture Archive/Terry Cioni; 2.4 Bruce Ayres/Tony Stone Images (left), Lori Adamski Peek/Tony Stone Images (right); 2.5 Patricia Healy; 2.8 Ontario Ministry of Tourism & Recreation; 2.9 CP Picture Archive/Andrew Vaughan; 2.10 CP Picture Archive/John Moore; 2.11 CP Picture Archive/Greg Baker; 2.16 Camera Press/Tom Hanley; 2.18 CP Picture Archive/Murad Sezer; 2.19 Jean-François LeBlanc, ACDI/CIDA (left), World Vision (right); p. 36 Sean Ellis/Tony Stone Images; 2.22 K. Dombi, ACDI/CIDA; 2.24 Nancy Durrell McKenna, ACDI/CIDA; 2.25 Ben Edwards/Tony Stone Images; 2.27 Johan Elzenga/Tony Stone Images; 2.28 Birgid Allig/Tony Stone Images; 2.30 CP Picture Archive

3.1 (Clockwise from top) Agriculture Canada/Prairie Farm Rehabilitation Administration, U.S. Environmental Protection Agency, Ontario Ministry of Natural Resources, Bruce Forster/Tony Stone Images, Ontario Ministry of Natural Resources, Ontario Ministry of Natural Resources; 3.2 Jeremy Walker/Tony Stone Images, David Frazier/Tony Stone Images, Ontario Ministry of Transport, Bruce Walker/Tony Stone Images; 3.3 © Canadian Space Agency, 2000/www.space.gc.ca; 3.5 Alejandro Balaguer/Tony Stone Images; 3.7 Robert Waldock; 3.9 Mark Williams/Tony Stone Images; 3.10 (a) Joseph Gladstone; (b) Carol Waldock (left), Leesa Price (right); (c) Environment Ontario; (d) Joseph Gladstone; (e) Carol Waldock (left), Leesa Price (right); (f) Ontario Ministry of Tourism & Recreation (left), Environment Ontario (right); (g) Lorne Resnick/Tony Stone Images; (h) Leesa Price; 3.11 Ben Osborne/Tony Stone Images; 3.13 © WorldSat International Inc., 1999/www.worldsat.ca (all rights reserved); 3.17 Ministère du Tourisme du Québec; 3.18 Port of Montreal; 3.20 Robert Frerck/Tony Stone Images

Pages 66–67 Imtek Imagineering/Masterfile; page 68 Gail Kenney; 4.4 David Hanover/Tony Stone Images; 4.6 Sutherland-Chan School/Ellen Prose; 4.8 Ontario Ministry of Food & Agriculture; 4.9 Ontario Hydro; 4.10 Ontario Ministry of Natural Resources; 4.11 Ontario Hydro; 4.12 Andrew Sacks/Tony Stone Images; 4.13 Pierre St-Jacques, ACDI/CIDA; 4.14 Joseph Gladstone; page 77 Lucasfilm Ltd.; 4.15 Randy Smith/Florida Atlantic University; 4.17 Ontario Hydro; 4.19 B. Lynne Milgram, PhD (left), Lew French (right); 4.20 National Aboriginal Achievement Foundation/Leona McIntyre; 4.22 Ontario Ministry of the Environment; page 83 MTPA Stock/Masterfile; 4.23 Gail Kenney

5.1 Steve Fitzpatrick/Masterfile; 5.3 Richard Smith/Tony Stone Images (top), Paul Chiasson, ACDI/CIDA (bottom); 5.4 Dale Wilson/Masterfile (top), David Paterson/Tony Stone Images (bottom); 5.7 B. Lynne Milgram, PhD; 5.9 CP Picture Archive/Mike Fiala; 5.10 Daniel J. Cox/Tony Stone Images; 5.11 B. Lynne Milgram, PhD; 5.12 Ontario Ministry of Food & Agriculture; 5.13 David Frazier/Tony Stone Images; 5.14 Andrew Sacks/Tony Stone Images; 5.15 Simon Norfolk/Tony Stone Images; 5.16 United Nations Film Library; 5.17 CP Picture Archive/Greg Baker (left), Leverett Bradley/Tony Stone Images (right); 5.18 Roger Tully/Tony Stone Images; 5.19 TVOntario; 5.22 Public Affairs Alberta; 5.24 Lew French (top), Leesa Price (bottom); 5.25 Tourism B.C.; 5.26 Lew French; 5.27 Leesa Price (left), Ontario Science Centre (right); 5.28 Ontario Ministry of Natural Resources; 5.29 Tony Page/Tony Stone Images; 5.31 TVOntario

6.1 Toronto Fire Services/Scott Cowden; 6.2 Paul Chesley/Tony Stone Images; 6.4 The Board of Trinity College, Dublin; 6.5 Western Canada Pictorial Index Inc.; 6.6, 6.7, 6.9 EuroDisney SCA; 6.13 Leesa Price; 6.15 CP Picture Archive/Ryan Remiorz; 6.18 B. Strong/World Vision

7.1 Leesa Price (left), B. Lynne Milgram, PhD (right); page 129 L.T. Webster/Libra Photographic; 7.3 Institute for Space & Terrestrial Science; 7.6 Gaden Choling Mahayana Meditation Centre; 7.7 CP Picture Archive/Mikica Petrovic; 7.8 Carol Waldock; 7.10 Canadian Food Inspection Agency; 7.11 Hafiz Alaoui; 7.15 National Archives of Canada/PA-128850; 7.17 CP Picture Archive/Junji Kurokawa; 7.18 Philip Maher/

World Vision; 7.25 Singapore Tourism Board; 7.26 V. Bonnell, University of California, Berkeley; 7.27 Singapore Tourism Board

8.1 Steve Matthews/World Vision; 8.2 CP Picture Archive/Ward Perrin; 8.6 David Young Wolff/Tony Stone Images; 8.9 National Film Board/Courtesy of the Ontario Black History Society; 8.12 B. Lynne Milgram, PhD; 8.14 Steve Reynolds/World Vision; page 158 L.T. Webster/Libra Photographic; 8.17 David Ward/World Vision (left), Diana Heroux/World Vision (right); 8.19 John Schenk/World Vision; 8.21 Andrea Booher/Tony Stone Images; 8.22 Francine Geraci; 8.23 World Vision; 8.25 Gaden Choling Mahayana Meditation Centre

9.1 Ontario Ministry of Agriculture & Food; page 168 L.T. Webster/Libra Photographic; 9.3 Jiri Hermann/BHP Diamonds Inc.; 9.4 Ian Samson/TVOntario; 9.5 Ontario Ministry of Mines & Northern Development ; 9.7 National Archives of Canada/C-3693; 9.9 Bruce Forster/Tony Stone Images; 9.10 B. Lynne Milgram, PhD; page 173 Gail Kenney; 9.11 Leesa Price; 9.12 Charles Gupton/Tony Stone Images (left), Masaharu Uemura/Tony Stone Images (right); 9.16 B. Lynne Milgram, PhD; 9.18 CP Picture Archive/Greg Baker; 9.20 Gaden Choling Mahayana Meditation Centre; 9.21 Chapters Online; 9.24 Tony Stone Images; 9.25 Gary John Norman/Tony Stone Images

10.10 CP Picture Archive/Paul Chiasson; 10.11 CP Picture Archive/Chuck Stoody; 10.12 CP Picture Archive/Rene Johnston; 10.13 Musée J. Armand Bombardier; 10.14 Spar Aerospace; 10.15 CP Picture Archive/Robin Wilhelm; 10.18 Lonnie Duka/Tony Stone Images; 10.20 Tom Tracy/Tony Stone Images; 10.24 Andrew Sacks/Tony Stone Images; 10.27 Port of Montreal

11.1 National Aeronautics and Space Administration; 11.2 Canadian Pacific Archives/NS.13561-2; 11.5 Canadian Atmospheric Environment Service; 11.6 CP Picture Archive/Andrew Vaughan; 11.9 UNESCO/Dominique Roger; 11.12 CP Picture Archive/Nancy King; 11.13 Saskatchewan Archives Board; 11.14 ACDI/CIDA; 11.16 World Vision; 11.17 Ministry of Foreign Affairs, Israel; 11.19 National Film Board/Ontario Black History Society (left), Ontario Black History Society (right); 11.20 Vancouver Public Library; pages 222–223 Robert Waldock; 11.23 CP Picture Archive/Chuck Stoody; 11.24 Keith Wood/Tony Stone Images; 11.25 CP Picture Archive/Paul Chiasson

12.1 Steve Matthews/World Vision; 12.3 CP Picture Archive/Peter Leibing; 12.4 CP Picture Archive; page 231 American Ballet Theatre/Martha Swope; 12.5 Robert Van Der Hilst/Tony Stone Images; 12.7 David Barbour, ACDI/CIDA (top), CP Picture Archive/Paul Chiasson (bottom); 12.8 CP Picture Archive; 12.9 Delip Mehta, ACDI/CIDA; 12.10 CP Picture Archive/ Fernando Proietti; 12.12 Gavin Hellier/Tony Stone Images; 12.14 Ontario Ministry of Tourism & Recreation (left), Toronto International Festival Caravan (right); 12.15 CP Picture Archive/Bayne Stanley (top), CP Picture Archive/Rosemary Gilliat (bottom); 12.16 CP Picture Archive/Chuck Stoody; 12.17 CP Picture Archive/Frank Gunn

13.1 Ontario Archives, Toronto (top); Ontario Ministry of Tourism & Recreation (bottom); 13.4 R. Ian Lloyd/Masterfile; 13.7 South African Tourism Board; 13.8 Donald Nausbaum/Tony Stone Images; 13.9 Department of Regional Industrial Expansion/Dilip Mehta; 13.10 TVOntario; 13.11 B. Lynne Milgram, PhD; 13.12 CP Picture Archive/Paul Chiasson; 13.13 CP Picture Archive/Tibor Illyes; 13.14 CP Picture Archive/Aranberri (left), CP Picture Archive/Javier Bauluz (right); 13.15 Ed Pritchard/Tony Stone Images; 13.16 Ontario Ministry of Tourism & Recreation; 13.18 CP Picture Archive/David Cheskin; 13.19 New Zealand High Commission; 13.21 CP Picture Archive/Andrew Vaughan; 13.24 Siegfried Eigstler/Tony Stone Images; 13.25 Baskin-Robbins International

14.1 TVOntario (left), CP Picture Archive/Jim Young (right); 14.3 John Fortunato/Tony Stone Images; 14.7 CP Picture Archive/Tim Krochak; 14.11, 14.12 Lew French; 14.13 CP Picture Archive/Paul Henry; 14.14 Don Smetzer/Tony Stone Images; 14.16 CP Picture Archive/Clement Allard; 14.17 B. Lynne Milgram, PhD, Lew French; 14.18 CP Picture Archive/Robert Wilson (left), CP Picture Archive/Andre Pichette (centre), Alfredo Caxaj (right); 14.19 Petro-Canada; 14.21 CP Picture Archive/Michelle MacAfee; 14.22 CP Picture Archive/Phill Snel (left), CP Picture Archive/ Vince Talotta (right); 14.23 Issac Erb & Son, St. John/National Archives of Canada

Page 320 Carol Waldock